GLOBAL ISSUES
for
GLOBAL CITIZENS

GLOBAL ISSUES *for* GLOBAL CITIZENS

AN INTRODUCTION TO KEY DEVELOPMENT CHALLENGES

Vinay Bhargava, Editor

THE WORLD BANK
Washington, D.C.

ISBN-10: 0-8213-6731-5
ISBN-13: 978-0-8213-6731-5
eISBN-10: 0-8213-6732-3
eISBN-13: 978-0-8213-6732-2
DOI: 10.1596/ 978-0-8213-6731-5

Library of Congress Cataloging-in-Publications data has been applied for.

Contents

v

Boxes

Figures

Tables

Foreword

Little more than a year ago, the World Bank held the first in its series of Global Issues seminars. Since then, through videoconferences with more than 20 participating universities, the series has brought hundreds of students from around the world into a real-time dialogue with each other and with development professionals representing the Bank's full range of economic and technical expertise. Many more students have participated indirectly, by accessing the videotaped sessions and lecture materials over the Internet. Through these discussions, participants on both sides have acquired a deeper understanding of some of the most urgent issues confronting humankind. This book grew out of the Global Issues seminars and is itself a testament to that two-way dialogue: the suggestion to compile the speakers' lecture notes into a book came from the students themselves.

Both the seminars and this book reflect the Bank's conviction that the seemingly intractable problems of our globalizing world—from entrenched poverty, to climate change, to new infectious diseases such as AIDS and avian flu—can be solved, but only with the informed participation of a global citizenry, cooperating toward global solutions through global institutions that they themselves own. In today's world, the unchecked spread of disease, hunger, pollution, and other menaces increasingly obscures established borders. Nations can no longer contain these forces, and experts can no longer—if they ever could—resolve them by prescribing technocratic fixes. By the same token, the general public can no longer simply outsource to government, at whatever level, the awesome responsibility of confronting these issues. Instead, we are all called, as responsible global citizens, to inform ourselves about these issues, to then inform others, and finally to get involved in seeking solutions.

One lesson that emerges from the book is that the global issues are very often interconnected, even if they may not seem so at first. Climate change, for example, threatens not only farms in developing countries but also fisheries all around the world, while at the same time contributing to the spread of deadly infectious diseases. Similarly, lack of education in many developing countries perpetuates poverty, which in turn keeps education out of reach for many, in a vicious cycle, even as widespread undernutrition robs many countries of education's potential returns. But another of the book's messages is that this interconnectedness can be at least as much opportunity as obstacle: if some global problems are mutually reinforcing, so, too, can be their solutions.

The book also reminds us that many global issues derive from the undersupply of global public goods. Like public goods at the local or the national level, such as roads and public schools, these are goods that are of value to everyone but that markets by themselves fail to deliver, because private providers cannot easily compel payment. Local and national governments can step in to provide these goods within their jurisdictions, but the problem in providing global public goods is precisely that no correspondingly global government exists or is likely to emerge. Yet, as the book also describes, more than a century of international cooperation has already led to some remarkable innovations in the provision of global public goods. From the founding of the International Telegraph Union over 140 years ago, to the creation of the World Bank itself in the 1940s, to more recent successes in protecting the ozone layer and eradicating smallpox, foresightful international leadership has time and again brought countries and concerned individuals together to meet urgent global needs. That kind of cooperative leadership in solving global problems is needed today more than ever.

I am proud that the World Bank took the initiative to convene these Global Issues seminars, and I am grateful both to the Bank staff who, under Vinay Bhargava's direction, organized and presented the seminars, and to the students—future global leaders—who engaged so energetically in the discussions and shared their own perspectives. I am especially grateful that my Bank colleagues have responded, with equal enthusiasm, to their students' urging to elaborate their presentations into this book, for the greater understanding of still other global citizens around the world.

Paul Wolfowitz
President
The World Bank
August 2006

Preface

W hat kind of future are we facing, and what kind of world will we leave for the next generation? These questions are demanding urgent attention in an increasingly interconnected world, where it is already apparent that many issues affecting people's lives locally have their origins globally. These global issues are as diverse as they are challenging; they range from climate change, to bird flu, to fair trade, to financial stability, to terrorism. Each of these issues affects a large number of people all around the planet. Addressing them requires collective action on the part of nations, and progress has been made, but effective mechanisms and institutions that can truly resolve these issues are in many cases lacking. Much more can and needs to be done.

This book is a compilation of articles by 27 experts at the World Bank, who have collaborated to provide some basic information on 17 of the global issues that matter most to the future shape of our world, as well as on three key elements of the global governance system: the United Nations, the international financial institutions, and global compacts. Our aim in publishing this volume is to help increase awareness and understanding of these global issues among the citizens of the world—and among college and university students in particular—so that they can participate in an informed way in the debate over these global issues and ultimately contribute to their solution.

Inspiration for the book grew out of the Global Issues Seminar Series that the World Bank offered during 2005 and 2006 to university students from Australia, Bulgaria, France, India, Japan, the Netherlands, Ghana, Lebanon, Pakistan, Sri Lanka, the Republic of Korea, South Africa, the United Kingdom, and the United States. During these weekly seminars, students from different countries were connected by live videoconferencing facilities for an interactive session with the Bank experts. The seminars were videotaped, and the videos, along with the text materials, have been placed on the

Bank's Web site so that anyone can access them (www.worldbank.org/globalseries). Many of the students suggested that the staff's lecture notes for the seminars be compiled in a book, to be used both as a reference and as a textbook for other courses and seminars in international studies.

The book's introductory chapter offers a definition of what constitutes a *global issue*, lists those issues that are most commonly recognized as such, discusses the main forces shaping these issues, and reviews the common forms of international action that currently exist to address them. The first three parts of the book are devoted to selected global issues in the areas of the global economy, global human development, and the global environment. Part Four discusses global governance—the mechanisms and institutions that the leaders of the world's nations have established to address these global issues jointly.

Each of the chapters that address a specific global issue begins by defining the issue and identifying what makes it global in scope. The chapter then moves on to explore the key underlying forces that shape the issue and the consequences of addressing or not addressing it, and then to a discussion of solutions, controversies, and international actions already under way or proposed. Each of the chapters ends with a brief review of the World Bank's own perspectives on the global issue in question and its role in seeking solutions.

One set of global issues that the book does not address are those related to the political aspects of global peace and security, such as arms proliferation, genocide, peacebuilding forces, de-mining, drug trafficking and other transnational crimes, and refugees. Although these are undoubtedly important matters, they are beyond the expertise and mandate of the World Bank.

During the seminar series, many participants asked: What can we do as individuals to make a difference on these global issues? Our response was that the process begins by recognizing that we are all global citizens as well as citizens of our own country, and that our civic duties extend in both dimensions. The next step is to begin to get to know the issue: this means going beyond the basic facts to understand the dynamics shaping the issue, the different points of view of those affected by it, what concrete actions are being taken and by whom, and what more needs to be done. The fact that you are reading this preface indicates that you have taken at least the first step toward understanding these issues. It is our hope that you will take this book along with you, and that it will help you as you proceed along that journey.

Understanding global issues is not the end of the journey, of course. Beyond awareness lies proactive involvement, for those who really wish to make a difference. Here we would like to draw upon a handy list compiled by the famous author and activist Jared Diamond, in his book *Collapse: How Societies Choose to Fail or Succeed:*

- Let your views be known to your elected representative and vote for those who show an inclination to help solve global issues.
- Influence policies of big companies by buying or refusing to buy their products and praising or embarrassing them on the basis of the companies' corporate social and environmental responsiveness.
- Talk to your family and friends about issues and get them involved.
- Develop support within your faith-based organizations.
- Make donations to an organization that is promoting actions on global issues that you would like to see happen.

Talking with family, writing a letter, buying a pound of fair trade coffee—these might not seem like giant strides on a global journey. But they are steps in the right direction, and the more such steps each of us takes, and encourages others to take, the closer we all come to a better life for all of humanity, locally and globally.

Vinay Bhargava
The World Bank
August 2006

About the Contributors

Kym Anderson is a Lead Economist in the International Trade Unit of the World Bank's Development Research Group. Before joining the Bank, he held academic appointments at the Australian National University and the University of Adelaide, where he was Foundation Executive Director of the Centre for International Economic Studies and holds a Personal Chair in the School of Economics.

Oscar Avalle heads the Office of the Special Representative of the World Bank to the United Nations. He was formerly the Bank's Operations Manager in Lima, and before that Special Assistant to the Bank's Vice President for the Latin America and the Caribbean Region. He has also worked at the Global Environment Facility. Before joining the Bank, he was a career diplomat representing Argentina in negotiations at the United Nations related to sustainable development and humanitarian affairs.

Jayshree Balachander is Senior Human Development Specialist in the Human Development Network of the World Bank's East Asia and Pacific Region. She is a specialist in country health policy dialogue; program development; and the design, implementation, and evaluation of projects for child and maternal health and nutrition and infectious disease control, with experience in Asia and Africa.

Vinay Bhargava is the Director of Operations and International Affairs in the External Affairs Vice Presidency at the World Bank. His areas of expertise are anticorruption, global issues management, and international financial multilateral institutions. He has over 25 years of experience in the design and implementation of development projects and programs in South and East Asia, West Africa, Eastern Europe, and the Middle East.

Punam Chuhan is Lead Economist in the Development Economics Vice Presidency of the World Bank. Her area of expertise is official development assistance. She represents the Bank in the Inter-Agency Task Force on Finance Statistics and has worked closely with other international organizations to establish new international standards on the measurement and reporting of debt and other financial obligations. She previously worked at the Federal Reserve Bank of New York.

Stijn Claessens is Senior Adviser to the Financial Sector Vice Presidency of the World Bank and Professor of International Finance Policy at the University of Amsterdam. His policy and research interests are firm finance and access to financial services, corporate governance, internationalization of financial services, and risk management. He has provided policy advice to emerging markets in Latin America and Asia and to transition economies.

Kevin Cleaver is the World Bank's Director for Agriculture and Rural Development and is responsible for managing the Bank's Agriculture and Rural Development Program globally. He previously held managerial positions in the Bank's Europe and Central Asia Region and its Africa Region. He joined the Bank as a Young Professional and before that worked for the government of Zaire.

Gaspard Curioni is a Junior Professional Associate in the Office of the Special Representative of the World Bank to the United Nations. Before joining the Bank he worked at the World Food Programme's New York office, where he followed interagency and intergovernmental processes in the development and humanitarian fields. He previously worked in the French foreign service and in the private sector.

Erwin De Nys is Rural Development Specialist in the Agriculture and Rural Development Department of the World Bank. Before joining the Bank, he served with the European Commission in the areas of agriculture, food security, and water management. He was also an Assistant Professor of Irrigation and Drainage at the Katholieke Universiteit Leuven in Belgium.

Gerhard Dieterle is the Forests Advisor to the World Bank and leads the Bank's Forestry Team in the Department of Environmentally and Socially Sustainable Development. He is a specialist in national and international forest and environmental policies, development policies, consultative processes, sustainable forest management, and forest conservation. He previously held positions with the German forest administration and the European Union.

Ian Goldin is Vice President, External Affairs, Communications, and United Nations Affairs, at the World Bank. He is responsible for managing the World Bank's global affairs programs and contacts with key constituencies and for overseeing the Bank's relations with the United Nations. He was previously the Director of Development Policy at the Bank, and before that he worked extensively in Africa, Asia, and Latin America and held senior management positions in both the private and the public sectors.

David Grey is the Senior Water Adviser for the World Bank's Africa and South Asia regions. He has worked on water issues in Africa, East and South Asia, the Middle East, Latin America, and Europe over the past 30 years.

Asli Gurkan is a Consultant to the External Affairs Department of the World Bank. She is the coordinator of the weekly Global Issues Seminar Series, with 20 participating universities in Africa, the Middle East, Europe, Asia and the Pacific, and North America. Before coming to the Bank, she was a research analyst working on Turkey's reform process in relation to its accession to the European Union.

Ruth Kagia is Director of the Education Department at the World Bank. She previously worked in the Bank's Africa and East Asia Regions, and she has extensive experience in the implementation of programs at the country level, having worked with governments in Africa in several capacities.

Kieran Kelleher is the Senior Fisheries Specialist in the Agriculture and Rural Development Department of the World Bank and is responsible for PROFISH, the Bank's global partnership on sustainable fisheries. He has been a fisherman, a fishery scientist, a fish farmer, a fish plant manager, and an adviser to international agencies and governments and has worked in more than 50 countries, primarily in Africa, Europe, and the Asia-Pacific region.

Karin Kemper is a Lead Water Resources Management Specialist at the World Bank. She has extensive work experience in the water sector and has carried out project investment work and research in Argentina, Bangladesh, Brazil, China, India, Mexico, Paraguay, Uruguay, and Zimbabwe. Her spe-

special interests include the institutional and economic aspects of water management, including river basin and groundwater management, water user participation, and decentralization.

Kazuhide Kuroda is a Senior Social Development Specialist in the Conflict Prevention and Reconstruction Unit of the Social Development Department at the World Bank, with experience in United Nations humanitarian operations. He has worked on natural resources and conflict issues and on demobilization and postconflict needs assessment for Bank country teams in Afghanistan, Cambodia, Iraq, and Liberia.

Yi-Kyoung Lee is a Health Specialist in the Human Development unit of the Africa Region at the World Bank. Since joining the World Bank as a Nutrition Specialist, she has worked on various health and nutrition projects and sector works in South Asia, East Asia, and Africa. Her interests include nutrition, HIV/AIDS, maternal and child health, and monitoring and evaluation.

John D. Nash is Advisor for Commodities and Trade in the Agriculture and Rural Development Department of the World Bank. He previously served in various positions in the Bank's Latin America and Europe and Central Asia regions and in its research group. Before joining the Bank, he served with the U.S. Federal Trade Commission as Assistant Director for Trade Regulation Rules and Economic Advisor to the Chairman and was an Assistant Professor of Economics at Texas A&M University.

Ian Noble is Leader of the Climate Change Team in the World Bank's Environment Department. He is an ecologist by training and was formerly a Professor of Global Change Research at the Australian National University. In Australia, he participated in the public policy debate over responses to climate change and served as a Commissioner in an inquiry into the future of the Australian forests and forest industries.

Nwanze Okidegbe is Rural Strategy Adviser in the Agriculture and Rural Development Department of the World Bank. He has managed a variety of projects and programs in agriculture and rural development, especially in Africa and Asia. His recent work has focused on implementation of the Bank's rural development strategy, quality assurance of projects and sector work, and coordination of global partnerships and programs.

Kyran O'Sullivan is a Senior Energy Specialist in the Infrastructure Vice Presidency of the World Bank. He has served the Bank on a variety of assignments in energy projects and sector work in Africa, the Middle East, and Eastern Europe. His recent work has focused on electricity access, impact evaluation, and monitoring.

Claudia Sadoff is the Lead Economist in the Agriculture and Rural Development Unit at the World Bank and serves as the Water Resources Anchor Team Leader. She previously worked with the United Nations Transitional Authority in Cambodia and the International Food Policy Research Institute and was a visiting Fulbright Scholar with the Thailand Research Development Institute in Bangkok.

Jamal Saghir is Director, Energy and Water, in the World Bank's Infrastructure Vice Presidency and Chair of the Energy and Mining Sector Board and the Water and Sanitation Sector Board at the Bank. Since joining the Bank, he has worked on a variety of private sector development, privatization, and restructuring assignments in Africa, Latin America, the former Soviet Union, and the Middle East and North Africa. He has held a variety of management positions with the Bank, including that of Sector Manager of the Middle East and North Africa Infrastructure Development Group. He has held his current position since 2001.

Meera Shekar is a Senior Nutrition Specialist with the Human Development Network at the World Bank, leading the repositioning of the nutrition agenda within the Bank and with its development partners. Before joining the Bank, she led the United Nations Children's Fund's Health, Nutrition and Water and Sanitation teams in Tanzania, the Philippines, and Ethiopia. She has worked on development issues across South Asia, East Asia, and Africa and has consulted extensively with the U.S. Agency for International Development, The Johns Hopkins University Population Communication Services, and other organizations.

Sona Varma is a Senior Economist in the Economic Policy and Debt Department at the World Bank, with previous experience in the Bank's South Asia Region and in the Bank's Finance Complex, mostly on Bangladesh and Sri Lanka. She is currently working on debt issues in low-income countries, notably on the Heavily Indebted Poor Countries Initiative, and on designing a framework for assessing debt sustainability.

Robert T. Watson is Chief Scientist and Senior Adviser in the Environmentally and Socially Sustainable Development Department Vice Presidency of the World Bank and is the Bank's senior spokesperson on global warming and climate change. He is the former Chairman of the Intergovernmental Panel on Climate Change, and before coming to the Bank, he was Associate Director for Environment in the Office of Science and Technology Policy in the Executive Office of the U.S. President.

Michael L. Weber is a freelance writer and research consultant specializing in marine and coastal conservation. He serves as program officer for oceans, coasts, and fisheries at the Resources Legacy Fund Foundation in Sacramento, California. He has directed programs on marine protected areas, sea turtle conservation, and fisheries conservation; has written dozens of articles and reports on marine conservation; and has advised in the production of television specials and exhibits on marine conservation.

Acknowledgments

This book was inspired by a World Bank-sponsored Global Issues Seminar Series that was launched in April 2005 and is ongoing. I want to express my profound appreciation to the local coordinators at the universities that participated in the seminar series during 2005 and 2006. They brought hundreds of students to participate and exchange views among each other across national and regional boundaries. They also encouraged us at the Bank to compile the seminar materials into this book, so that many more people around the world can be informed about and get involved in the global issues agenda. These coordinators include Yoshiaki Abe (Waseda University, Japan), Michèle Belot (University of Essex, United Kingdom), Elena Chernikova (Kent State University, United States), Ivanka Djakova (University of Sofia, Bulgaria), Alex Fischer (Central European University, Hungary), Kennedy Fosu (University of Ghana), Ho-Jung Ha (Korean Development Institute), Liz Ingram (Australian National University), Kenneth Jackson (University of Auckland, New Zealand), Muhammad Kamran Naqi Khan (Hamdard University, Pakistan), Tatsuo Kinbara (Hiroshima University, Japan), Dmytro Kulchitsky (American University of Beirut, Lebanon), Boris Najman (Sorbonne University, France), Keiichi Ogawa (Kobe University, Japan), Morgenie Pillay (Rhodes University, South Africa), Jean-Philippe Platteau (University of Namur, Belgium), Georgeta Pourchot (Virginia Tech University, United States), Nicky Pouw (University of Amsterdam, the Netherlands), Deyan Radev (University of Sofia, Bulgaria), Linda Robertson (Kent State University, United States), Yannis Stivachtis (Virginia Tech University, United States), Shalika Subasinghe (Sri Lanka Distance Learning Centre), Maree Tait (Australian National University), and Tracy Williams (University of Sussex, United Kingdom).

This book would not have been possible without the passion and dedication of the World Bank experts who shared their knowledge with us in the seminar series. They made special efforts not only to interact with students from around the world in many different time zones but also to convert their lecture notes into the chapters in this book. They share a common interest in making the world a better place for all of us to live, and I want to thank them and their managers for their cooperation and contributions. Their names and affiliations are listed in the "About the Contributors" pages.

The book has benefited extensively from the inputs of peer reviewers both inside and outside the World Bank. Their insights and comments helped us improve the depth, scope, and consistency of the book's coverage. We are deeply grateful to Olusoji O. Adeyi, Jock Anderson, Laura Bailey, Ian Bannon, John Briscoe, Karen Brooks, Csaba Csaki, Angelique DePlaa, Yuri Dikhanov, Mark Dorfman, Cinnamon Dornsife, Gershon Feder, Bernard Harborne, Santiago Herrera, Rafik Hirji, Patrick Honohan, Rama Lakshminarayan, Don Mitchell, Tawhid Nawaz, Sanjay Pradhan, and Meike van Ginneken.

I also would like to acknowledge the support of World Bank country offices and distance learning centers around the world for hosting the seminar series in their facilities, including the Development Learning Centers in Tokyo, Colombo, and Canberra and the Bank country offices in Accra, Beirut, Colombo, and Paris.

I am extremely grateful to Asli Gurkan for her skillful coordination of the Global Issues Seminar Series since the fall of 2005, for her adept management of this book's compilation process, and for her timely editorial assistance. I am extremely grateful also to Michael Treadway for his excellent developmental editing and his adaptability to multiple requests and deadlines. Without their aptitude, hard work, and commitment, this book would simply not have been possible.

Thanks also go to members of the World Bank's Office of the Publisher who were closely involved from the start, namely, Santiago Pombo and Stephen McGroarty, and to other members of the External Affairs Team— Maya Brahmam, Angelica Silvero, Hui Mien Tan, and Caroline Vagneron— for contributing to the success of the seminar series.

Finally, I am extremely grateful to Ian Goldin, Vice President, External Affairs Department, Communications, and United Nations Affairs at the World Bank, who has been an enthusiastic supporter of the Global Issues Seminar Series and of this book project.

Vinay Bhargava
Washington, D.C.

Abbreviations

ADB	Asian Development Bank
AfDB	African Development Bank
AIDS	Acquired immuno deficiency syndrome
AMC	Advance market commitment
APL	adaptable program loan
CAF	(World Bank) Conflict Analysis Framework
CARICOM	Caribbean Community
CDC	(United States) Centers for Disease Control and Prevention
CDD	community-driven development
CDM	Clean Development Mechanism
CGIAR	Consulative Group on International Agricultural Research
CPF	Collaborative Partnership on Forests
CPIA	country performance and institutional assessment
DAC	Development Assistance Committee (of the OECD)
DPL	development policy loan
EBRD	European Bank for Reconstruction and Development
ECOSOC	(United Nations) Economic and Social Council
EEZ	exclusive economic zone
EFA	Education for All
EITI	Extractive Industries Transparency Initiative
FAO	Food and Agriculture Organization of the United Nations
FATF	Financial Action Task Force on Money Laundering
FDI	foreign direct investment
G-8	Group of Eight (major industrial countries)
GCAP	Global Call to Action Against Poverty
GCIM	Global Commission on International Migration
GDP	gross domestic product
GEF	Global Environment Facility
GM	genetically modified

GNI	gross national income
GNP	gross national product
GOPAC	Global Organisation of Parliamentarians Against Corruption
GtC	gigatons of carbon
HDI	Human Development Index
HIPC	heavily indebted poor countries
HIV	human immunodeficiency virus
IAEA	International Atomic Energy Agency
IBRD	International Bank for Reconstruction and Development
ICSID	International Centre for Settlement of Investment Disputes
IDA	International Development Association
IDB	Inter-American Development Bank
IEA	International Energy Agency
IFC	International Finance Corporation
IFF	International Finance Facility
IFI	international financial institution
IMF	International Monetary Fund
IOSCO	International Organization of Securities Commissions
IPCC	Intergovernmental Panel on Climate Change
JI	Joint Implementation
LICUS	Low-Income Countries Under Stress
LSMS	Living Standards Measurement Survey
LULUCF	land-use, land-use change, and forestry
MDB	multilateral development bank
MDGs	Millennium Development Goals
MDRI	Multilateral Debt Relief Initiative
MIGA	Multilateral Investment Guarantee Agency
MPA	marine protected area
NGO	nongovernmental organization
ODA	official development assistance
OECD	Organisation for Economic Co-operation and Development
OED	(World Bank) Operations Evaluation Department
PACI	Partnership Against Corruption Initiative
PCF	(World Bank) Post-Conflict Fund
ppb	parts per billion
ppm	parts per million
PROFISH	Global Program on Fisheries
PRSC	poverty reduction strategy credit

PRSP	Poverty Reduction Strategy Paper
PWYP	Publish What You Pay
RPG	regional public good
S&DT	special and differential treatment
SARS	severe acute respiratory syndrome
SDRM	sovereign debt reduction mechanism
SPS	sanitary and phytosanitary
UN	United Nations
UNAIDS	Joint United Nations Programme on HIV/AIDS
UNCAC	United Nations Convention Against Corruption
UNDP	United Nations Development Programme
UNECA	United Nations Economic Commission for Africa
UNEP	United Nations Environment Programme
UNESCO	United Nations Educational, Scientific and Cultural Organization
UNFCCC	United Nations Framework Convention on Climate Change
UNFF	United Nations Forum on Forests
UNICEF	United Nations Children's Fund
WEC	World Energy Council
WEHAB	water, energy, health, agriculture, and biodiversity
WHO	World Health Organization
WSSD	World Summit on Sustainable Development
WTO	World Trade Organization
WWF	World Wildlife Fund

Introduction to Global Issues

VINAY BHARGAVA

M ore than at any other time in history, the future of humankind is being shaped by issues that are beyond any one nation's ability to solve. Climate change, avian flu, financial instability, terrorism, waves of migrants and refugees, water scarcities, disappearing fisheries, stark and seemingly intractable poverty—all of these are examples of *global issues* whose solution requires cooperation *among* nations. Each issue seems at first to be little connected to the next; the problems appear to come in all shapes and from all directions. But if one reflects a moment on these examples, some common features soon become apparent:

- Each issue affects a large number of people on different sides of national boundaries.
- Each issue is one of significant concern, directly or indirectly, to all or most of the countries of the world, often as evidenced by a major United Nations (UN) declaration or the holding of a global conference on the issue.
- Each issue has implications that require a global regulatory approach; no one government has the power or the authority to impose a solution, and market forces alone will not solve the problem.

These commonalities amount almost to a definition of *global issue,* and awareness of them will help throughout this book in identifying other such issues besides those named above. First, however, a few other definitions and distinctions will further clarify just what we mean by global issues.

I would like to thank Cinnamon Dornsife, Michael Treadway, Jean-François Rischard, and Asli Gurkan for their advice and comments on earlier versions of this chapter.

Some Definitions

Global issues, globalization, and global public goods are related but differing concepts. *Globalization* generally refers to the increasing integration of economies around the world, particularly through trade, production chains (where parts for a final good, such as an automobile, are produced in one country and assembled in another), and financial flows. The term increasingly also refers to the movement of people and of information (including not only financial and other raw data but ideas, fashions, and culture as well) across international borders. Globalization can be understood as a driving force affecting many global issues, from migration to fair trade to debt relief.

The concept of *global public goods* is a more recent one, and indeed its dimensions and implications are still being worked out by researchers and policy analysts. The International Task Force on Global Public Goods has defined *international public goods* (a term that includes both global and regional public goods) as goods and services that "address issues that: (i) are deemed to be important to the international community, to both developed and developing countries; (ii) typically cannot, or will not, be adequately addressed by individual countries or entities acting alone; and, in such cases (iii) are best addressed collectively on a multilateral basis."[1] By this definition, most but not all of the global issues addressed in this book involve the creation of—or the failure to create—global public goods. We will return to the topic of global public goods later in the chapter.

What Global Issues Do We Face Today?

Global issues are present in all areas of our lives as citizens of the world. They affect our economies, our environment, our capabilities as humans, and our processes for making decisions regarding cooperation at the global level (which this book will call *global governance*). These issues often turn out to be interconnected, although they may not seem so at first. For example, energy consumption drives climate change, which in turn threatens (a) marine fisheries through changes in ocean temperature and chemistry and (b) other food resources through changes in rainfall patterns. For purposes of this book, we group global issues into the five thematic areas shown in table 1.1. Of course, there are also other possible categorizations and other approaches to global issues.[2]

Not all of the issues listed in table 1.1 are discussed in this book. Rather, we have tried to cover the most important ones in each of the categories in table 1.1 where the World Bank has expertise. Global issues in the area of

TABLE 1.1 A List of Global Issues by Thematic Area	
Thematic area	**Global issues**
Global economy	International trade,* financial stability,* poverty and inequality,* foreign aid,* debt relief,* international migration,* food security,* intellectual property rights
Global Human development	Universal education,* communicable diseases,* humanitarian emergencies, hunger and malnutrition,* refugees
Global environment and natural resources	Climate change,* deforestation,* access to safe water,* loss of biodiversity, land degradation, sustainable energy,* depletion of fisheries*
Peace and security	Arms proliferation, armed conflict, terrorism, removal of land mines, drug trafficking and other crime, disarmament, genocide
Global governance	International law, multilateral treaties, conflict prevention,* reform of the United Nations system,* reform of international financial institutions,* transnational corruption,* global compacts,* human rights

Note: Asterisks indicate that a chapter on this global issue is included in this book.

peace and security are also very important but are beyond the expertise and mandate of the World Bank. The book therefore has four parts, covering the global economy, global human development, the global environment and natural resources, and global governance. Each part has several chapters, each of which covers one of the global issues listed in table 1.1.

Each chapter begins by defining the issue and identifying what makes it global in scope. The chapter then explores the key underlying forces that shape the issue, the consequences of addressing or not addressing it, and possible solutions, controversies, and international actions already under way or proposed. Each chapter ends with a brief review of the World Bank's own perspectives on the issue and its role in seeking solutions. What follows is a brief introduction to the four thematic areas and the global issues discussed within each.

The Global Economy

National and regional economies around the world are becoming increasingly integrated with each other through trade in goods and services, transfer of technology, and production chains. The interconnectedness of financial markets is also expanding rapidly. Such integration offers greater opportunity for people to tap into more and larger markets around the world, and so increase both their incomes and their ability to enjoy all that the world economy has to offer.

At the same time, however, economic integration poses serious inherent risks: in a globalized world economy, an adverse event such as a financial crisis in one part of the world can easily spread to other parts, just as a contagious disease spreads from person to person. An example of such contagion was the East Asian financial crisis of 1997–98, in which a financial and currency crisis in Thailand quickly triggered similar upheavals in the Republic of Korea, Indonesia, and elsewhere, prompting international intervention to avert a global crisis. (See chapter 3 for more about the East Asian and other financial crises.) Another example involves the globalization of trade and labor markets: concerns about the fairness of recent international trade agreements and about the effects of freer trade on jobs and working conditions led to violent protests at the World Trade Organization meeting in Seattle in 1999; these protests helped change the dynamic of the latest round of international trade negotiations. (See chapter 7 for a discussion of these ongoing negotiations.) There are also concerns that the world economy is growing in an unbalanced way, with rising inequalities in incomes and opportunities.

Part One of the book is devoted to those global issues that fall under the heading of the global economy. Of the many issues that could be addressed, the book considers the following: *poverty and inequality, financial stability, aid, debt, migration, trade,* and *food security.*

Poverty and Inequality

Substantial progress has been made in recent decades in reducing poverty— the proportion of people living in extreme poverty worldwide has halved since 1980. Yet poverty remains deep and widespread: more than a billion people still subsist on less than one dollar a day, and income per capita in the world's high-income countries, on average, is 65 times that in the low-income countries.

Income is not the only measure of poverty, nor is it the only one for which the recent numbers are grim. Over three-quarters of a billion of the world's people, many of them children, are malnourished. Whereas the rich countries have an average of 3.7 physicians per 1,000 population, the low-income countries have just 0.4 per 1,000. Maternal mortality in childbirth in many low-income African countries is more than 100 times higher than in the high-income countries of Europe. Vast numbers of people also struggle to survive in squalid, depressing living conditions, where they lack both opportunity to better their lives and the social recognition and voice to demand such opportunity. These, too, are real and important aspects of poverty.

Accompanying widespread poverty is widespread inequality, again as measured both by income and by other yardsticks. Measured in absolute terms, the income gap between rich and poor countries has widened over the past several decades. The economic divide within countries is likewise large.

In an increasingly interdependent world, the high prevalence and stubborn persistence of poverty and inequality in developing countries—the subject of chapter 2 of this volume—have implications for all countries. Deep deprivation weakens the capacity of states to combat terrorism, organized crime, armed conflict, and the spread of disease, and these in turn can have severe economic, environmental, and security consequences for neighboring states and the global community. Poverty and inequality and their associated outcomes can no longer be contained within national boundaries. This makes them a global problem of huge proportions, and it means that alleviating poverty and reducing inequality are critical to maintaining and strengthening regional and global stability. That is why the UN has made reducing world poverty a top priority—it is a target under the first of the Millennium Development Goals (MDGs) adopted at the UN Millennium Summit—and that is why the World Bank takes as its fundamental mission to build a world free of poverty.[3]

Financial Stability

The emergence of a global, market-based financial economy has brought considerable benefits to those middle-income countries at the forefront of economic reform and liberalization—the so-called emerging market economies. Thanks largely to the opening of the financial sector in these countries, investors in other countries can now better diversify their investment choices across domestic and international assets, increasing their expected rate of return. Businesses within these countries, meanwhile, are better able to finance promising ideas and fund their expansion plans. As a result, financial resources worldwide are invested more efficiently, boosting economic growth and living standards on both sides of these transactions.

But, as chapter 3 argues, the globalization of financial markets has proved to be a double-edged sword. Even in those countries where liberalization has been a tonic for economic growth, it has also raised the real risk of financial crisis. The most controversial aspect of financial liberalization involves the liberalization of portfolio flows, especially short-term borrowing. The dangers were brought into sharp focus during the East Asian financial crisis of the late 1990s, mentioned above. The failure of financial systems in that episode imposed high economic and social costs, such as rampant unemployment, increased migration, social conflict, and social instability—and not only in the countries directly affected. In the wake of this and other crises, an urgent debate has been launched over reform of the international financial architecture to reduce the chances of further financial instability.

Aid for Development

Foreign aid has been one of the foundations of international cooperation for many decades. A large part of such aid is intended to promote development in low- and middle-income countries: almost every country in the world has benefited from aid at some time in its development history. Aid comes from both government sources (in which case it is called official development assistance) and private sources. Among government sources are the bilateral aid programs of national governments, such as the U.S. Agency for International Development, and international financial institutions, such as the International Monetary Fund and the World Bank. Private sources include a growing number of charitable and other nongovernmental organizations, among others. Besides directly financing a vast range of development activities, aid also comes in the form of debt relief for the world's heavily indebted countries.

Aid for development plays, and is expected to continue to play, a vital role in addressing many of the global issues discussed in this book. Meanwhile the growth of global programs and funds and the emergence of new bilateral and private donors are increasing the channels by which aid is delivered. With this expansion in the volume and sources of aid, more and better coordination among donors will be essential if aid is to be delivered effectively. Chapter 4 discusses the basic concepts of international assistance, the forces shaping aid for development, the various criticisms levied against existing aid programs, international responses to increase the volume and the effectiveness of aid flows, and the prospects for increasing worldwide aid and for better monitoring of its use and impact.

Debt Relief and Debt Sustainability

For the world's poorest countries, foreign aid and the ability to take on foreign debt present a valuable opportunity to invest in their own development. But foreign borrowing poses great disadvantages as well as great advantages. On the one hand, when the proceeds of public borrowing are invested wisely, directed at the right policies and programs, they can indeed promote more rapid development. On the other hand, too much borrowing, or any borrowing that is not undertaken prudently, can act as a drag on the economy, as precious funds must then be devoted to debt service rather than to serving the country's development needs. As chapter 5 explains, debt that is rising rapidly relative to a country's output or exports can threaten that country's very future.

This threat became increasingly and painfully evident in the case of a number of low-income countries in the 1980s and 1990s. Their plight sparked an international advocacy campaign, popularly know as the Jubilee movement, to forgive the debts of the poorest countries with huge debt burdens. This campaign led in turn to the launch of the Heavily Indebted Poor Countries (HIPC) Initiative in 1996, to address the excessive debt burdens of the world's poorest nations. Since then, 38 of these countries—32 of them in Sub-Saharan Africa—have qualified or potentially qualify for HIPC assistance, and of these, 18 are now receiving irrevocable debt relief and 10 are receiving interim relief. The rest have been beset by persistent social difficulties that make debt relief infeasible for now. However, at their summit in Gleneagles, Scotland, in 2005, the leaders of the Group of Eight major industrial nations pledged to eventually write off 100 percent of the debt of the poorest African countries. In line with this proposal, officially known as the Multilateral Debt Relief Initiative, efforts are under way to provide $37 billion in debt relief to countries that are at the HIPC completion stage.

International Migration

Increasing flows of people across national borders are both a contributor to and a consequence of a more interconnected world. About 180 million people worldwide already live outside their country of birth, and pressure for international migration will continue, driven by differences in demographics and real incomes between countries. Research shows that although the largest economic gains from immigration accrue to the immigrants themselves, the international migration of labor can also benefit both the countries receiving immigrants and the countries sending them, and that on balance it boosts world income and reduces poverty. In the receiving countries, migrants can fill labor shortages in certain industries. In the sending countries, they can help ease unemployment and other social pressures while increasing financial inflows, in the form of remittances from the migrants to their families back home. Remittances also help level out the distribution of income both within and across countries. Worldwide remittances have doubled in the past decade, reaching $216 billion in 2004, according to official statistics, of which $151 billion is estimated to have gone to developing countries. Actual remittances are most likely higher, because remittances through informal channels fail to be counted.

Migration is not without its costs, however. For the migrants themselves, the journey itself and the search for fair employment and humane treatment in the host country can be arduous and risky. The host country government may bear added costs to assimilate the migrants, and wages for some native workers may fall. The home country may suffer a loss of valuable skilled workers. The sum of these and other costs depends, of course, on the number of migrants, and so the major issues surrounding international migration today, which chapter 6 examines, are how to help countries adapt to large-scale migration and how to improve its global development impact. Equitable migration is also ultimately linked to other broader issues such as poverty reduction and human rights, making it a global concern.

International Trade

In an ever more integrated world economy, international trade matters more than ever before. As chapter 7 argues, a robust and equitable trading system is central to the fight against global poverty, because it drives economic growth and provides jobs in developing countries where they are sorely needed. Measured by the volume of goods and services traded, world trade continues to grow, and just since 2000, the exports of developing countries as a group have increased their share of world markets by more than a fifth, from 19 percent to 23 percent. Yet growth in trade in many low-income countries has long been held back by protectionist policies in the more developed countries. Many rich countries offer subsidies to politically favored domestic industries such as sugar, textiles, apparel, and steel. These subsidies are a serious barrier to low-income countries' exports.

The Doha Development Round of multilateral trade talks, now under way under the auspices of the World Trade Organization (WTO), is the first such round to place developing country interests at the center of the negotiations. Although progress on the Doha round stalled following the collapse of the September 2003 WTO Ministerial Conference in Cancún, Mexico, WTO members have committed themselves to make progress as the talks proceed. Delivering on the promise of lowering tariffs as well as nontariff barriers in both developed and developing countries could stimulate worldwide increases in income that would lift an estimated 144 million people out of poverty.

Food Security

In a world of growing prosperity and agricultural abundance, about 800 million people still do not get enough to eat. Eliminating hunger is thus one of the most fundamental challenges facing humanity. The challenge is a complex one—so much so that this book devotes two chapters to unraveling its multiple dimensions. As chapter 8 explains, the task of reducing hunger—another one of the targets under the first of the MDGs—is shaped by interlinked issues of food availability, access to food, food security, and food distribution. Food availability refers to the supply of food, whether at the global, regional, national, or local level, without regard to the ability of individuals to acquire it. Sources of supply may include production within the household, domestic commercial food production, food stocks accumulated in earlier periods, commercially purchased imports, and food aid. There are presently no signs of a food availability problem at the global level. In fact, global food production has more than kept pace with growing world population in recent decades, increasing in per capita terms by 0.9 percent annually and even faster in such populous developing countries as China and India.

In most circumstances, the main cause of food insecurity is not lack of availability but lack of access at the household level: because of weak purchasing power and insufficient household agricultural production—both characteristics associated with poverty—millions of people cannot obtain enough of the food that is available locally to meet their dietary needs. And even access to sufficient food at the household level does not guarantee that all individuals will have an adequate food intake. That depends upon the distribution of food among household members, methods of food preparation, dietary preferences, and mother-child feeding habits—issues taken up further in chapter 11.

Global Human Development

Part Two of the book covers three global issues related to the development and preservation of human capability: *communicable diseases, education,* and *malnutrition.* The Human Development Reports team of the UN Development Programme has defined the task of human development as "creating an environment in which people can develop their full potential and lead productive, creative lives in accord with their needs and interests."[4] Building human capabilities through education, health services, and access to resources and knowledge is fundamental to human development. Most of the actions needed lie within the domain of national governments, but broad-based human development also has significant externalities, or spillover effects, that make it a global issue. Education, good health, and good nutrition are all vital not only for the earning capacity and general well-being of individuals but also for the prosperity of national economies and, in a globalizing world, for the global economy. Controlling the global spread of diseases is determined in part by the effectiveness of national public health programs, but also by the degree of international cooperation in containing outbreaks, and the weakest link in the chain determines the risk for all. The importance of education, health, and nutrition both for individuals and for human society at all levels explains why several of the MDGs focus on these human development issues.

Communicable Diseases

HIV/AIDS, tuberculosis, and malaria are just a few of the infectious diseases that continue to plague humankind, especially in the developing world. Meanwhile new threats such as avian flu and severe acute respiratory syndrome (SARS) continue to emerge. With essential vaccines and immunizations still underprovided in many developing countries, communicable diseases are an international public health issue that has caught the attention of the global public and its leaders. There is increasing global awareness that communicable diseases do not respect national borders and that how these diseases are dealt with in developing countries has consequences both for global public health and for the global economy.

As chapter 9 reports, this view is well grounded in years of research, which has produced some important breakthroughs but also reported some dismaying findings: 40 million people worldwide are now infected with HIV, and those infected experience a decline in life expectancy of 6 to 7 years on average; communicable diseases represent 7 of the top 10 causes of child mortality in developing countries, even though 90 percent of these deaths are avoidable. Improvements in global public health not only promise relief from human suffering on a vast scale but also have important economic benefits, as reductions in mortality, reduced incidence of disease, improved nutrition leading to improved intellectual capacity, and other gains feed through to a larger, more productive, and more capable world labor force.

Education

In today's global economy, education has become more vital than ever before in determining whether people, their local communities, and their countries achieve their potential and prosper. The world economy is undergoing changes that make it much more difficult for individuals in any country to thrive without the skills and tools that a quality education provides. This is particularly important for the poor, who rely on their skills and labor as their way out of poverty.

As chapter 10 explains, these changes present new challenges and opportunities for educators and educational systems, and the stakes are tremendously high. The choices that countries make today about education could lead to sharply divergent outcomes in the decades ahead. Countries that respond astutely should experience extraordinary educational progress, with major social and economic benefits, including catch-up gains for the poor and marginalized. Countries that fail to recognize the challenge and respond to it risk stagnating or even slipping backward, widening social and economic gaps and sowing the seeds of unrest.

Malnutrition

As chapter 11 reminds us, malnutrition remains the world's most serious health problem and the single biggest contributor to child mortality. Nearly one-third of all children in the developing world are either underweight or stunted, and more than 30 percent of the developing world's population suffer from micronutrient deficiencies. Without investments to reduce malnutrition, many countries will fail to achieve the MDGs, and other major international efforts in health may be derailed. In Sub-Saharan Africa, malnutrition rates are increasing, and in South Asia, which has the highest prevalence of undernutrition of any region, the situation is improving only slowly.

There is now unequivocal evidence that workable solutions to the malnutrition problem are available. An example is the strikingly low cost at which micronutrients could be provided to those in need of them: one estimate is that *all* of Africa's micronutrient needs could be met for a mere $235 million a year. Indeed, interventions such as these have been shown to be excellent economic investments. The May 2004 Copenhagen Consensus of eminent economists, which included a number of Nobel laureates, concluded that, among a lengthy list of interventions proposed to meet the world's myriad development challenges, nutrition interventions pay some of the highest returns.

Global Environment and Natural Resources

Part Three of the book focuses on issues related to conserving and more equitably sharing the planet's environmental and natural resources in ways that meet present needs without undermining future uses. This is the essence of environmental sustainability—a concept reflected in yet another of the MDGs. Resources such as a stable world climate, energy, clean and fresh water, fisheries, and forests are all part of the global commons, and all are already under stress. Those stresses will only become more intense as world population and incomes increase, and as today's developing countries follow consumption paths taken decades earlier by the developed countries. Yet addressing the challenges of sustainable resource use is hampered by a sobering reality: many of the world's resources are global public goods, which means (as discussed below) that individuals and individual nations acting only in their self-interest will fail to take fully into account the implications of their consumption for the well-being of other people and other countries. In the absence of foresightful and globally coordinated policies, exploitation of these resources can easily become a race to grab whatever one can grab before nothing is left. The chapters in this part of the book discuss these issues of how to manage shared global resources and use them in a sustainable fashion.

Climate Change

Virtually all climate scientists now agree that climate change is occurring and is due largely to human activity, and that further change is inevitable. Recent studies indicate that human activity over the past 100 years has triggered a historically unprecedented rise in global surface temperatures and ocean levels, with a worrisome acceleration particularly over the past two decades. The consequences will affect billions of people, particularly in poor countries and in subtropical regions, through decreases in agricultural productivity, increased incidence of flooding and of severe weather events, an expanded range of waterborne diseases, loss of biodiversity, and a number of other effects. Beyond this, if the global climate is pushed far out of balance, it may become launched on an irreversible course toward catastrophe, with worldwide repercussions.

Thus, as chapter 12 argues, there is an urgent need to develop an effective response to climate change. That response will necessarily be twofold, requiring, on the one hand, internationally coordinated efforts to prevent still further climate change, and on the other, cost-effective adaptations to a world in which a changing climate is certain to affect the livelihoods of all, and especially the poor.

Energy

The world economy of 2035 will be three to four times its present size, thanks largely to rising incomes in developing countries. Even if dramatic improvements in energy efficiency are achieved, this vastly expanded activity will consume much more energy than the world uses today. Pressures to supply enough fossil fuel, biomass, and electricity to meet world demand will therefore only get worse. As chapter 13 explains, world economic activity must become radically less carbon intensive, to avoid not only environmental disaster through climate change but also health disasters on an epic scale, as cities in the developing world choke under a fog of pollution. A shift to renewable energy and low- or no-carbon fuels is essential, as are the development and adoption of energy-efficient technologies.

Water

During the past century, while world population has tripled, the use of fresh water for human consumption, agriculture, and other activities has increased sixfold. Some rivers that formerly reached the sea no longer do so—all of the water is diverted to human use before it reaches the river's mouth. Half the world's wetlands have disappeared in the same period, and today 20 percent of freshwater species are endangered or extinct. Many important aquifers are being depleted, and water tables in many parts of the world are dropping at an alarming rate. Worse still, world water use is projected to increase by about 50 percent in the next 30 years. It is estimated that, by 2025, 4 billion people— half the world's population at that time—will live under conditions of severe water stress, with conditions particularly severe in Africa, the Middle East, and South Asia. Currently, an estimated 1.1 billion people lack access to safe water, 2.6 billion are without adequate sanitation, and more than 4 billion do not have their wastewater treated to any degree. These numbers are likely to only grow worse in the coming decades.

This potentially bleak outlook makes water supply a critical issue and one that cuts across national and regional economies and many productive sectors. Many observers predict that disputes over scarce water resources will fuel an increase in armed conflicts. The issue has fortunately caught the attention of policy makers and, as discussed in chapter 14, efforts are under way at both the national and the international level to address water scarcity issues.

Fisheries

The continuing depletion of the world's marine fisheries is a global issue of increasing concern. Fish is an important food for billions of people and provides a livelihood for an estimated 200 million worldwide. Fishers follow migrating schools of fish from sheltered bays and estuaries to the open ocean and from one sea to another, harvesting a global resource that benefits all but is managed by none. Small-scale fishers from Senegal and Ghana fish in the waters of many other countries in West Africa and in the Gulf of Guinea; European and Asian industrial tuna fleets operate throughout the Atlantic, Indian, and Pacific Oceans. Nations, too, act much like individual fishers, each seeking its own individual benefit from the common resource. In the past half century, the growth of human populations and economies, the spread of new technologies such as fishing nets made from synthetic materials, and the motorization of fishing fleets has contributed to the decline of many fisheries, jeopardizing ecological and economic sustainability for coastal communities around the world.

Chapter 15 depicts the situation of the world's fisheries today as a classic "tragedy of the commons." Without effective international regulation, fisheries accessible to more than one country, including those on the high seas, are declining as each vessel tries to take as much as it can of what remains. Yet efforts to provide such regulation have been beset with problems. Many existing international instruments designed to regulate high-seas and transboundary fishing are weak. The existing Law of the Sea Convention and its subsidiary instruments have important gaps, and effective enforcement of measures for responsible high-seas fishing has proved elusive. The World Bank and other organizations have started a major global initiative under a global partnership program called PROFISH to focus attention on the actions needed.

Forests

The world's forests cover about 25 to 30 percent of its land surface, or between 3.3 billion and 3.9 billion hectares, depending on the definitions used. It is estimated that during the 1990s the world suffered a net loss of 95 million hectares of forests—an area larger than República Bolivariana de Venezuela—with most of the losses occurring in the tropics. These losses matter because forests provide a complex array of vital ecological, social, and economic goods and services.

From an ecological point of view, forests are the repository of the great bulk of terrestrial biodiversity. In some countries in the Asia-Pacific region, forest destruction is responsible for global biodiversity losses on the order of 2 to 5 percent per decade, resulting in inestimable harm to ecosystem stability and human well-being. Forests also contain large amounts of sequestered carbon, and their destruction or degradation (especially by burning) is thought to contribute between 10 and 30 percent of all carbon dioxide gas emissions into the atmosphere. Deforestation is thus a major factor in global warming. In addition, mismanagement of woodlands in humid tropical and subtropical countries contributes significantly to soil losses equivalent to 10 percent of agricultural output in those countries each year. From an economic and social point of view, about 60 million people (mainly indigenous and tribal groups) are almost wholly dependent on forests, and another 350 million people who live within or adjacent to dense forests depend on them heavily for subsistence and income. In developing countries, about 1.2 billion people (including more than 400 million in Africa) rely on open woodlands or agroforestry systems that help to sustain agricultural productivity and generate income. Some 1 billion people worldwide depend on medicines derived from forest plants or rely on common-property forest resources for meeting essential fuel wood, grazing, and other needs.

As chapter 16 argues, conservation and production must coexist if the full potential of forests for poverty reduction and protection of the global environment is to be realized. Much of the world's forest area will inevitably be used for productive purposes. But large areas must be preserved intact for their ecological and cultural value.

Global Governance

The need for a global governance system comprising international institutions, agreements, and regulations has long been recognized. After World War I, the League of Nations was created as the first attempt at such a global system. However, the League proved ineffective, and after World War II a new international system was designed,[5] with the UN, the World Bank, the International Monetary Fund (IMF), and the General Agreement on Tariffs and Trade (succeeded in the 1990s by the WTO) as its cornerstones. This system remains in place today as the primary means for addressing the global issues agenda.

However, the inherited system suffers from many problems such as lack of perceived legitimacy, lack of resources, lack of effective enforcement mechanisms, and lack of representativeness. As global issues and challenges have intensified, demands for reform to make these global governance mechanisms more effective have grown ever more urgent, and many proposals have been offered in response. Some progress has also been made in the adoption of global compacts, in which countries agree to work together toward global development goals and to prevent and resolve violent conflicts. Part Four of the book discusses two key issues in global governance (conflict prevention and international actions to curb corruption), the two principal groups of global governance institutions (the UN system and the international financial institutions), and the main global compacts and the processes that led to them.

Conflict and Development

Some 1.1 billion people are either affected currently by violent conflict or at extremely high risk of being affected in the foreseeable future. The majority of violent conflicts today are intrastate, or civil, rather than interstate, or between nations, and the prevalence of both kinds of conflict is declining. Most of the world's conflicts now occur in low-income countries, particularly in Africa.

With globalization, however, the persistence of conflict anywhere has ripple effects that range far and wide. Neighboring countries, in particular, suffer reduced income and increased incidence of disease, and often they must absorb large numbers of refugees fleeing the conflict. Civil conflicts frequently result in large territories lying outside the control of any recognized government, which may then become epicenters of crime and disease. In the post-September 11 world, these areas are also often linked to terrorism, making them a truly global concern. These concerns have prompted world leaders to initiate new measures under the auspices of the UN, including a new Peace-building Commission. This and other measures are discussed in chapter 17.

Corruption

Chapter 18 addresses what former World Bank President James Wolfensohn called the "cancer of corruption"—the abuse of public institutions for private gain. Recent studies have shown conclusively what has long been widely assumed, namely, that corruption is detrimental to both the economic and the political well-being of countries. Corruption creates distortions and inefficiencies in public administration and in private economic activity, and it increases inequality: it unfairly benefits the few with access to the powerful, while especially harming the poorest. In 2004 the World Bank estimated that, worldwide, more than $1 trillion, or the equivalent of 3 percent of gross world product, is paid in bribes each year. This form of corruption takes place at both the national and the international level. The victims are usually people in developing countries, whose precious foreign aid and investment are siphoned off from badly needed development projects and into the pockets of corrupt government officials, their family members or cronies, or corrupt brokers or middlemen. Recent years have seen a major step forward to address transnational corruption and its effects, with the launch of the UN Convention Against Corruption.

The United Nations System

Effective management of global issues requires effective international cooperation, and the UN is the principal body within which such cooperation takes place. The Charter of the UN sets out the basic principles of international relations and entails obligations on all its member states. According to the Charter, the UN has four purposes: to maintain international peace and security, to develop friendly relations among nations, to cooperate in solving international problems and in promoting respect for human rights, and to serve as a center for harmonizing the actions of sovereign nations. The UN itself consists of six principal organs: the General Assembly, the Security Council, the Economic and Social Council, the Trusteeship Council, the International Court of Justice, and the Secretariat. The extended UN family, however, is much larger, encompassing various agencies, funds, programs, and other bodies, such as the UN Children's Fund (UNICEF) and the UN Development Programme. In addition to these are the specialized agencies, such as the World Health Organization, the World Bank, and the International Monetary Fund, which are administered autonomously but are considered part of the UN system.

The UN today faces many challenges to its effectiveness and is undertaking a variety of reforms in response. The success or failure of these reforms will have significant implications for the global issues discussed in this book. The organization also suffers from an unfortunate rift between developed and developing countries, which will make movement on reform extremely difficult going forward. Chapter 19 reviews the numerous efforts over the years of the UN Secretariat, the other UN bodies, the member states, and their advisers to reform the system so as to improve coordination among the various bodies and so better serve the UN mission.

International Financial Institutions

Addressing global issues requires international cooperation in the economic as well as the political sphere. Whereas the latter is primarily the domain of the UN system, as described just above, the mobilization of economic and financial cooperation, including transfers of resources, to address global issues falls mainly within the purview of the international financial institutions (IFIs). IFIs are institutions that provide financial support and professional advice for economic and social development activities in developing countries, or that promote international economic cooperation and stability—or both. They include the IMF, the World Bank, and the four regional development banks: the African Development Bank, the Asian Development Bank, the Inter-American Development Bank, and the European Bank for Reconstruction and Development. (The World Bank and the regional development banks are also called multilateral development banks.) As with the UN, there are many proposals on the table for reform of the IFIs, to enable them to play a more effective role in the global issues agenda. Chapter 20 provides an overview of the IFIs, the role they play in addressing global issues, and the main proposals to improve their effectiveness.

Global Compacts

At the start of the 21st century, world leaders laid out, in remarkable unison, a series of global compacts for a sustainable world, including most prominently the Millennium Development Goals. The most recent global summits have sought to evaluate progress toward the MDGs and to advocate the creation of institutional mechanisms to deal with the global development challenges ahead. Global compacts have great potential to prevent the world from growing further out of balance. However, progress so far has been slow, and there are real concerns that the targets will not be achieved by the established deadlines.

Chapter 21 discusses the global initiatives of recent decades that triggered the consolidation of a global development agenda through global compacts. It highlights the issues and controversies that have influenced these efforts to make a better world for all. Besides the MDGs, the key meetings and compacts covered include

- The WTO ministerial conference in Doha, Qatar, in 2001
- The International Conference on Financing and Development in Monterey, Mexico, in 2002
- The World Summit on Sustainable Development in Johannesburg, South Africa, also in 2002
- The UN World Summit of 2005.

What Are the Forces Shaping Today's Global Issues?

The global issues identified in the previous section are not static but rather dynamic, and their evolution in the coming years will be shaped by many factors. The forces driving these issues, the consequences thereof, and the appropriate solutions vary from issue to issue, but certain broad forces are common to many of them. These include demographics, growth of the global economy, technology and innovation, global interdependencies, and global advocacy.

Demographics

After doubling from 3 billion in 1960 to 6 billion in 2000, the world's population is expected to increase to 8 billion by 2030. It should then stabilize in the 21st century at 9 billion to 10 billion, which would be 20 to 30 percent fewer than forecast in the 1960s and 1970s. Most of this growth will occur in developing countries; population in the developed countries as a group will actually decline. Meanwhile the dependency ratio—the number of nonworking people supported by the average worker—will decline in the developing countries, boosting their ability to save and so to raise productivity. This in turn will increase their capacity to finance on their own the investments needed to meet basic human needs, maintain and improve public health, educate the next generation, and create job opportunities.

However, given that some 2.5 billion to 3 billion people in developing countries (about half the current world population) now live on less than two dollars a day, the ability of these countries to take care of all their people is at present extremely limited and will remain so for some time to come. Unless the richer nations help them through increased aid and trade, growing social discontent and outright conflict in developing countries will fester and eventually spill across their boundaries. The developed world cannot simply build a wall and turn its back on what is happening in the developing countries. Demographics will combine with the other forces to find their way through such barriers, whether made of bricks and mortar or of institutionalized indifference.

Economic Growth

Even if we assume, conservatively, real global economic growth of 3 percent a year, the global economy will grow from $35 trillion in 2005 to $75 trillion in 2030 (both figures are at 2001 market exchange rates and prices).[6] This vast expansion of output will have major consequences for both production and consumption, particularly of food, water, and energy, and will make today's environmental stresses still more acute. Within this expanding global economy, the developing countries as a group are projected to grow at 5 percent a year in real terms, while industrial country growth is projected to be just 2.5 percent a year. In this scenario, the share of the developing world in gross world product climbs substantially from just over a fifth to a third, with a major share going to China.

Although the share of the developing countries in world income rises significantly in this scenario, and absolute poverty in the world declines, the gap in income per capita between the rich and the poor countries nonetheless widens. Without deliberate intervention, persisting inequality both within and across countries will retard global development.[7]

Scientific and Technological Innovation

Future breakthroughs in science and technology have the potential to dramatically improve the health and productivity of the world's poor, mitigate climate change and environmental degradation, and feed a larger world population in a sustainable manner. Whether they actually will do so depends in large measure on collective decisions about the funding, implementation, and dissemination of technological innovation. Some technologies may also make global issues harder to grapple with. For example, the safe long-term disposal of nuclear waste is becoming a global issue, and some emerging technologies (such as genetic engineering) are beginning to pose legal and ethical dilemmas.

Increasing Interconnectedness and Interdependence

The ever-greater interconnectedness of people around the world—the very spirit of globalization—can be seen in the growth of international migration, tourism, and education, and in increased traffic on telephone exchanges, satellite television and radio, and of course the Internet. Unfortunately, that same interconnectedness also manifests itself in an increase in diseases that spread across borders, in international terrorism, in threats to the global environment, and in myriad other ways. The growing *interdependence* of people and communities worldwide can be seen in terms of expanded economic integration through trade and capital flows; in growing public security concerns related to drug trafficking, transnational crime, terrorism, and human rights; and in concerns about the overuse of world resources and the preservation of the environment. These two forces— interconnectedness and interdependence—are themselves interrelated and mutually reinforcing: growing interconnectedness increases awareness of our interdependence, and vice versa. Both are powerful drivers of increased concern about global issues and demand for effective action. The fact that different nations, communities, and individuals experience the benefits and costs of this increasing globalization differently generates controversies; it also complicates, and sometimes undermines, the effective and timely res- olution of global issues.

Global Advocacy

The continuing revolution in communications technologies and networks, cited just above, is enabling the global flow of information to all corners of the world instantaneously. People in today's world know much more, and in real time, about what is going on elsewhere in the world than their grandpar- ents or even their parents could have imagined. We are all becoming more and more aware of the differences between the world's haves and its have- nots, the interconnections between local human activity and global ecology, and the increased vulnerability of all of us everywhere to diseases, crises, and conflicts arising anywhere. Some nations are throwing the doors open to these new communications technologies, while others are trying, usually in vain, to control their spread.

The flow of information through these new communications technologies is neither one-way nor top-down. Rather, the new technologies are empow- ering people everywhere to express their views to a global audience (for exam- ple, through blogs) and enabling them to connect with like-minded persons to promote social (or in some cases antisocial) activities and advocate for their causes. This phenomenon has serious implications for the manner in which global issues are addressed and for the maintenance of peace and security across borders. Growth in instant worldwide communications is generating a parallel growth in public advocacy and activism, elevating formerly local or regional issues to global status, while mobilizing public opinion and demand for action on a global scale. For many of the global issues discussed in this book, instant communications and advocacy are already playing a crucial role in global policy making; examples include the debt relief movement, the climate change movement, the campaign to make poverty history, and the international drive for new vaccines.

Why Care About Global Issues?

It may be only a fortunate coincidence that the new communications technologies that have made such global grassroots interaction possible are the same technologies that have shown us the uses to which such interaction can and should be put—and that it is urgent to do so. Thanks in part to these technologies and the information they impart, we know not only that migration is an issue in Guatemala, and sea-level rise an issue in Maldives, and debt relief an issue in Uganda. Rather, our instantaneous technology allows us to consider these disparate issues simultaneously, side by side, and to understand that they are all issues of great importance whose impact is felt everywhere—that they are indeed global issues.

And that means they are *our* issues. Because these issues are global, the consequences of action, inaction, or inadequate action on these issues will, by definition, be felt globally—not just somewhere on the other side of the world, but here, where we live. If that is not sufficient reason to care about these issues, and to use our newfound interconnectedness to join with others and do something about them, then what in the world is?

But what do we really know about those consequences just alluded to? One thing we can say is that although they will vary from global issue to global issue, there is also significant interaction *between* issues and consequences. The consequences of inaction can be grouped into economic, social, security, health, and environmental effects:

- *Economic consequences.* If the world and its leaders fail to address such global economic issues as fairness in international trade, greater equality of income and opportunity, financial stability, sustainable debt, and corruption, the growth and stability of the global economy could be undermined and overall prosperity reduced. These consequences—weaker growth and greater inequality—would grow, feeding frustration and social stress. The insistence of the antiglobalization movement on turning back the clock would grow stronger, for example, and its protests more disruptive.
- *Social consequences.* As populations grow, as communities around the world become more and more interconnected, and as global flows of information accelerate and expand their bandwidth, more and more of the world's people will know more and more about what is going on outside their local communities and national borders. Those suffering from inequality and deprivation will become increasingly aware of the

better lives that others elsewhere lead. The slowing growth of world population and the rise in developing countries' share of world income provide a great opportunity to address crucial human development issues such as health and education, social issues such as inclusiveness and social cohesiveness, and governance issues such as institutional accountability. Failure to address these issues adequately could have serious implications for civil peace and harmony in societies all around the world.

- *Security consequences.* The widening gap between rich and poor, together with intensifying competition for increasingly scarce natural resources, both nationally and internationally, will fuel conflict and extremism, which will inevitably spill across national borders. Lagging development could also lead to the failure of states, some of which would likely become havens for terrorists or drug cartels. The damage would soon spread to other states, developing and developed, that remain otherwise intact.
- *Health consequences.* Failure to address malnutrition and the spread of preventable and communicable diseases would perpetuate and indeed increase human suffering and mortality wherever these scourges strike. The unchecked spread of disease would also have economic consequences, through reduced productivity and an increased disease burden, and these, too, would spread beyond national borders.
- *Environmental consequences.* Today's patterns of production and consumption cannot simply be scaled up to a world with $75 trillion or $100 trillion in annual gross product. Something will have to give, and that something is likely to be our shared environment. If today's developing countries replicate the consumption patterns of today's rich countries, great damage to the global environment, and to the planet's ability to sustain life and growth, is in store. The technologies needed to change these consumption patterns and develop alternatives are among the most valuable of global public goods, yet their development is now largely neglected. If present trends in the deterioration of biodiversity continue, the world of tomorrow will be biologically much poorer than that of today, even if the many poor communities dependent on fragile ecosystems can be moved to alternative locations and livelihoods. The financing needed to compensate these communities, so as to preserve biodiversity for the benefit not only of the countries involved but of the world, is huge—well beyond the means of those countries alone.

How Are Today's Global Issues Being Addressed?

It is clear that how today's global issues are addressed, or not addressed, will have a profound impact on the shape of the future world in which we all will live. Yet, as noted above, there is no global government to address these global issues, set global public policies and priorities, collect taxes on a world-wide basis, and allocate resources accordingly. Thus progress on most of these issues depends on a deliberate—and deliberative—process of building international consensus for collective action. This consensus can be expressed in many forms, for example:

- *International agreements signed by both industrial and developing countries.* Programs based on international agreements enjoy strong legitimacy, thanks to their formal authorization, especially when there is strong participation of developing countries in their design and implementation, and when there are equitable governance agreements. Examples include the MDGs and the 1987 Montreal Protocol on the control of ozone-depleting chlorofluorocarbons.
- *International law.* The International Law Commission of the United Nations prepares drafts on various aspects of international law, which can then be incorporated into conventions and submitted for ratification by the member states. Once a nation has ratified a convention, it is legally bound thereto. Thus the ratification constitutes consensus. Some of these conventions form the basis of law governing relations among states, such as conventions on diplomatic relations and the Geneva Conventions.
- *Declarations signed by participants at international conferences.* These declarations represent a less explicit and less binding form of international consensus than formal conventions or treaties and are largely oriented toward advocacy.
- *Actions of the G-8, G-20, G-77, and other such groupings.* The declarations of these intergovernmental groups are similar to international conferences in that they advocate and mobilize their members to take action, whether it is on doubling aid for Africa, debt relief, or any of a number of other issues. Of course, these statements signify consensus only among their members, not a global consensus. The economic and political power of the group (greatest for the G-8, less for the others) largely determines its potential to engage in effective problem solving on global issues. Their choice of issues on which to focus may in turn be driven by the advocacy efforts of civil society and other organizations.

- *Civil society campaigns and associations.* In some instances, global
  action is driven by civil society campaigns such as the Jubilee movement, the Live Aid concerts, the Global Call to Action Against
  Poverty, and the Make Poverty History campaign. Some well-known
  annual global forums such as the World Economic Forum and the
  World Social Forum also frequently focus on global issues and can
  profoundly influence the debate.
- *Global partnerships.* Often partnerships to address global issues are
  established by groups of donors, including governments, private sector
  and civil society organizations, and international organizations. Some
  recent examples in the health field are the Global Alliance for Vaccination and Immunization; Roll Back Malaria; the Global Fund to Fight
  AIDS, Tuberculosis, and Malaria; and the Partnership for Maternal,
  Newborn, and Child Health. Many of these partnerships promote
  ownership among developing countries by focusing on issues of relevance to them and by demonstrating that they can have an impact.
- *Global governance institutions.* Nations of the world have set up many
  international organizations with mandates to work on a wide array
  of global issues in the economic, social, cultural, education, health,
  and other fields. Among these multilateral organizations are the UN
  and its agencies, the IMF, the WTO, the World Bank and the regional
  development banks, and the International Labour Organization. All
  of these are involved in managing global issues as mandated by their
  governance bodies, which consist of representatives of the member
  nations.

What Makes Global Issues So Difficult to Address?

Dissatisfaction with the current structures for addressing global issues is widespread. Many people feel that some of the most important global issues are
not being addressed adequately, and they worry that the current generation
may leave the planet in worse shape than when it was inherited. The public
goods nature of many global issues, which was touched upon earlier in this
introduction, is a key reason why action commensurate with the challenge
can be slow to emerge.

Public goods are defined by two characteristics: the benefits they produce
can be enjoyed without paying for them (nonexcludability), and consumption
of the good by one person does not detract from its consumption by another
(nonrivalrousness). An often-cited example of a public good is a lighthouse—
but perhaps a more timely example would be a global positioning satellite

(GPS). The signal from such a satellite can be captured by anyone with a GPS receiver (which must normally be paid for, but the signal itself need not), and so it is nonexcludable; the number of people who can access the signal simultaneously is effectively limitless, and so it is nonrivalrous as well. Most types of knowledge and know-how are also public goods, after any patent or copyright restrictions on their use have expired. Global commons are goods or resources that are usually of natural origin, such as wilderness forests or ocean fisheries. They share the characteristics of public goods to a certain extent: they are largely nonexcludable, and they are nonrivalrous to the extent that their use does not exceed their capacity to regenerate themselves. When usage passes a certain point, the resource will be degraded or even destroyed.

Markets, whether national or international, typically fail to provide public goods: since it is impossible to make the user pay for them, there is no incentive for businesses to produce them. Nor are markets by themselves able to address the problem of managing global commons. At the national level, governments step in to provide many public goods, paying for them through taxes and other revenues. However, in the case of global public goods, no global tax or other mechanism exists to finance their production and supply. Countries looking only to their own narrow self-interest will be unlikely to agree on which global public goods should be provided, or on how to share the burden of financing them. At the same time, there is overproduction of global public "bads," such as communicable diseases, drug smuggling, climate change, and human rights abuses.

Global public goods have nonetheless been provided, some more successfully than others. *Global Monitoring Report 2003* (World Bank and IMF 2003) cites the following examples, starting with the most successful: aviation safety, postal systems, the Internet, the eradication of smallpox, advances in agricultural research, and protection of the ozone layer.[8] Examples where success has so far proved elusive include the prevention of climate change and the sustainable use of fisheries. Institutional arrangements such as UN peacekeeping programs, global funds such as the Global Environment Facility, and research groups such as the Consultative Group on International Agricultural Research have emerged and are very active in addressing global issues. These, too, are public goods, and their modest successes thus far are welcome and need to be expanded.

What the World Bank Is Doing About Global Issues

Over the past few years the World Bank has put significant resources into activities related to global issues, including the creation of global public goods. One important vehicle for such activities is the MDGs, which the Bank vigorously supports along with its country members, the UN system, and numerous other organizations. The Bank is increasingly being called upon to take a lead role in addressing global issues because of its global membership and reach, its power to convene technical and financial expertise, its ability to mobilize resources, and its multisectoral experience and institutional knowledge. As the only global institution among the multilateral development banks, the World Bank has increased its support for global programs rapidly in recent years. The Bank is now participating in some 70 different programs involving the following global issues (some of which are covered in this book), among others:

- Biodiversity
- Climate change
- Coastal and marine management
- Conflict prevention and postconflict reconstruction
- Corruption
- Debt relief
- Disaster management
- Energy
- Environment
- Financial sector
- Fisheries and aquaculture
- Forests and forestry
- Health, nutrition, and population
- HIV/AIDS
- Hunger
- Land resources management
- Malaria
- Natural resources management
- Poverty reduction
- Protection of the ozone layer (the Montreal Protocol)
- Renewable and rural energy
- Safe motherhood
- Sustainable development
- Tuberculosis
- Water resources management
- Water supply and sanitation.

The Bank's support for global programs—as distinct from the single-country projects and programs that make up the bulk of its work—began three decades ago, with the establishment of the Consultative Group on

International Agricultural Research (CGIAR). The Bank serves as both convener and donor to CGIAR, as well as a lender to developing countries for complementary activities. CGIAR, which brings together leading agricultural research institutes from around the world, has had some notable successes in creating global public goods such as the high-yielding varieties of crops that were the backbone of the Green Revolution. A major expansion of the Bank's work on global issues began in the late 1990s, when the Bank increased its orientation toward global partnerships and associated program support activities. This change in policy reflected the Bank's recognition of the rapid pace of globalization and the sharply increased attention to global issues within the development community. In September 2000, the Development Committee of the Bank and the IMF endorsed the Bank's priorities in supporting global public goods; those priorities focus on five areas: public health, protection of the global commons, financial stability, trade, and knowledge.

Finally, in addition to its own programs, the World Bank is active in many global partnership programs that address global issues. Through its participation in these programs, the Bank plays an important role in collective action on a variety of global issues. Besides CGIAR, examples include the Global Fund to Fight AIDS, Tuberculosis, and Malaria; the Global Environment Facility; and the Consultative Group to Assist the Poorest. The Bank looks forward to continuing and strengthening these partnerships while continuing to pursue its own initiatives on global issues—alongside its traditional country-based projects, many of which also contribute to building a healthier global community.

Notes

1. The International Task Force on Global Public Goods (http://www.gpgtaskforce.org) was created through an agreement between France and Sweden signed in April 2003. The Task Force's mandate is to assess and prioritize international public goods, both global and regional, and make recommendations to policy makers and other stakeholders on how to improve and expand their provision.
2. See, for example, Lomborg (2004), Rischard (2002), and the Web site Facing the Future (http://www.facingthefuture.org). An alternative list of global issues can be found at http://www.un.org/issues.
3. The full list of MDGs appears in chapter 21 of this book; for more on the MDGs go to http://www.un.org/millenniumgoals.
4. The team consists of leading scholars, development practitioners, and experts from around the world and is supported by the Human Development Report Office of the UN Development Programme. For more details go to http://hdr.undp.org/hd.
5. For a comprehensive discussion of the evolution of the international system and its strengths and weaknesses, see chapter 2 of Dervis and Ozer (2005).
6. This section draws on Wolfensohn and Bourguignon (2004).
7. See World Bank (2006a).
8. World Bank and International Monetary Fund (2003, chapter 12).

Selected Readings and Cited References

Dervis, Kemal, and Ceren Ozer. 2005. *A Better Globalization: Legitimacy, Governance, and Reform.* Washington, DC: Center for Global Development.

Diamond, Jared. 2005. *Collapse: How Societies Choose to Fail or Succeed.* New York: Penguin Group. (See especially chapters 14 and 16.)

Lomborg, Bjorn, ed. 2004. *Global Crises, Global Solutions.* Cambridge, United Kingdom: Cambridge University Press.

Rischard, Jean-François. 2002. *High Noon: Twenty Global Problems, Twenty Years to Solve Them.* New York: Basic Books.

Sachs, Jeffrey D. 2005. *The End of Poverty: Economic Possibilities for Our Time.* New York: Penguin Press. (See especially chapter 1.)

Stiglitz, Joseph E. 2003. *Globalization and Its Discontents.* New York: Norton. (See especially chapter 2.)

Wolfensohn, James, and François Bourguignon. 2004. "Development and Poverty Reduction: Looking Back, Looking Ahead." Paper prepared for the October 2004 Annual Meetings of the World Bank and the International Monetary Fund, World Bank, Washington, DC. (See especially Parts 1 and 2.)

World Bank. 2003. *World Development Report 2003: Sustainable Development in a Dynamic World.* New York: Oxford University Press. (See especially the Overview.)

————. 2006a. *World Development Report 2006: Equity and Development.* Washington, DC.

————. 2006b. *The Road to 2050: Sustainable Development for the 21st Century.* Washington, DC.

World Bank and International Monetary Fund. 2003. *Global Monitoring Report 2003.* Washington, DC.

PART ONE

The Global Economy

The globalization of the world economy is the epic of our era and a driving force behind many global issues outside the economic realm as well. Not only nations and private enterprises around the world but also the people within them—individual workers and consumers—are today ever more interconnected through trade in goods and services, finance, migration, and in other ways. As the chapters of this part of the book show in considerable detail, globalization is a double-edged sword. It brings with it a vast expansion of opportunities to interact with our fellow human beings for our mutual benefit, but it also poses great risks: an invidious concentration of wealth, financial instability and crushing debt burdens, and increased tensions among cultures, to name just a few. Hence a common theme of these chapters is the urgency of enhanced international cooperation to manage the risks of globalization responsibly while reaping the promised benefits of greater material prosperity.

2

Poverty and Inequality

PUNAM CHUHAN

Poverty in developing countries remains deep and widespread. Despite substantial progress in recent decades in reducing poverty—the proportion of people living in extreme poverty has halved since 1980—more than a billion people still subsist on less than one dollar a day. Over three-quarters of a billion people, many of them children, are malnourished. Each year nearly 11 million children die from malnutrition or disease before reaching their fifth birthday; most of these deaths would be easily preventable in any developed country. Over half a million women die every year in childbirth from lack of appropriate health care, malnourishment, or disease. More than 100 million children of primary school age, the majority of them girls, do not attend school.

Staggering as these numbers are, the inequalities in income and other measures both between and within countries are overwhelming as well. Income per capita in the world's high-income countries, on average, is 65 times that in the low-income countries. Rich countries have 3.7 physicians per 1,000 population, compared with just 0.4 per 1,000 in low-income countries. Maternal mortality in childbirth in many low-income African countries is more than 100 times higher than in the high-income countries of Europe. Even though the recent trend in the distribution of world income shows a decline in inequality, it remains quite high: the population-weighted Gini index is over 50 for the world as a whole. (The Gini index is a standard measure of inequality and is discussed further below.) The economic divide within countries is likewise large, particularly in Africa and Latin America.

In an increasingly interdependent world, the high prevalence and stubborn persistence of poverty in developing countries have implications for all countries. Deep deprivation weakens the capacity of states to combat organized crime, armed conflict, terrorism, and the spread of disease, and these in turn can have severe economic, environmental, public health, and security consequences for neighboring states and the global community. Poverty and its associated outcomes can no longer be contained within national boundaries. This makes poverty a global problem of huge proportions, and it implies that alleviating poverty is critical to maintaining and strengthening regional and global stability.

In recognizing this challenge, the international community has committed itself to a global partnership to promote development and reduce poverty. In 2000, the United Nations (UN) adopted the Millennium Development Goals (MDGs)—targets to be achieved by 2015—against which the global community can measure progress toward reducing poverty, and in 2002, the international community adopted the Monterrey Consensus, which created a new framework of mutual accountability between developed and developing countries for meeting these goals. The MDGs call for a dramatic reduction in poverty relative to 1990 levels and the promotion of sustained development. For the billion people in the world who live on less than a dollar a day, a future free of poverty, illiteracy, extreme vulnerability to disease, and lack of opportunities is only possible with sustained development; development holds the key for world peace and security as well. Yet despite a remarkable consensus on the actions and policies needed to achieve these goals, much remains to be done.

This chapter discusses the various dimensions of poverty and inequality and offers a sense of the scope of the problem and the direction of recent trends. It also discusses the international community's response to spur development and alleviate the scourge of poverty. The chapter then highlights the forces shaping the debate over poverty and inequality. Finally, it addresses the recent global actions aimed at accelerating progress on poverty reduction.

Concepts and Measures of Poverty and Inequality

An extensive and growing literature analyzes poverty and inequality. When one studies the evolution of poverty and inequality; the relationship among growth, poverty, and inequality; and the impact of globalization on the poor, it is useful to have an understanding of the underlying methodological issues. Some of the key aspects of definition and measurement are summarized below.

Definitions

The conventional notion of poverty is narrow, characterizing it in terms of deprivation or lack of essential goods and services. In this view, poverty is defined as income or consumption of commodities that is below some minimum threshold. This narrow characterization of poverty is not new. More than a century ago, Seebohm Rowntree used a survey on earnings and expenditures to estimate that 10 percent of residents of the city of York, England, lived in poverty—that is, below the minimum amount needed to subsist.

But what makes poor people poor is not just deprivation of income or of things to consume; often they are illiterate, have high health risks, and live in squalid conditions as well. A broader view of poverty encompasses these non-income dimensions of poverty such as education, health, prevalence of disease, gender equality, and access to water and sanitation. These dimensions are included in the MDGs and are recognized in the World Bank's *World Development Report 2000/2001,* which defines poverty as a "pronounced deprivation in well being."

An even broader view of poverty is the "capability approach" to well-being promulgated by Nobel laureate Amartya Sen (2000). This approach extends the notion of poverty to include vulnerability to risk, lack of voice in society, and powerlessness. Sen argues that what is important to well-being is the capability to function in society.[1] Key capabilities include not only adequate resources for essential needs—food, shelter, clothing—but also access to education, good health, security from violence and other risks, and political participation and voice. Poverty arises when people lack these basic capabilities to function in the society in which they live.

Closely related to poverty is inequality, or the gap between the poor and the rich. Inequality has to do with the distribution of *outcomes* such as income, wealth, consumption, or other dimensions of well-being.[2] It is different from equity, which is essentially about the distribution of *opportunities*— economic, political, and social; *World Development Report 2006* (World Bank 2006) argues that inequity in opportunities affects economic development and that greater equity can over time promote stronger growth. The focus of this chapter is on equality in income and other outcomes.

Measurement

Because poverty has these various dimensions, monetary and nonmonetary, and because it is such a complex phenomenon, there is no single perfect measure of poverty. The various measures are complementary, and the choice of which measure to use will depend upon the purpose it is to be used for. So, to measure poverty, one must first define an indicator of well-being. A standard approach is to derive income or consumption per capita from household surveys, which must be well designed in order to provide relevant and representative information. The World Bank has developed the Living Standards Measurement Survey (LSMS) to obtain reliable household income and consumption information; data collected from the LSMS are widely used in poverty analysis. The next step is to establish a threshold of income or consumption that represents the minimum acceptable level for subsistence. This threshold, called the poverty line, will vary from country to country and can be defined either in absolute monetary terms or relative to some baseline. For example, the poverty line in the United States is set in absolute terms (currently about $19,000 for a family of four), whereas the European Union proposes a relative poverty line, defined as household income less than 50 percent of the national mean.

The final step is to generate an aggregate measure, based on the poverty line, of the incidence of poverty in the economy. The most common indicator is the headcount index, which is simply the proportion of the population living under the poverty line. This indicator, however, does not measure the depth of poverty among the poor—it counts a person (or household) just below the poverty line the same as a desperately poor person living far below the line. One measure that does address this dimension of poverty is the poverty gap, which weights the headcount index, on a scale of zero to one, by the average shortfall of the poor household from the poverty line. The further the person (or household) is from the poverty line, the larger the weight; for example, someone who is exactly at the poverty line gets a weight of zero, while someone halfway between the poverty line and zero gets a weight of 0.5.

Because they differ from country to country, national poverty lines are not useful in comparing poverty across countries. For that, a single uniform poverty threshold is required. The approach most often used today is that first applied by *World Development Report 1990* (World Bank 1990), namely, the proportion of people living on less than a dollar a day. To derive this "international poverty line," the 1990 report converted national poverty lines into a single "international dollar" measure using 1985 purchasing power parities (PPPs),[3] and the poverty line that was most typical of those among low-income countries was selected. The current international poverty line that is comparable to the one-dollar-a-day line in 1985 is actually equal to $1.08 a day in 1993 consumption purchasing power parity terms (but is still referred to as one dollar a day).[4] Another poverty threshold that is commonly used in international poverty comparisons is two dollars a day.

The Human Development Index (HDI), developed by the United Nations Development Programme (UNDP) in 1993, is a composite measure of well-being based on life expectancy at birth, knowledge (in terms of adult literacy and gross enrollment in primary, secondary, and tertiary education), and income per capita (measured as gross national product per capita at PPP). The UNDP uses the HDI to provide an annual ranking of countries on these three dimensions. A value below 0.5 represents low development. Most African countries rank among the lowest on the HDI, and the trend for these countries is far from favorable.

Several measures have been developed to analyze the scope and extent of income inequality. These measures typically compare the income of an individual or a group with that of another individual or group. Like poverty, inequality can be expressed in absolute or relative terms—that is, in terms of the absolute gap between individuals or groups or the relative gap. The relative measures most commonly used today are the Lorenz curve and the Gini coefficient. The Lorenz curve plots the cumulative percentage of total income received against the cumulative percentage of recipients, starting with the recipient with the lowest income. If incomes were perfectly uniformly distributed, so that every recipient has exactly the same income, each point along the curve would be higher than the point to the left of it by a constant amount, and thus the curve would trace a straight diagonal line. The Gini coefficient (or Gini index, which is simply the Gini coefficient multiplied by 100) is a summary statistic derived from the Lorenz curve. It measures the area between the actual distribution of income, as depicted by the Lorenz curve, and the diagonal line that depicts perfect income equality; the Gini coefficient is scaled so that it ranges from 0 to 1, with 0 representing absolute equality in distribution and 1 representing complete inequality.

The distribution of income can also be described in terms of the percentage of total income received by various quantiles of the population, where a *quantile* refers to some fraction of the population ordered by income from lowest to highest. For example, the *bottom quintile* refers to the one-fifth of the population with the lowest incomes, the *bottom decile* to the lowest tenth, and so on.

Inequality can be measured within a country, between or across countries, or globally (across all people of the world).[5] Inequality is commonly expressed in terms of income,[6] but it can be applied to other indicators of poverty as well:

- Within-country inequality measures the distribution of income or consumption with respect to individuals or groups living in the same country.
- Between-country inequality measures the income gap between people in different countries, assuming each receives the average income for his or her country. There are two concepts of inequality between countries, and the choice of which concept to use will again depend upon the purpose: *Intercountry inequality* compares mean income per capita

across countries, focusing on the distribution of unweighted country means. Thus a country with a large population such as India has the same weight as a country with a tiny population such as Fiji. This measure provides little information about inequality among the people of the world. *International inequality* considers both the country's mean income per capita and the size of its population. Thus it represents the distribution of country means weighted by population. Although this measure does not take account of income distribution within a country, it is useful in assessing income disparities among the people of the world.

- Global inequality focuses on the incomes of individuals and their distribution. Here, the individual, not the country, is the unit of observation. This measure relies on national income distributions based on countries' household survey data to estimate a global income distribution. The data requirements for compiling this measure are much greater than for the other two measures.

Poverty and Inequality as Global Issues

The high prevalence of poverty in the developing world and the pronounced deprivation faced by millions living in developing countries have brought poverty and inequality to the forefront of the global agenda. Since 1980, international attention has been increasingly sharply focused on reducing poverty worldwide. More recently, the focus has widened to include equality and equity as well.

The latest data available show that over a billion people in the developing world were living in extreme poverty (on less than a dollar a day) in 2002, 450 million fewer than in 1981 and 200 million fewer than in 1990 (table 2.1). (Although poverty is a worldwide phenomenon, the focus of this chapter is on developing countries.) The greatest reduction in absolute poverty has occurred in East Asia, where the number of poor declined by three-quarters during 1981–2002; South Asia has also made strong inroads in reducing the number of poor. Not all regions have participated equally in this improvement, however. Sub-Saharan Africa has seen a near doubling in the number of poor—from 164 million to 303 million—and the number of people living on less than a dollar a day has risen in Latin America and in developing Europe and Central Asia as well. Prospects are bright for a continued decline in overall poverty, to the point where, by 2015, only 10 percent of the developing world's population will be living on less than a dollar a day—well below the MDG target of 14 percent.

TABLE 2.1 People Living on Less Than a Dollar a Day, by Developing Region, 1981, 1990, and 2002

Region	Millions			As percentage of total population			
	1981	1990	2002	1981	1990	2002	MDG 2015[a]
East Asia and the Pacific	796	472	214	57.7	29.6	11.6	14.8
China	634	375	180	63.8	33.0	14.0	
Europe and Central Asia	3	2	10	0.7	0.5	2.1	0.3
Latin America and the Caribbean	36	49	47	9.7	11.3	8.9	5.7
Middle East and North Africa	9	6	5	5.1	2.3	1.6	1.2
South Asia	475	462	437	51.5	41.3	31.2	20.7
Sub-Saharan Africa	164	227	303	41.6	44.6	44.0	22.3
All developing countries	1,482	1,218	1,015	40.4	27.9	19.4	14.0

Source: World Bank, World Development Indicators.
a. The MDG for poverty calls for a halving of the proportion of the population living on less than a dollar a day from 1990 levels by 2015.

But not all regions will achieve the goal of halving extreme poverty. Sub-Saharan Africa is the region most at risk: nearly half of those countries are off track to achieve the income poverty MDG, and an additional 40 percent lack sufficient data to allow an evaluation of their prospects. There has also been overall progress on reducing hunger, yet only 33 out of 77 countries with reliable data on malnutrition are on track to achieve the MDG target for hunger. Here, too, Africa is seriously off track.

Progress in reducing poverty has thus been uneven. Some countries and regions have seen a remarkable decline in poverty, while others have actually experienced an increase. Figure 2.1 shows how poverty reduction has progressed, or not, in selected countries. Each symbol in the figure represents a country, and its position with respect to the vertical axis shows the percentage of that country's population in extreme poverty in 1981, while its position with respect to the horizontal axis shows the corresponding percentage in 2001. Thus, countries that have reduced poverty by this measure will lie above the diagonal line, countries that have seen an increase will lie below it, and countries that have seen no change in poverty will lie directly on the diagonal. As the figure shows, the greatest improvement has occurred in the Asian economies, most notably in Cambodia, China, India, Pakistan, and Vietnam; only one East Asian country and one South Asian country fall below the

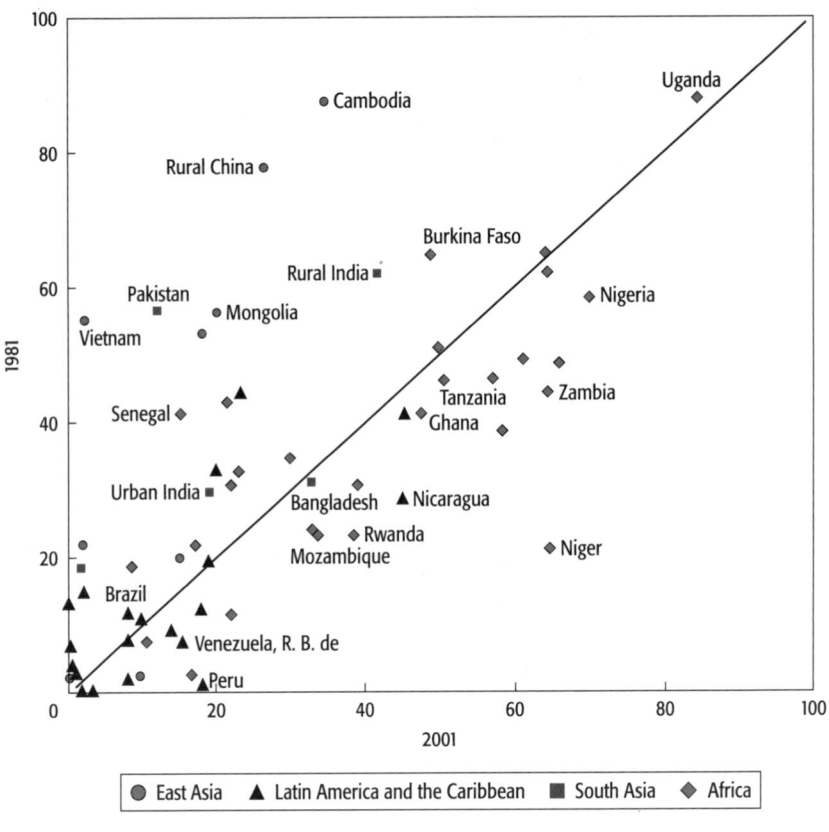

FIGURE 2.1 Share of Population Living on Less Than a Dollar a Day in Selected Countries, 1981 and 2001
Percent

Source: Author's construction using the World Bank's PovcalNet (http://iresearch.worldbank.org/PovcalNet/jsp/index.jsp).

diagonal line. Most of the African countries, in contrast, saw a long-term slippage in poverty reduction, including several that experienced relatively rapid economic growth and some poverty reduction in the 1990s, such as Ghana, Mozambique, and Tanzania. The performance of the Latin American economies was mixed, with nearly half seeing an increase in the proportion of people living on less than a dollar a day.

Progress on the human development MDGs (those addressing education, gender equality, child and maternal mortality, and communicable disease) has been mixed. All regions are off track on at least some of the goals, and although some countries in South Asia and Sub-Saharan Africa are meeting some of the goals, these regions are largely off track on all of them. On the goal of universal primary education, progress has been encouraging: the number of countries that have achieved or are on track to achieve this goal has increased, as has the rate of growth in the primary completion rate. Gender disparities in primary and secondary education are also narrowing. By contrast, the pace of reduction in child mortality has been slow: only 20 percent of developing countries are on track to reduce child mortality rates by two-thirds of their 1990 levels by 2015. Gains toward this goal have been particularly slow in Sub-Saharan Africa. Maternal mortality rates remain unacceptably high in many developing countries as well, although some countries in East Asia and Latin America have substantially improved maternal health through better health facilities and an increase in the number of trained birth attendants. Diseases such as HIV/AIDS, malaria, and tuberculosis continue to exact a heavy toll on populations in Sub-Saharan Africa. Although the prevalence of HIV/AIDS has stabilized, the death rate from this disease is on the rise.

Progress on the environmental MDG is likewise mixed. Despite strong progress in some regions, many countries are off track toward the goal of reducing by half the proportion of people without sustainable access to safe drinking water and basic sanitation by 2015. The situation in Sub-Saharan Africa is particularly critical: 64 percent of the population lack access to an improved water source, and 37 percent lack access to improved sanitation facilities.

Views differ on whether the decline in absolute poverty worldwide has been accompanied by greater equality in the distribution of income. The answer depends upon the concept of equality that is used. In terms of intercountry inequality—that is, when all countries are weighted equally—income inequality has increased since the 1980s. But in terms of international equality—when the more populous countries have larger weights—the gap between countries has narrowed. This favorable result is driven by the strong economic growth in China and India during this period.

A 2004 study used data from 138 countries during 1980–2002 to show how the world distribution of income changed over that period.[7] If one takes only differences between countries into account, in 2002 the poorest 40 percent of the world's population received slightly more than 10 percent of world income, while the wealthiest 10 percent received nearly 40 percent (figure 2.2). The population-weighted world Gini index (assuming equal income within countries) was over 50. Although the distribution of world income is thus quite unequal, the recent historical trend shows a decline in inequality: the

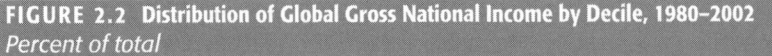

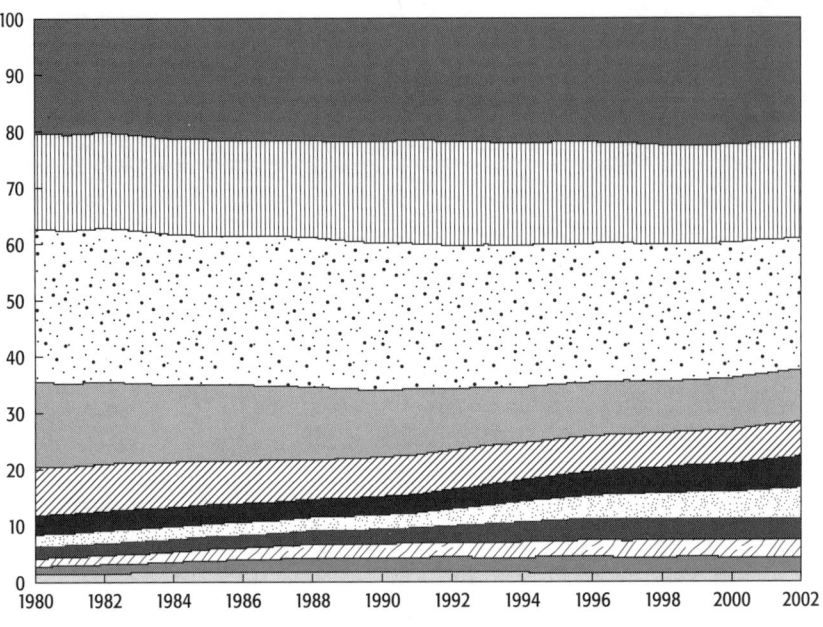

FIGURE 2.2 Distribution of Global Gross National Income by Decile, 1980–2002
Percent of total

Source: Bourguignon, Levin, and Rosenblatt 2004.
Note: The top two strata represent the top 5 percent and the second 5 percent, respectively, of the population; the remaining strata represent the eighth through the first (lowest) deciles, respectively. Gross national income is measured in 1995 international dollars (dollars adjusted for PPP).

poorest 40 percent of world population have nearly doubled their share of world income, while the richest 10 percent have seen only a small increase in their share. Not all of the lower deciles saw an improvement, however. The second through the sixth deciles gained income share, but the poorest decile and the seventh and eighth deciles all saw a decline in income share on balance.

By contrast, global inequality measures, which combine cross-country differences and income distribution within countries, show mixed results for trends in inequality in the 1990s. Some studies estimate that the world Gini index has declined by between 3 and 4 points, whereas other studies find either no change or an increase in inequality.[8] The differences in results most likely stem from differences in data and assumptions used to compute the inequality measure. Despite these differences in findings regarding the trend, all studies find global inequality to be very high: the world Gini value for the

1990s is about 65, indicating that between-country inequality is sharply greater than within-country inequality. The richest 5 percent of the world's population receive about a third of world income (measured in PPP terms), while the poorest 5 percent receive only 0.2 percent.[9]

Within-country inequality is high in many developing countries. Nearly 60 developing countries have a Gini index of 40 or more; by comparison, the high-income countries of Europe typically have Gini values of 25 to 35. Gini indexes reveal that countries in Sub-Saharan Africa and in Latin America and the Caribbean appear to be the most unequal in the world. Evidence also suggests that public spending on education and health is often regressive, with the poorest quintiles receiving much smaller shares than the richer quintiles.

Several factors explain why poverty and inequality are global issues. First, as this part of the chapter has shown, poverty remains widespread, and it is readily apparent that, unless action is taken to reduce poverty, the situation will dramatically worsen. Second, there is an increasing recognition that developed and developing countries need to work together to make poverty history; the poor countries cannot achieve the MDGs on their own. Rich countries can help poor countries accelerate progress on reducing poverty by providing resources—aid—to scale up service delivery and investment in much-needed infrastructure. Moreover, by removing barriers to trade that discriminate against developing countries, rich countries can help spur growth and accelerate poverty reduction in the developing world.

Forces Shaping the Agenda

The poverty and inequality agenda today is being shaped by two broad forces: global concern over fairness, and globalization. The persistence of deep poverty and of inequality not only has fueled a sense of deprivation and injustice among the poor themselves but has also violated a basic sense of fairness in those who are not poor. People everywhere have a general sense of fairness as it applies to themselves and others, which is rooted in the concept of social justice. This shared notion of fairness reflects widely held moral and ethical values of the world community and forms the basis of the international system of human rights. Persistent poverty, large inequalities between and within countries, and lack of opportunity are not consistent with this sense of fairness.

The forces of globalization mean that the problem of poverty is no longer contained within national boundaries. With increasing interdependence through trade, migration, and financial integration, the actions of people in one country have consequences for people in other countries. Concerns for

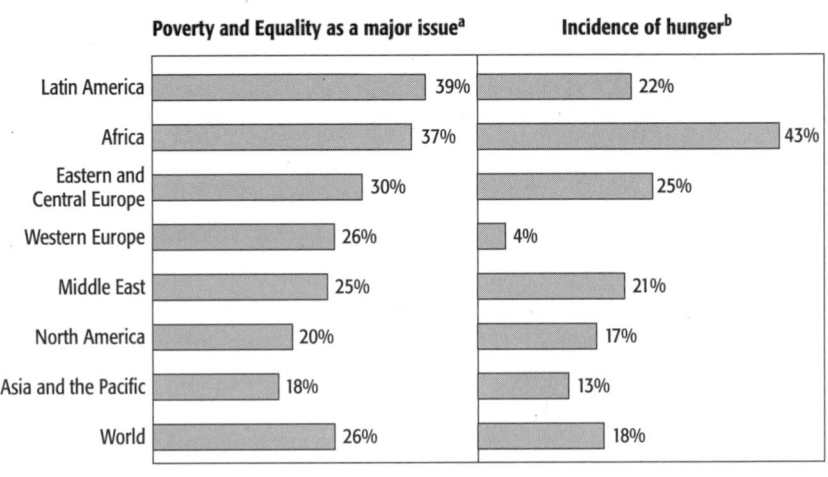

FIGURE 2.3 **World Opinion on Poverty and Equality as a Major Issue and on the Incidence of Hunger**

Source: Gallup International 2005.
a. Respondents were asked, "What do you think is the most important problem facing the world today?"
b. The percentages equal the share of respondents who said that they or their families had often or sometimes not had enough to eat in the preceding 12 months.

both fairness and globalization are contributing to an increasing awareness among the citizens of the world's rich countries that they need to help improve the well-being and opportunities of the citizens of poor countries, especially if they are to reduce global inequalities.

A worldwide survey conducted by Gallup International in 2005, covering more than 65 countries and over 50,000 people, reports that more than one in four people view either poverty or inequality as the most pressing global problem (figure 2.3). This perception is evident across all world regions as well: in Latin America poverty or inequality was ranked as the most important problem by 39 percent of those surveyed, in Africa by 37 percent, in Eastern and Central Europe by 30 percent, and in Asia and the Pacific by 18 percent. All regions also report evidence of hunger. At 43 percent, Africa has the highest incidence of people or families who lack adequate food to eat. The numbers for other regions are lower but still substantial.

Advocacy groups have played an important role in building consensus on key public actions by the international community. Their campaigns on critical issues such as debt relief and a fair global trading system have raised awareness among citizens of rich and poor countries alike. Advocacy groups have been particularly effective in campaigning to reduce the debt burden of the poorest countries: the international coalition Jubilee 2000, which called for the cancellation of poor countries' debt by the year 2000, played a key role in the Heavily Indebted Poor Countries (HIPC) Initiative; the international coalition Make Poverty History successfully campaigned in 2005 for canceling poor countries' debt through what subsequently became known as the Multilateral Debt Relief Initiative (MDRI).

World leaders have acknowledged the global threat posed by deep poverty. A 2004 UN report lists poverty, communicable diseases, and degradation of the environment among the top six threats to international peace and security facing the world in the 21st century.[10] The report takes a comprehensive view of collective security. It addresses the security concerns of all states, not just rich states but poor and weak ones as well. It also recognizes an interconnectedness of poverty, civil war, and possibly terrorism[11]: extreme poverty, hunger, and a high incidence of infectious diseases can create conditions for domestic unrest, armed conflict, and failed states.[12] The report argues that the foremost way to promote security is through development. Development reduces poverty and strengthens the state's capacity to govern, and so reduces the threats of organized crime, civil war, and terrorism. Attaining the MDGs is therefore essential to improving global security.

By 2015, world population is expected to increase by over three-quarters of a billion. Virtually all of this growth (95 percent) will occur in developing countries, and many of these people will be born into poverty; simulations show that a third more people could be rescued from poverty if growth is - pro-poor rather than distributionally neutral.[13] Poor countries and the global community must act now so as to provide a better future for all.

Globalization and the Poor

Two controversial issues in the debate over poverty and inequality are whether globalization benefits or harms the poor and whether the extent of inequality adversely affects poverty reduction and thus is bad for the poor.

Does Globalization Harm the Poor?

The impact of globalization on poverty has generated considerable debate. Globalization has many facets, including foreign trade, cross-border financial flows, international migration, temporary movement of service providers, and information flows. The focus here is on openness to trade. Although absolute poverty has declined as the world has globalized, some view globalization as unfair to the poor. Anti-globalizers argue that openness to trade has led to greater poverty and to rising disparities between and within countries.

The standard macroeconomic perspective is that openness to trade reduces poverty by stimulating economic growth, which is central to poverty reduction. Another indirect way through which trade liberalization impacts poverty is by boosting productivity, which is necessary for fostering long-term growth. There are a variety of other channels through which trade liberalization can directly alleviate poverty: by lowering the prices of households' consumption baskets (including through lower tariffs), raising wages and employment, and increasing government revenue and spending.[14]

Several studies, however, suggest that the linkages between globalization and poverty are not so straightforward.[15] The outcome is influenced by other factors, including the degree of labor mobility across sectors; access to credit markets for the poor, so they can avail themselves of profitable investment opportunities; and access to technical know-how and training programs. Thus globalization can in some situations have a negative impact on the poor, especially in the near term. This points to the need to have appropriate policies in place to ensure that the poor gain from globalization.

A recent survey of the empirical literature found that no simple generalizations can be made about the impact of openness to trade on poverty.[16] The evidence broadly supports the view that, in the long run, trade liberalization reduces poverty on average, and there is no evidence of a generally negative impact on poverty. This is not to say, however, that the employment and wages of the poor have never suffered, or that declining fiscal revenues have never caused spending on the poor to be curtailed, where trade has been liberalized. The empirical evidence also shows that poor households are less able than better-off households to take advantage of new economic opportunities or to protect themselves against negative shocks.

As noted earlier, whether economic inequality has declined or not depends upon what is being measured—that is, the underlying concepts. Not surprisingly, those who claim that economic disparities have widened as a result of trade liberalization generally base their argument on absolute as opposed to relative differences in equality.[17] In fact, studies have shown that, on average, the impact of openness to trade on the distribution of the growth of income is neutral.[18] Thus trade liberalization on average does not affect relative inequality, but it does widen absolute inequality. This is not to say that some countries have not seen a widening of within-country relative inequality during growth spurts. Indeed, in India and China some productive sectors have grown disproportionately faster than others, and this unequal growth has benefited certain groups over others: urban residents and the well educated, for example, saw their incomes rise more than did rural residents and the unskilled.

Inequality Matters for the Pace of Future Poverty Reduction

While recognizing global inequality as a problem, the international community has been mostly focused on reducing absolute poverty. For example, the MDGs measure the numbers of people living in deprivation and do not address distribution issues directly. However, a growing literature argues that inequality can affect the pace of poverty reduction.[19] One way it can do so is through reducing the effectiveness of growth in achieving poverty reduction. The response of poverty reduction to economic growth depends on inequality, so that two otherwise identical economies with very different income distributions will have very different poverty reduction responses to growth. The country with high initial income inequality is likely to see a smaller positive impact of growth on poverty reduction than the country with low initial income inequality.[20] Change in the initial income distribution can affect the pace of poverty reduction as well.

Recent Actions by the International Community

There is today a broad consensus within the international community on how to reduce poverty and reach the MDGs. The consensus rests on a framework of mutual accountability between developed and developing countries. This consensus recognizes the need to harness global forces to tackle poverty through

- Better access of developing country producers to developed country markets
- Better access to international financial resources to boost investment in health, education, and infrastructure and to reduce vulnerability to external shocks and natural disasters
- Debt relief to free up resources for investing in health, education, water and sanitation, and to reduce debt overhang
- Adapting technological and scientific advances and medical research to directly benefit the poor.

For their part, developing countries need to pursue sound policies and make a commitment to good governance, which is central to development. Governments in developing countries need to be accountable to their citizens for the delivery of services such as health, education, and infrastructure and for their use of resources. Strengthening the quality of developing countries' public financial management is central to this framework. Building on this consensus, there is an urgent need for all parties—developed and developing countries alike—to scale up their action.

Development and the world's poor took center stage in the world arena in 2005. This "Year of Development" kicked off with the UN Millennium Project and reached a high point with the UN World Summit in September. During 2005, the international community sharpened its focus on aid, debt relief, trade liberalization, and security. At their summit in Gleneagles, Scotland, the leaders of the Group of Eight countries pledged to double their aid to Africa— an increase of $25 billion a year—by 2010, and donors worldwide agreed to expand their aid to all developing countries by about $50 billion. Major progress was also made in 2005 in extending and deepening debt relief to the poorest countries through the MDRI. This initiative will cancel 100 percent of the debt that heavily indebted poor countries owe to the African Development Fund, the International Development Association (IDA), and the International Monetary Fund (IMF), delivering over $50 billion in debt relief (in nominal terms).[21] Donors need to ensure that they deliver on their aid commitments and that more of the increment in aid is available for reducing poverty.

The UN World Summit in September 2005, which saw the largest gathering of world leaders in history, drew sharp attention to the interconnectedness of economic development and security. One of the summit outcomes was the creation of the UN Peacebuilding Commission, which will bring together key international actors to marshal resources, advise on postconflict peacebuilding and recovery strategies, and focus attention on reconstruction and institution-building efforts to help lay a solid foundation for sustained development. The work of this commission will be critical to meeting the special challenge facing fragile states, in which government and the rule of law are weak.

Despite world attention, recent progress on multilateral trade liberalization has been modest. The Doha Development Round of multilateral trade negotiations, which began in 2001, has great potential for spurring growth and fighting global poverty. Welfare gains to developing countries from complete liberalization of merchandise trade (see chapter 7) are conservatively estimated at $86 billion a year by 2015, according to *Global Monitoring Report 2006* (World Bank and IMF 2006). Of course, not all poor countries are expected to benefit equally, and some might lose in the near term. Nevertheless, the answer is not to postpone trade reform but rather to assist poor countries in meeting the adjustment costs of competing in freer markets, and to implement measures to improve their investment climates.

Despite the opportunities offered by trade liberalization, members of the World Trade Organization have so far been unable to make progress on modalities for market access for agricultural and nonagricultural products; as a consequence, the Doha round's deadlines have repeatedly been missed. Members face a challenge to conclude the negotiations in 2006. All parties must redouble their efforts to reach an ambitious conclusion of the Doha round: key items are for the European Union to expand access to its agricultural market, for the European Union and the United States to reduce their domestic support to agriculture, and for developing countries to further liberalize their manufacturing and services sectors.

To further influence the global response to poverty, poor countries also need to exert greater influence in international forums. An active debate is ongoing on the appropriate share and representation of developing countries in international financial institutions.

The Role of the World Bank in Poverty Reduction

The World Bank's mission is to work for a world free of poverty. The Bank is helping developing countries and their people achieve the MDGs and sustained development through a two-pillar strategy: building a climate for investment, jobs, and sustainable economic growth; and investing in and empowering poor people to participate in development. The development strategy recognizes that strong growth requires an economic environment that is conducive to investment, job creation, and productivity growth. It also recognizes that economic growth cannot be sustained without human development. Thus, investing in education, health, and gender equality and achieving the MDGs are vital in helping to empower people so that they can better participate in the development process.

The World Bank helps countries reduce poverty and sustain development by providing financial assistance—concessionary financing through loans and grants from its affiliate IDA, and nonconcessionary financing through the International Bank for Reconstruction and Development (IBRD)—as well as a wide range of policy advisory and analytical services and technical assistance. In conducting these activities, the Bank tailors its support to the needs of the recipient country. The Bank's programs help to foster economic and financial stability, enhance the investment climate and the development of the private sector, promote more open international trade, improve infrastructure services, strengthen governance and fight corruption, and promote environmental sustainability. Through its programs the Bank also supports education, promotes gender equality, improves health outcomes, and combats communicable disease.

IDA is the largest source of concessional financial assistance for the world's poorest countries. Traditionally, IDA provided assistance in the form of highly concessional credits, but since fiscal 2003, it has expanded the use of grants for the poorest and most deeply indebted countries. IDA commitments totaled $8.7 billion in fiscal 2005. Africa received $3.9 billion, followed by South Asia at $2.9 billion and East Asia and the Pacific at $1.1 billion. The sectors receiving the largest support were public administration, including law and justice, $2.2 billion; health and social services, $1.3 billion; and transportation, $1.1 billion. IDA allocates resources to individual countries on the basis of their need and performance. The performance factors include the quality of policies and institutions, with a particular emphasis on governance.[22] IBRD commitments were $13.6 billion in fiscal 2005.

The Bank works closely and continuously with national governments, bilateral donors, other international institutions, the private sector, civil society organizations, and other stakeholders to improve the effectiveness of its development activities. Through these sustained, cooperative efforts it hopes to come ever closer to achieving its goal of a world free of poverty.

Notes

1. See Sen (1999, especially chapters 3 and 4).
2. See Atkinson and Bourguignon (2000) for a detailed discussion of economic inequality.
3. The PPP exchange rate states the number of units of local currency required to purchase the same basket of goods and services that can be purchased for one dollar in the United States.
4. Current practice is to use a single consumption level or gross domestic product PPP for a country. The International Comparisons Program will produce poverty comparisons where, for the first time, there will be separate conversion factors for each income group—that is, there will be income-specific baskets.
5. See Milanovic (2006) and Ravallion (2003).
6. An added complication is that income-per-capita measures based on the national accounts can be quite different from those based on disposable income from household surveys. This means that inequality measures will be sensitive to the data source.
7. Bourguignon, Levin, and Rosenblatt (2004).
8. See Milanovic (2006). Dikanov and Ward (2001) and Bourguignon and Morrison (2002) find a decline of about 1 point in the Gini index. Bhalla (2002) suggests that the decline is about 3 to 4 points.
9. Milanovic (2006).
10. United Nations (2004).
11. Krueger and Maleckova (2003) find little evidence of a direct link between poverty and terrorism.
12. There is a considerable literature on the links between poverty and conflict; see, for example, Collier and Hoeffler (2002) and Humphreys and Varshney (2004). The empirical evidence suggests that poverty and slow growth increase the risk of conflict and that conflict worsens poverty by imposing a steep financial cost on an economy and adversely affecting growth.
13. Dikhanov (2005).
14. See Easterly (forthcoming), Winters, McCulloch, and McKay (2004), and Winters (forthcoming) for detailed discussions of the channels through which globalization affects the poor.
15. Harrison (forthcoming).
16. Winters, McCulloch, and McKay (2004).
17. See Ravallion (2003) and Deaton (2004) for a discussion of these issues. Ravallion (2003) argues that quality-of-data issues also contribute to the controversy over the impact of globalization.
18. See Dollar and Kraay (2002).

19. See World Bank (2005), Aghion, Caroli, and Garcia-Penalosa (1999), Dikhanov (2005), and Ravallion (2005b).
20. Ravallion (2005b).
21. The cutoff date for debt relief was the end of 2004 for the African Development Fund and the IMF, and the end of 2003 for IDA.
22. See World Bank and IMF (2006).

Selected Readings and Cited References

Aghion, Philippe, Eva Caroli, and Cecilia Garcia-Penalosa. 1999. "Inequality and Economic Growth: The Perspectives of the New Growth Theories." *Journal of Economic Literature* 37(4): 1615–60.

Atkinson, Anthony B., and François Bourguignon, eds. 2000. *Handbook of Income Distribution*, vol. 1. Amsterdam: Elsevier Science.

Bhalla, Surjit. 2002. *Imagine There's No Country: Poverty, Inequality, and Growth in the Era of Globalization.* Washington, DC: Institute for International Economics.

Bourguignon, François, Victoria Levin, and David Rosenblatt. 2004. "Declining International Inequality and Economic Divergence: Reviewing the Evidence through Different Lenses." *Economie Internationale* 1000: 13–25.

Bourguignon, François, and Christian Morrisson. 2002. "Inequality Among World Citizens: 1820–1992." *American Economic Review* 92 (4): 727–44.

Collier, Paul, and Anke Hoeffler. 2002. "On the Incidence of Civil War in Africa." *Journal of Conflict Resolution* 46 (1): 13–28.

Deaton, Angus. 2004. "Measuring Poverty." Manuscript Research Program in Development Studies. Princeton, NJ: Princeton University.

Dikhanov, Yuri. 2005. "Trends in Global Income Distribution, 1970–2000, and Scenarios for 2015." Human Development Report Office Occasional Paper, United Nations Development Programme, New York.

Dikhanov, Yuri, and Michael Ward. 2001. "Evolution of the Global Distribution of Income, 1970–99." United Nations Development Programme, New York.

Dollar, David, and Aart Kraay. 2002. "Growth is Good for the Poor." *Journal of Economic Growth* 7: 195–225.

Easterly, William. Forthcoming. "Globalization, Poverty, and All That: Factor Endowment versus Productivity Views." In *Globalization and Poverty*, ed. Ann Harrison. Chicago: University of Chicago Press.

Gallup International. 2005. "Voice of the People 2005: Hunger and Poverty." Available at http://www.voice-of-the-people.net.

Harrison, Ann. Forthcoming. "Globalization and Poverty." In *Globalization and Poverty*, ed. Ann Harrison. Chicago: University of Chicago Press.

Humphreys, Macartan, and Ashtoush Varshney. 2004. "Violent Conflict and the Millennium Development Goals: Diagnosis and Recommendations." Presented at the MDG Poverty Task Force Workshop, Bangkok, June.

Krueger, Alan B., and Jitka Maleckova. 2003. "Education, Poverty and Terrorism: Is There a Causal Connection?" *Journal of Economic Perspectives* 17 (4): 119–44.

Milanovic, Branko. 2002. "Can We Discern the Effect of Globalization on Income Distribution?" Policy Research Working Paper, World Bank, Washington, DC.

_____. 2006. "Global Inequality: What It Is and Why It Matters." Washington, DC: World Bank.

Ravallion, Martin. 2003. "The Debate on Globalization, Poverty and Inequality: Why Measurement Matters." *International Affairs* 79 (4): 739–54.

_____. 2005a. "A Poverty-Inequality Trade-off?" Policy Research Working Paper 3579, World Bank, Washington, DC.

_____. 2005b. "Inequality Is Bad for the Poor." Policy Research Working Paper 3677, World Bank, Washington, DC.

Sen, Amartya, 1999. *Development as Freedom.* New York: Knopf.

United Nations. 2000. "Resolution Adopted by General Assembly: 55/2 United Nations Millennium Declaration." United Nations, New York.

_____. 2001. "Road Map Towards Implementation of the United Nations Millennium Declaration." Report of the Secretary General, United Nations, New York.

_____. 2004. *A More Secure World: Our Shared Responsibility.* Report of the High-level Panel on Threats, Challenges and Change. New York: United Nations.

United Nations Development Programme. 2005. *Human Development Report 2005.* New York: United Nations.

Winters, Alan L. Forthcoming. "Trade and Poverty in Africa." *Journal of Development Studies.*

Winters, Alan L., Neil McCulloch, and Andrew McKay. 2004. "Trade Liberalization and Poverty: The Evidence So Far." *Journal of Economic Literature* 42: 72–115.

World Bank. 1990. *World Development Report 1990: Poverty.* New York: Oxford University Press.

_____. 2000. *World Development Report 2000/2001: Attacking Poverty.* Washington, DC.

_____. 2005. *World Development Report 2006: Equity and Development.* Washington, DC.

World Bank and International Monetary Fund. 2006. *Global Monitoring Report 2006.* Washington, DC.

Selected Web Links on Poverty and Inequality

MacArthur Network	http://www.wws.princeton.edu/rpds/macarthur
Make Poverty History	http://www.makepovertyhistory.org
Poverty Action Lab	http://www.povertyactionlab.com
UN Millennium Development Goals	http://www.un.org/millenniumgoals
UN Millennium Project	http://www.unmillenniumproject.org
World Bank PovertyNet	http://www.worldbank.org/poverty

3

The Search for Stability in an Integrated Global Financial System

STIJN CLAESSENS

T he growing interconnectedness of national financial systems is a key dimension of globalization. Today virtually every country in the world is linked to the global financial system, and many firms, individuals, and countries enjoy the benefits of access to global financial markets for financing their investment and consumption needs. On the investor side, even small players in the global marketplace, such as individual investors, can direct their wealth around the world almost as easily as moving pieces on a chessboard—a privilege that formerly only the biggest firms and the richest people enjoyed. This increased freedom of financial movement has benefited all involved by facilitating trade, enhancing the diversification of assets, and expanding the resources available for development.

Counterbalancing this greater freedom and opportunity, however, are the dangers inherent in financial markets. National and international financial markets can experience booms and busts. Firms, industries, and even whole countries can go in and out of financial fashion, subject to the whims of a scattered and contentious population of investors, who often behave more like an angry herd than the rational *homo economicus* of economic theory. Whole economies can be left trampled and broken in the wake of such stampedes. Effective mechanisms are needed to harness these flighty markets and ensure that their vital energy is directed to productive, not destructive, purposes.

National financial systems, especially in the world's rich countries, have developed such mechanisms to varying degrees. They include central banks, capital market and insurance regulators, bank deposit insurance regimes, and bankruptcy systems, among many others. But many developing countries are

The author thanks Patrick Honohan for his very useful comments.

still struggling to develop such institutions. And no strong analogues to most of these institutions yet exist at the global level, although, as the international financial system becomes increasingly globalized, their absence is ever more keenly felt. This chapter explores the ongoing integration of the global financial system and the ongoing challenge of making it work for the benefit of all.

Financial Integration Yesterday and Today

The global integration of financial systems, with all its opportunities and dangers, is a topic of enormous current interest, but by no means a new one. National financial systems, especially those of the major industrial countries, were by some measures almost as closely intertwined in the first decade of the past century as they are in the first decade of this century. A long period of weak financial integration occupied much of the early and middle decades of the 20th century—long enough perhaps to create the perception that global financial interconnectedness is the exception rather than the norm. But that period of low global integration now appears to have been an interruption in a very long-term trend toward an ever more globalized world financial system.

Figure 3.1 is adapted from a chart constructed by Maurice Obstfeld (1998), a long-time student of international financial integration and the coauthor of a leading international economics textbook. The figure shows dramatically the rise, fall, and recovery of global financial integration since 1860. (How exactly Obstfeld measures integration is a technical matter; one can say that it is based on net international flows of money and credit in a given year, and that it is measured in a consistent way over the entire 140-year period.) Integration is seen to rise steeply, and even accelerate, in the last four decades of the nineteenth century. This was the period of the international gold standard, when each of the world's major industrial countries fixed the price of gold in its own currency: for example, the price of gold in the United States was set at $20.67 an ounce. By doing so, countries automatically fixed the price of each other's currencies in terms of their own—that is, their exchange rates. The ability to exchange one currency for another at a predictable rate engendered confidence among would-be international investors, encouraging them to take the risk of sending their capital abroad. It is probably no coincidence that the period from 1880 to 1914 was also a period of unprecedented economic growth, with relatively free trade not only in capital but also in goods and labor.

With the outbreak of World War I, however, this integrated world financial system collapsed as major belligerents resorted to inflationary finance.

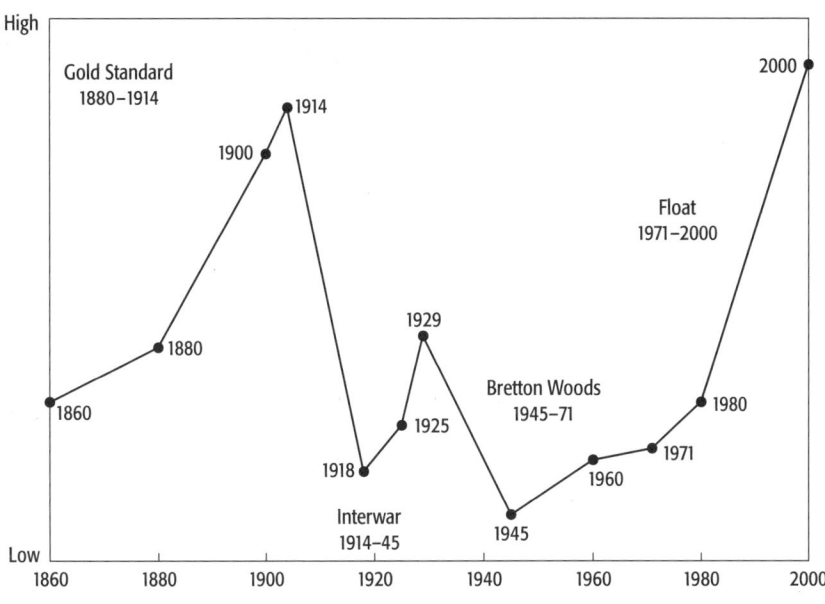

FIGURE 3.1 International Financial Integration as Measured by Capital Flows, 1860–2000

Source: Obstfeld and Taylor 2002. Reprinted with permission.
a. See the source for a description of how integration is measured.

The gold standard was briefly reinstated from 1925 to 1931 as the Gold Exchange Standard, but integration struggled to rebound. It plunged again with the onset of the Great Depression, reaching new lows by the end of World War II. After that war ended in 1945, integration by Obstfeld's measure began a steady recovery; again not coincidentally, this period of reintegration also followed the creation of the Bretton Woods international monetary regime a few years after the war. That arrangement once again linked national currencies to gold, this time indirectly via links to the U.S. dollar, as the U.S. government promised to redeem other central banks' holdings of dollars for gold at a fixed rate of $35 an ounce.

After 1970, despite the breakup of the Bretton Woods regime and the shift to floating exchange rates, integration surged: between 1980 and 2000, Obstfeld's measure rose more than in any previous 20-year period in the figure. However, its level at the end of that period was only marginally higher than its previous peak in 1914. Financial integration seemed to have come full circle from the long hiatus of world wars and depression, and in recent years it appears poised to continue its long-term upward trend.

Figure 3.2 uses differences in international interest rates to demonstrate the same historical cycle of financial integration, disintegration, and reintegration at a higher level than before. The *law of one price* says that two sellers cannot charge very different prices for the same good if buyers can purchase it from one seller as easily as from the other. Therefore, if countries are financially integrated, so that borrowers can borrow abroad as easily as in their own country, interest rates in the two countries should converge, since the interest rate is simply the price one pays to borrow money. Savings should flow from countries with less demand for money and credit to countries with greater demand, equalizing the interest rates in the two countries, after adjusting for any differences in expected inflation rates between their currencies. By the same token, if two countries are not closely integrated financially, average interest rates in the two countries can diverge and remain far apart indefinitely.

It follows that one can measure financial integration by the extent to which international interest rates move in tandem, or, equivalently, the extent to which differences in interest rates remain close to zero. Figure 3.2 plots the difference in average real (that is, inflation-adjusted) interest rates between the United States and the United Kingdom over most of the same period

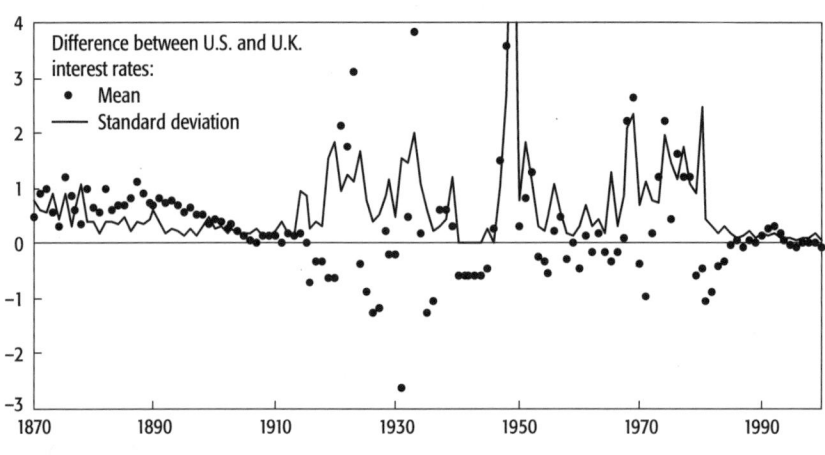

FIGURE 3.2 International Financial Integration as Measured by Interest Rate Differentials
Percentage points[a]

Source: Obstfeld and Taylor 2002. Reprinted with permission.
a. Smaller differences in mean interest rates indicate greater integration.

shown in figure 3.1. From 1870 until about the outbreak of World War I, the average difference in interest rates, shown by the solid line, was usually below 1 percentage point (with the interest rate in the United States, the country with the greater demand for funds, consistently above that in the United Kingdom). The standard deviation of the difference in interest rates (a measure of the variation in this difference over the course of a year, shown by the dots in figure 3.2) was also quite small. From 1914 until about 1980, however, the difference between U.K. and U.S. interest rates was usually both large and highly variable. After 1980, stability returns: the difference is even smaller and more stable than it was before 1914. This evidence from interest rates is thus quite consistent with the pattern observed in figure 3.1: countries were closely financially integrated before World War I and after 1980, and not in the period in between.

Yet a third way of demonstrating the historical pattern of financial integration is by looking at gross international asset positions. The first two figures were based on flows of capital, that is, the amount entering or leaving a country in a given year. Figure 3.1 measured these flows directly, and figure 3.2 indirectly, through the effect of these flows (or lack of flows) on interest rates—that is, through prices. Figure 3.3 now looks at how much of the

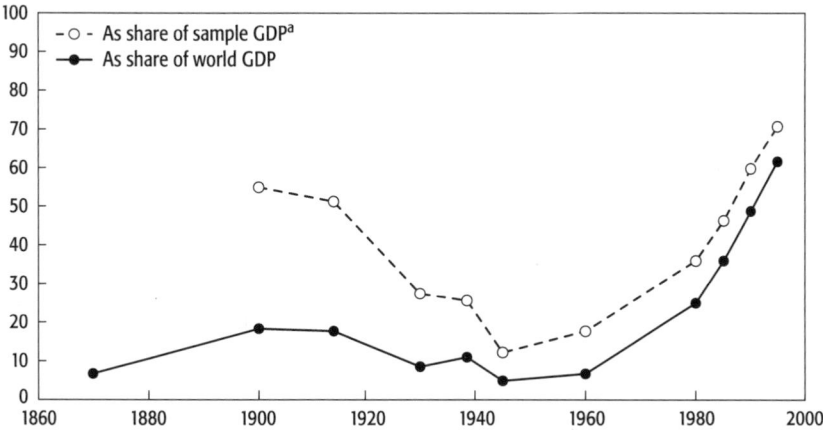

FIGURE 3.3 International Financial Integration as Measured by the Stock of Foreign Capital
Percentage of total

- ○ - As share of sample GDP[a]
- ● - As share of world GDP

Source: Obstfeld and Taylor 2002. Reprinted with permission.
a. Sample of industrialized countries.
GDP = gross domestic product

total *stock* of global capital is owned by someone residing in a different country from that in which the capital is invested—this is how *foreign* capital is conventionally defined. These stocks of foreign capital represent the accumulated capital flows of current and past years, less any reflow to the country of origin, much as the level of a reservoir reflects the accumulation of rainfall in the surrounding area over some past period, less any water released from the reservoir.

When this stock measure of foreign capital is taken as a ratio to gross domestic product (GDP), for a sample of countries that are mostly highly developed today, the pattern is again one of high integration in the early 1900s, a sharp decline during the two world wars and the years in between, and a sharp increase once again after World War II. Also as in the first two figures, financial integration is seen to have only recently risen above its previous peak. Capital assets held by investors outside the country of destination amounted to just over half of the sample GDP in the early 1900s, but only about 10 percent by 1945, rising to about two-thirds of sample GDP by 1990.

However, when the denominator is world GDP rather than the combined GDPs of the sample countries, the gross foreign asset position is much smaller: 20 percent or less in the earlier period, rising to about 60 percent in the later period. This way of looking at the data shows that international financial integration in the past was more limited to today's highly developed industrial countries, whereas today capital is invested in many more countries, far beyond anything experienced in the first great era of financial globalization—this will be discussed further below.

The Forces Driving Today's Global Capital Flows

Figure 3.3 showed that a lot more capital is held outside its country of origin today than just 30 or 40 years ago. Indeed, by scaling to GDP, the figure actually understates this growth in the foreign capital stock, because world GDP itself has grown severalfold since 1970, just as it grew severalfold from 1860 to 1970. If the figure instead reported all assets in dollars, even inflation-adjusted dollars, today's foreign capital stock would dwarf anything seen during the first era of financial integration, before 1914.

In either of those earlier periods, one might reasonably have made the case that gross foreign capital holdings mainly reflected imbalances in countries' current accounts. In other words, some countries were importing more goods and services from abroad than they were exporting, and foreign capital stocks mostly represented countries' borrowing and other liabilities to finance that excess of imports. Something different was clearly happening by the mid 1980s, however, and especially after about 1990. From less than 25 percent of world GDP, gross foreign asset positions surged to well over half of world GDP by 2000, with no sign of leveling off. This means that the average resident of the average country holds outside its borders an amount of wealth equal to half a year's income. That is clearly far more than the financing of current account imbalances can explain. What could be driving these huge increases in gross foreign capital stocks?

The most likely answer is diversification. Prudent investors avoid putting all their investment eggs in one basket, so that the loss of one basket does not imply the loss of all one's eggs. At the national or regional level, this argues for spreading one's wealth geographically and across industries, so that one's fortune is not wiped out by a single bad harvest in one state or province or the bankruptcy of a single company or industry. The same logic applies on a global scale: not all countries will experience extended periods of poor (or good) economic performance at the same time; therefore diversification across countries can further protect one's portfolio. This desire to diversify can explain why investors would invest large shares of their wealth in countries other than their own; more than that, it can also explain why they would invest even in countries whose investment opportunities are similar to those available at home.

The motivation to invest overseas was different in earlier eras such as the turn of the 20th century. Development, and specifically the high returns expected from investing in the fast-growing developing countries of that time, was the main motive behind most foreign investment—not diversification, although that played a role as well. The greater share of international capital flows went from the rich industrial countries of that time to poorer countries to build infrastructure and develop industry. The recipient countries were usually the colonies or former colonies of the rich countries. The United Kingdom was the most important supplier of this development capital, and the United States—then still largely undeveloped—was the most important recipient. Today, in contrast, although there is again a large flow of capital into developing countries, this is dwarfed by the amount of capital flowing from rich countries to other rich countries, many of which are *both* important senders and important recipients of capital.

This shift in the direction of capital flows is evident in figure 3.4. Each pair of bars represents the set of countries whose incomes per capita lay, in either 1913 or 1997, within a certain range of income per capita relative to that in the United States. Thus, for example, the pair of bars in the far left of the figure represents the poorest countries, those whose incomes per capita were

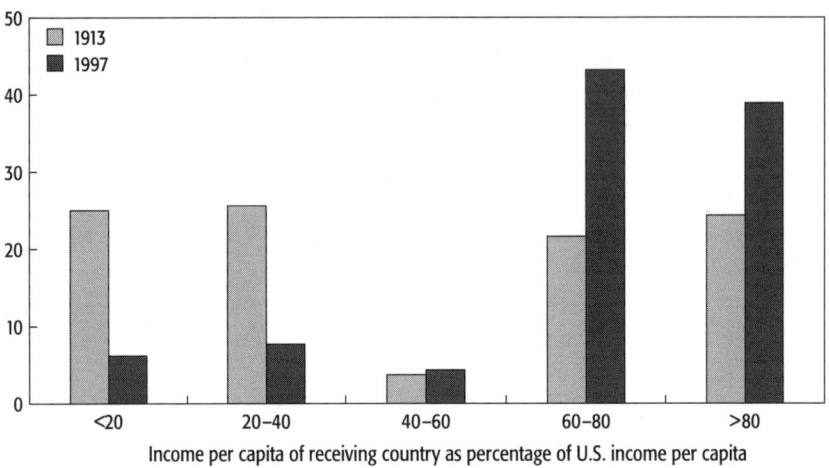

FIGURE 3.4   Shares of Global Foreign Capital by Income Range of Recipient Country
*Percent*ᵃ

Income per capita of receiving country as percentage of U.S. income per capita

Source: Obstfeld and Taylor 2002. Reprinted with permission.
a. Shares are of gross stocks.

less than one-fifth of U.S. income per capita in the indicated year. The height of the bars represents the percentage share of the total foreign capital stock residing in that set of countries in either 1913 or 1997. Since all possible levels of income are represented in the figure, the sum of the bar heights for each year equals 100 percent, by definition. Thus, for example, in 1913 about a quarter of all of the world's foreign capital (which, again, means capital held outside its country of origin) went to the poorest countries.

The figure shows that foreign capital was distributed very differently around the world in the first era of financial globalization than in the second. In 1913, the poorest countries of the world were home to almost exactly the same amount of foreign capital as the next poorest group (those with income per capita between 20 and 40 percent of U.S. income per capita), and together these two groups were home to slightly more foreign capital than the rich and moderately rich countries (those with income per capita at least 60 percent of the U.S. level). (The low share of foreign capital in the countries in the middle pair of bars perhaps indicates that few countries fell into that category.) In 1997, however, the world's top two groups of rich countries claimed roughly 80 percent of the world's gross foreign capital, or four times as much as the rest of the world combined. This, too, is hard to square with the idea that most capital flows in recent decades have been for purposes of development and higher rates of return; rather, investors in the rich countries have been sending most of their capital to other rich, already-developed countries, presumably for purposes of diversification.

If gross flows and diversification are so much more important today in international financial markets, the question that must still be answered is: What has changed? Why is there so much capital movement that does not lead to net increases in investment? Why has diversification emerged as a dominant force only in the current era of globalization? What prevented investors back then from spreading their capital liberally around the whole world, diversifying their holdings in other rich countries *as well as* seeking out high rates of return in developing countries? The answer behind the increase in gross capital flows seems to be threefold: technological advance, specialization, and deregulation, with all three closely linked to globalization.

The role of technology is perhaps the easiest to understand. As is well known, advances in telecommunications have made it far easier and faster to send money and credit around the world than ever before, and easier and quicker to bring that capital home when needed. Just as important, improvements in telecommunications—and in particular the Internet—make it far easier to know what is happening in markets all around the world. Information about markets, including markets in other countries, is after all the lifeblood of international finance. Sound investment requires the ability to monitor the use of one's capital by those to whom it has been entrusted; those who forgo such monitoring are unlikely for long to have capital to risk. New technology has also led to a revamping of industrial structures in the financial sector, allowing nonbank entities such as utilities (and telecommunications firms themselves) to market financial services. The evolution of ever-faster telecommunications with ever-greater bandwidth has thus contributed greatly to investors' ability to diversify their holdings worldwide. All of these trends have been affecting the rich countries most, leading to increased capital flows among them.

With increased globalization also comes increased specialization in the provision of financial services. Economies of scale are possibly more important in finance than in any other industry. The incentive to exploit these scale economies drives the growth of a few major financial centers such as New York, London, and Tokyo and concentrates the issuance and trading of financial instruments in these global hubs. The concentration of both borrowing and lending services in these global financial capitals—and often in a handful of large financial conglomerates headquartered there—partly explains the growth of large foreign capital positions in the rich countries.

The third driving force, deregulation, itself has three important dimensions: deregulation of products, deregulation of domestic markets, and deregulation of cross-border financial transactions. The deregulation of products is partly seen in the bewildering array of new financial instruments that financial institutions now offer, some of which—for example, in the exchange rate arena—help build safe and efficient international financial markets. At the same time, financial markets themselves are being deregulated, for example, as institutions formerly confined to one small part of the financial services domain are allowed to enter others. Commercial banks in many countries are now being allowed to expand into investment banking, insurance, brokerage, and other financial services. In addition, deregulation has spurred a wave of mergers and acquisitions of financial companies, creating megafinancial corporations that can efficiently exploit the increased economies of scale mentioned above. Cross-border mergers of financial companies have increased to the point where they now make up 30 percent of all such mergers. Finally, deregulation of international transactions has made it possible for leading financial institutions in the developed countries and elsewhere to operate more freely in less-developed markets, bringing in best practices while also contributing to the concentration of activity in the large financial centers. In some emerging markets, foreign banks control 50 percent or more of the banking system.

More Opportunity—But Also More Instability: The Consequences of Financial Globalization

The various forms of financial liberalization can foster the development of the financial sector in developing countries. In turn, a well-functioning financial sector can help boost private sector–led growth, the most important driver of poverty reduction. And, indeed, a more developed financial sector has been shown to speed countries' economic development. There is much evidence today of a strong and causal relationship between the depth of a country's financial system (as measured, for example, by the supply of private credit or stock market capitalization relative to GDP) on one hand, and such key economic indicators as investment, growth, poverty, and total factor productivity, on the other hand. Many empirical tests have shown financial development to be one of the few robust determinants of the growth of countries.

But finance matters for the well-being of people even beyond its contribution to economic growth: it can help individuals smooth their income over time, ensure against risks, and broaden investment opportunities. Finance can be particularly important for the poor, because a well-functioning financial sector provides them with access to credit and other financial services. Indeed, recent evidence has shown that a more developed financial system can help reduce poverty and income inequality.

These gains also exist at the international level. More financially integrated countries—that is, countries that have opened themselves up to a greater degree to international financial markets—have been found to have higher levels of investment. Many researchers have found a positive effect on GDP growth, as well as reduced volatility, from international risk sharing facilitated through international financial market liberalization.

On the other hand, global capital flows also pose serious risks, in the form of greater vulnerability to currency crashes, surges in inflation, falls in output, increases in unemployment, and so forth. Financial crises can burden countries with crippling costs, hinder development, and increase poverty. The decade of the 1990s saw many such crises, which raised questions about whether international financial markets were working as they should. The crisis in the European Exchange Rate Mechanism in the fall of 1992 was followed by the Mexico crisis of 1994–95, the East Asian crises of 1997–98, and crises in Russia and Brazil later in 1998. Already in the first years of the 21st century there has been a severe crisis in Argentina, further financial turmoil in Brazil, and a crisis in Turkey. It is thus still a matter of controversy whether the net effects of international financial integration on growth and volatility are positive. More generally, there remains a perception that countries' development financing needs are poorly matched with the amount of available capital and with the forms in which that capital is available to them. There is also much disappointment and skepticism among policy makers and interested citizens worldwide about the contribution of the international financial system to global development.

International Initiatives to Enhance Global Financial Stability

The financial crises of the 1990s—with the East Asian crises of 1997–98 as the main trigger—made it clear that action was needed to strengthen the international financial system, to prevent further crises and possibly a global financial meltdown. Not only a whole region but indeed the whole of the global financial system had been seriously shaken by the turbulence. There ensued a lengthy and often-heated debate over what has come to be called the *international financial architecture,* or the whole of the system that monitors, coordinates, regulates, and otherwise influences cross-border capital flows and domestic financial systems.

The choice of metaphor has proved remarkably appropriate: as the debate has evolved, close analogues to real architectural issues and processes continue to emerge. A few examples: What should be the sequence of reforms—should we fix the banking system before dealing with insurance and equity markets? (Should we call in the plumbers first, or wait until the electricians are done?) Do we need new international regulatory bodies, or can we work with existing ones? (Should we add on to the house or improve what is already there?) Should we undertake sweeping and possibly risky structural changes, or should we try to get by with merely cosmetic ones? (Should we call in an interior decorator to make things look better, even if the house is falling apart?) Should we rely mainly on free financial markets to regulate themselves, or should we impose tight governmental controls? (Do we want the style to be American Modern or Classic European?) One thing that is certain is that the new financial architecture has many rooms and corridors, only a few of which this chapter can explore.

One generally accepted broad principle in the redesign of the international financial architecture has been to retain its basic market orientation. The free operation of financial markets has, on balance, served the world economy well. But, as recent history has reminded us, financial markets have certain dynamics that other markets do not, which can lead to instability under some circumstances. And instability in one market in one country can have spillover effects on markets in other sectors and other countries. Thus, there remains a role for official or semiofficial institutions at the international level and for a genuinely global public policy.

However, any effort to maintain and improve stability in global financial markets must start from one basic fact: no international body has the legal authority to exercise direct control over international transactions under normal circumstances. There is, for example, no global central bank analogous to, say, the U.S. Federal Reserve or the European Central Bank that can provide liquidity globally, nor is any international agency empowered to provide deposit insurance, mandate uniform accounting standards, or legislate financial disclosure requirements for firms issuing equity or bonds. And there is little likelihood of the countries of the world agreeing to establish such global financial governing bodies in the foreseeable future. The International Monetary Fund (IMF) is perhaps the closest to an organization with an international mandate, but its power derives mostly from its ability to step in and impose rules on countries already in crisis, as a condition of receiving the IMF's emergency lending. The IMF can and does monitor the transactions of countries in global financial markets and issue warnings when appropriate, and it conducts regular surveillance of countries' policies and prospects, but there is little it can do to directly prevent a financial crisis or force countries to change policies. Legal authority for regulating financial systems continues to reside mainly at the national, not the international, level.

Given this reality, proposals to reform and reinforce the international financial architecture have had a twofold focus. The first is to encourage countries to voluntarily agree on and enforce common standards for financial regulation and supervision; the second is to improve monitoring and surveillance of countries and international financial markets by the IMF and other international institutions.

Much progress has already been made in setting new international financial standards and getting them adopted by countries around the world. Indeed, no fewer than 60 such standards have been promulgated, although only about 12 have been widely adopted; these are considered the core international standards, and countries today are being monitored for compliance with these standards by the IMF or the World Bank, or both.

Much of the impetus for standards setting for banking systems has come from the Basel Committee on Banking Supervision, which has concluded standards for banking, dealing mostly with capital requirements, national supervision, and disclosure of risks. The Organisation for Economic Cooperation and Development (OECD), for its part, has promulgated standards for corporate governance. Standards have also been developed by the IMF for fiscal and monetary policy transparency on the part of national governments, by the International Association of Insurance Supervisors for insurance regulation, by the International Organization of Securities Commissions for securities market regulation, and most recently by the Financial Action Task Force on Money Laundering. Standards for national bankruptcy procedures have also been issued—an important development because, as discussed below, efforts to establish an international bankruptcy court have so far failed to reach fruition. These are just a few of the major international standards already in existence; for a more complete list, see table 3.1.

Increased macroeconomic and financial surveillance has been largely within the purview of the IMF. In addition to their surveillance efforts, the IMF and the World Bank have embarked on two new initiatives. The first is the Financial Sector Assessment Program. This program identifies strengths and vulnerabilities in countries' financial systems, determines how key sources of risk are being managed, and ascertains needs for developmental and technical assistance in countries' financial sectors. The second is the Reports on the Observance of Standards and Codes. As the name indicates,

TABLE 3.1   Standards and Codes Relevant for the International Financial Architecture

Area of concern	Standard or code and organization responsible
Policy transparency	
Data transparency	Special Data Dissemination Standard and General Data Dissemination System (IMF)
Fiscal transparency	Code of Good Practices on Fiscal Transparency (IMF)
Monetary and financial policy transparency	Code of Good Practices on Transparency in Monetary and Financial Policies[a] (IMF)
Financial sector regulation and supervision	
Banking	Core Principles for Effective Banking Supervision (Basel Committee on Banking Supervision)
Securities	Objectives and Principles for Securities Regulation (International Organization of Securities Commissions)
Insurance	Insurance Supervisory Principles (International Association of Insurance Supervisors)
Payments systems	Core Principles for Systemically Important Payment Systems (Committee on Payments and Settlements Systems) Recommendations for Securities Settlement Systems[b] (Committee on Payments and Settlements Systems)
Market integrity	
Corporate governance	Principles of Corporate Governance (Organisation for Economic Co-operation and Development)
Accounting	International Accounting Standards (International Accounting Standards Board)
Auditing	International Standards on Auditing (International Federation of Accountants)
Insolvency and creditor rights	Standard based on Principles for Effective Insolvency and Creditor Rights Systems (World Bank) and Legislative Guide on Insolvency Law (United Nations Commission on International Trade Law)
Other	
Money laundering and terrorist financing	40+9 Recommendations (Financial Action Task Force)

Source: Financial Stability Forum. For links to full descriptions of the standards and codes, see http://www.fsforum.org/compendium/key_standards_for_sound_financial_system.html.
a. Usually assessed under the Financial Sector Assessment Program, a joint program of the IMF and the World Bank.
b. For countries with significant securities trading.

these are regular reports on how well countries are implementing and adhering to the various new standards.

Beyond these two programs, both international financial institutions are heavily involved in financial sector development. The World Bank's focus is on building robust and inclusive financial systems that offer services to all members of society. Specific objectives are to increase access for the under-served, reduce the risk of financial crisis, enable longer-term finance, and smooth the financial effects of natural disasters and other shocks. The World Bank Group, through its five component institutions, offers its public- and private-sector clients in the developing world a broad menu of complementary products and instruments with which to build sound and efficient financial systems. These include financial instruments (loans, investments, and guarantees), advisory services (assessments, technical assistance, capacity building, and economic and sector work), knowledge generation and dissemination, and partnerships.

An important historical fact about the international standards approach, and one that has led to some criticism of it, is that the standards have been shaped for the most part by the world's developed countries. Leadership in this area has come mainly from the Group of Seven (now Eight) and the Group of Ten, whose membership consists of the largest industrial countries. The developed countries are also more influential within the World Bank and the IMF than would be the case if voting rights in those organizations were determined by population, or by "one country, one vote" as in the United Nations. Developing countries, consequently, have had relatively little input in the standards discussion: few emerging markets are represented in the Financial Stability Forum (a body set up after the crises of the late 1990s, which brings together national authorities, international financial institutions, and others), and the newly created Group of Twenty, which does include developing countries, has had relatively little input thus far in standards setting. In the view of some, the current balance of influence amounts to financial regulation without representation.

The dominance of the developed countries in the standards-setting process was to some extent inevitable: it was these countries, with their already well-developed financial markets, that were mostly at the forefront of the issues. They also had most of the resources and expertise needed to undertake a thorough review of the existing systems, and they had already been working in concert to develop common standards, through forums such as the Basel process and the OECD. Thus, the global promulgation of standards was largely seen as just a matter of bringing these already existing or in-process standards to the rest of the world.

Yet it is not without merit to argue that the standards process has unfairly left the developing countries on the outside looking in. Not only did the process give greater weight to the interests of developed country governments, but it also gave representatives of the financial and corporate sectors of those countries an opportunity to lobby for their own private interests. As a consequence, the current set of standards is arguably not neutral between developed and developing countries but tends rather to favor the former, which are the global economy's traditional lenders, over the latter, the traditional borrowers. Moreover, the process has tended to leave out some countries, like Brazil, China, India, and Russia, that were small players in the world economy when the process began but have become major players since, and will be even more important in the near future.

As a result, the poorer countries of the world have had to adapt or catch up to a set of standards that they had little voice in creating, even as they are making prodigious efforts to build and expand their often still weak domestic financial systems. At best, one can say that they had few outmoded national standards to scrap and replace. But these countries have good reason to wonder if the new global standards are designed in their interest, and this raises issues about the standards' legitimacy. For example, the standards promote free entry by foreign banks and other financial institutions into national financial markets. Although this may help developing countries import state-of-the-art technology and worldwide best practice, it clearly works to sustain the financial dominance of the developed countries, in which nearly all the world's leading banks are headquartered. More broadly, whereas the new standards typically constrain national autonomy, they put no such constraints on private global investors' choices. Perhaps most worrisome of all, the standards tend to presume that a one-size-fits-all approach is best, without taking into consideration the very real differences between countries in terms of size, development, history and culture, and financial sophistication.

Arguably, one adverse consequence of this perceived lack of legitimacy has already occurred, namely, the failure to create an international bankruptcy court. Such an institution (or a similar sovereign debt reduction mechanism [SDRM]) would have great potential to prevent future financial crises, or at least mitigate their destructiveness, by bringing to situations of country illiquidity and insolvency the same structure and discipline that now applies *within* countries with effective reorganization and bankruptcy laws. Often the prospect of a country's default on its debt actually precipitates a crisis, as investors run for the door to be first to sell off their holdings, because they fear that, if they wait, there will be nothing left to sell. Like Chapter 7 or Chapter 11 procedures in the United States, an international bankruptcy institution could, in effect, call a timeout in such a situation. This would give the country a chance to recover its footing, or at least allow for an orderly restructuring of financial claims. Unfortunately, the SDRM proposal has so far gone nowhere, in part because of opposition from the U.S. administration, but also because emerging market economies have failed to support it. Some of these countries fear that this new institution, too, would be tailored to the developed countries' preferences and interests rather than their own.

In the meantime, financial crises have continued. They have occurred with less frequency and less of a propensity for spillover than during the 1990s, but the crises that have occurred have sometimes been severe, as in Argentina and Turkey. There have been some near misses as well. Meanwhile, the crises that have occurred continue to be managed in the same contentious, ad hoc way as were earlier crises.

A most obvious consequence of the lack of universal support for the redesigned international financial architecture is that some countries have been amassing huge foreign exchange reserves as a buffer against a future crisis. China, India, the Republic of Korea, and other countries have all expanded their reserves severalfold since 1997. This buildup of reserves relates to the form of exchange rate management that these countries have adopted. With fixed exchange rates, countries accumulate or lose foreign reserves depending on the movement of capital into or out of the country. Views on what the right exchange rate model is for emerging markets have varied over time. Some years ago, a fully fixed exchange rate or a currency peg was considered an attractive option for developing countries. However, after the 1990s currency crises, the option, at the other end of the spectrum, a floating, freely determined rate, came to be considered more attractive. The thinking these days leans toward *managed floating plus,* where countries allow the currency to float, target a reasonable inflation rate to tie down price expectations, and make some additional reforms, such as limiting foreign exchange exposure in the banking system.

Although a floating exchange rate regime is nowadays the preferred model, in practice many countries continue to manage their exchange rates, and this explains why some countries are accumulating such large foreign exchange reserves. Countries with floating exchange rates do not need to accumulate reserves. Their fear of floating relates to the desire to build up foreign exchange buffers against a continued threat of instability. As the new international financial architecture remains imperfect and lacks legitimacy in the eyes of some, countries prefer to pile up reserves as a form of self-insurance. This is costly, however, as these developing countries, which arguably should be importers of capital to finance their development, become exporters of capital instead. Because the risks of a major future crisis remain considerable, the longer-run issues of the legitimacy of the international financial architecture need to be addressed to find a structural solution.

Selected Readings and Cited References

Barth, James, Gerard Caprio, and Ross Levine. 2005. *Rethinking Bank Supervision and Regulation: Until Angels Govern*. Cambridge, UK: Cambridge University Press.

Claessens, Stijn. 2003. "The International Financial Architecture: What is New(s)?" Inaugural Speech, Vossius Press, University of Amsterdam, October 22, 2002.

Claessens, Stijn, and Geoffrey R. D. Underhill. 2005. "The Need for Institutional Changes in the Global Financial System: An Analytical Framework." Discussion Paper 4970, Centre for Economic Policy Research, London.

Eichengreen, Barry. 2004. "Financial Stability." In *Copenhagen Consensus: Global Crises, Global Solutions*, ed. Bjorn Lomborg. Cambridge, UK: Cambridge University Press.

Financial Standards Forum website.

International Monetary Fund. 2005. *Global Financial Stability Report: Market Developments and Issues*. Washington, DC.

Obstfeld, Maurice. 1998. "The Global Capital Market: Benefactor or Menace?" *Journal of Economic Perspectives* 12 (4): 9–30.

Obstfeld, Maurice, and Kenneth Rogoff. 2001. "The Six Major Puzzles in International Macroeconomics: Is There a Common Cause?" In *NBER Macroeconomics Annual 2000*, ed. Ben S. Bernanke and Kenneth Rogoff. Cambridge, MA: MIT Press.

Obstfeld, Maurice, and Alan M. Taylor. 2002. "Globalization and Capital Markets." Working Paper 8846, National Bureau of Economic Research, Cambridge, MA.

_____. 2004. *Global Capital Markets: Integration, Crisis, and Growth*. Cambridge, UK: Cambridge University Press.

Schinasi, Garry. 2005. *Safeguarding Financial Stability: Theory and Practice*. Washington, DC: International Monetary Fund.

World Bank. "Preventing and Minimizing Crises." Chapter 2 of *Finance for Growth: Policy Choices in a Volatile World*. Washington, DC.

Selected Web Links on International Finance and Financial Crises

Information sources

IMF factsheet on international financial architecture	http://www.imf.org/external/np/exr/facts/arcguide.htm
Roubini Global Economics Monitor	http://www.rgemonitor.com
World Bank page on financial sector resources	http://www.worldbank.org/finance
World Bank page on financial research	http://econ.worldbank.org/programs/finance
World Bank page on international financial architecture	http://www.worldbank.org/ifa

International organizations

Bank for International Settlements	http://www.bis.org
Financial Stability Forum	http://www.fsforum.org/home/home.html
International Monetary Fund	http://www.imf.org/external/np/exr/facts/ sc.htm
Organisation for Economic Co-operation and Development	http://www.oecd.org

International standards-setting bodies and other groupings

Basel Committee on Banking Supervision	http://www.bis.org/bcbs/index.htm
Committee on the Global Financial System	http://www.bis.org/cgfs/index.htm
Committee on Payment and Settlement Systems	http://www.bis.org/cpss/index.htm
International Accounting Standards Board	http://www.iasc.org.uk
International Association of Insurance Supervisors	http://www.iaisweb.org
International Organization of Securities Commissions	http://www.iosco.org/iosco.html

4

Development Aid: Key to Balanced Global Development

PUNAM CHUHAN AND VINAY BHARGAVA

F oreign aid has been one of the pillars of international cooperation for many decades. Aid is provided from both government (official development assistance [ODA]) and private sources, most of it for the purpose of promoting development, where it plays a vital role in addressing many of the global issues discussed in this book. This chapter will discuss some basic concepts relating to aid, recent trends and innovations in aid flows, the importance of aid to development, some common criticisms of aid and how it is given, international efforts to provide more and better aid, and the prospects for increasing aid for development (the new aid architecture).[1]

Concepts

Several interrelated terms are commonly used in discussions about foreign aid and will be used in this chapter as well. The list below draws on an excellent glossary put together by the Development Assistance Committee of the Organisation for Economic Co-operation and Development (OECD) to define some key concepts (see the list of selected Web links at the end of the chapter):

- *Aid commitment.* A firm obligation expressed in writing and backed by the necessary funds, undertaken by an official donor to provide specified assistance to a recipient country or multilateral organization.
- *Debt restructuring.* Any action officially agreed to between creditor and debtor that alters the terms previously established for repayment. This may include forgiveness (cancellation of the loan) or rescheduling, which may be implemented either by revising the repayment schedule or by extending a new refinancing loan.

- *Grant element.* A measure of the concessionality of a loan, determined by the difference between the interest rate on the loan and the market interest rate (currently the conventional reference rate is assumed to be 10 percent a year).
- *Grant.* A transfer made in cash, goods, or services for which no repayment is required.
- *Loan (or credit).* A transfer for which repayment is required.
- *Official development assistance.* Grants or loans provided on concessional financial terms (with a grant element of at least 25 percent) by the official sector (a government or government-owned institution) with promotion of economic development and welfare as the main objective.
- *Tied aid.* Official development assistance that may only be used to procure goods or services from the donor country or from a group of countries that does not include substantially all developing countries.

Aid for development comes from a number of sources: the bilateral aid agencies or programs of governments, such as the U.S. Agency for International Development and the Swedish International Development Cooperation Agency; international financial institutions, such as the African Development Bank, the International Development Association, and the International Monetary Fund's Poverty Reduction and Growth Facility (see chapter 20); and nongovernmental organizations. The largest organized group of donors is the OECD Development Assistance Committee (DAC).[2] Aid finances a wide range of development activities as well as debt relief for heavily indebted countries (see chapter 5).

Current Trends

After falling substantially in the second half of the 1990s, ODA has rebounded as donors deliver on the aid commitments they made at the Monetary Financing for Development Conference in 2002 and thereafter. Assistance from DAC countries exceeded $106 billion in 2005, up from less than $80 billion in 2004 and about $62 billion in 2001. Although nominal net ODA has more than doubled from 1997 to 2005, the increase measured in real terms (taking account of inflation and exchange rate movements) is a more modest 55 percent, for an average annual growth rate over those years of 11.6 percent (figure 4.1). Growth in ODA accelerated in 2005, partly in response to special factors, notably the implementation of Paris Club debt agreements for Iraq and Nigeria. However, not all of this new ODA represents additional resources that can be used for development; for example, debt relief involves a net transfer of resources if debt is being serviced—that is, not in arrears—but is closer to a mere accounting exercise if it is not.

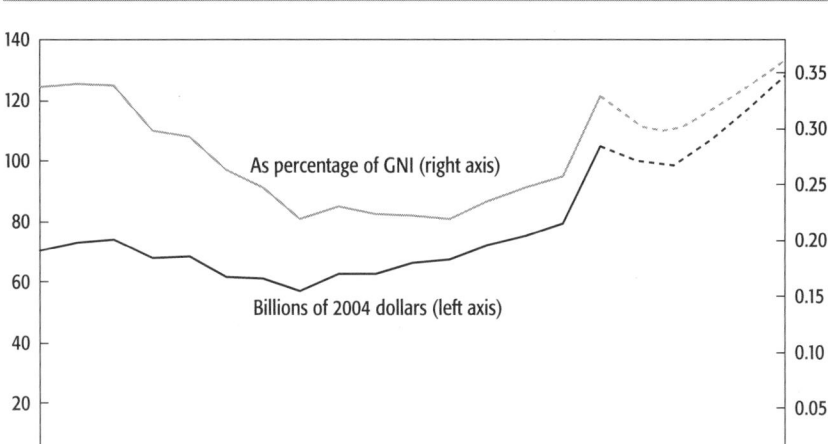

FIGURE 4.1   Net Official Development Assistance Provided by Development Assistance Committee Member Countries, 1990–2010

Source: Organisation for Economic Co-operation and Development 2006.
Note: Data for 2006–10 are projections.
GNI = gross national income

These increased aid flows mirror an increase in the DAC countries' aid effort: their ODA as a share of their combined gross national income (GNI) climbed from 0.22 percent to 0.33 percent in 2001–05 (figure 4.1). However, this is still well short of the target ratio of 0.7 percent of GNI that rich countries pledged in 1970 to move toward, and that all developed countries were urged to achieve under the Monterrey Consensus. Only five donors— Denmark, Luxembourg, the Netherlands, Norway, and Sweden—have met that target. Even with the increase in ODA, development assistance is a fraction of major donors' military spending. Military spending by the five largest DAC donors was $648 billion in 2005, more than nine times their net ODA spending of $71 billion, according to the Stockholm International Peace Research Institute.[3] World military spending that year was $1 trillion.

Countries other than DAC members contribute an increasing share of total aid. ODA from non-DAC donor countries that report flows to DAC nearly tripled in nominal terms in 2001–04, to $3.7 billion. Saudi Arabia accounts for the largest share of assistance by this group. Other donors that are beginning to emerge in importance include the Republic of Korea, Kuwait, Taiwan (China), and Turkey. Non-DAC donors that are members of the European Union are committed to meeting country-level ODA targets to which the European Union has agreed collectively; they are also beginning to provide larger volumes of aid. Meanwhile, some major emerging market economies, such as China and Russia, are playing an increasing role. Data on assistance from these newly emerging non-DAC donors are incomplete, however, making it difficult to obtain comprehensive information on the volume and prospects of that assistance. The World Bank is partnering with DAC and with the United Nations Development Programme to gather better information on aid from non-DAC donors.

Private giving is increasing as well. Grants from nongovernmental organizations (NGOs) out of their own resources grew by more than 50 percent in 2001–04, to more than $11 billion. (NGOs also often serve as a conduit of aid resources from official donors; these flows are not included in the $11 billion figure.) Private giving surged in 2005 in response to a string of natural catastrophes such as the Indian Ocean tsunami of December 2004 and the South Asia earthquake of October 2005. Global private giving for tsunami-related humanitarian relief was $5.1 billion, or 38 percent of the $13.4 billion in total amounts pledged.[4] This growth in private donor funds also reflects the success that NGOs have had in influencing policy on an array of development issues, from debt reduction to the environment, social programs, and women's rights.

Aid continues to be the largest source of external financing for low-income countries, especially in Sub-Saharan Africa. Totaling about $25 billion in 2004, assistance to Africa far outpaced nondebt private financial flows such as foreign direct investment ($11.4 billion) and inward remittances ($7.7 billion). The prospects for attracting more direct investment to the region are improving, however, as several African countries undertake tough reforms to liberalize their economies and promote macroeconomic stability. Nevertheless, much remains to be done to enhance their investment climate. Thus, in the near to medium term, increases in ODA will remain critically important for the region.

Innovations in Funding Development Assistance

Innovative financing mechanisms could augment traditional aid and improve its predictability. Progress on developing and implementing several of these mechanisms is ongoing: the International Finance Facility for Immunization (IFFIm) is being established as a pilot International Finance Facility (IFF); a pilot advance market commitment (AMC) proposal is being developed; and an increasing number of countries are moving forward with legislation to impose an airline departure tax, with the revenue to be used for ODA.

IFF, which was first proposed by the United Kingdom in 2003, would be designed to frontload aid flows in the short term to help countries reach the

Millennium Development Goals (see chapter 21). Donors would make off-budget pledges of future increases in aid commitments. IFF would then raise funds on private capital markets by issuing AAA-rated bonds backed by these pledges, and the proceeds would be provided to developing countries through existing aid programs. IFF would draw down donor pledges to pay off the bonds over time.

Technical aspects of the IFF proposal are being addressed through IFFIm, which will channel funds pledged by France, Italy, Norway, Spain, Sweden, and the United Kingdom through the existing governance structure and country programs of the Global Alliance for Vaccines and Immunization. Work to implement the IFFIm structure is under way. In addition, France and the United Kingdom are evaluating the implementation of a full IFF for health and education, partly funded by the airline departure tax.

AMCs for vaccines could complement the IFFIm program to strengthen global immunization efforts. Under an AMC, donors would guarantee a set envelope of funding at a given price for a new vaccine that meets specified target requirements. AMCs are designed to provide financial incentives to the private sector to develop vaccines for diseases that disproportionately affect the world's poor. The finance ministers of the Group of Eight countries are supporting the development of an AMC pilot, which is likely to be launched by the end of 2006.

Among proposals to generate additional revenue for aid funds, the airline departure tax has gained steady support. France has passed legislation enabling collection of an airline departure levy, with revenue estimated at €200 million a year. Over a dozen countries have said they will implement the tax, and others plan to follow suit. The United Kingdom indicated its intention to use part of the revenue from its existing air passenger duty to provide a long-term stream of finance to IFFIm and other IFFs. Many countries have welcomed France's proposal to use departure tax revenue and other contributions to fund an International Drug Purchase Facility, which would provide long-term, predictable finance to purchase and lower the prices for drugs used to treat the major pandemics affecting the world's poorest countries.

Does Aid Make a Difference for Development?

Theory suggests that development assistance can lower poverty by boosting economic growth. One way in which aid can affect growth directly is by easing the short- and medium-term resource constraints facing poor countries, thereby enabling these countries to make much-needed investments in their infrastructure, the productive sectors, and social services (investing in health and education increases the productivity of labor). Also, when aid takes the form of technical assistance, it can facilitate the transfer of new technology and knowledge. To the extent that it can influence the other drivers of growth, such as the quality of institutions and governance, aid can indirectly influence growth and poverty reduction as well.

In many low-income countries, especially in Sub-Saharan Africa, most external development inflows come in the form of aid. Accordingly, these countries are particularly dependent on increased aid if they are to achieve the Millennium Development Goals—and they are vulnerable to aid shortfalls. Developed countries can help developing countries alleviate poverty by providing more and better aid.

Some analysts have argued that aid is needed to help poor countries out of what these analysts call a *poverty trap*. Developing countries often lack a minimum amount of capital—infrastructure, human capital, and public administration—to support modern production activity. Without capital, the economic environment remains weak, constraining private sector activity (including the investment that would create such capital) and resulting in low or negative economic growth. These economies are thus caught in a trap in which low saving, low productivity of investment, and poor health cause poverty to persist. The key to breaking out of the poverty trap, in this view, is a large infusion of investment in physical and human capital, funded predominantly by external sources, given the limited domestic capacity to save. Such a scaling up of aid at the initial low level of the capital stock would yield increasing returns to additional aid (as one would expect from investment theory), with diminishing returns to investment setting in only beyond some minimum capital stock threshold.

Jeffrey Sachs and his colleagues claim that many low-income countries in Africa are in, or vulnerable to, a poverty trap because of their physical geography (many are small, are landlocked or lack good natural harbors, and are far from developed country markets), and because they suffer from low productivity in agriculture and a severe disease burden.[5] To boost economic activity and growth in Africa, public investment in basic infrastructure and human capital is needed to raise the capital stock above a minimum threshold. And because domestic resources are insufficient to support such an investment program, a substantial amount of aid will be required. Once basic health, agriculture, and infrastructure needs are met, poor countries will be able to boost domestic investment and foster growth, thus escaping the poverty trap.

The recent empirical evidence on the contribution of aid to development is mixed, however. Cross-country studies support three broad alternative views of the linkages between aid and economic growth.

One set of studies finds that the relationship between aid and growth is positive but that the returns to aid diminish as aid increases (because of limits to absorptive capacity and other constraints).[6] An extension of this work suggests that the type of aid matters. Aid is not homogeneous: some aid does not directly foster economic growth in the short run but is instead provided for humanitarian purposes or to promote democracy, establish judicial and other essential institutions, and improve education and health. And so it is likely to affect growth over a longer period. One recent paper argues that *only* aid that directly fosters growth in the near term, such as spending on infrastructure and the productive sectors, should be included in assessing the relationship between aid and growth.[7] This *short-impact* aid was found to have a positive affect on growth in Sub-Saharan Africa: short-impact aid above the average for developing countries lifted growth in annual income per capita by half a percentage point. The paper concludes that although growth in Africa was disappointing over the period studied (1973–2001), it would have been worse in the absence of aid.

Another set of studies finds that the effect of aid depends on the quality of policies and institutions or on other country characteristics. The most influential of these studies, by Craig Burnside and David Dollar, finds that aid has a more favorable impact on economic growth when countries have better policies and institutions in place.[8] Other studies find evidence that aid raises growth in countries with adverse terms of trade shocks,[9] and that aid can be effective in countries experiencing difficult economic environments such as natural disasters and falling terms of trade.[10] Although subsequent studies have questioned the Burnside-Dollar results, donors have embraced their view of how aid works, which has thus influenced the selectivity with which aid is allocated in the emerging aid architecture.

A third set of studies finds no effect, or even a negative effect, of aid on growth. This could happen if the aid supported unproductive projects, encouraged graft and corruption, promoted rent seeking by an elite group, or postponed much-needed reforms. (Broadly speaking, *rent seeking* refers to the ability of economically well-positioned individuals or companies—for example, natural monopolies—to reap high profits from their favored position rather than from any advantage in efficiency.) Aid might also have undermined private sector activities by weakening the external competitiveness of the economy—that is, through Dutch disease.[11] Increased aid can put pressure on the recipient country's currency to appreciate, as aid increases demand for nontraded goods (schools, hospitals, and other infrastructure for development). This pushes up the prices of nontraded goods relative to those of traded goods and draws domestic resources from the production of the latter to the former. Although currency appreciation can thus undermine both export growth and overall growth, especially in the short run, the actual outcome depends upon the supply response of the economy. If that response is strong, the resulting gains in productivity will outweigh any loss from declining export competitiveness.

This mixed empirical evidence has fueled the debate on the usefulness of aid. Some analysts have been sharply critical of aid, arguing that it has been wasteful, supporting corrupt governments and perpetuating bureaucracies while failing to help the poor. Aid skeptics maintain that the real constraints on growth are weak governance and inappropriate policies in developing countries, not resource availability. William Easterly claims that although donors have provided $568 billion in aid to Africa over four decades, African economies are as poor today as they were at the start.[12] He points in particular to the poor record of aid in African economies such as the Democratic Republic of Congo, Côte d'Ivoire, and Somalia. Aid failed in these and other countries, in his view, because of a lack of feedback and accountability—two elements that are critical if aid is to work. Aid agencies must be subject to evaluation by outside, independent evaluators and be held accountable for results.

While accepting that aid has sometimes failed, some supporters of increased aid argue that it is largely the donors who are to blame. Donors have used foreign aid to pursue various objectives that had more to do with furthering the donors' own interests than with directly promoting economic development. One study finds that political and strategic considerations, more than economic development, underlie donors' aid allocations.[13] They find that two major determinants of aid are ties from the colonial past (countries tend to give aid to their former colonies) and political alliances. Also, countries that democratize receive more aid at the margin. Given all these other factors that have gone into the aid decision, it is not surprising to find cases where aid has not worked to reduce poverty or promote development. As a contrast, supporters draw on several examples of countries that appear to have used aid well, experiencing surges in economic growth after receiving large infusions of aid. Notable examples are Botswana and Korea in the 1960s and Ghana, Mozambique, Tanzania, and Uganda in more recent years.

There is also growing evidence that aid can be effective in fragile states and especially in countries recovering from violent conflict. Analyses show that growth in these economies is particularly responsive to the quality of policies, institutions, and governance. During the first postconflict decade—and particularly about five years after the end of conflict—aid appears to be effective in supporting growth as well.[14] The reason is that postconflict countries can effectively handle increased aid only later in the process, when their absorptive capacity has increased. Thus, more aid sustained over a longer period is more likely to produce a turnaround in these countries. The priority in the early stage should be to build institutions that can effectively manage public spending. Often, however, aid has been inadequate and ill timed, phasing out (after the stage of disarmament and demobilization) just when it should be phasing in.

Common Criticisms of Aid Practices

Some have argued that more aid is not the main issue but rather the quality of that aid. In this view, how aid is allocated and delivered by donors, and constraints on developing countries' capacity to absorb the additional resources, will determine aid's effectiveness. Analysts, aid advocates, NGOs, and others have identified many ways by which aid could be made more effective. The main criticisms of current aid practices are summarized below.

Debt Relief Does Not Always Add New Resources

Nearly half the increase in net ODA from 2001 to 2004 came in the form of debt relief and technical cooperation, more than a quarter was for emergency assistance, and only a tenth for flexible forms of financing (table 4.1). As

TABLE 4.1 Composition of and Increase in Net Official Development Assistance, 2001–04

Source of ODA	Net ODA (billions of 2004 dollars)			Increase (billions of 2004 dollars)		Share of increase in DAC ODA, 2001–04 (percent)
	2001	2003	2004	2003–04	2001–04	
DAC members						
Special-purpose grants	29.6	40.6	38.4	−2.2	8.8	73
Debt forgiveness	3.5	9.1	7.1	−2.0	3.6	30
Technical cooperation	17.0	19.7	18.8	−0.9	1.9	15
Food aid and emergency relief	5.5	8.0	8.5	0.5	3.0	25
Administrative costs	3.7	3.8	4.0	0.2	0.3	2
Flexible bilateral ODA[a]	14.8	13.2	16.0	2.8	1.2	10
Contributions to multilateral institutions	23.0	21.4	25.1	3.8	2.1	17
Total	67.4	75.1	79.5	4.4	12.1	100
Non-DAC members	1.6	3.7	3.7	0.0	2.2	
Grants by NGOs from own resources	8.7	10.9	11.4	0.5	2.6	

Source: Development Assistance Committee of the Organisation for Economic Co-operation and Development database.
Note: Numbers may not sum to totals because of rounding.
a. DAC members' ODA less special-purpose grants less contributions to multilaterals.

noted above, debt relief represents additional financial resources if the debt is actually being serviced, but it amounts to little more than an accounting exercise if it is not. In that case, it contributes zero new resources but is merely a recognition of the fact that the debt will not be repaid. A study by ActionAid International estimates that a substantial amount (over 60 percent, and more for some of the larger donors) of ODA from DAC countries is "phantom" aid that does not represent a real resource transfer to the recipient.[15] Debt relief, technical assistance, tied aid, and aid that is not targeted for poverty reduction are included in this definition of phantom aid. By this measure, only $27 billion of the $69 billion in aid provided by DAC countries in 2003 represented a resource transfer. In computing its Index of Donor Performance, the Center for Global Development uses a net resource transfer concept instead of a net flows concept to adjust the quantity of ODA flows; thus, it excludes forgiveness of non-ODA loans from the ODA statistics.[16]

There was a shift toward flexible forms of financing in 2004, but the broad pattern observed over the past few years is expected to continue in the near term, as debt forgiveness for Iraq and Nigeria are reflected in ODA flows. For example, 2005 data show that over a fifth of ODA represented debt relief, with Iraq and Nigeria receiving about $19 billion in debt forgiveness. Beyond the near term, as donors deliver on commitments, a larger share of ODA is expected to represent actual resource transfers.

Technical Cooperation and Tied Food Aid Are Inefficient

The modality through which donors deliver aid matters. Technical cooperation accounts for a third of bilateral aid flows and remains a key donor tool for supporting capacity building. Yet the effectiveness of such aid has come into question: technical cooperation is often criticized as excessively expensive, because of the high cost of hiring international experts. It may also worsen the problem of brain drain in developing countries, if foreign experts are used instead of the best and brightest people available locally. Technical cooperation is also widely viewed as too fragmented and uncoordinated.

If it is to support sustainable capacity development, technical assistance should be made more effective and aligned with the newer paradigm for capacity building outlined, for example, in a recent World Bank report.[17] This will require recipients to have more ownership and control over such assistance, so that it can be provided where it is really needed. In addition, the focus of technical assistance should be on building capacity at the level of institutions, organizations, and individuals. Depending on country circumstances, donors should shift away from technical assistance toward providing more aid in flexible form—that is, as resources that can be used to finance recurrent expenditures in health and education and investment in much-needed infrastructure and productive capacity.

A similar issue arises with bilateral food aid. Although food is a small component of total aid (about 5 percent), it remains an important tool for providing emergency assistance and for addressing hunger and malnutrition.[18] Most food aid is tied, which raises the issue of whether untying it can lower the cost. A recent OECD study finds that providing direct transfers in kind is at least 30 percent more costly for donors than unrestricted financial assistance.[19] Nor is tied food aid cost-effective for the recipient country: transfer of food in kind was found to be about 50 percent more costly than locally procured food, and 33 percent more costly than food imports from a third country. It appears that financial assistance or more flexible sourcing of in-kind assistance is preferable, except where local procurement might not be an option (especially in areas with food shortages) or where well-functioning internal markets are lacking, or where weak trade links could hamper imports from third countries.

Geopolitical and Strategic Considerations Drive Much of the Aid, Rather Than Need

Much of the increment in ODA has been directed to geopolitically strategic countries: front-line states such as Iraq and Afghanistan accounted for over half of the increase in net ODA from all donors during 2001–04 (figure 4.2). Although recent evidence shows that bilateral donors are allocating more aid to poorer countries and to better performers—those with stronger policies and institutions—there is considerable variation across donor countries, with some of the larger donors among the least selective in terms of these criteria. Also, bilateral donors are in general less selective than multilateral donors. Bilateral donors need to ensure that assistance to countries that need the most help in achieving the Millenium Development Goals (MDGs), is not crowded out by other donor objectives.

Donor Fragmentation Reduces Aid Effectiveness

Donor fragmentation—many donors, each with a small share of total aid, leading to the diffusion of aid across multiple small, independent, uncoordinated projects—remains a problem. Such fragmentation can lower the quality of aid provided, through several well-known mechanisms: high transaction costs for recipients, because more time is taken up meeting donor requirements; failure to capture returns to scale, as too many small projects are each subject to large fixed costs; and a reduced stake on the part of the

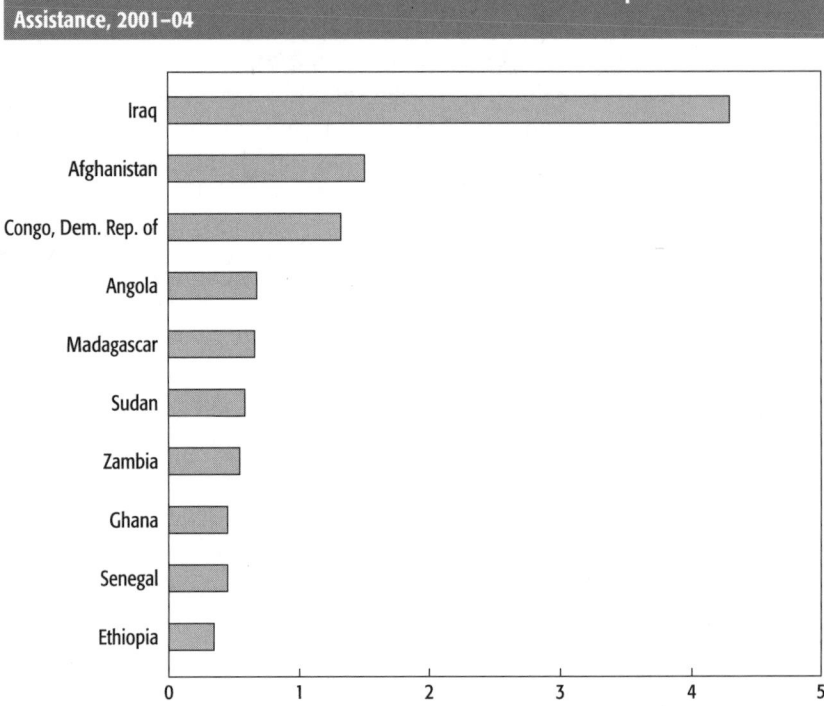

FIGURE 4.2 Distribution of the Increase in World Official Development Assistance, 2001–04

Source: Development Assistance Committee of the Organisation for Economic Co-operation and Development database.
Note: Figure shows only the 10 countries with the largest increases in net ODA.

donors in the overall country outcome. Evidence from donor shares in annual aid distribution indicates that donor fragmentation has been rising. The degree of fragmentation, computed from these shares, is moderately correlated with the size of ODA relative to recipients' GNI, suggesting that greater aid dependency is associated with greater fragmentation. Donor fragmentation for Africa is higher than that for developing countries as a whole. On average, a recipient country in Sub-Saharan Africa received foreign aid from 25 different donors a year during 1980–2002.[20] Although major donors concentrate their aid in a few countries, they tend to provide some aid in every country in the region.

Volatility of Aid Flows Reduces Aid Effectiveness

When aid flows vary dramatically and unpredictably from year to year, it puts considerable stress on the ability of recipient countries to plan and use resources well, and the result can be a loss of aid's effectiveness. The problem can be particularly severe for countries that receive large volumes of aid, because these countries cannot usually offset the shortfall by borrowing abroad or domestically. One study finds that aid shortfalls are mostly offset by reductions in government spending, and sometimes by increases in taxes.[21] Other researchers find that aid is relatively more volatile than fiscal revenue or economic output.[22] Moreover, this relative volatility of aid grows with aid dependency. The uncertainty of aid also makes it difficult for recipients to maintain macroeconomic stability through consistent policies. Aid flows need to be disbursed in a more predictable and timely way if recipient countries are to use these flows effectively.

Constraints on Absorptive Capacity Limit the Scope for Scaling Up

Recipients' absorptive capacity and other constraints limit the amount of additional resources that can be effectively provided. Capacity constraints can manifest themselves at many levels (from national policy and public budget management to local service delivery) and in many ways (macroeconomic management, institutional capacity, infrastructure, human capital, and social and cultural factors). But these constraints are not equally binding; some, such as weak public expenditure management, can be eased in the near term, while others, such as shortages of skilled health and education service providers and weak quality of political checks and balances, may take longer. Also, efforts to remove these constraints can be mutually reinforcing, with improvements in one area spurring change in others. All these aspects of capacity constraints point to the importance of properly sequencing interventions in capacity building.

Aid Fosters Dependency

In many low-income countries, aid finances a large share of government expenditure, sometimes over 50 percent. In order to lower dependency on foreign aid, which is inevitably temporary, domestically generated government revenue will need to rise. The concern is that aid can undermine the state's ability to mobilize domestic resources. Large aid inflows may reduce the government's incentive to raise revenue at home; aid also lowers the government's reliance on its citizens for revenue, and this may make the government less accountable to its citizens and may insulate it from domestic pressure to spend prudently and effectively.

Corruption Causes Much Aid to Be Wasted

There is an increasing recognition that corruption is a development issue—that corrupt practices in a country can impede its growth and poverty reduction. As chapter 18 documents, corruption and embezzlement occur worldwide on a large scale—amounting to as much as $1 trillion by one estimate.[23] Zaire's President Mobutu Sese Seko alone embezzled an estimated $5 billion, and Nigeria's President Sani Abacha stole an estimated $2 billion to $5 billion. The recent report on the United Nations Oil-for-Food program for Iraq found evidence of $1.8 billion in kickbacks from oil companies and suppliers to the Iraqi government.[24]

The sheer size of aid flows to developing countries opens multiple opportunities for resources to be diverted to improper uses. The primary responsibility for preventing this rests with the national authorities of the countries on both sides of the aid transaction, but ultimate responsibility lies with their citizens; in recipient countries, this means establishing strong national governance systems and combating corruption at the local level. Nevertheless, global factors can influence corruption even at this level. Donors and international financial institutions are essential parts of the global governance framework, especially for poor countries. It is up to them to move to bolster their own anticorruption controls, improve transparency, encourage adherence to internationally recognized standards and codes, and work with their clients to encourage domestic accountability.

How the International Community Is Responding to the Aid Challenge

Donors are keenly focused on increasing aid and its effectiveness. As this chapter has shown, they are already delivering more assistance, and the prospects for scaling up aid further have brightened. Moreover, there is an increasing recognition that, for achieving the MDGs, how aid is allocated and delivered is as important as how much aid is provided. Aid is more effective when it is aligned with recipients' development priorities, when it reduces transaction costs through harmonized and coordinated donor processes, when it is more predictable, and when there is a clear focus on results. The last several years have seen substantial changes in country-level delivery processes.

Increasing the Volume of Aid

At their July 2005 summit in Gleneagles, Scotland, the leaders of the Group of Eight leading industrial countries committed to increase aid to Africa by $25 billion a year by 2010, more than doubling assistance to the region. DAC members have also agreed to expand aid to all developing countries by about $50 billion a year by 2010. These promises would raise DAC donors' ODA to 0.36 percent of their GNI in 2010. In May 2005, DAC members of the European Union (EU) set an intermediate target for their collective ODA-GNI ratio of 0.56 percent for 2010, and they revised their target for 2006 upward to 0.42 percent, from 0.39 percent.[25] These pledges represent a near doubling of assistance, to $81 billion (in 2004 dollars) by 2010 for this donor group. Countries also reaffirmed their commitment to raise their ODA to 0.7 percent of GNI by 2015. If all DAC countries' commitments are delivered upon, ODA measured in 2004 dollars would be just under $100 billion in 2006 and would rise to about $128 billion by 2010.

To achieve these targets, ODA will have to expand at an accelerated pace. Total ODA will need to grow 50 percent faster (in real terms) from 2004 to 2010 than it did on average from 2001 to 2004; the pace of growth will need to triple for those EU members that are also DAC countries. Implementation of Paris Club debt agreements for Iraq and Nigeria are expected to boost aid volumes in the near term (through 2006). Beyond that, more of the increase in ODA will represent a real transfer of resources, perhaps raising difficulties for donors that deliver a large share of their aid through debt relief. For several countries, the acceleration in the growth of ODA required to meet commitments might be much greater. Coming at a time when public budgets are under pressure, could introduce some uncertainty in medium-term aid volumes.

The prospect of significant additional amounts of aid make improved monitoring of commitments and flows all the more important. Careful monitoring is needed not only to assess progress in implementing promises but also to build momentum for emulating best practice. Just as important, monitoring can help clarify the scale of resources that will become available over the medium term, and how this scaling up will translate into availability of resources at the country level. By providing such information reliably over the next few years, monitoring can facilitate improvements in the transparency and coordination of aid and help improve its predictability. Donors recognize the challenge of providing three-year forward projections on aid at the country level and have asked DAC to undertake an effort to collect such information.

Scaling up will also require better coordination among aid delivery channels—bilateral funds, global funds, multilateral funds, and private funds. The growth of global programs and funds and the emergence of new bilateral and private donors are increasing both the number and the bandwidth of delivery channels. More coordination among donors will be essential to delivering this assistance effectively. For example, global funds need to support country-led development strategies and priorities and not undermine the capacity of national authorities for coherent planning, financing, and service delivery. Likewise, bilateral donors need to shift toward delegated cooperation, so as to make use of the comparative advantages of individual donors. The first step to achieving better coordination will be better sharing of information on planned donor activities.

Focusing on Harmonization, Alignment, and Results

Donors have sharpened their focus on improving aid delivery. The Paris Declaration on Aid Effectiveness, endorsed by officials of about 90 countries and 27 aid agencies in March 2005, gave a boost to the aid effectiveness agenda. Through the Paris Declaration, which built on the 2003 High Level Forum on Harmonization in Rome and the 2004 Roundtable on Managing for Development Results in Marrakech, donors and partners agreed to mutual accountability in carrying out the partnership agreements made by both sides. Building on the principles of ownership, alignment, harmonization, managing for results, and mutual accountability, the agenda set by the Paris Declaration specifies monitorable, time-bound actions to improve the quality of aid. Broad-based support for this agenda has translated into progress at the global level, as evidenced by the adoption of global targets for 2010 for the 12 indicators in the Paris Declaration. Much remains to be done, however, as indicated by the gaps between the preliminary baselines and the agreed global targets.[26] Progress in implementing the Paris framework at the country level has been mixed—only a few countries have seen substantive progress in the customization of several Paris indicators and targets to the country context. Vigorous implementation of the Paris agenda is needed to deliver more effective development assistance.

Mutual accountability of donors and partners is the cornerstone of the new international aid architecture.[27] Along with higher aid volumes, the new architecture calls for better aid coordination, more effective aid delivery, and a sharper focus on results. It also recognizes the centrality of governance and institutions, the importance of strengthening public sector management, and the need to address absorptive capacity constraints. Faster progress in implementing this partnership framework is needed for achieving the MDGs.

The Role of the World Bank

The World Bank is a vital source of financial assistance to developing countries around the world. The World Bank also plays a leadership role in the global aid community through its analytic and advisory work. The International Development Association (IDA) is the affiliate of the World Bank that helps the world's poorest countries by providing resources—concessional finance and grants—for programs aimed at boosting economic growth and improving living conditions. IDA credits are interest-free loans with repayments stretched over 35 to 40 years, including a 10-year grace period. In 2002, IDA began providing a significant portion of its resources in the form of grants, which are anticipated to account for approximately 30 percent of IDA's commitments in the coming years.

The allocation of IDA's resources is determined primarily by each borrower's rating in the annual country performance and institutional assessment (CPIA). In addition to CPIA, portfolio performance and governance also feature in the allocation process. Together with these factors, population and income per capita also determine IDA allocations. IDA plays a leading role at the country level, working with countries and donors to help coordinate programs. Many IDA programs are co-funded with other donors. During the 12-month period ending June 30, 2005, IDA approved $8.7 billion for 160 new operations in 66 countries. Cumulative credits outstanding as of June 30, 2005, were $120.9 billion.

IDA's assistance is intended to improve the lives of the people living in poor countries. To measure the degree to which IDA is helping these countries grow and reduce poverty, IDA introduced a system for measuring results in 2002, as part of the policy framework for the 13th replenishment of IDA resources (IDA-13).[28] This system was designed to strengthen the focus of IDA's activities on development outcomes and to help inform IDA donors about the effectiveness of IDA's assistance. The system has been strengthened as part of the negotiations for the 14th replenishment of IDA's funds (IDA-14), and the enhanced system took effect in July 2005. The IDA-14 results-measurement system is designed to show aggregated results across IDA countries, reflect the priorities and processes of national poverty reduction strategies, assess IDA's contribution to development results, and link to the MDG's framework. It measures results on two levels: aggregate country outcomes and IDA's contribution to country outcomes.

Along with financing development activities and influencing country policies and programs, the Bank supports development through its analytic and advocacy work on donor country policies and actions. Particularly important is its work with respect to improving the paradigm for delivering aid, strengthening the selectivity of aid allocation, developing principles for effective international engagement in fragile states, enhancing monitoring and evaluation, sharpening the focus on results, and providing debt relief to the poorest countries. The World Bank collaborates with its various partners when addressing these and other major global development issues.

Notes

1. This chapter draws on chapter 3 of World Bank and International Monetary Fund (2006).
2. The DAC has 22 member countries: Australia, Austria, Belgium, Canada, Denmark, Finland, France, Germany, Greece, Ireland, Italy, Japan, Luxembourg, the Netherlands, New Zealand, Norway, Portugal, Spain, Sweden, Switzerland, the United Kingdom, and the United States.
3. Stockholm International Peace Research Institute (2005).
4. Inderfuth, Fabrycky, and Cohen (2005).

5. Sachs and others (2004).
6. Dalgaard, Hansen, and Tarp (2004); Hansen and Tarp (2001).
7. Clemens, Radelet, and Bhavnani (2004).
8. Burnside and Dollar (2000).
9. Collier and Dehn (2001).
10. Guillaumont and Chauvet (2001). *Terms of trade* refers to the ratio of the price of a typical basket of a country's exports to that of a typical basket of its imports. When its terms of trade are falling, the country can buy fewer imports with a given quantity of its exports than before.
11. In its classic form, Dutch disease occurs when a country has an abundance of a valuable natural resource (natural gas in the case of the Netherlands in the 1950s), and strong foreign demand for that resource causes its currency to appreciate, which in turn makes the country's other exports less competitive, so that those industries decline. Using cross-country evidence, Rajan and Subramanian (2005) find a significant adverse impact on labor-intensive and exportable manufacturing industries from aid surges and an associated real appreciation of the currency.
12. Easterly (2006).
13. Alesina and Dollar (2000).
14. Collier and Hoeffler (2004).
15. Action Aid International (2004).
16. The Center for Global Development's Index of Donor Performance combines both quantitative and qualitative measures to adjust the ODA of DAC donors. It attempts to quantify some of the dimensions of aid quality by favoring selectivity on the basis of need and quality of governance, penalizing tying of aid, and penalizing project proliferation. It also makes an adjustment for tax policies that support charitable giving.
17. World Bank (2005).
18. Generally speaking, food aid is provided under three types of circumstances: during emergency situations in which food supply has been disrupted or the local food market has been destroyed; for humanitarian purposes to prevent hunger in poor households; and through sales in local markets, with the proceeds providing budget support.
19. Organisation for Economic Co-operation and Development (2005b).
20. World Bank and International Monetary Fund (2005).
21. Gemmell and McGillivray (1998).
22. Bulir and Hamann (2003); Bulir and Lane (2002).
23. Kaufmann (2005).
24. Independent Inquiry Committee into the United Nations Oil-for-Food Programme (2005).
25. According to the Council of the European Union (2005), the objective for 2010 for each of the EU member states that are part of DAC is 0.51 percent, and that for the 10 newest EU members is 0.17 percent.
26. Organisation for Economic Co-operation and Development (2005a).
27. Bourguignon and Leipziger (2006).
28. Because IDA assistance is in the form of grants and concessional loans, it is not self-financing, and member countries must replenish its funds from time to time. The thirteenth replenishment in IDA's history was agreed to in 2002, and the fourteenth in 2005.

Selected Readings and Cited References

ActionAid International. 2004. "Real Aid: An Agenda for Making Aid Work." Johannesburg.

Alesina, Alberto, and David Dollar. 2000. "Who Gives Foreign Aid to Whom and Why?" *Journal of Economic Growth* 5(1): 33–63.

Bourguignon, François, and Danny Leipziger. 2006. "Aid, Growth, and Poverty Reduction: Toward a New Partnership Model." World Bank, Washington, DC.

Bulir, Ales, and A. Javier Hamann. 2003. "Aid Volatility: An Empirical Assessment." *IMF Staff Papers* 50: 65–89.

Bulir, Ales, and Timothy Lane. 2002. "Aid and Fiscal Management." Working Paper WP/02/112, International Monetary Fund, Washington, DC.

Burnside, Craig, and David Dollar. 2000. "Aid, Policies, and Growth." *American Economic Review* 90(4): 847–68.

Clemens, Michael, Steven Radelet, and Rikhil Bhavnani. 2004. "Counting Chickens When They Hatch: The Short-Term Effect of Aid on Growth." Working Paper 44, Center for Global Development, Washington, DC.

Collier, Paul, and Jan Dehn. 2001. "Aid, Shocks, and Growth." Policy Research Paper 2688, World Bank, Washington, DC.

Collier, Paul, and Anke Hoeffler. 2004. "Aid, Policy, and Growth in Post-Conflict Societies." *European Economic Review* 48(5): 1125–45.

Council of the European Union. 2005. "Millennium Development Goals: EU Contribution to the Review of the MDGs at the UN2005 High Level Event—Conclusions of the Representatives of the Governments of the Member States Meeting within the Council." Document 9266/05. Brussels.

Dalgaard, Carl-Johan, Henrik Hansen, and Finn Tarp. 2004. "On the Empirics of Foreign Aid and Growth." *Economic Journal* 114(496): 191–216.

Easterly, William. 2003. "Can Foreign Aid Buy Growth?" *Journal of Economic Perspectives* 17(3): 23–48.

————. 2006. *The White Man's Burden: Why the West's Efforts to Aid the Rest Have Done So Much Ill and So Little Good.* London: Penguin Press.

Easterly, William, Ross Levine, and David Roodman. 2003. "New Data, New Doubts: A Comment on Burnside and Dollar's 'Aid, Policies, and Growth.'" Working Paper 9846, National Bureau of Economic Research, Cambridge, MA.

Guillaumont, Patrick, and Lisa Chauvet. 2001. "Aid and Performance: A Reassessment." *Journal of Development Studies* 37(6): 66–92.

Gemmell, Norman, and Mark McGillivray. 1998. "Aid and Tax Instability and the Government Budget Constraint in Developing Countries." CREDIT Research Papers 98/1, Centre for Research in Economic Development and International Trade, Nottingham, United Kingdom.

Hansen, Henrik, and Finn Tarp. 2001. "Aid and Growth Regressions." *Journal of Development Economics* 64(2): 547–70.

Independent Inquiry Committee into the United Nations Oil-for-Food Programme. 2005. *Report on Programme Manipulation.* October 27.

Inderfuth, Karl F., David Fabrycky, and Stephen P. Cohen. 2005. "The Tsunami Report Card." *Foreign Policy.* www.foreignpolicy.com/story/cms.php?story_id=3314.

Kaufmann, Daniel. 2005. "Myths and Realities of Governance and Corruption." In *Global Competitiveness Report 2005–2006,* ed. Augusto Lopez-Claro, Michael E. Porter, and Klaus Schwab. Geneva: World Economic Forum.

Organisation for Economic Co-operation and Development. 2005a. "Baselines and Suggested Targets for the 12 Indicators of Progress—Paris Declaration on Aid Effectiveness." Paris.

————. 2005b. "The Development Effectiveness of Food Aid: Does Tying Matter?" Paris.

————. 2006. *2005 Development Co-operation Report*. Paris.

Rajan, Raghuram, and Arvind Subramanian. 2005. "What Undermines Aid's Impact on Growth?" Working Paper WP/05/126, International Monetary Fund, Washington, DC.

Roodman, David. 2005. "An Index of Donor Performance." Working Paper 67, Center for Global Development, Washington, DC.

Sachs, Jeffrey D., with John W. McArthur, Guido Schmidt-Traub, Margaret Kruk, Chandrika Bahadur, Michael Faye, and Gordon McCord. 2004. "Ending Africa's Poverty Trap." *Brookings Papers on Economic Activity* 1: 117–216.

Stockholm International Peace Research Institute. 2005. "Recent Trends in Military Expenditure." Stockholm. www.sipri.org/contents/milap/milex/mex_trends.html.

United Nations. 2002. "Report of the International Conference on Financing for Development." New York.

World Bank. 2005. "Building Effective States: Forging Engaged Societies." Report of the World Bank Task Force on Capacity Development, Washington, DC.

World Bank and International Monetary Fund. 2005. *Global Monitoring Report 2005*. Washington, DC.

————. 2006. *Global Monitoring Report 2006*. Washington, DC.

Selected Web Links on Foreign Aid

Agence Française de Développement	http://www.afd.fr/jahia/Jahia/lang/fr/pid/1
Center for Global Development	http://www.cgdev.org
Deutsche Gesellschaft für Technische Zusammenarbeit	http://www.gtz.de/en
Development Assistance Committee of the Organisation for Economic Co-operation and Development	http://www.oecd.org/dac
Development Assistance Committee of the Organisation for Economic Co-operation and Development Glossary	http://www.oecd.org/glossary/0,2586,en _2649_33721_1965693_1_1_1_1,00.html
EuropeAid	http://ec.europa.eu/comm/europeaid/ index_en.htm
Japan International Cooperation Agency	http://www.jica.go.jp
Overseas Development Institute	http://www.odi.org.uk
Swedish International Development Cooperation Agency	http://www.sida.se
U.K. Department for International Development	http://www.dfid.gov.uk
U.S. Agency for International Development	http://www.usaid.gov
World Bank page on aid effectiveness research	http://www.worldbank/aid

5

Debt Relief, Debt Sustainability, and Growth in Low-Income Countries

SONA VARMA

familiar saying in finance is that when a small borrower can't pay, it's the borrower's problem, but when a big borrower can't pay, it's the lender's problem. By the same token, when dozens of impoverished borrowing countries around the world can't pay, it's a global issue. Debt sustainability—the ability of a country to meet its debt service obligations without resort to exceptional financing or a major correction in its balance of income and expenditure—is an important precondition for that country's economic stability. Without it, investors both domestic and foreign will not continue to invest in the country and its people, and without investment, economic growth and development will slow and stall. But because repayment of debt depends on growth and development in the debtor country, when many such countries see their economies become unstable and thus fail to grow, those who lent to those countries are put at risk as well. This means that a country's debt sustainability matters not only to the debtor country itself but also to its creditors. And when such lenders see their financial positions weakened, their ability to lend to other, healthier borrowing countries becomes compromised, possibly causing that growth to stall as well. It is in this sense that unsustainable debt in the world's poorest countries is an issue of global concern.

Unlike middle-income countries, low-income countries rely mostly on official aid to finance their development. However, many have proved

Valuable inputs in the preparation of this chapter were received from Soniya Mitra, Mark Roland Thomas, and Luca Bandiera of the World Bank and Christina Daseking of the International Monetary Fund.

unable to use the loans offered to them on highly concessional terms, often decades ago, to generate sufficient growth to repay those loans.[1] At first, some creditors addressed the problem by offering what was euphemistically called *precautionary lending,* intended to maintain positive net transfers to borrowing countries and keep them from defaulting. However, this only postponed resolution of the growing problem of unsustainable debt burdens. Gradually, it became clear that something had to be done, and on a global scale, to relieve the debt burdens of these desperately poor countries. The alternative was that a large proportion of humanity would face a grim economic future, with consequences for the rest of the world economy as well.

Meanwhile some politicians, civil society organizations, and religious groups had been seeking to place debt relief at the forefront of the global agenda. Together they played a key role in lobbying for multilateral debt relief, and ultimately in the creation of the Heavily Indebted Poor Countries (HIPC) Initiative in 1996 and its enhancement in 1999. Activist civil society groups such as Jubilee International held numerous debt relief campaigns worldwide, which painted debt as evil and pointed out the large size of many poor countries' debt service burdens compared with what they could afford to spend on health and education. Jubilee 2000 was a highly effective global lobbying campaign that managed to put this relatively arcane issue on the negotiating table throughout the world.

These campaigns exerted strong political pressure on the leaders of the industrialized nations to take action. They played an important role in the June 2005 proposal by the finance ministers of the Group of Eight (G-8) major industrial countries, which called for the International Development Association (IDA, the World Bank's concessional lending affiliate), the International Monetary Fund (IMF), and the African Development Fund (AfDF, the African Development Bank's concessional lending affiliate) to cancel 100 percent of the debt owed to them by all HIPCs worldwide.

The United Nations' Millennium Declaration and the associated Millennium Development Goals (MDGs), by focusing the world's attention on the plight of the poorest, have also played an important role in the recognition of debt as a global issue. Meeting the MDGs by the target date of 2015 will require substantial financial flows to developing countries. For many low-income countries, these resources need to be provided on sufficiently concessional terms to avoid a renewed risk of debt distress. Moreover, as countries, donors, and other stakeholders struggle to find these resources, some have legitimately questioned why countries that are unable to meet the basic needs of their people should have to repay their debts to countries that are far more prosperous.

How Did Countries Become Overindebted?

The debt crisis in low-income countries is partly the result of disappointing economic growth and the use of large volumes of borrowed funds—as opposed to grants—in the struggle against poverty. As economists Serken Arslanalp and Peter Henry argue,[2] the poorest countries did not suffer from a debt overhang, a situation where too much debt exerts a drag on economic performance. Instead, they were unable to put large amounts of net external financing to good use for growth and poverty alleviation, because they lacked the basic infrastructure that forms the basis for profitable economic activity: things like well-defined property rights, roads, schools, hospitals, and clean water. In a global environment in which many economies were prospering from growing trade and financial integration, these desperately poor countries were thus left further behind. Among the countries meeting the official criteria for designation as a HIPC, debt ratios rose from moderate levels to dangerously high levels as export and gross domestic product (GDP) growth faltered: on average, the net present value of debt as a ratio to exports was below 250 percent (the HIPC threshold) in the early 1980s, but by the mid 1990s, it had risen to some 800 percent of exports (and 160 percent of gross national income; figure 5.1). The debt problem in

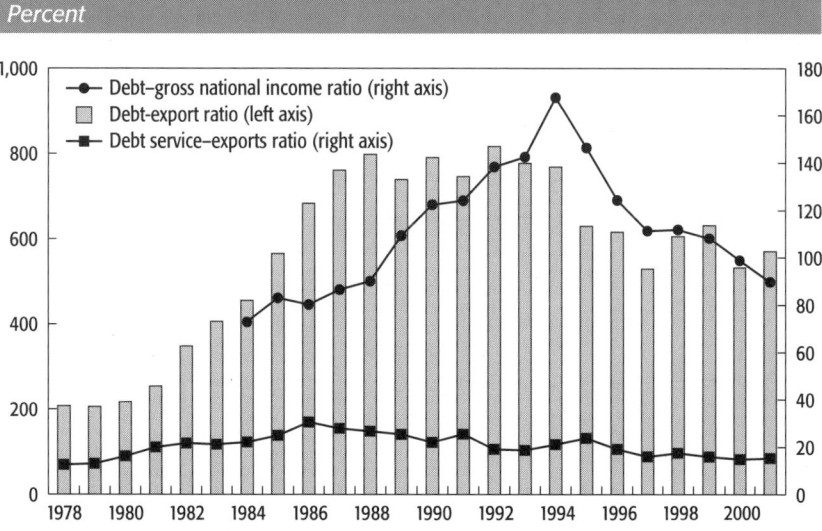

FIGURE 5.1 Debt Ratios in Heavily Indebted Poor Countries, 1979–2001
Percent

Source: International Monetary Fund 2003, using data from World Bank 2003, the World Bank Debtor Reporting System, and IMF staff estimates.
Note: Data are for 42 low-income countries for which data were available.

low-income countries is a clear reminder of the challenges that lie ahead in translating new borrowing into growth-enhancing projects and policies.

Several factors were responsible for the disconnect between borrowing and growth in most of the crisis countries. Perhaps the foremost of these were severe shocks such as droughts or prolonged declines in prices of primary commodities—the predominant export category for many low-income countries. Commodity prices fell sharply at the start of the 1980s and remained low for many years. Other factors included, depending on the country, waste of resources due to policy deficiencies, poor governance, or weak institutions; inadequate debt management (reflected in unrestrained lending and borrowing on unfavorable terms); nonconcessional lending and refinancing policies on the part of creditors, primarily in the early years, motivated in part by the desire of some creditor countries and their export credit agencies to promote their exports[3]; and political factors, such as civil war and social strife, which often had devastating economic consequences.[4] Some borrowed resources were simply embezzled by corrupt governments and never used for the purposes for which they were intended. This debt, also known as "odious debt" (box 5.1), has been an important focus of attention by debt relief activists, who argue that poor countries should not have to repay these illegitimate debts contracted by corrupt regimes. In addition, as already noted, the debt crisis developed in slow motion and largely invisibly, as bilateral creditors at first used stopgap solutions to deal with—or to paper over—their borrowers' payment difficulties.

The reasons behind the unsustainable rise in these low-income countries' debt offer important lessons for preventing debt crises in the future. Although the specifics again differ from country to country, a common theme is that lending and borrowing decisions were predicated on growth projections and marginal returns on invested resources that never materialized. Figure 5.2 shows that if the low-income countries as a group had experienced real GDP growth at an annual rate of 5 percent since 1980, their average debt-to-GDP ratio would have been about 50 percent in 2000, much smaller than the actual ratio. A 5 percent real growth rate is a relatively modest target for a developing country, yet only a little more than one in three low-income countries achieved that rate of growth during the period.

The Consequences of Excessive Debt

Heavy and unsustainable debt burdens in low-income countries have various adverse consequences not only for the borrowers but also for their creditors and the global aid architecture.[5] The need to repay debt reduces what

BOX 5.1 Odious Debt

Odious debt is generally understood as debt taken on by a country that serves the interests of the ruler or the ruling regime (typically a nondemocratic one) rather than the country as a whole and its people. When, as so often happens, the ruler or regime that incurred the debt is overthrown or otherwise replaced, the question immediately arises as to whether the country should be held liable for that debt, from which, by definition, it has received no benefit.

The issue of odious (or illegitimate) debt is a particularly thorny one for several reasons. The concept itself is not well delimited either in law or in practice, and there are no internationally accepted rules, frameworks, or conventions in place to define and deal with it. What, for example, constitutes an illegitimate regime? Some kleptocratic dictatorships enjoy the support at least of a large minority of the population, and, on the other hand, even democratically elected leaders can be thoroughly corrupt. In the latter case, shouldn't the voters have monitored the rulers' actions and called them to account when they misborrowed or misspent?

Let us assume that the regime was illegitimate. Money being fungible, can it be convincingly established that none of the debt was used for legitimate purposes? If that cannot be established, and the debt has to be apportioned as to legitimate and illegitimate uses, how does one do that? How does one determine how much of the debt was beneficial and how much went into the pockets of the rulers and their cronies?

Other questions involve the lenders. Should they forfeit their claim on the grounds that they should have realized they were lending to an illegitimate regime? What if their home country government encouraged or even pressured them to lend? Should the lenders have anticipated that the debt might someday be labeled as illegitimate and that they might be compelled to write it off? Might not such ex post determinations give rise to a moral hazard, discouraging lending to any country whose political institutions are at all questionable?

Internationally accepted norms and standards that answer these questions need to be developed before any discussion of how to operationalize them can occur. Yet it is far from clear who should set such international standards, how they would be applied, or how they would be mediated in the event of a dispute.

the debtor country can spend internally on investment in education, health, infrastructure, and other poverty-reducing activities; this in turn reduces its growth potential and thus its future ability to service the debt. And because external debt must nearly always be repaid in foreign currency, debt service may siphon off a large share of a country's foreign exchange holdings, limiting its ability to import capital goods and thus further hindering growth. As already noted, a large debt overhang also dampens incentives to invest in the debtor country, because potential investors realize that higher taxes will

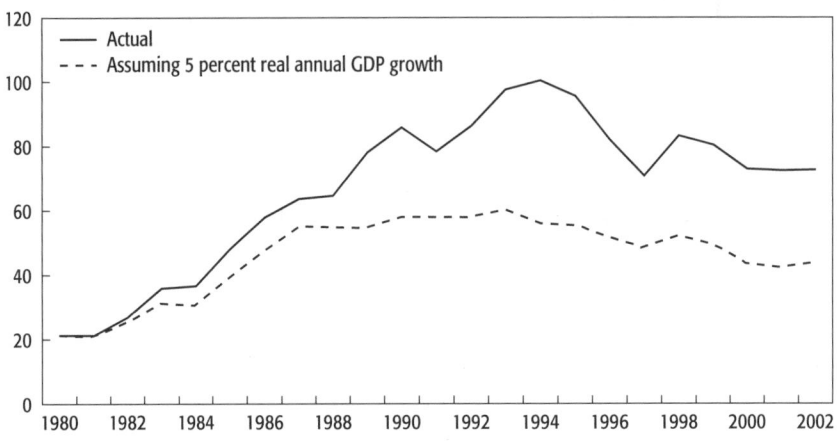

FIGURE 5.2 Actual and Simulated Debt-GDP Ratios in Low-Income Countries, 1980–2003
Percent

Source: World Bank, *Global Development Finance* Statistics.
Note: Debt ratios are expressed in net present value terms.

likely be imposed on the returns on their investment in order to service the debt. Investors may also fear that onerous debt servicing obligations may result in foreign exchange rationing for imports, or even currency controls. Multinational companies that invest directly in a developing country by building factories or other operations there often rely heavily on parts and other resources imported from their operations in other countries to make their products; thus foreign exchange rationing could threaten their operations. Finally, when a rising share of revenue must be devoted to debt service, the government's ability to implement reforms is weakened. The result can be a severe loss of credibility that undermines public support for policy reform and brings the government under pressure to renege on its debt service obligations.

For their part, when creditors must provide debt relief to their borrowers with heavy debt burdens, they are left with fewer of their finite resources to finance new investment. Moreover, creditors are often hesitant to lend to countries that have required large-scale debt relief in the recent past, for fear the cycle will merely repeat itself. This tends to result in a shift from lending to grant financing, which is seldom available on the same scale that the lending would have been. Indeed, as debt relief for low-income countries has increased in recent years, a number of bilateral creditors have already shifted toward greater grant financing.

The International Community's Response

The international community was admittedly slow to recognize and respond to the debt problem at its roots. But eventually, it did come to grips with the issue and began to provide relief, first from debt owed to official bilateral creditors (that is, the governments of industrialized countries) and later from debt owed to multilateral financial institutions such as the World Bank. Steps are also being taken to put a framework in place that is intended to prevent a recurrence of the problem.

Bilateral Creditors

The initial responses to the debt crisis in low-income countries were predicated on the belief that the problem was temporary. Bilateral creditors, who initially held the bulk of the debt in low-income countries, addressed the emerging debt-servicing problems through new net lending and flow rescheduling, first on commercial and subsequently on increasingly concessional terms. Net transfers to these countries (grants and loans minus debt service paid) remained positive, averaging 13 percent of GDP for the average borrowing country over 1984–96, but because a large share of the new flows came in the form of new debt rather than grants, they did little to relieve the debt burden. (For the group as a whole, the ratio of aggregate net transfers to the countries' combined GDP—that is, the GDP-weighted average flow—was 7 percent, reflecting proportionately smaller flows to the larger economies in the group.) This strategy also distracted the attention of both debtors and donors from more fundamental economic issues and, by pushing debt service payments into the future, added to the debtors' solvency problems.

The acknowledgment that the debt *stocks* of these countries—that is, the still-unpaid debts resulting from past borrowing—were effectively unsustainable, and that indebtedness itself could be among the factors impeding investment and growth, started to take hold only in the early 1990s, when the Paris Club began to consider stock-of-debt operations. (The Paris Club is the organization of industrial country creditors that negotiates debt and debt service relief with developing country borrowers.) The realization that low-income countries needed larger and larger amounts of debt relief culminated in 1996 in the HIPC Initiative, with its comprehensive treatment of all the outstanding obligations of eligible low-income countries, as discussed below.[6]

Multilateral Creditors

It soon became apparent that bilateral debt relief was insufficient to alleviate the payment difficulties faced by the poorest countries. Indeed, as bilateral debt relief through the Paris Club took hold, an increasing share of low-income countries' debts came to be owed to multilateral lenders such as the World Bank, IMF, and the regional development banks such as the African Development Bank (AfDB). Various stakeholders intensified their campaign for the multilateral creditors to cancel the debts owed to them, arguing that the burden of debt service was further impoverishing low-income countries by diverting their scarce resources away from poverty-alleviating expenditures. In response to these campaigns, the World Bank and IMF launched the HIPC Initiative in 1996, which created a framework within which all creditors, including multilateral creditors, could provide debt relief to the world's poorest and most heavily indebted countries.

Today, 40 countries are potentially eligible to receive HIPC assistance. Of these, 29 are already receiving debt service relief totaling more than $59 billion, of which the World Bank's contribution to date is about $14 billion. The resulting lower debt-service payments have allowed debtor governments to spend more on initiatives related to poverty reduction, including basic health, education, and infrastructure. With HIPC relief, poverty-reducing expenditures in these countries are expected to rise from less than twice their debt service payments to more than four times (figure 5.3).

Recent Initiatives

In June 2005, the G-8 proposed to augment debt relief to those HIPCs that have reached their HIPC completion point, leading to 100 percent cancellation of the debt they owed to IDA, IMF, and AfDB. (Under the HIPC Initiative, a country reaches the completion point, and is granted irrevocable debt relief, when it has implemented the reforms it has previously agreed to, has satisfactorily implemented a Poverty Reduction Strategy, and has maintained sound macroeconomic policies.) This proposal, later named the Multilateral Debt Relief Initiative, was recently endorsed by the shareholders of the World Bank, IMF, and AfDB. Post–completion point HIPCs received debt cancellation under this initiative from IMF effective January 2006, and IDA debt cancellation became effective as of July 1, 2006. AfDB will also deliver debt relief under this initiative in the course of 2006.

The main objective in canceling this debt is to provide additional resources to help the HIPCs reach the MDGs. With this additional debt relief, HIPCs' debt ratios will fall considerably (figure 5.4), leading to an average annual

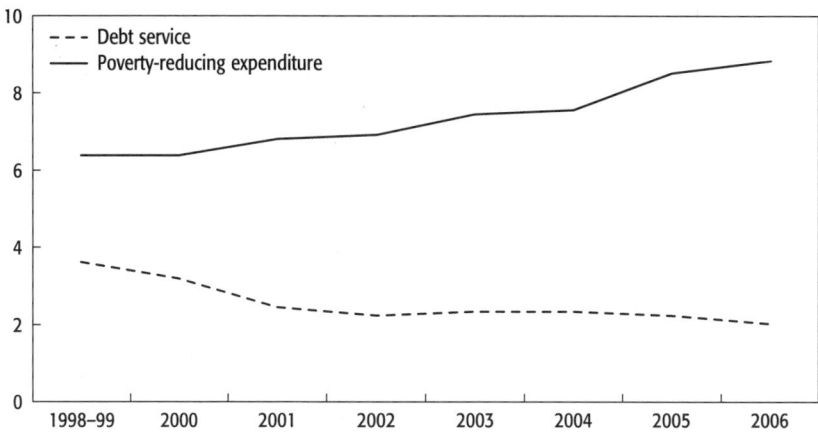

FIGURE 5.3 Debt Service and Poverty-Reducing Government Expenditure in HIPCs
Percent of GDP

Source: World Bank and International Monetary Fund 2006.

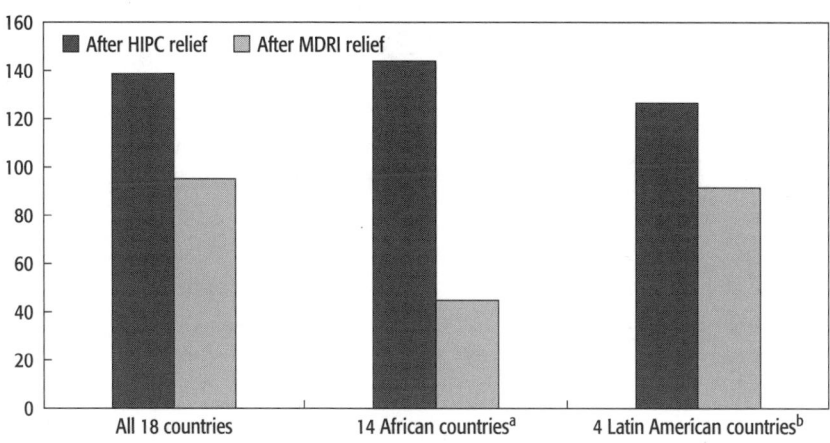

FIGURE 5.4 Debt-Export Ratios in HIPC Completion Point Countries before and after Relief under the Multilateral Debt Relief Initiative
Percent

Source: World Bank, Global Development Finance Statistics, and Staff Estimates.
a. Benin, Burkina Faso, Ethiopia, Ghana, Madagascar, Mali, Mauritania, Mozambique, Niger, Rwanda, Senegal, Tanzania, Uganda, and Zambia.
b. Bolivia, Guyana, Honduras, and Nicaragua.
MDRI = Multilateral Debt Relief Initiative

reduction in debt service payments of about $1 billion in these countries, with larger amounts after that. The cost to the World Bank of financing the initiative is estimated to be $37 billion, and the total initiative is expected to cost about $50 billion, effectively doubling the debt relief provided by the HIPC Initiative. For IDA and AfDB, debt cancellation is being financed entirely by additional donor resources.

In addition, the World Bank and IMF are implementing a forward-looking debt sustainability framework for low-income countries that aims to contain the risk of future debt crises by preventing a renewed buildup in external debt. The Bank and IMF approved this framework in early 2005 to ensure that low-income countries are provided resources on terms commensurate with their risk of debt distress. Staff of the two institutions are using this framework to jointly analyze debt sustainability in those countries eligible for assistance from IDA, and IDA has adopted the framework as the basis for grant allocation under the fourteenth replenishment of its funds (IDA-14). By current estimates, about 40 countries could receive part or all of their IDA allocation in the form of grants, because of concerns related to medium-term debt sustainability. Overall, about 30 percent of IDA-14 resources could be provided as grants between mid-2006 and mid-2008. Although further debt cancellation will significantly reduce debt ratios in the HIPCs, a strong forward-looking framework that mitigates the risk of recurring debt problems remains important to preserving sustainability in these countries as well as in those not qualifying under the initiative.

Is Debt Relief Really the Answer? Arguments For and Against

Now that substantial debt relief has been extended to a large number of HIPCs, it is worth reviewing the experience and asking whether, in retrospect, the initiative was both the right and the effective thing to do.

There are four basic arguments for providing debt relief to low-income countries. The first is the moral argument, strongly promoted by the Jubilee campaign and some other advocates: put simply, poor countries should not have to devote scarce resources to repaying rich creditors. Although this argument resonates strongly with anyone who feels compassion for the plight of the world's poor, it would essentially mean no further lending to poor countries, which would then be limited to accessing grant resources to finance their development. This would imply a shrinking of the total resources available to help poor countries invest and grow.

The second argument is that poor countries need to reduce their debt overhang in order to spur growth. In this context, the HIPC Initiative has sharply reduced debt service and laid the basis for debt sustainability in the qualifying countries. However, as mentioned above, the evidence on whether a true debt overhang exists in low-income countries is mixed at best.

A third argument is the *efficient lending* argument: debt relief is an efficient way of cleaning up the balance sheet in the event that lenders have overlent, partly in an effort to ensure positive net flows to poor countries. If provided in this context, however, debt relief might create a moral hazard: if the efficient lending argument was valid last time, why should it not be valid again the next time? Such reasoning might lead developing countries— possibly the same ones as before—to borrow heavily and recklessly in the future, in the expectation that they will once again receive debt relief should the perception again arise that creditors have overlent.

Perhaps the most reasonable economic argument for debt relief is that it can be an important alternative source of financial flows to countries that desperately need financing to meet their basic needs, in a world where such flows to the poorest countries are limited. Debt relief offers a vehicle for the international community to provide the additional resources needed to meet the MDGs in a predictable and easily accessible form. For example, some of the resources that African countries currently spend on debt service (around $2 billion annually) could surely be better used in pursuit of the MDGs: this is the main argument behind the Multilateral Debt Relief Initiative described above. In the view of Jeffrey Sachs, director of the Earth Institute at Columbia University, among others, some of these needs can indeed be met with relatively modest amounts of financing, and in such cases debt relief may be sufficient on its own to provide the necessary resources.

But this argument also has its shortcomings. Debt relief can only generate a limited amount of resources, especially for HIPCs, much of whose debt has already been forgiven, and most of whose remaining debt is at very low interest rates. As figure 5.5 shows, between 1999 and 2003, HIPCs paid the equivalent of only a fraction of their total official development assistance in the form of debt service.

To the extent that the poorest countries continue to face difficulties in maintaining debt sustainability, debt relief can be beneficial. But debt relief cannot guarantee debt sustainability. And for accomplishing the broader objectives of growth and sustainable development, debt relief is a limited tool, in several ways:

- Because, as just noted, the resources that can be generated from debt relief are limited by the existing stock of debt, the potential gains from debt relief are modest compared with those from trade liberalization

FIGURE 5.5   Debt Service and Official Development Assistance for 28 Highly Indebted Poor Countries, 1999–2003
Billions of dollars

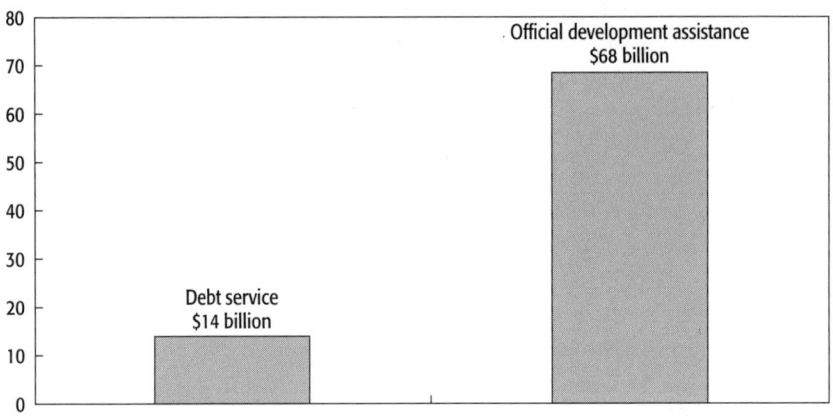

Source: Daseking (n.d.).
a. Data are for the 28 countries that had reached the decision point under the HIPC program.

and increased access to markets (a major part of the agenda under the Doha round of international trade negotiations).

- The benefits of debt relief can quickly be erased if relief is not accompanied by sustained improvement in policies and a prudent new strategy for future borrowing. The history of debt relief is full of countries that failed to reform their policies and so began once again to build up debt after having their debts forgiven.

- If donors provide debt relief by reallocating resources already earmarked for aid, the recipient countries will see no net increase in resources. Although the HIPC Initiative was supposed to provide resources that were additional to existing aid programs, donors have to some extent simply reallocated their new aid flows toward the initiative. In the future, a necessary condition should be that the donor community increase its overall aid envelope, and not reduce other aid flows to finance debt relief.

Finally, one must not overlook some other serious issues that continue to plague the effectiveness of debt relief. One of these is equitable treatment. Given limited donor resources, debt relief to some countries tends to divert funds away from other poor countries that have managed their debts responsibly. For example, between 1999 and 2003, HIPCs received nearly five times more aid per capita than other low-income countries. Equally important is the issue of moral hazard, discussed briefly above: the expectation of future debt relief may cause governments to engage in irresponsible borrowing in the hope that it will someday be forgiven.[7] Empirical analyses have in fact indicated a strong positive relationship between debt distress (and hence the need for debt forgiveness) and poor policy and institutions.[8] The presence of moral hazard strengthens the argument that strong policy performance must be a precondition for debt relief.

Notes

1. Financing from the International Development Association, the World Bank's concesssional lending arm, is provided at 0.75 percent annual interest with a 10-year grace period and 40-year maturity. Most other multilateral lenders provide similarly concessional terms. The debt issues of middle-income countries are discussed elsewhere in this volume.
2. Arslanalp and Henry (2004).
3. For a discussion of the historical role and objectives of export credit agencies, see Stephens (1999).
4. For a discussion of these factors and the specific experience of 10 low-income countries, see Brooks, Cortes, Fornasari, Ketchekman, and Metzgen (1998).
5. This section draws heavily on Moss and Chiang (2003).
6. The Paris Club provided its first concessional stock-of-debt operation in 1995 to Uganda. For a brief history of debt relief to low-income countries, see Daseking and Powell (1999).
7. See Easterly (2002).
8. See Kraay and Nehru (2004).

Selected Readings and Cited References

Arslanalp, Serkan, and Peter Henry. 2004. "Helping the Poor to Help Themselves: Debt Relief or Aid." NBER Working Paper 10230, National Bureau of Economic Research, Cambridge, MA.

Brooks, Ray, Mariano Cortes, Francesca Fornasari, Benoit Ketchekmen, and Ydahlia Metzgen. 1998. "External Debt Histories of Ten Low-Income Developing Countries—Lessons from Their Experience." Working Paper 98/72, International Monetary Fund, Washington, DC.

Daseking, Christina. n.d. "Debt Relief for Poor Countries: Rationale and Expectations." International Monetary Fund, Washington, DC.

Daseking, Christina, and Robert Powell. 1999. "From Toronto Terms to the HIPC Initiative: A Brief History of Debt Relief for Low-Income Countries." Working Paper 99/142, International Monetary Fund, Washington, DC.

Easterly, William. 2002. "How Did the Heavily Indebted Poor Countries Become Heavily Indebted? Reviewing Two Decades of Debt Relief." *World Development* 30 (10): 1677–96.

International Development Association and International Monetary Fund. 2004. "Debt Sustainability in Low-Income Countries—Proposal for an Operational Framework and Policy Implications." Washington, DC.

International Monetary Fund. 2003. "Debt Sustainability in Low-Income Countries: Towards a Forward-Looking Strategy." Policy Development and Review Department paper SM/03/185, International Monetary Fund, Washington, DC.

Jayachandran, Seema, and Michael Kremer. 2006. "Odious Debt." *American Economic Review,* 96 (1): 82–92.

Kraay, Aart, and Vikram Nehru. 2004. "When is Debt Sustainable?" Policy Research Working Paper 3200, World Bank, Washington, DC.

Moss, Todd, and Hadley S. Chiang. 2003. "The Other Costs of High Debt in Poor Countries: Growth, Policy Dynamics and Institutions." Issue Paper on Debt Sustainability 3, Center for Global Development, Washington, DC.

Pattillo, Catherine A., Hélène Poirson, and Luca Ricci. 2002. "External Debt and Growth." Working Paper 02/69, International Monetary Fund, Washington, DC.

Stephens, Malcolm. 1999. *The Changing Role of Export Credit Agencies.* Washington, DC: International Monetary Fund.

United Nations Millennium Project. 2004. "A Practical Plan to Achieve the Millennium Development Goals." United Nations, New York.

World Bank. 2003. *Global Development Finance 2003.* Washington, DC: World Bank.

World Bank and International Monetary Fund. 2006. *Global Monitoring Report 2006.* Washington, DC.

Selected Web Links on Debt and Debt Relief

Development Finance International/ Debt Relief International	http://www.development-finance.org
European Network on Debt and Development	http://www.eurodad.org
International Cooperation for Development and Solidarity	http://www.cidse.org
Jubilee Debt Campaign UK	http://www.jubileedebtcampaign.org.uk
Jubilee USA Network	http://www.jubileeusa.org
NetAid	http://www.netaid.org
United Nations Millennium Project	http://www.unmillenniumproject.org
World Bank page on debt	http://www.worldbank.org/debt

6

Globalizing with Their Feet: The Opportunities and Costs of International Migration

IAN GOLDIN

L ong before the world had heard of international investment or even trade, people were choosing migration as a way to escape poverty and find a better life. It was, after all, the emigration of primitive hunter-gatherers from central Africa to settle in the fertile valleys of Egypt and Mesopotamia that gave rise to civilization itself. Ever since then, migrants have made room for themselves wherever dynamic and productive economies have emerged around the world, making those economies still more dynamic and productive.

When the Netherlands established itself as the hub of the world economy in the 1600s, no less than a quarter of the population of Amsterdam was foreign born. Two centuries later, the invention of the steamship made possible an era of mass migration to the booming Americas and, to a lesser extent, Australasia: already by the 1840s some 300,000 migrants were crossing the Atlantic each year from Europe alone, and by 1900 that figure had risen to

This chapter draws on work on migration in *Globalization for Development: Trade, Finance, Aid, Migration and Policy* (World Bank and Palgrave Macmillan, 2006), which I co-authored with Kenneth Reinert, who has proved to be an excellent collaborator in every respect. I also am deeply grateful to Andrew Beath, who provided outstanding research assistance and a substantive contribution, including through the development of the typology and data reflected in this chapter.

1.4 million. In the present century, as the cost of travel has continued to drop, millions still leave their homelands to seek opportunity abroad—from Indian *techies* seeking high-paying jobs in the information sector, to Filipino nurses filling gaps in industrial-country health care systems, to low-skilled Indonesians and Pakistanis laboring in the oilfields of the rich Gulf states.

Like trade and investment, migration need not be a zero-sum exercise, merely transferring to one country what it takes from another. Rather, it is a way of matching opportunity with need, supply with demand, in a way that—potentially at least—benefits all by allocating resources more efficiently and revealing comparative advantage, in this case of individuals perhaps more than of nations. Migrants tend to go where their talents and skills can be put to best use and earn the best return. As they do, they contribute to economic growth in the countries that welcome them; they also bring with them practices and customs that enrich the culture of the host country—imagine London without its curry restaurants or Miami without its ubiquitous salsa beat. At the same time, migrants usually send a large share of their earnings back to family members, thereby reducing poverty in their home countries; they also promote the diffusion of new technologies to their homelands, helping those countries advance and prosper. The resulting rich mix of peoples and ideas is the face of globalization itself.

If international migration has the potential to provide economic gains for everyone involved, how large might those gains be? It is obviously difficult to estimate the impact of migration on a global scale, but one such estimate finds that even a modest increase in migration flows could boost global output by $150 billion a year. That may not seem an enormous payoff in a world economy that produces some $30 trillion a year, but even small improvements would yield gains equivalent to those predicted from liberalization of world-wide trade in goods.

But again, like trade and investment, migration is not without its costs and risks, the most obvious of which are incurred by the migrants themselves. Emigrants leave family, friends, and a familiar culture behind for what is sometimes only a vague hope of employment abroad. They often must pay a large fraction of their annual income just to make what can be an extremely hazardous journey, must spend even more to overcome barriers to their entry, and, once arrived, must deal with hostility or exploitation on the part of some of their hosts.

The costs to the host country of a large inflow of migrants may also be considerable—which is one reason why the barriers are there in the first place. Migrants may compete for jobs with native-born workers (although, as indicated below, the net long-term impact of migrants on employment tends to be positive), and they may use taxpayer-funded social services (although the evidence suggests that migrant families often pay more in taxes than they claim in benefits and that they do not consume more of such services than do native-born families of similar income). Add to this an array of language and cultural differences and other frictions, and it is scarcely surprising when residents of host countries complain about migrants—a concern one hears voiced even in countries that were themselves built on relatively recent migration, such as the United States and Australia.

Finally, and often underestimated, are the costs to the countries that the migrants have left behind. Migration has very significant personal and social costs. Emigration may skim off a large share of a country's best workers and innovative leaders, leaving the country even less well equipped than before to manage the development shortcomings that prompted the emigration.

Clearly, global migration presents countries—and the world as a whole—with difficult problems but also immense opportunities. But these problems and opportunities are not shared across countries in equal proportions, and indeed some of the problems will surely exceed any one country's ability to solve them, least of all the poorest countries. Making migration work to the betterment of all countries and peoples is therefore likely, as with so many other global challenges, to require increased international cooperation, a greater effort to understand the issues, and, finally, concerted action.

The Forces Driving Migration and the Forces Inhibiting It

Broadly speaking, people migrate when they come to believe their lives will be better in another country than in their own. But this simple and obvious statement obscures what is really a complicated decision for each individual or family, with the outcome depending on a number of interrelated factors. Ultimately, the choice is based on some kind of cost-benefit analysis, however informal: people will migrate if they are reasonably confident that the sum of the changes, positive and negative, they endure by migrating will increase their overall satisfaction—their utility, to use the standard economic jargon—relative to what it will be if they do not migrate.

The typical individual considering whether to emigrate is probably correct in surmising that migration will raise his or her income. But the prospect of higher income is not the only item on the benefit side of the ledger. Prospective rural migrants may also harbor dreams of a more exciting and fulfilling life in a large foreign city. Those who already have family living overseas will yearn to be reunited with them. Besides these *pull* factors encouraging migration, there are also *push* factors. One of these, of course, is endemic poverty and hardship at home or, in the extreme, the threat of starvation, perhaps brought on by natural disaster or environmental degradation. Civil strife and other forms of political turmoil also exert pressure to migrate, especially for members of groups on the losing side. A financial crisis may suddenly destroy large numbers of jobs and chill economic expansion, compelling the jobless to leave or face a drastic decline in their standard of living. Less dramatic and thus less well recognized, but also important, are changes in social or economic policy in the home country that make life more difficult for some at the margin. In Mexico in the 1990s, for example, cuts in farm subsidies and the increased agricultural competition brought on by the North American Free Trade Agreement put economic pressure on many small Mexican farmers, especially those cultivating marginally productive land. In all these cases, migration offers an escape from an intolerable situation. (Box 6.1 provides a taxonomy of the types of migrants according to the various motives for migration.)

Against these benefits to the migrant must be balanced the costs he or she bears. As already noted, the travel expense alone poses a huge obstacle to many would-be migrants, especially those from the poorest countries and the poorest groups within countries. In a world where over a billion people live on less than a dollar a day, saving up the hundreds of dollars needed for an airline ticket to the United States or Western Europe is for many out of the question. Making matters worse, those from the poorest countries and groups are also less likely to benefit from *chain migration:* unlike migrants from many middle-income countries, they typically lack access to social networks of previous migrants in the destination country, who can both lend the transportation fare and help the new migrants establish themselves once arrived.

As a consequence, most migrants to the world's rich countries come not from among the world's poorest but from middle-income countries or from the middle and upper reaches of the income distribution in low-income countries. Economists specializing in migration issues speak of a *migration hump.* Very few U.S. immigrants earned less than $1,000 in annual income (adjusted for international purchasing power differences) in their home countries, and very few earned more than $15,000. The vast majority lie in between these levels of income (see figure 6.1). Migration, apparently, is not a solution well targeted to mass poverty, nor does it seem to have great appeal to most people who are already well off at home. (Again, these data are for migration to the United States only; the picture may be different elsewhere, for example in Europe, where international distances tend to be smaller and barriers, at least within the European Union, are lower.)

BOX 6.1   A Taxonomy of Migration

International migrants can be characterized along several dimensions, such as their reason for migrating and the duration of their expected stay in the host country. Of course, the resulting categories may overlap: in particular, people may migrate for more than one reason, and the true reason for their seeking to migrate may be difficult to discern. The following are a few commonly used terms to describe different types of migrants.

Permanent settlers are persons who, whatever their reason for migration, intend to reside permanently in the host country, possibly becoming citizens there.

Economic migrants are those who migrate primarily for economic reasons—that is, to improve their material standard of living, apart from any other consideration—whether or not they intend to take up permanent residence.

Family migrants are those whose principal motive is to reunite with family and loved ones who have migrated previously, whether or not they intend to take up permanent residence.

Expatriates are persons who migrate with the intention of returning home after some undefined period in the host country, which may be long or short, and who retain their citizenship in the home country. They are distinguished from *permanent settlers* by their intention to return, and from *guest workers* in that their stay is indefinite.

Guest workers are persons who are allowed to enter a host country to work for a defined, limited period.

Asylum seekers are persons who migrate on their own accord for noneconomic reasons—specifically, out of a well-founded fear of state persecution in the home country—and claim entitlement, under the 1951 Geneva Convention on Refugees, to resettlement in one of the countries that are signatories of the convention.

Refugees are persons who flee their homeland, usually temporarily, in response to disruption of any sort, including official or unofficial persecution but also for economic reasons or because of natural calamity, and who therefore are not necessarily entitled to asylum under the 1951 Geneva Convention.

Undocumented migrants, or illegal migrants, are those who cross borders without official permission by the destination country.

Visa-free migrants are those who migrate freely between countries within a recognized single labor market such as the European Union.

Source: Authors.

The costs of migration to the migrant do not end with arrival in the destination country. There are still the costs associated with any move to a new domicile, whether within a neighborhood or across an ocean. For immigrants

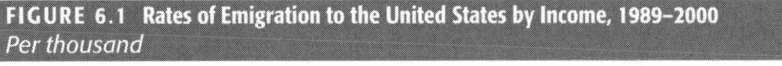

FIGURE 6.1   Rates of Emigration to the United States by Income, 1989–2000
Per thousand

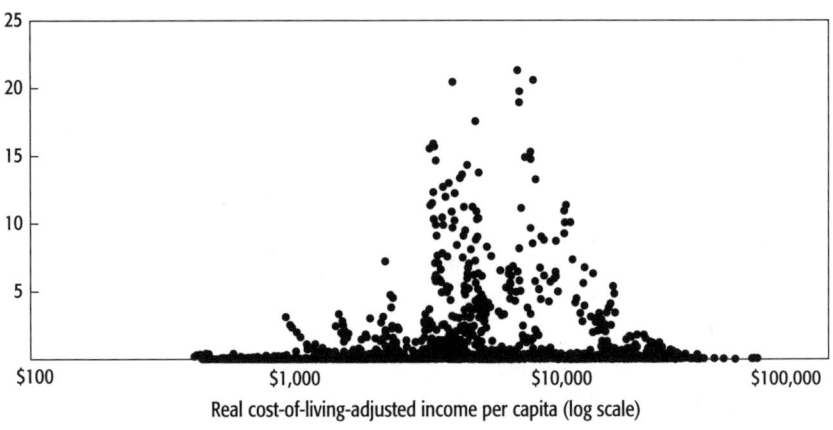

Real cost-of-living-adjusted income per capita (log scale)

Source: Goldin and Reinert with Beath 2006 (p. 167). Data are authors' calculations based on data from the U.S. Department of Homeland Security and the World Bank.
Note: "Real cost-of-living-adjusted income per capita" represents gross domestic product per capita (in constant 1995 dollars) adjusted for purchasing power parity. Each dot represents a country-year combination showing one country per year. The migration patterns observed between source countries and the United States may not necessarily represent those observed between source countries and other destination countries.

these costs may be higher because they are unfamiliar with local markets for the goods and services they need, and they may even find themselves cheated or defrauded. Immigrants often also suffer the noneconomic costs of incomplete acceptance into, or even outright exclusion from, their adopted society.

This description of the costs and benefits facing would-be migrants has thus far left out one crucial dimension, namely, risk. All of the above considerations are subject to great variation across individual outcomes, and typically the would-be migrant lacks the information needed to accurately assess the various probabilities. Entry to the destination country may be granted, or it may be denied; jobs may be plentiful or scarce; wages may be generous or miserly; working conditions may be good or intolerable. The migrant may face harassment from officials, abuse or exploitation by unscrupulous employers, and hostility and even violence from native-born peers. (Box 6.2 describes further some of the abuses that migrants, especially low-skilled migrants, all too often suffer.) All of these contingencies, in a country the migrant has probably never visited, are difficult to predict, and this leads many potential migrants to discount heavily any estimate of the potential benefits of emigrating. Such risk aversion in the face of uncertainty may help explain why, even in Puerto Rico, where any native-born worker can freely move to the U.S. mainland and expect, on average, to triple his or her salary, three out of four nevertheless elect to stay on the island.

The Consequences of Migration for Source and Destination Countries: Benefits and Costs

The previous section discussed the pros and cons of migration from the point of view of the migrants. But how does emigration affect the homeland that the migrants leave behind? Again, close observation reveals both benefits and costs.

Benefits to Source Countries

A significant economic benefit from migration for the home country is the inflow of remittances: earnings that the emigrant workers send back (as transfers, not as loans) to families and friends at home. Worldwide, these are substantial in magnitude and growing: remittances to all developing countries have been estimated at about $160 billion, up from less than $5 billion in 1975 and about $100 billion in 2003. (These numbers are not adjusted for inflation, and the observed increase may partly reflect greater diligence in monitoring all money flows in the wake of the September 11 attacks.) Latin America and South Asia have seen remittances roughly double in just the past decade, to

TABLE 6.1 Economic Importance of Remittances by Developing Region and in Selected Countries, 2003

Region and country	Remittances received		Remittances as percentage of		
	Total[a]	per capita[b]	GDP	FDI	ODA
Latin America and the Caribbean	24,153	64	2	93	634
Mexico	14,595	143	2	135	14,148
Jamaica	1,259	477	16	175	36,599
Haiti	811	96	30	10,397	406
South Asia	15,959	19	4	518	433
India	17,406	16	3	408	1,847
Bangladesh	3,191	23	6	3,114	229
Sri Lanka	1,309	68	7	572	195
East Asia and Pacific	19,532	11	1	33	285
Philippines	7,880	97	10	2,470	1,069
Tonga	66	647	40	2,454	240
Vanuatu	53	252	19	279	163
Middle East and North Africa	14,400	52	2	338	219
Morocco	3,628	120	8	159	694
Lebanon	2,700	600	14	754	1,182
Jordan	2,201	415	22	585	178
Sub-Saharan Africa	4,901	8	1	59	27
Nigeria	1,676	12	3	140	528
Lesotho	184	103	16	439	232
Cape Verde	92	196	11	622	64
Europe and Central Asia	12,818	27	1	36	135
Poland	2,314	61	1	56	194
Bosnia and Herzegovina	1,178	285	17	309	219
Moldova	465	110	24	796	399

Source: World Bank data.
FDI = foreign direct investment
GDP = gross domestic product
ODA = overseas development assistance.
a. Millions of dollars.   b. Dollars.

about $24 billion and $16 billion, respectively (table 6.1); meanwhile, remittances to Sub-Saharan Africa have grown steadily but remain below $5 billion—consistent with the observation that the lowest-income countries send relatively few emigrants.

Globally, remittances sent through official channels approximate foreign direct investment (FDI) as a source of hard currency for developing countries. But in many developing countries, remittances loom larger in the national accounts than do either FDI or foreign aid: remittances to Haiti, for example, were four times that country's foreign aid in 2003, and over 100 times its (admittedly meager) FDI; even in Mexico, in recent decades one of the developing world's investment magnets, remittances exceeded FDI by fully a third. Remittances account for 10 percent or more of national income in a long list of developing countries, including El Salvador, Eritrea, Jamaica, Jordan, Nicaragua, and the Republic of Yemen.

Unlike most FDI, however, remittances are often distributed widely through the source country's economy: 15 percent of Filipino households, for example, and 34 percent of households in the Dominican Republic receive payments from family and friends working abroad. In part because of their wide social reach, remittances have been found to have a powerful impact on poverty reduction and on overall consumption in the recipient countries. And because remittances do not vary with the strength of the local economy, they tend to be stable over time, even countercyclical (if more money is remitted when times are tough)—a particular benefit in countries going through recession or a financial crisis.

Another, less visible benefit of emigration for many source countries—in Eastern Europe and the former Soviet Union, for example—is partial relief from the economic and social pressure of supporting a large underemployed population. Not only is the burden reduced for governments of having to provide social services to those jobless workers who emigrate, but emigration may also defuse social tensions that would otherwise build among idle, mostly young workers who lack opportunities at home.

Finally, another intangible benefit to source countries derives from the social and business networks that their expatriates build while abroad. These networks expand the bandwidth, as it were, of economic interaction with the richer host economy, enabling still more emigrants to seek employment there while also stimulating increased trade and investment. Here, a good example is the sophisticated city-state of Singapore, whose large emigrant Chinese population has contributed significantly to the recent progress of less developed China. The arrival of skilled, energetic migrants in a host country also alerts other entrepreneurs and investors there to the economic opportunities presented by the underused human capital remaining in the home country. This may lead to increased FDI in the latter. Perhaps most important for the long run, these networks encourage the transfer of technology from the typically more advanced host country to the more backward home country, as returning emigrants bring back the knowledge and skills they have acquired during their foreign sojourn, and as FDI expands. The examples of Israel and Taiwan (China) illustrate the significance of a large diaspora, in terms of both investment and political support.

Costs to Source Countries

But emigration can also impose high and sometimes unpredictable costs on those left behind. As already noted, in the poorest countries it is mostly the relatively well off—who tend also to be the most highly skilled—who emigrate; host countries may amplify this tendency by *cherry picking* the most skilled emigrants out of the multitudes seeking entry. Yet often the departure of these relatively affluent and skilled individuals creates a scarcity of desperately needed skills back home, in medicine and education, for example. It also deprives the country of much-needed tax revenue. More broadly, the loss of potential leaders and innovators can undermine the home economy's dynamism and growth potential, and even its social cohesion. Often these skilled emigrants acquired their skills through free or heavily subsidized public education in the home country. In such cases, it is the residents of the wealthy host countries who reap what the taxpayers of the poorer source country have sown—this amounts to a perverse subsidy of the rich by the poor.

Nor is this *brain drain* a small-scale phenomenon. One study found that of some 2 million scientists and engineers born and educated in developing countries, about 400,000—one-fifth—were now employed in research and development in high-income countries. In all, about 3 million university graduates from developing countries are living outside the developing world. Smaller countries tend to suffer the greatest outflow, especially when they are geographically close to a large developed country or region: Guyana, for example, has lost 70 percent of its university graduates to the United States; 65 percent of Gambians with university degrees—as well as 51 percent of Somalis, 45 percent of Sierra Leonians, and 44 percent of Ghanians—have also emigrated. India and China have lost only about 4 percent of their college graduates, but because these tend to be the cream of the crop, the impact is nonetheless great: the income earned by the relatively few Indian expatriates in the United States alone is equivalent to 10 percent of India's national income. India's income tax revenue would be as much as a third higher had these emigrants stayed in India. It is estimated that the total worldwide wealth transfer due to brain drain is between $45 billion and $60 billion.

Benefits to Destination Countries

One could make a prima facie case that immigration is on balance good for the host countries simply by noting that, just like the Netherlands in the 17th century, many of the world's boom countries today have large immigrant populations. In Singapore, the richest country in Southeast Asia, immigrants make up a quarter of the workforce; the two wealthiest countries in Europe, Luxembourg and Switzerland, also have the largest proportions of immigrant workers; in Dubai, perhaps the most dynamic economy in the Middle East, migrant workers actually outnumber the native-born nine to one.

But correlation does not necessarily imply causation: are these countries prospering because they welcome migrants, or do migrants come because these countries are prospering? Teasing out the true contribution of immigrants to growth involves some difficult econometrics. At the very least, though, one can say that immigration has not prevented these economies from growing rapidly and, conversely, that it takes more than just dismantling the border controls for host countries to realize the benefits of immigration.

On theoretical grounds, however, it is much more than plausible that immigration has indeed boosted growth where immigrants have been welcomed. Low-cost immigrant labor can lower production costs, thus encouraging new domestic business formation while also attracting business capital from abroad. Immigrants may also bring in skills and expertise that are in short supply in the host country, possibly stimulating innovation throughout whole sectors. And the bandwidth effect spoken of earlier—the broadening of trade and investment links because of increased migration—works in both directions, benefiting the host country as well as the migrants' home countries. Finally, by lowering the average age of the population, immigrants may also contribute to the long-term survival of public pension systems in host countries, as discussed further below.

Costs to Destination Countries

Not everyone in the developed world finds these arguments persuasive, of course. The most commonly heard argument against immigration in developed countries is that immigrants take jobs away from some native workers and lower wages for the rest. This is certainly consistent with elementary economic theory, which holds that an increase in the quantity of labor supplied will reduce its price (that is, wages) and that at the lower price some workers will choose to withhold supply (that is, become unemployed), all else being equal. There is also plenty of anecdotal evidence of immigrants taking jobs that native-born workers were unwilling to take at the offered wage. But all other factors are not equal, and it turns out that whether immigration lowers wages and raises joblessness in the aggregate, at a national or a regional level, is again a difficult question to answer empirically.

For one thing, migrants and native-born workers are seldom perfect substitutes for one another: often migrants lack the fluency in the host-country language required for some jobs, and some jobs are so unattractive and poorly paid that they would go unfilled if only native-born workers were available. Also, in countries like the United States with a long history of migration, new immigrants may simply replace old ones, leading to little if any net change in the immigrant share of the workforce or the population. Native-born workers also have other options than competing head to head with new immigrants: for example, they can go back to school to acquire new skills that the migrants lack, or they can become migrants themselves, moving to other regions of the country where immigration is lower or abroad. Of course, these options have costs of their own.

As for the impact on wages, most studies have found that the average wage of native-born workers is only slightly lower in markets with large numbers of immigrants. But average prices may also be lower than they would be otherwise, thanks precisely to the immigrants' willingness to work hard for low pay. In addition, businesses may be attracted to cities and regions where immigration has lowered average labor costs, increasing the dynamism of the local economy and perhaps ultimately equalizing wages across regions at a higher level than before.

Another common complaint among opponents of immigration in the rich countries is that immigrants inevitably become a net burden on government and society, consuming more in public services than they contribute in tax revenue. For example, an influx of immigrant families may place a burden on local school systems, which, even if sufficient funding were available, cannot always expand their facilities fast enough to keep pace with the growing demand. Public health care systems may likewise be hard put to accommodate the arrival of large numbers of mostly uninsured immigrants.

That immigrants impose a net burden on their host communities may indeed be the case sometimes, but other times not; in the end this, too, is an empirical question, and the answer likely depends both on the immediate circumstances and on the time horizon. One leading immigration economist calculated that illegal immigration into California created a net burden on California taxpayers of about $2 billion to $3 billion a year, or roughly 3 percent of that state's budget. But many studies of European immigration find large net benefits to the host country, in part because undocumented immigrants cannot easily claim the public services to which they would be entitled if they were legal. A study of the United Kingdom found that, were it not for the tax revenue accruing from the immigrant population, public services would have to be cut sharply or the income tax raised by a full percentage point.

A longer view of the budget impact of immigrants paints a somewhat different picture, however. It is well known that, with their countries' aging populations, nearly all developed country governments will soon be hard pressed to meet their obligations to retirees in full. A falling ratio of current workers to retirees will mean that either the payroll taxes that fund public pensions and medical care for the aged will have to be raised, or those services will have to be reduced. Increased immigration offers a way to escape this dilemma, or at least to blunt its horns. By allowing more immigrants of working age to enter, aging developed countries can push the declining worker-retiree ratio back upward. Indeed, since the typical migrant tends to be in the early years of his or her working life, immigration can bring in a large cohort of workers who will remain in the workforce for many decades to come—the greatest comparative advantage of migrants, from this perspective, may be their youth. A thorough present-value calculation may even determine that the net fiscal costs of subsidizing immigrants today, through such public services as free education and food assistance, will be more than paid back when these young immigrants mature into productive members of their adopted society.

But the costs to the destination country, like those for the source country and the migrants themselves, cannot be reduced to economic considerations alone. There are many other dimensions. First and foremost is the impact on the local culture of a large influx of immigrants from quite different cultures and the ability of individuals and communities to sustain their identities while accepting the entry and diversity of others. The networks of migrants and clustering to maintain community connections and support, at times revealed in differences in language and culture, may lead to de facto segregation of immigrants in ethnic enclaves. If a relative weakness in education and opportunities tend to keep these enclaves poorer than the surrounding communities, the resulting social inequality may contribute to increased isolation and perceptions or experience of higher crime and other antisocial behaviors. The recent attention given to the question of immigration in virtually all the rich countries reflects the importance of these complex noneconomic factors.

National and Global Strategies for Migration

The analysis thus far can be summarized as follows: the host countries of migrants—as well as the migrants themselves—are more likely to benefit from migration, on net, than to lose from it. As with any economic transformation, some individuals and possibly some groups will be made worse off, but, in principle at least, part of the net gains from migration can be used to compensate these losses. For the sending or home countries and communities of the migrants, the net effect cannot be ascertained in advance as the implications, for example, of increased remittances and diaspora benefits, need to be considered in light of the implications of brain drain and loss of entrepreneur and social fabric. In general, in high-unemployment environments, migration of lower skilled migrants is likely to have a broadly positive impact, whereas the impact of higher skilled migrants may on balance be negative. These conclusions will sound familiar to students of economic policy or to anyone who has studied the welfare effects of international trade. And indeed, from a policy perspective, the implications appear to be quite similar: better to accept and adapt to migration, while regulating it effectively, than to try to reduce it or ban it, on the one hand, or to allow free entry to all comers, on the other. The question then becomes how should countries adapt, and how can they regulate effectively?

The question is urgent, because more people around the world wish to migrate—and can migrate—than ever before in history. The close to 200 million people who today live outside the country of their birth is actually a low figure by historical standards relative to total population, but flows have grown rapidly in recent decades, and the trend is clearly upward. Globalization has made millions in the developing world more aware of the higher standard of living that people in the industrialized world enjoy, and development has lowered the international and financial cost and travel times involved and raised living standards to the point where migration is considered by many. Unless policies change in the countries that receive migrants, therefore, traditional methods of border control will inevitably come under great strain, the burden on taxpayers in those countries will increase, and the seamy side of migration—the human smugglers, the exploiters, the human traffickers—will expand and thrive.

A New Multilateral Initiative: The Global Commission on International Migration

The urgency and growing importance of the issues of migration, remittances, and brain drain have led to widespread recognition that migration is indeed a global issue and that international action is needed to address the challenges to the source and host countries and, even more important, the social and economic challenges to the migrants themselves. This recognition, in turn, led to the launch by the United Nations of the first multilateral initiative on migration, the establishment of a Global Commission on International Migration (GCIM) with the following mandate:

- Placing international migration on the global agenda
- Analyzing gaps in current policy approaches to migration and examining interlinks with other issue-areas

- Presenting recommendations for action to the United Nations Secretary-General.

GCIM issued its report in October 2005. It found that the international community had failed to realize the full potential of international migration and had not risen to the many opportunities and challenges such migration presents. Greater coherence, cooperation, and capacity are required for more effective governance of migration at the national, regional, and global levels.

The GCIM report provided a concise yet wide-ranging analysis of key migration issues, stressing that migration and related policies must be based on shared objectives and a common vision. The commission proposed a comprehensive, coherent, and global action framework based on six broad principles for action, along with a number of related recommendations covering the role of migrants in a globalizing labor market, migration and development, irregular (often referred to as illegal) migration, migrants in society, human rights of migrants, and governance of migration.

The report further noted that the recent expansion in the scale and scope of migration seems certain to continue for the foreseeable future and may well accelerate, given the growing developmental, demographic, and democratic disparities that exist between different regions of the world. Migration is driven by powerful economic, social, and political forces, and states must acknowledge this reality.

The six broad principles that GCIM proposed for international action are as follows:

- People should be able to migrate by choice rather than out of necessity, in a safe and authorized manner and because their skills are valued and needed.
- The role of migrants in promoting economic growth, development, and poverty reduction should be recognized and reinforced; migration must become an integral part of global development strategies.
- States, exercising their sovereign right to decide who enters their territory, should cooperate with each other in an effort to stem irregular migration, while fully respecting the rights of migrants and refugees and readmitting those citizens who choose to return to their home country.
- Long-term and authorized migrants should be effectively integrated in the societies where they settle, so as to accommodate social diversity and foster social cohesion; migrants must be aware of their rights and respect their legal obligations.

- The human rights framework affecting international migrants should be implemented more effectively, so as to improve protections and labor standards for migrants.
- Migration policies should be enhanced by improved coherence and strengthened capacity at the national level, by greater cooperation at the regional level, and by more effective dialogue and consultation among governments and between international organizations at the global level.

World Bank Initiatives on Migration and Remittances

There is an urgent need for more research and data that view migration from a development perspective. A World Bank research program is currently engaged in data gathering and analysis on the development impact of international migration, with the aim of identifying policies, regulations, and institutional reforms that developed and developing countries can adopt to ensure that migration results in improved development outcomes. Complementing this research is ongoing work by the Bank on remittances, to improve the collection of data on remittances, reduce the costs of sending remittances and strengthen the relevant financial infrastructure; to better understand the development impact of remittances; and to enhance the integrity of money transfer systems.

The Bank and the International Monetary Fund are leading a working group of national statistical agencies, formed at the request of the Group of Eight, to better record remittances in countries' national accounts. Its draft report is due in 2006. The Bank has made its research available to GCIM for which it has prepared a policy paper on the portability of social security benefits for temporary migrant workers. Bank staff have also contributed to the Group of Twenty's deliberations on migration and remittances. As part of international efforts to reduce the cost of remittances, the Bank co-chairs, with the Bank for International Settlements, a taskforce on international policy coordination for remittance payment systems.

A research volume titled *International Migration, Remittances, and the Brain Drain* (Ozden and Schiff 2005) was recently published by the World Bank, comprising four case studies on the impact of remittances on poverty in certain countries and four chapters on the brain drain. The book also contains the largest database on the brain drain in print, along with analyses of its impact.

The Bank's *Global Economic Prospects 2006: Remittances and Migration,* the latest in the annual Global Economic Prospects series, reports the staff's analysis of a scenario in which international migration increases sharply. It considers the impact of such an increase on the migrants themselves and their countries of origin; the change in the size of remittances and the resulting impact; the implications of greater remittances for development at the household level; and the transactions costs associated with such remittances.

Selected Readings and Cited References

Global Commission on International Migration. 2006. *Migration in an Interconnected World: New Directions for Action.* New York.

Goldin, Ian, and Kenneth A. Reinert, with Andrew Beath. 2006. "Migration." In *Globalization for Development: Trade, Finance, Aid, Migration and Policy.* Washington, DC: World Bank and Palgrave Macmillan.

Hatton, Timothy, and Jeffrey Williamson. 2005. *Global Migration and the World Economy.* Cambridge, MA.: MIT Press.

Human Rights Watch. 2004. "Bad Dreams: Exploitation and Abuse of Migrant Workers in Saudi Arabia." *Human Rights Watch* 16 5(E).

Lucas, Robert. 2005. *International Migration and Economic Development.* Northampton, United Kingdom: Edward Elgar.

Ozden, Caglar, and Mauriec Schiff, eds. 2005. *International Migration, Remittances, and the Brain Drain.* Washington, DC: World Bank.

World Bank. *Global Economic Prospects 2006: Remittances and Migration.* Washington, DC.

Selected Web Links on Migration

Center for Migration Studies of New York	http://cmsny.org
European Research Centre on Migration and Ethnic Relations (Utrecht University)	http://www.ercomer.org/wwwvl
Global Commission on International Migration	http://www.gcim.org
Institute for the Study of International Migration (Georgetown University)	http://www.georgetown.edu/sfs/programs/isim
International Labour Migration Database (International Labour Organization)	http://www.ilo.org/public/english/protection/migrant/ilmdb/ilmdb.htm
International Organization for Migration	http://www.iom.int
Organisation for Economic Co-operation page on international migration	http://www.oecd.org/topic/0,2686,en_2649_37415_1_1_1_1_37415,00.html
Office of the United Nations High Commissioner for Refugees	http://www.unhcr.org
U.S. Census Bureau page on geographical mobility and migration	http://www.census.gov/population/www/socdemo/migrate.html

7

Trade Reform and the Doha Development Agenda

KYM ANDERSON AND JOHN D. NASH

Awealth of evidence, accumulated over many years, shows that market openness and integration with the world economy promote economic growth and reduce poverty.[1] Provided that foreign exchange markets are also operating well, a country's trade policy is the key link in the transmission of price signals from the world marketplace to the national economy. These signals allow the country's resources to be allocated in a manner consistent with its comparative advantage in production, thereby increasing efficiency. An open trade regime also encourages the import of modern technologies that can boost productivity growth. History shows that no country has achieved rapid growth and lifted large numbers of its citizens out of poverty while isolated from the world economy. To paraphrase Arvind Panagariya, professor of economics at Columbia University and a leading expert on international trade, although trade openness is not by itself *sufficient* to trigger growth, it is clearly necessary.[2]

It is especially critical that developing countries harness this engine of growth and poverty reduction for the benefit of their agriculture, for several reasons. First, agriculture is hugely important for these countries. Around 63 percent of the population in low-income countries live in rural areas, and agriculture and the processing of agricultural goods account for 30 to 60 percent of gross domestic product (GDP) in these countries and an even larger share of employment. Second, poverty is predominantly a rural phenomenon: close to three-quarters of the world's poor (defined as those living on less than a dollar a day) reside in rural areas, and the rural poor worldwide will outnumber their urban counterparts for at least another generation. In the first 21 countries that have prepared Poverty Reduction Strategy Papers, the rural poverty rate exceeded the urban rate in all but 3, by margins ranging from 7 to 43 percent.

Some developing countries have already seized the opportunities offered by global agricultural trade to generate dynamic rural growth and achieve dramatic poverty reduction. For example, Chile's rural poverty rate fell from 53 percent in 1987 to 23 percent in 2000, thanks largely to an export-oriented agricultural growth strategy that provided not only new farm jobs in horticultural industries but also part-time, off-farm job opportunities to other farm families in such activities as packing, processing, and transporting the new exportable products.

But in most developing countries agricultural trade has not fulfilled its potential. Developing countries have approximately doubled the share of manufactures in their exports to both industrial and other developing countries in the past two decades, and they have increased the share of agricultural goods in their exports to other developing countries by close to half. Yet during the same period, the share of agricultural goods in their exports to high-income countries actually fell (table 7.1). This suggests that barriers in the high-income countries are obstructing agricultural trade. Indeed, a formidable array of policy instruments exists in both developed and developing countries to tax or otherwise restrict agricultural imports, notwithstanding recent reforms.

Most high-income countries rely on a combination of border measures (tariffs, export subsidies, or quantitative import restrictions) and direct production subsidies to protect and support their farmers (figure 7.1). All of these measures reduce market opportunities for developing countries. Developing

TABLE 7.1   Product Composition of Merchandise Trade in Developing Countries
Percentage of total

Product type	1980–81	1990–91	2000–01
Agricultural goods and processed food			
To other developing countries	9.5	8.9	13.4
To high-income countries	25.8	23.3	22.9
Total	35.3	32.2	36.3
Other primary goods	45.3	45.1	30.3
Other manufactured goods			
To other developing countries	6.6	7.5	12.3
To high-income countries	12.7	15.2	21.1
Total	19.3	22.7	33.4

Source: COMTRADE data.

FIGURE 7.1 **Rates of Agricultural Protection from Border Measures and Direct Payments to Farmers, 2004**
Percentage by which gross payments are raised

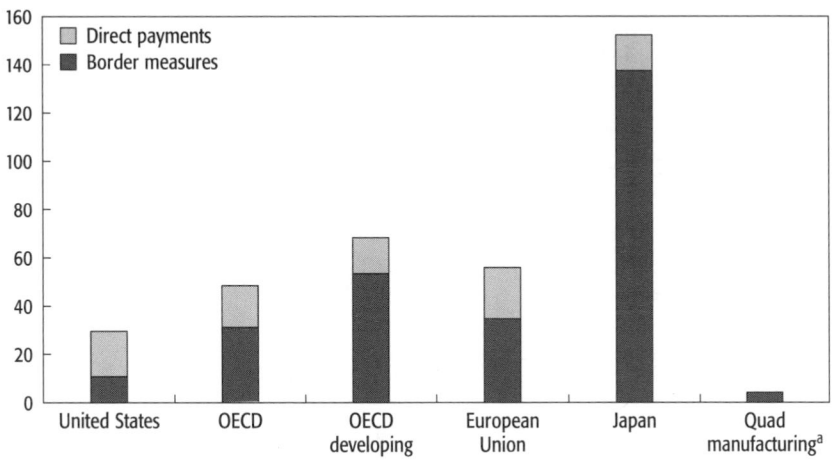

Source: International Monetary Fund 2004; data from OECD Agriculture Market Access Database.
a. Canada, the European Union, Japan, and the United States.
OECD = Organisation for Economic Co-operation and Development

countries are likewise guilty, although, compared with developed countries, they tend to protect their farmers more through import tariffs than through direct support. Many developing countries have liberalized their trade regimes since the 1980s, but liberalization has advanced much further in manufacturing than in agriculture (table 7.2).

Developed countries do not, as a rule, impose high tariffs on the tropical products that are the traditional exports of most developing countries. (Sugar is an exception: because it can be produced from sugar beets and other temperate crops, most developed countries have high barriers against imported sugar.) But the barriers they do maintain are nonetheless important, even for tropical commodity producers, for two reasons. First, their tariff structures on these tropical products are often *escalated*—the higher a product is on the processing chain, the higher the tariff. (Tariffs are typically higher on processed chocolate than on cocoa beans, for example.) By discouraging the import of higher-value-added products, these tariffs keep exporting countries dependent on production of these low-value-added, primary products, which are also subject to high price volatility. Second, protection against nontraditional exports discourages developing country producers from diversifying

TABLE 7.2 Average Applied Import Tariffs by Sector and Region, 2001
Percent[a]

	Importer		
Product category and exporter	**High-income countries[b]**	**Developing countries[c]**	**World**
Agriculture and food			
High-income countries	18.0	18.0	17.8
Developing countries	14.0	18.0	15.6
All countries	16.0	18.0	16.7
Textiles and wearing apparel			
High-income countries	8.0	15.0	12.0
Developing countries	7.0	20.0	9.3
All countries	8.0	17.0	10.2
Other manufactures			
High-income countries	2.0	9.0	4.1
Developing countries	1.0	7.0	2.5
All countries	1.0	8.0	3.5

Source: Anderson, Martin, and van der Mensbrugghe 2006a.
a. Ad valorem equivalents.
b. Regions include the newly industrialized East Asian customs territories of Hong Kong (China), Republic of Korea, Singapore, and Taiwan (China) as well as the transition economies that joined the European Union in April 2004. The European Union is assumed to be a single customs territory.
c. Data are import-weighted averages incorporating tariff preferences granted to developing countries.

into these products. So, although in theory farmers of developing countries could escape the rural poverty trap by diversifying, in reality high trade barriers by developed countries prevent them.

Until the Uruguay Round, which concluded in 1994, agriculture remained outside the purview of multilateral trade talks under the General Agreement on Tariffs and Trade. The Uruguay Round Agreement on Agriculture began a process of making trade-distorting instruments in agriculture more transparent and less of a hindrance to trade. A number of loopholes, however, have limited the agreement's impact in increasing trade opportunities for developing countries. The current Doha Development Round of multilateral trade negotiations, conducted under the auspices of the World Trade Organization (WTO), recognized from the beginning that agriculture would be central to the negotiations, and this has proved to be the case.

An important reason to liberalize trade through multilateral negotiations is the fact that liberalization is a global public good, such that its benefits are not adequately internalized in the decision processes of individual liberalizing countries. Trade policy reforms (such as lowering of tariffs) as well as investments in trade machinery (such as customs reform and ports) can have significant externalities, or spillover effects, from the country undertaking the reform or making the investment to other countries. All countries benefit from one country's trade reforms and trade-related investments, and these benefits are increased when undertaken by a number of countries concurrently. However, because the liberalizing country does not realize the full benefits of its own reform and investment, it may undertake less of both than is best for all. This kind of positive externality of reform can be internalized through the liberalization undertaken in the WTO negotiations.

The Arguments for (and Against) Removing Trade Barriers

The standard analysis of national gains from international trade emphasizes the fact that countries' costs of production of various goods and services differ, as do the preferences of their residents for those different goods and services. Thus economic benefits can arise when each country specializes in the goods and services that it is relatively good at producing and exchanges them for the goods and services in which other countries similarly specialize. A country's economy becomes more productive as those industries in which it has an advantage in production compared with other countries expand, drawing resources from other industries that lack such comparative advantage, which then grow more slowly or contract.

The gains from increased trade tend to be greater, as a share of national output, for smaller economies, particularly where economies of scale in production were not fully exploited before trade reform, and where consumers (including firms importing intermediate inputs) value variety, so that intra- as well as interindustry trade can flourish. In such cases the more efficient firms within the expanding industries tend to take over the less efficient ones. The gains from trade are also greater when, before reform, trade barriers allowed imperfect competition to prevail in the domestic marketplace; this, too, is more common in smaller economies where each industry tends to consist of only one or a few firms.

To this standard analysis need to be added links between trade and economic growth. There are several channels through which increased openness to trade can affect an economy's growth rate. These include the scale of the market when knowledge is embodied in the products traded, the degree of redundant knowledge creation that is avoided through openness, and the effect of knowledge spillovers.

Economies that are more open tend to attract more investment from abroad, which raises their stock of capital. More-open economies also tend to be more innovative, because of greater trade in intellectual capital (information, ideas, and technologies, sometimes but not always in the form of purchasable intellectual property). Trade liberalization can thereby lead not just to a larger capital stock and a one-time increase in productivity but also to higher *rates* of capital accumulation and productivity growth in the reforming economy because of the way reform energizes entrepreneurs. It is widely agreed, however, that for those higher growth rates to be sustained, several other things are needed: effective institutions to allocate and protect property rights, freely functioning domestic factor and product markets, and macroeconomic and political stability.

Why Do Countries Retain Protectionist Policies?

If the economic gains from removing trade distortions are so evident, why do most countries retain protection from foreign competition for at least some of their industries? A number of possible reasons have been identified: to provide temporary shelter from competition for infant industries, to prevent or reduce unemployment, to maintain a favorable balance of payments, or to raise tax revenue. But all of these are almost always found wanting, because an alternative domestic policy instrument is available to meet the same objective more effectively or more cheaply.

The most compelling explanation for the persistence of trade barriers is one based on political economy. The changes in product prices that result from trade liberalization or cuts in subsidies necessarily change the prices for the services of productive factors: land, labor, and capital. Hence, even though the country's total income and wealth are expected to grow when trade distortions are reduced, not everyone will gain. Some industries and their workers will be made less well off than before, and in most countries the social safety net, if it exists at all, typically provides only partial compensation for such losses. Moreover, these expected losses in jobs, income, and wealth tend to be concentrated in the hands of a few industries and workers, who are therefore prepared to support politicians who resist reform. However, the gains for consumers, although larger in the aggregate than the aggregate losses, are distributed widely and thus are small for each consumer; hence it is not worthwhile for consumers to get together to lobby for reform. Export firms and other potential gainers from increased export opportunities may be better positioned to act as a political counterbalance to protectionist forces, but under the status quo before reform they tend to be weaker than the antireform forces, and indeed the eventual gainers cannot always be identified in advance of the reform itself. All this stacks the deck in favor of the prereform status quo.

Agriculture seems to be particularly resistant to reform in many countries. One reason is that many farmers, understandably, would prefer not have to give up a familiar, traditional livelihood that their families may have practiced for generations. Meanwhile, many urban dwellers are evidently willing to support them in this preference, often because farming has an important place in the country's history and culture.

Even so, it is ironic that agricultural trade policy is so contentious, given the farm sector's small and declining importance in the global economy. Agriculture's share of global GDP has fallen from around 10 percent in the 1960s to little more than 3 percent today (although, when food processing is added, the share doubles to 6 percent). In developed countries agriculture accounts for only 1.8 percent of GDP and only a slightly larger share of employment. Mirroring that decline, agriculture's share of global merchandise trade has fallen over the past three decades, from 22 percent to 9 percent, and in developing countries from 42 percent to 11 percent. Agriculture and food together account for only 7 percent of global trade in goods and services combined.

However, 52 percent of employment in developing countries is in agriculture, and 44 percent of all jobs globally are on farms. As will be discussed below, agricultural trade liberalization offers enormous potential benefits to these farmers. True, as with any trade reform, those benefits do not come without costs. Reform will force some industries to shrink or close while others expand, and the costs of adjustment for firms and workers in the downsized industries may not be trivial even if they are dwarfed by society's overall gains. There are also social costs. Many of those disemployed by reform will become eligible for government social support, such as unemployment payments and retraining grants, and in the meantime crime may increase, with its attendant costs. These one-time costs need to be weighed against the ongoing economic benefits from reform. The private and social costs of adjustment tend to be smaller, the longer the phase-in period of the reform. Also, the annual change in an industry's terms of trade under phased trade reform is typically dwarfed by changes due to exchange rate fluctuations, technological improvements, preference shifts, and other normal economic developments. Hence most estimates of the costs of reform indicate that they are minor relative to the benefits.

Trade liberalization has also lately attracted considerable resistance from some nongovernmental organizations (NGOs)—witness their prominence during the demonstrations outside the WTO ministerial meeting in Seattle in 1999. Some NGOs see trade reform as contributing to world economic dominance by multinational firms, and certain unpleasant aspects of globalization as inflicting grievous social and environmental ills in rich and poor countries alike. But just as the traditional, economic arguments for trade protection have been found wanting, so, too, have the social and environmental ones, both conceptually and empirically. For example, increased trade has caused no systematic *race to the bottom* in the environmental or labor standards of rich countries, and foreign corporations operating in poor countries often set higher environmental and labor standards for themselves than do their domestic competitors. Nor has trade growth been a major contributor to wage stagnation among unskilled workers in developed countries.[3]

One further contentious issue that has become more prominent in recent debates has to do with whether low-income countries would in fact gain from agricultural reform by high-income countries. One reason they may not is that, if they themselves are net food importers, they may have to pay more for food on international markets if developed country subsidies and protection are cut. Another reason is that, as food exporters become able to access freely those protected high-income markets abroad (through various trade preference schemes), food-exporting low-income countries might receive less for their produce as domestic prices come down in those currently protected rich countries. These arguments are valid, but they are only part of the story. The other part depends on what happens to the prices of developing countries' other imports and exports—including, for example, their exports of cotton, which currently have to compete with highly subsidized cotton produced in high-income countries, especially the United States. This is a complex empirical question that can only be addressed using a mathematical model of the global economy (see below).

Actions Already Under Way to Promote Freer Trade—and Actions Still to Come

One way to reduce trade protectionism is through better dissemination of more-convincing information about the benefits to consumers, exporters, and the overall economy from reducing subsidies and other trade distortions. Such information could help bring greater balance to a debate too often dominated by the views of single-issue NGOs, labor unions, and others, who tend to focus only on the (often overstated) costs of reform to their constituents. Already the spread of more-balanced assessments of the benefits and costs of trade reform has led some countries to make such reforms unilaterally. These include not only numerous developing countries but also some richer countries such as Australia and New Zealand. More recently, several major NGOs, together with the Secretariat of the Organisation for Economic Co-operation and Development, have focused on providing better information about the wastefulness of environmentally harmful subsidies; their efforts have already had an impact, such as in reducing coal mining subsidies in Europe.

Another way is through technological innovation. The information and telecommunications revolution of the past two decades, for example, has dramatically lowered the costs of doing business across national borders. The resulting trade opportunities have encouraged exporters to mobilize to counter the antitrade lobbying of import-protected groups and NGOs.

One country's trade opening may also favorably influence the policy stance adopted by others, by raising international prices, stimulating foreign investment, and providing greater market access abroad for those countries' exporters. Such opening also adds to the evidence of the net gains to be won at relatively low cost (particularly when reforms are phased in) from trade reform, thus providing solid empirical ammunition against the alarmists.

A coincidence of this and the previous two types of shocks has given rise to the latest wave of globalization, which has raised not only the rewards to those economies that practice good economic governance but also the cost of tolerating poor governance. Just as financial capital can now flow into a well-managed economy more easily and quickly than ever before, so can it be withdrawn more quickly if confidence in that economy's governance is shaken—as the East Asian financial crisis of the late 1990s demonstrated all too clearly. A crucial element of good economic governance is a commitment to a permanently open international trade and payments regime, along with sound domestic policies such as secure property rights and prudent monetary and fiscal policies.

Governments seeking to open their economies are increasingly considering a range of bilateral, regional, and multilateral negotiating opportunities, because they recognize that the potential exchange of market access concessions can tip the political equilibrium in trade's favor, both at home and abroad. If country A were to allow more imports unilaterally, it might harm its import-competing producers more than it helps its exporters; but if country A instead lowers its trade barriers in exchange for its trading partners lowering theirs, its exporters will be made better off. Their added benefit may then exceed the import-competing producers' loss by enough to make the political calculus tilt in favor of reform. When politicians in country A's trading partners likewise see opportunities to gain from such an exchange, the prospects for trade negotiations are ripe.

It stands to reason that the gains from market access negotiations are potentially greater, nationally and globally, when more countries are involved and when more products and issues are covered. That is precisely the logic behind the wide-ranging negotiations now under way among nearly 150 WTO member countries in the Doha Round. As that process, however, becomes increasingly cumbersome, many countries choose to negotiate bilaterally or regionally as well, in the hope of still faster and deeper integration. Preferential free trade areas involving just a subset of countries may fail to make all participants better off, however, because such agreements, rather than expanding trade, may actually divert trade from lower-cost suppliers outside the agreement; nonparticipants may, of course, be made worse off, too. Hence any proposed trade agreement should undergo a careful empirical analysis of the likely net gains.

What Can the Doha Development Round Contribute?

The gains from reducing unwarranted government intervention in markets have been well known ever since Adam Smith wrote *The Wealth of Nations* more than two centuries ago.[4] Even so, greater dissemination of empirical results on the net benefits of reducing trade distortions can still promote liberalization by balancing the often-exaggerated claims of its opponents. Such studies can also identify the domestic policy reforms that should accompany trade reform, to guarantee that not only does aggregate national welfare improve but also that as few people as possible are left behind and that harm to the environment is minimized. In an ideal world such information would persuade all governments to fully liberalize their trade unilaterally. Although that outcome may be unlikely, it provides a benchmark against which all opportunities for partial trade liberalization can be measured.

Of the opportunities for freer trade available today, the one most nearly within reach is a nonpreferential, legally binding partial liberalization achieved within the Doha Round. That round was launched in 2001 with the intention of completing negotiations at the end of 2004. But the issues associated with agriculture have been so controversial that a successful conclusion is not yet certain, and the completion date has been moved back to 2007 at the earliest.

What Are the Prospective Gains from Full Trade Liberalization?

What would be the economic impact of removing all merchandise trade barriers and agricultural subsidies globally? The most recent study to model these effects uses a newly released database on protection and the latest version of the World Bank's Linkage model of the global economy.[5] It also provides comparable estimates of partial reforms as proposed for the Doha Round. The following are among the study's key messages.

The potential gains from further global trade reform are huge, even if one ignores the dynamic gains and the gains from greater economies of scale and increased competition. Freeing all merchandise trade and eliminating agricultural subsidies is estimated to boost global welfare by nearly $300 billion a year by 2015 (table 7.3), plus any effects from increased productivity.

Developing countries would gain disproportionately. Developing countries would enjoy almost 30 percent of the global gains (table 7.3), well above their one-fifth share of global GDP. Their welfare would increase by 0.8 percent, compared with just 0.6 percent for the developed countries. The reason for their larger share is partly that existing developing country tariffs are relatively high, and so their reduction leads to substantial efficiency gains. In addition, their exports are more concentrated in farm and textile products (table 7.1), which will benefit disproportionately as current developed country tariffs are reduced under the agreement.

Benefits could be as great from South-South as from South-North trade reform. Trade reform by developing countries themselves will be almost as important economically to those countries as reform by the developed countries (table 7.4, bottom panel). If developing countries instead delay their own reforms, or undertake less reform than the developed countries, they may fail to realize the full potential gains.

Agriculture is where liberalization is needed most. By far the greatest cuts in bound tariffs and subsidies are required in agriculture, where rates of assistance remain very high relative to those in other sectors. Food and agricultural policies are responsible for almost two-thirds of the global gain currently forgone because of merchandise trade distortions (table 7.4, top panel), despite agriculture's small shares of world trade and GDP noted earlier. And agricultural trade reform is as important for the developing countries as for the world as a whole: almost two-thirds of their potential gains come from global agricultural liberalization, compared with just one-quarter from textiles and clothing and one-tenth from other merchandise liberalization (table 7.4, bottom panel). Moreover, these gains ignore the social and environmental benefits from boosting agriculture in developing countries: in

TABLE 7.3 Estimated Impact of Full Liberalization of Global Merchandise Trade, by Country and Region, 2015[a]

Country or region	Estimated increase in real income (billions of 2001 dollars)		Estimated total increase in real income as share of baseline income (percent)
	Total	**Because of change in terms of trade only**	
Australia and New Zealand	6.1	3.5	1.0
Europe[b]	65.2	0.5	0.6
United States	16.2	10.7	0.1
Canada	3.8	−0.3	0.4
Japan	54.6	7.5	1.1
Republic of Korea and Taiwan (China)	44.6	0.4	3.5
Hong Kong (China) and Singapore	11.2	7.9	2.6
Argentina	4.9	1.2	1.2
Bangladesh	0.1	−1.1	0.2
Brazil	9.9	4.6	1.5
China	5.6	−8.3	0.2
India	3.4	−9.4	0.4
Indonesia	1.9	0.2	0.7
Mexico	3.6	−3.6	0.4
Russian Federation	2.7	−2.7	0.6
South Africa	1.3	0.0	0.9
Thailand	7.7	0.7	3.8
Turkey	3.3	0.2	1.3
Vietnam	3.0	−0.2	5.2
Rest of South Asia	1.0	−0.8	0.5
Rest of East Asia	5.3	−0.9	1.9
Rest of Latin America and the Caribbean	10.3	0.0	1.2
Rest of Europe and Central Asia	1.0	−1.6	0.3
Middle East and North Africa	14.0	−6.4	1.2
Selected countries in Sub-Saharan Africa[c]	1.0	0.5	1.5
Rest of Sub-Saharan Africa	2.5	−2.3	1.1
Rest of world	3.4	0.1	1.5

(Continues on the following page)

TABLE 7.3 (Continued)

Country or region	Total	Because of change in terms of trade only	Estimated total increase in real income as share of baseline income (percent)
High-income countries	201.6	30.3	0.6
Developing countries	85.7	−29.7	0.8
Middle-income countries	69.5	−16.7	0.8
Low-income countries	16.2	−12.9	0.8
East Asia and Pacific	23.5	−8.5	0.7
South Asia	4.5	−11.2	0.4
Europe and Central Asia	7.0	−4.0	0.7
Middle East and North Africa	14.0	−6.4	1.2
Sub-Saharan Africa	4.8	−1.8	1.1
Latin America and the Caribbean	28.7	2.2	1.0
World	287.3	0.6	0.7

(Estimated increase in real income, billions of 2001 dollars.)

Source: Anderson, Martin, and van der Mensbrugghe 2006a (table 12.4).
a. Increases are measured relative to baseline.
b. Europe includes the 25 members of the European Union plus the members of the European Free Trade Association.
c. They are Botswana, Madagascar, Malawi, Mozambique, Tanzania, Uganda, Zambia, and Zimbabwe. These countries accounted for 14 percent of Sub-Saharan African GDP in 2001, while South Africa accounted for 36 percent and the rest of Sub-Saharan Africa accounted for 50 percent.

TABLE 7.4 Distribution of Estimated Welfare Effects of Full Trade Liberalization, by Source and Product Group, 2015[a]
Percent

Source of welfare effect	Agriculture and food	Textiles and clothing	Other manu-factures	All goods
	Share of total effects on global welfare			
Changes in developed country policies	46	6	3	55
Changes in developing country policies	17	8	20	45
Changes in all countries' policies	63	14	23	100
	Share of total effects on developing countries' welfare			
Changes in developed country policies	30	17	3	50
Changes in developing country policies	33	10	7	50
Changes in all countries' policies	63	27	10	100

Source: Anderson, Martin, and van der Mensbrugghe 2006a (table 12.6).
a. Developing countries include the transition economies of Eastern Europe and the former Soviet Union.

addition to reducing poverty, those benefits include less crowding of cities and less industrial pollution.

What Are the Prospective Gains from Partial Liberalization?

The same study that produced the above findings also examined the July 2004 WTO Framework Agreement and identified a range of scenarios that might emerge from the Doha Round. The study draws the following conclusions:

- In addition to phasing out farm export subsidies (involving less than $5 billion a year globally), countries should make large cuts in legally bound domestic farm support commitments (currently involving payments of a little under $100 billion a year) and agricultural tariffs (involving far greater transfers than do subsidies) to ensure cuts in applied rates of protection, which are typically set well below legally bound rates.
- Even large cuts in bound tariffs will accomplish little if the category of *sensitive products* receives lesser cuts, because countries will then simply classify their most protected goods as sensitive.
- Cuts in cotton subsidies would help cotton-exporting developing countries enormously: developing countries' share of global cotton exports would rise from just over half to as much as 85 percent.
- Lowering barriers to imports of nonagricultural goods and services in developing countries would help balance the exchange of concessions between them and the developed countries.
- Most developing countries would gain from partial liberalization in the Doha Round, and the rest could gain as well if they also reform their own trade policies.
- Farm output and employment would grow in developing countries under all likely Doha scenarios; only in the most protected countries of Western Europe, northeast Asia, and the United States would they fall, and even then by only small amounts (table 7.5).

In short, much is to be gained from liberalizing merchandise trade—and especially agricultural trade—in the Doha Round, and a disproportionate share of that gain would go to developing countries. Moreover, it is the poorest in these countries—farmers and unskilled laborers—who appear most likely to gain from liberalization.[6] However, the political sensitivity of farm support programs, coupled with the complexity of the measures introduced in the Uruguay Round Agreement and of the modalities set out in the Doha Framework Agreement, ensure that the devil will be in the details.

TABLE 7.5 Effects of Comprehensive Doha Trade Reform on Agricultural Output and Employment Growth, by Country and Region, 2005–15
Percent a year[a]

Country or region	Growth in agricultural output		Growth in agricultural employment	
	Baseline	Doha scenario[b]	Baseline	Doha scenario
Australia and New Zealand	3.5	4.4	0.4	1.1
Canada	3.5	4.3	0.2	1.0
United States	2.2	1.7	−0.8	−1.4
Europe[c]	1.0	−0.4	−1.8	−2.8
Japan	0.5	−1.4	−2.7	−4.1
Republic of Korea and Taiwan (China)	2.2	1.6	−1.3	−2.1
Argentina	2.9	3.6	0.9	1.6
Bangladesh	4.2	4.2	1.1	1.2
Brazil	3.3	4.4	1.1	2.2
China	4.3	4.3	0.8	0.8
India	4.3	4.4	1.0	1.0
Indonesia	3.0	3.0	−0.7	−0.6
Mexico	3.9	4.1	2.0	2.4
Russian Federation	1.5	1.4	−2.3	−2.3
South Africa	2.5	2.7	0.0	0.1
Thailand	−0.1	0.4	−4.6	−4.3
Turkey	3.0	3.1	−0.5	−0.5
Vietnam	5.8	5.9	3.9	4.0
Rest of South Asia	4.8	4.9	2.0	2.1
Rest of East Asia	3.7	3.8	0.2	0.3
Rest of Latin America and the Caribbean	4.4	5.3	1.9	2.7
Rest of Europe and Central Asia	3.3	3.4	0.0	0.1
Middle East and North Africa	4.0	4.1	1.5	1.6
Selected countries in Sub-Saharan Africa[d]	5.3	5.4	3.0	3.0
Rest of Sub-Saharan Africa	4.6	4.8	2.2	2.3
Rest of world	5.0	5.5	2.4	2.8

Source: Anderson, Martin, and van der Mensbrugghe 2006a (tables 12.12 and 12.13).
a. Annual averages.
b. The details of this partial reform scenario are described in Anderson, Martin, and van der Mensbrugghe (2006a).
c. Europe includes the 25 members of the European Union plus the members of the European Free Trade Association.
d. They are Botswana, Madagascar, Malawi, Mozambique, Tanzania, Uganda, Zambia, and Zimbabwe.

Why Trade Reform May Not Be Enough

Reduction of formal trade barriers is a necessary condition for the sustainable expansion of trade, but it may not be sufficient, as other constraints can reduce exporters' ability to take advantage of new opportunities. The importance of resolving these behind-the-border issues is increasingly being recognized, and the aid for trade agenda is aimed at doing just that (see below). Within agricultural trade, food safety and agricultural health standards are often cited as possible impediments to developing country exports. The development of these sanitary and phytosanitary (SPS; *phytosanitary* refers to plant health and sanitation) standards has been a prerequisite for the explosion of growth in trade of high-value agricultural products. But there is concern that standards will undermine the competitive progress already made by some developing countries and present insurmountable barriers to new entrants into the high-value food trade. There is particular concern about the following issues:

- Emerging food safety and agricultural health measures will be applied in a discriminatory manner.
- Developing countries lack the administrative, technical, and other capacities to comply with new or more stringent requirements.
- The costs incurred to reach compliance will undermine the comparative advantage of developing countries in the high-value food trade.
- Institutional weaknesses and compliance costs will further marginalize weaker economic players, including smaller countries, enterprises, and farmers.
- Inadequate support is available for capacity building in this area, despite the provisions made in the WTO Agreement on the Application of Sanitary and Phytosanitary Measures.

Experience shows, however, that even though new or more stringent standards by importers can serve as a trade barrier, they can also act as a catalyst for progressive change. Where the investment climate is good, stricter standards can provide a stimulus for investments in supply-chain modernization, provide increased incentives for the adoption of better safety and quality control practices in agriculture and food manufacturing, and help clarify the appropriate and necessary roles of government in food safety and agricultural health management. This can contribute to more sustainable and profitable trade over the long term. Exporters are best able to exploit opportunities when actions to address SPS problems are embedded in an overall competitiveness strategy from the outset, rather than taken on an ad hoc basis in response to a crisis. The private sector must take the lead in complying with SPS measures, but weak government SPS administration in exporting countries may add to the transaction costs of complying with importers' standards. Many countries face a need to build capacity in this field.

How Is the World Bank Helping?

Historically, the World Bank has been involved in trade policy chiefly through its country-based programs. The Bank has long supported the efforts of its client countries to integrate into the world trading system by reforming their own trade policies. In the 1980s, the trade regimes of many developing countries were demonstrably unsuccessful in generating growth, and they frequently contributed to macroeconomic crises. They also created strong biases against private sector development and an export-led growth strategy and generated opportunities for corruption. The Bank made structural adjustment loans available to support reform, and, partly as a result, many countries did significantly open their economies. Between 1995–97 and 2001–03, the simple average of agricultural tariffs fell by 23 percent among low-income countries and by 15 percent among middle-income countries, compared with 30 and 25 percent, respectively, for tariffs on manufactures.

Since the 1980s, exports from developing countries—both to industrialized countries and to other developing countries—have boomed, although agricultural exports to industrialized countries have lagged behind. The focus has now shifted from trade policy reform as such to institutional issues, including the performance of customs agencies and product quality and certification.

In addition, the World Bank has used its lending to support investments in behind-the-border measures, to overcome trade bottlenecks caused by inadequate institutions or infrastructure. Growth in trade-related operations in recent years has been quite impressive. Actual and projected commitments for new trade operations for the three-year period from fiscal 2004 through 2006, at $2.9 billion, exceed those for all ongoing trade operations approved over the preceding eight-year period ($2.4 billion). Of particular interest here are projects that addressed increasingly complex food safety, agricultural health, and other standards, which, as already noted, developing countries must meet in order to exploit opportunities in markets for high-value-added products. Currently, the Bank has 15 ongoing projects with standards components, and another 15 projects are under preparation. In the past these projects have generally been designed to address shortcomings in institutional capacity and to finance some infrastructure—government and private—to

> ### BOX 7.1 Senegal's Agricultural Export Promotion Project
>
> In light of ongoing global changes in the global food industry and an increased emphasis on food safety and standards, marketing rather than production issues were determined to be the most important factor limiting Senegal's agricultural export expansion in the mid 1990s. Specific areas where attention was identified as needed were market information and intelligence; quality, shipping, and packaging tests; new product tests; and export infrastructure. Senegal's reputation as a reliable and safe exporter needed to be rebuilt after it was lost in the 1980s, and a combination of hard (physical infrastructure) and soft (capacity building) investments was needed to achieve this. Project components included both, and the design proved effective in demonstrating the export potential of the Senegalese horticultural sector.
>
> The project succeeded in doubling exports, after Senegalese producers successfully passed 60 tests of pesticide residue on fruits and vegetables carried out on random samples. Capacity building under the program included the training of 1,360 members of the two major producer-exporter associations, establishment of a central data and information center, initiation of regular publication of an exporter bulletin, and establishment of a Web site, http://www.iflexsenegal.org, with information on fruits and vegetables available for export. On the physical infrastructure side, a state-of-the-art cold storage facility was designed and constructed at Dakar's airport, and an innovative packaging center was completed in Sangalkam. Both facilities were designed through an innovative and inclusive process that closely involved stakeholders, enhanced institutional capacity, and generated momentum for increased private sector investment in the industry. The project was closed in mid 2004, and a recent evaluation judged it to be successful, with a high probability that its accomplishments would be sustained.

improve the ability of food exporters and processors to meet quality and food safety standards (box 7.1). But recently some projects have gotten under way to address threats to global health and trade that arise from diseases of animal origin such as avian influenza, and more such projects are being prepared. The Bank has also teamed with WTO, other international organizations, and several bilateral partners to establish a Standards and Trade Development Facility, to provide grant financing for innovative capacity-building programs, especially in low-income countries.

Beyond the traditional trade agenda, increasing attention has focused recently on the adjustment costs that trade liberalization can impose on developing countries. Countries facing such costs should be assured of transitional support. The World Bank and the International Monetary Fund (IMF) are ready to provide adjustment assistance under existing mechanisms (including lending, for example, through IMF's recently inaugurated Trade Integration Mechanism). Where these costs are particularly severe, the Bank and IMF are prepared to coordinate with other donors to bring in additional assistance, in the form of grants or loans as appropriate. Likely candidates for assistance could include countries adversely affected by the end of textile quotas, countries affected by erosion of developed country trade preferences, net food-importing countries, and countries undertaking major trade reforms.

The World Bank also has an extensive program of technical assistance for countries dealing with trade-related problems. In the low-income countries much of this is undertaken through a multidonor initiative known as the Integrated Framework for Trade-Related Technical Assistance. The Bank has taken the lead in the majority of the Diagnostic Trade Integration Studies that are the first stage of assistance within this framework. These studies identify barriers to enhanced trade and integration and identify any needed projects or follow-up technical assistance. More in-depth work then follows to prepare the projects or undertake the assistance.

Although the World Bank is itself neither a member of WTO nor a party to the Doha negotiations, it has been closely involved in client countries' accession processes, providing both technical assistance and capacity building. In addition, since the beginning of the Doha Round, the Bank has advocated reaching an ambitious agreement that would significantly lower trade barriers. It has argued, both in its public statements and elsewhere, that agriculture is key to a pro-development outcome and that the industrialized countries must show leadership in making this happen. But developing countries also should take advantage of this opportunity to reduce their own trade barriers. This advocacy—together with the Bank's other work in trade policy—is underpinned by an extensive program of research, which has provided much of the evidence on the possible results of the Doha Round cited above. The Bank plans to continue to do all it can to make the global trading system more development-friendly and to help developing countries take full advantage of the opportunities that liberalized trade offers.

Notes

1. Recent surveys of the effects of market opening and economic integration include Dollar and Kraay (2004), Winters (2004), and World Bank (2002).
2. Panagariya (2004).
3. Two recent books, by Bhagwati (2004) and Wolf (2004), provide comprehensive yet very readable discussions of the positive net effects of freer trade, as well as rebuttals of trade liberalization's opponents.
4. On the intellectual history of the virtues of free trade, see Bhagwati (1988, chapter 2) and Irwin (1996). Bhagwati notes that the virtues of division of labor and exchange were cited 24 centuries ago in Plato's *Republic*.
5. See Anderson, Martin, and van der Mensbrugghe (2006a) for details of the model and its findings.

6. For more on the potential antipoverty consequences of the Doha Round, see Hertel and Winters (2005, 2006).

Selected Readings and Cited References

Aksoy, M. Ataman, and John C. Beghin, eds. 2004. *Global Agricultural Trade and Developing Countries*. Washington, DC: World Bank.

Alderman, Harold. 2001. "What Has Changed Regarding Rural Poverty Since 'Vision to Action'?" Rural Strategy Background Paper 5, Agriculture and Rural Development Department, World Bank, Washington, DC.

Anderson, Kym. 2005. "On the Virtues of Multilateral Trade Negotiations." *The Economic Record* 81 (4): 414–38.

Anderson, Kym, and Will Martin. 2005. "Agricultural Trade Reform and the Doha Development Agenda." *The World Economy* 28 (9): 1301–27.

————, eds. 2006. *Agricultural Trade Reform and the Doha Development Agenda*. London: Palgrave Macmillan; Washington, DC: World Bank.

Anderson, Kym, Will Martin, and Ernesto Valenzuela. 2006. "The Relative Importance of Global Agricultural Subsidies and Market Access." Forthcoming, in *World Trade Review* 5 (3), November.

Anderson, Kym, Will Martin, and Dominique van der Mensbrugghe. 2006a. "Market and Welfare Implications of the Doha Reform Scenarios." In *Agricultural Trade Reform and the Doha Development Agenda*, ed. Kym Anderson and Will Martin. London: Palgrave Macmillan; Washington, DC: World Bank.

————. 2006b. "Would Multilateral Trade Reform Benefit Sub-Saharan Africa?" *Journal of African Economies* 15 (forthcoming). Circulated as World Bank Policy Research Working Paper 3616, Washington, DC, June 2005.

Anderson, Kym, and Warwick McKibbin. 2000. "Reducing Coal Subsidies and Trade Barriers: Their Contribution to Greenhouse Gas Abatement." *Environment and Development Economics* 5 (4): 457–81.

Bhagwati, Jagdish N. 1988. *Protectionism*. Cambridge, MA: MIT Press.

————. 2004. *In Defense of Globalization*. Cambridge, MA: MIT Press.

Coe, David T., Elhanan Helpman, and Alexander W. Hoffmaister. 1997. "North-South R&D Spillovers." *Economic Journal* 107: 134–39.

Dollar, David, and Aart Kraay. 2004. "Trade, Growth and Poverty." *Economic Journal* 114: F22–F49.

Hertel, Thomas W., and L. Alan Winters. 2005. "Estimating the Poverty Impacts of a Prospective Doha Development Agenda." *The World Economy* 28 (8): 1057–71.

————, eds. 2006. *Poverty and the WTO: Impacts of the Doha Development Agenda*. London: Palgrave Macmillan; Washington, DC: World Bank.

International Monetary Fund. 2004. "Agricultural Trade: Reaping a Rich Harvest from Doha." *Finance and Development* 41 (4). Washington, DC.

Irwin, Douglas A. 1996. *Against the Tide: An Intellectual History of Free Trade*. Cambridge, MA: MIT Press.

_____. 2002. *Free Trade Under Fire*. Princeton, NJ: Princeton University Press.

Jaffee, Steven, Kees van der Meer, Spencer Henson, Cees de Haan, Mirvat Sewadeh, Laura Ignacio, John Lamb, and Mariana Bergovoy Lisazo. 2005. *Food Safety and Agricultural Health Standards: Challenges and Opportunities for Developing Country Exports*. Report 31207, Poverty Reduction and Economic Management Trade Unit and Agriculture and Rural Development Department, World Bank, Washington, DC.

Panagariya, Arvind. 2004. "Miracles and Debacles: In Defence of Trade Openness." *The World Economy* 27 (8): 1149–71.

_____. 2005. "Agricultural Liberalization and the Least-Developed Countries: Six Fallacies." *The World Economy* 28 (9): 1277–99.

Ravallion, Martin. 2002. "On the Urbanization of Poverty." *Journal of Economics* 68: 435–42.

van der Mensbrugghe, Dominique. 2005. "LINKAGE Technical Reference Document: Version 6.0," World Bank, Washington, DC. http://www.worldbank. org/prospects/linkagemodel.

Winters, L. Alan. 2004. "Trade Liberalization and Economic Performance: An Overview." *Economic Journal* 114: F4–F21.

Wolf, Martin. 2004. *Why Globalization Works*. New Haven, CT: Yale University Press.

World Bank. 2002. *Global Economic Prospects and the Developing Countries: Making Trade Work for the Poor*. Washington, DC: World Bank.

Selected Web Links on Trade and Development

World Trade Organization — http://www.wto.org

Integrated Framework for Trade-Related Assistance to Least Developed Countries — http://www.integratedframework.org

Trade Integration Mechanism (IMF factsheet) — http://www.imf.org/external/np/exr/facts/tim.htm

8

The Challenge
of Food Security:
Strategies to Reduce
Global Hunger
and Malnutrition

KEVIN CLEAVER, NWANZE OKIDEGBE, AND ERWIN DE NYS

I n a world of growing prosperity and agricultural abundance, about 800 million people still do not get enough to eat. Eliminating hunger and malnutrition is thus one of the most fundamental global challenges facing humanity. Besides alleviating human suffering from hunger, better nutrition in low- and middle-income countries will result in healthier people who are more capable to contribute to a thriving global economy, participate in world trade, and be less dependent on foreign assistance. A healthier population may also require fewer resources devoted to health care. For these reasons the United Nations has set, as one of its Millennium Development Goals, the goal of cutting in half the number of hungry and malnourished people worldwide by 2015. The international community and developing countries must work together to achieve this goal.

Malnutrition and its associated disease conditions can be caused by eating too little, eating too much, or eating an unbalanced diet that lacks necessary nutrients. Broadly speaking, two different types of malnutrition exist: undernutrition, and overweight and obesity. Undernutrition is defined as failure to consume adequate energy, protein, or micronutrients to meet basic

The authors would like to thank Jock R. Anderson, Csaba Csaki, and Gershon Feder for their excellent comments in improving this chapter.

requirements for body maintenance, growth, and development. This is the leading nutrition problem in low-income countries and is characterized by low height for age (stunting), low weight for height (wasting), and low weight for age (underweight).

Overweight and obesity are both labels for ranges of weight that are greater than what is generally considered healthy for a given height. (There is no universally agreed definition, but by one commonly used measure, obesity refers to weight exceeding the upper limit of normal body mass index by more than 20 percent.) The key causes of overweight and obesity are increased consumption of energy-dense foods high in saturated fats and sugars, along with reduced physical activity. Overweight and obesity are strong risk factors for major diet-related noncommunicable diseases, such as type II diabetes, cardiovascular disease, hypertension, stroke, and certain types of cancer.

Although undernutrition and obesity problems coexist in developing countries, this paper focuses on undernutrition only, and from the perspective of agricultural policy and food security in its different dimensions. Other perspectives on malnutrition are covered in chapter 11 and should not be considered as competing concepts but rather as complementary.

The Global Scale of Malnutrition

Undernutrition is a major global problem that is inextricably linked with poverty. Data show that the proportion of undernourished people in the developing world (about 17 to 20 percent of the population) remained fairly constant from 1990–92 to 2000–02. As figure 8.1 reveals, the vast majority of the world's undernourished people live in Asia (60 percent of the total) and Africa (28 percent), where undernutrition has decreased very little over the past decade (by 4 percent in Asia and 3 percent in Sub-Saharan Africa). The extent of undernutrition has been studied best among children, in extensive surveys conducted since the 1970s. Data from the World Health Organization show that the prevalence of stunting in preschool children in developing countries worldwide fell from 47.1 percent in 1980 to 32.5 percent in 2000. Thus, although the trend is positive, child undernutrition remains a major global problem.

In Africa, although the prevalence of stunting likewise declined, from 40.5 percent in 1980 to 35.2 percent in 2000, the absolute number of stunted children increased by more than one-third over the same period. Within Africa, stunting is most prevalent in eastern Africa, where, on average, 48 percent of preschool children are affected. In western Africa, the

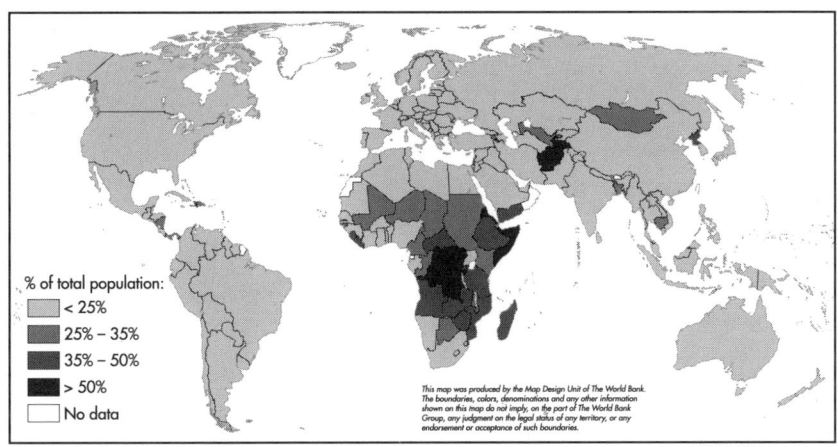

IBRD 34985 AUGUST 2006

FIGURE 8.1 Estimated Prevalence of Undernourishment in the Developing World, 2001–03ᵃ
Percent

% of total population:
  < 25%
  25% – 35%
  35% – 50%
  > 50%
  No data

This map was produced by the Map Design Unit of The World Bank. The boundaries, colors, denominations and any other information shown on this map do not imply, on the part of The World Bank Group, any judgment on the legal status of any territory, or any endorsement or acceptance of such boundaries.

Source: Food and Agriculture Organization of the United Nations 2004.
ᵃUndernourishment is defined as the proportion of the population that is unable to acquire sufficient calories to meet daily caloric requirements.

prevalence of stunting has changed little (from 36.2 percent to 34.9 percent), whereas northern Africa has shown considerable improvement (from 32.7 percent to 20.2 percent). Meanwhile, Asia has made substantial progress: stunting there decreased from 60.8 percent in 1980 to 43.7 percent in 2000. Yet stunting remains widespread, particularly in South Asia, where child malnutrition is extremely common.

The effects of undernutrition on child mortality in developing countries are devastating. It has been estimated that protein-energy undernutrition is a causative factor in 49 percent of the approximately 10.4 million annual deaths among children under five years of age. Undernutrition also has a significant economic impact. The economic loss to a nation where undernutrition is prevalent can be estimated in terms of lost productivity per individual worker. For example, the annual economic loss in Nigeria due to all forms of malnutrition in children under age five in 1994 has been estimated by this method at $489 million, or about 1.5 percent of gross domestic product (GDP). The economic costs of undernutrition are of a similar order of magnitude in other developing countries (see figure 8.2).

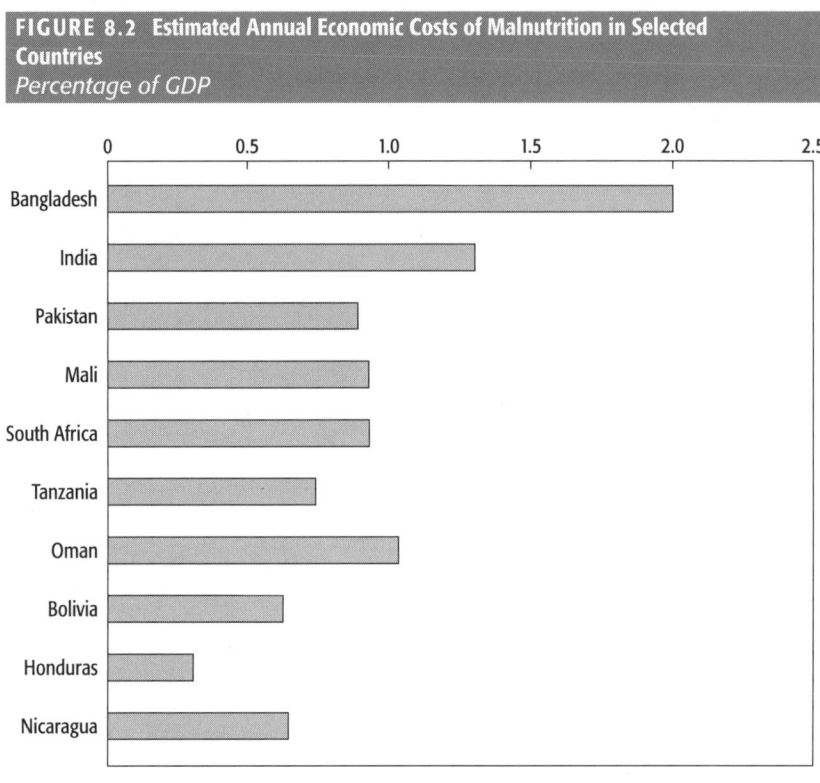

FIGURE 8.2   Estimated Annual Economic Costs of Malnutrition in Selected Countries
Percentage of GDP

Source: World Bank 2005.

The Forces Shaping the Problem of Undernutrition

The discussion in this section is guided by the notion of food security as defined at the 1996 World Food Summit in Rome (box 8.1). Food security is a multilayered concept, determined by several factors, including food availability, access to food, and food consumption, each working at several levels: global, regional, national, household, and individual.

Food Availability

Food availability refers to the supply of food, whether at the global, regional, national, or local level, without regard to the ability of individuals to acquire it. Sources of supply may include production within the household, domestic commercial food production, food stocks accumulated in earlier periods, commercially purchased imports, and food aid. There are presently no signs

BOX 8.1 The World Food Summit's Definition of Food Security

The World Food Summit was held in Rome in 1996, with the aim of renewing global commitment to the fight against hunger. The Food and Agriculture Organization of the United Nations (FAO) called the summit in response to widespread undernutrition and growing concern about the capacity of agriculture to meet future food needs. The conference produced two key documents, the Rome Declaration on World Food Security and the World Food Summit Plan of Action.

The broader concept of food security is reflected in the World Food Summit definition: "food security, at the individual, household, national, regional and global levels is achieved when all people, at all times, have physical and economic access to sufficient, safe and nutritious food to meet their dietary needs and food preferences for an active and healthy life." It recognized that poverty is "a major cause of food insecurity and that sustainable progress in poverty eradication is critical to improving access to food," but noted that "conflict, terrorism, corruption and environmental degradation also contribute significantly to food insecurity."

Source: Overseas Development Institute 1997.

of a food availability problem at the global level. In fact, global food production has more than kept pace with increasing world population in recent decades, increasing in per capita terms by 0.9 percent annually and even faster in such populous developing countries as China and India.

Important changes are occurring in food production and in trade patterns between different regions of the world. There is a trend toward greater food imports in many developing regions: Sub-Saharan Africa is a region of particular concern in this regard. This trend reflects the poor performance of the agricultural sector in the region, where yields for cereals (1 ton per hectare), roots and tubers (8 tons per hectare), and pulses (0.5 ton per hectare) are well below world—and even developing country—averages. The main culprits are lags in technological change, problems in input supply, and the region's marginal position in global trade and investment. Each of these proximate causes of poor performance in turn stems from a wide variety of problems confronting African agriculture, including poor infrastructure, domestic policies that are often hostile to agriculture, trade barriers in industrial countries, unsuitable climate, and weak education systems. Food availability is also lowest in Sub-Saharan Africa, at 2,195 kilocalories (kcal) per capita per day, and has remained almost stagnant over the past four decades (table 8.1). In contrast, the supply of energy per capita has risen dramatically in East Asia (by almost 1,000 kcal per capita per day, mainly in China) and in the Middle East and North Africa (by over 700 kcal per capita per day).

TABLE 8.1 Food Availability by World Region, Selected Years
Kilocalories per person per day

Region	1964–66	1974–76	1984–86	1997–99
Developing countries	2,054	2,152	2,450	2,681
Middle East and North Africa	2,290	2,591	2,953	3,006
Sub-Saharan Africa	2,058	2,079	2,057	2,195
Latin America and the Caribbean	2,393	2,546	2,689	2,824
East Asia	1,957	2,105	2,559	2,921
South Asia	2,017	1,986	2,205	2,403
Industrialized countries	2,947	3,065	3,206	3,380
World	2,358	2,435	2,655	2,803

Source: Food and Agriculture Organization of the United Nations 2002.

At the national level, food availability has often been viewed mistakenly as a food self-sufficiency problem. As a result, government food security strategies have frequently emphasized increased domestic food production, largely through the distribution of Green Revolution technologies, as the key means for addressing malnutrition. However, domestic production strategies are not necessarily the best way to increase availability: some degree of reliance on imports may be a less costly way of procuring domestic food needs. In this sense, globalization may help to improve food availability worldwide. Moreover, increased food availability at the national level does not ensure increased access to food at the household level. As the economist and Nobel laureate Amartya Sen argues, "starvation is the characteristic of some people not *having* enough food to eat. It is not the characteristic of there *being* not enough food to eat."[1]

Access to Food

Access to food refers to the ability of households to obtain food, whether through home production, commercial purchase, or transfers. In most circumstances, the main cause of food insecurity is not lack of availability but lack of access due to weak purchasing power and insufficient household agricultural production—both characteristics associated with poverty. Access to food is a large problem in South Asia, where, although crop yields and food availability are higher than in Sub-Saharan Africa, access to food remains limited by low income per capita ($380 a year on average) and the large share of the population (43 percent) living in poverty.

Differences in malnutrition also exist between urban and rural populations. Analyses indicate that although average levels of stunting are consistently greater in rural areas, large differences by socioeconomic status exist within both urban and rural groups. These differences are commonly greater in the urban areas: the most disadvantaged urban children have rates of stunting that are, on average, only slightly lower than those of the most disadvantaged rural children.

However, even access to sufficient food at the household level does not guarantee that all individuals have adequate food intake. That depends also upon the distribution of food among household members, methods of food preparation, dietary preferences, and mother-child feeding habits.

Food Consumption

Food consumption refers to the quantity and quality of food ingested at the household or the individual level. Although often measured in terms of food expenditure, it is conceptually closer to "food intake" as measured by calories or by quantities of different nutrients consumed. Nutritional status, in turn, refers to a person's physical condition as a result of the ingestion, absorption, and utilization of nutrients. Nutritional status thus depends not only on food intake but also on the body's ability to use these nutrients, which may be influenced by other health factors.

Empirical evidence suggests that one cannot simply assume strong and straightforward links all along the pathway from food production to nutritional outcomes. For instance, increased food availability may not lead to increased food access, if the former is achieved in such a way that it does not increase the real incomes of low-income households. Also, many factors other than household food production and income may affect rural food consumption, such as resource allocation patterns within households. Similarly, many factors other than food consumption, such as infectious disease, may affect nutritional status.

The challenge for policy makers and analysts concerned with achieving food and nutrition security is to understand how these various determinants—food availability, access to food, and food consumption—are linked to one another; how closely they are related in various contexts; and what important intervening variables affect the links of these variables to nutritional outcomes. Although research on food preparation and diets is first and foremost a local and country-level activity, the production of global agricultural public goods (for example, by the Consultative Group on International Agricultural Research, the worldwide alliance of agricultural research centers) can provide considerable economies of scale, especially in an age of rapid advances in information technology and biotechnology. Sharing of information and best practices may therefore improve nutrition globally.

Controversies and Alternative Views

No one disputes the responsibility of national governments and the international community to combat hunger and malnutrition. The question is how to achieve better nutrition. This section presents some alternative perspectives on and approaches to this question, such as the role of food aid, school feeding programs, and the use of agricultural biotechnology.

Food Aid

Food aid is the international provision of food commodities, usually the surplus of donor countries, for free or on highly concessional terms. Food aid is a contentious issue, because although it can clearly help some of the neediest in society, it may also cause economic harm to others. A key challenge regarding food aid lies in determining whether it can be an effective component of development policies aimed at achieving food security and improved nutrition.

On the one hand, food aid can fill the gap when food availability from local production and commercial imports is insufficient and markets fail to respond to demand; this generally occurs only in acute food-supply shocks. On the other hand, it is argued, food aid may undermine agricultural production by reducing domestic prices for farm produce, which now has to compete with food aid. In addition, food aid may create a disincentive to invest in agricultural inputs, processing plants, and markets, thus impeding economic development. Because both these arguments have some truth to them, food aid must be carefully managed so as to minimize the negative impacts.

Donors need to clarify their policy on the use of food aid, because it is generally recognized that food aid-in-kind sent by industrial countries, often at great cost, is not the best way for developing countries to attain long-term food security. In certain situations food aid may be essential to the well-being of vulnerable segments of the population, if it is provided on time, cheaply, and in a manner that does not destroy local production incentives. Arguments for or against the use of food aid should be made on the grounds of its efficiency as an instrument to address specific objectives and situations, such as preserving lives during natural and human-made disasters and protecting vulnerable social groups such as refugees, disabled people, or AIDS orphans. Food aid should be handled in a way that avoids disrupting local markets and production and should be linked to longer-term strategies for agricultural rehabilitation and development. Alternatives to food aid delivered from donor countries should be considered. For example, it may be preferable for donors to provide cash to recipient governments with which to buy food on the international market. Another alternative is for donors to buy food in nearby developing countries with adequate food supply and then donate it to poor, food-short countries.

School Feeding Programs

The provision of free or subsidized food to children in school is another contentious issue, because it is not clear that school feeding programs are a cost-effective investment for improved nutrition. Many governments justify such programs for their supposed nutritional benefits. However, the consensus in the research community is that such aid may come too late: the damage caused by undernutrition to human growth, brain development, and human capital formation is greatest—and largely irreversible—during gestation and the first two years of life. Any such investments after this critical period are much less likely to improve nutrition. For these reasons, the United Nations (UN) Millennium Project Task Force on Hunger does not view school feeding as a direct nutritional intervention.

School feeding programs can, however, sometimes be justified on other than nutritional grounds, as providing an incentive for children to go to school and to perform better. It can reduce a child's hunger during the school day, allowing him or her to be more attentive in class. A comprehensive food-for-schooling program can also ensure that children who attend school are given food rations to take home, offering economic incentives for poor families to release children from household or labor obligations so that they can attend school. The evaluation of school feeding programs in Bangladesh, for example, has shown increased participation in (by 20 to 30 percent) and duration of (between 0.4 and 1.4 years) schooling. This increase, however, was not clearly reflected in either nutrient intakes or anthropometric indices such as stunting and wasting. In conclusion, from a nutritional point of view, earlier intervention during gestation and the first two years of life is a more effective means of dealing with undernutrition in children.

Agricultural Biotechnology

Biotechnology has tremendous potential to improve agriculture and food production in developing countries. In Africa, several countries are putting in place structures and capacities for research and development in biotechnology. Improvements in productivity are beginning to emerge from the applications of biotechnology. For example, the application of tissue culture to address constraints of availability to farmers of adequate disease-free planting materials and rapid improvement in crop production is now commonplace in several countries. The demand for such materials is high, and the impact on the incomes of small farm households is becoming increasingly noticeable. The importance of genetic modification in increasing the production of transgenic food crop varieties with resistance to pesticides, insects, and diseases, and its impact on reducing the prohibitive costs to farmers of agricultural chemical inputs and yield losses, cannot be ignored.

However, major differences exist between countries in relation to the level of application, and many countries, developed and developing, are fearful of the impact of agricultural biotechnology. In 2002–03, when a number of southern African countries suffering from food shortages rejected food aid in the form of genetically modified maize, a highly polarized debate over the role of biotechnology came to the surface, which continues today (box 8.2).

BOX 8.2 The Debate over Genetically Modified Maize in Zambia

Zambia made its position on genetically modified (GM) food clear in 2002, when it rejected food aid from the United States during that year's drought and subsequent food crisis because the aid could not be confirmed to be GM free. The Zambian government banned the import, sale, and use of GM products, citing health, environmental, and trade concerns. The following year a team of southern African scientists, which the member nations of the Southern African Development Community (SADC) had asked to investigate the potential effects of planting and eating GM crops, concluded that the crops posed no immediate risk to humans and animals. They advised the southern African nations to embrace the technology because of its potential to increase agricultural yields. However, they also warned that the potential environmental risks remained a challenge. They therefore recommended that GM technologies be evaluated in African environments, and they called for African nations to develop their own capacity to regulate and test GM products.

In sharp contrast to the SADC team's findings, Zambia's own team of scientists recommended that the country should maintain its stand against GM food, because "GM crops can cause resistance to antibiotics and compromise immunity in people with poor health status." In 2005, when southern Africa was in the grip of its third severe drought since 2000, the Zambian government maintained its position on GM food. At the same time, the Zambian media (together with other journalists in eastern and southern Africa) issued a declaration outlining their resolve to make their coverage of biotechnology-related issues more balanced, accurate, and analytical to educate the public about technology. This came after the release of a report that criticized the Zambian media for being one-sided on GM issues and uncritical of the government line.

This debate about biotechnology has created fear, mistrust, and general confusion among the public, and participants have often failed to seek the views of policy makers and stakeholders in developing countries. The controversy over the characteristics of genetically modified (GM) crops and the implications of their use have tended to overshadow consideration of the many other contributions that cutting-edge agricultural research and non-GM techniques can make to increasing crop productivity, as well as developing and propagating new crop varieties. In fact, the debate should not be whether developing countries need biotechnology, but how biotechnology can be promoted, supported, and applied in safe and sustainable ways that contribute to improved agriculture and to social and economic welfare. Developing countries need to develop long-term policies on biotechnology that promote the assessment of and targeted research into their specific needs; improve and enhance their own scientific capacities and technological infrastructure; and integrate biotechnology risk management into their environmental, health, and agricultural interventions.

What Countries and the International Community Can Do

Because undernutrition is related to poverty and lack of development in so many ways, a wide variety of development actions are needed to improve food security and nutrition. Some of these can be undertaken by national governments; others must be addressed by the international community. Detailed strategies and actions at the country level can only be defined through a country-specific analysis of the forces driving undernutrition. This chapter can therefore make only a few general recommendations.

Domestic Policies and Investment

Undernutrition can be often attributed to shortcomings in the domestic political framework or the domestic economic environment. Several studies have shown that the rate of rural poverty reduction is strongly influenced by the rate of agricultural growth. This is not surprising given the importance of agriculture as a source for employment and income for the rural poor.

In order to bring about food security, governments should put in place policies and institutions that foster growth and reduce poverty and that balance the interests of food consumers in low prices with those of producers and investors in high returns. This requires a clear strategy to ensure that economic growth is pro-poor and that the poor have access to productive assets, markets, institutions, and services. As the incomes of the poor rise, generally they purchase more and better food. This will not cure the problem of hunger and undernutrition, because the cause is not just low income. It will, however, contribute to a solution at the household level.

The literature on agriculture and food security offers a number of general recommendations for how governments could reform their policies and increase their investments in agriculture in order to achieve food security, including the following:

- Promoting an integrated policy approach to hunger education
- Restoring the budgetary priority of the agricultural and rural sectors
- Linking nutritional and agricultural interventions
- Increasing poor people's access to land and other productive resources
- Empowering women and girls
- Creating vibrant partnerships to ensure effective policy implementation.

An integrated and multisectoral policy approach is essential, because countries frequently lack a clear policy or strategy to address each of the three dimensions of food security. Also, institutional roles, mandates, and initiatives toward improved nutrition are often diffused across a range of ministries, donor-funded projects, nongovernmental organizations, monitoring networks, and the private sector. The drafting of Poverty Reduction Strategy Papers provides a good opportunity for multisector planning and mainstreaming of food security in all areas of domestic policy.

National governments must also make a commitment to increase public funding to the sectors essential in combating undernutrition, in particular the agricultural and rural sectors. The Maputo Declaration on Agriculture and Food Security in Africa, adopted by the African Union in July 2003, is an example of such a commitment. This declaration endorsed a recommendation that African countries invest at least 10 percent of their budget in agriculture and rural development.

Again, however, general recommendations for agricultural policy reform are difficult to provide, because the causes of food insecurity and malnutrition are often country-specific. Broadly speaking, the best policies and investments are best that promote agriculture and food market development and rural infrastructure, and that stimulate private investment in agriculture and in agroprocessing. In addition to these long-term general policies and investment for agricultural development, improved social safety nets can offer protection to poor people and other vulnerable groups by providing direct access to food through feeding programs for mothers and infants, school meals and school gardens, and food-for-work and food-for-education programs.

Removal of Internal and Regional Barriers to Agricultural Trade

Trade is an essential element of food security. An export-led agricultural strategy focusing on areas of comparative advantage is likely to generate stronger growth and increased incomes and may be a better way to bring about food security. A strong external trade position also helps achieve food availability at the national level by strengthening the capacity to import.

However, low-income countries, which today account for less than 0.5 percent of global trade, have been largely excluded from the benefits of trade liberalization. Their export industries continue to face both internal obstacles (lack of a secure legal framework; and weaknesses in infrastructure, information flows, and human resources) and market access restrictions imposed by industrialized countries (tariffs, quotas, and technical barriers to trade). It is essential that developed countries make greater concessions to open their markets to all types of products from low-income countries. Also needed is greater capacity for trade, achieved by tackling the many obstacles and helping exporters meet product standards, safety requirements, and certification procedures.

Conversely, liberalization may result in increased exposure to foreign competition and the removal of government support for certain sectors. These adverse impacts may have negative consequences for food security in the short term. In view of these risks, rules for special and differential treatment (S&DT) for developing countries are being negotiated within the World Trade Organization. In the agricultural negotiations, S&DT measures relate mainly to export competition, domestic support, and market access. These measures must allow developing countries to pursue agricultural policies that support their development goals and poverty reduction strategies, as well as their food security and livelihood concerns.

Regional integration can help achieve food security by expanding marketing opportunities, integrating food markets, and facilitating food transfer from areas of surplus to areas of shortage. Beyond the benefits of free trade areas and customs unions, regional cooperation is vital to solving common problems related to food insecurity. Environmental problems, agricultural pests and diseases, agricultural research, and infrastructure often have a cross-border dimension that requires effective regional cooperation.

The results of regional cooperation in developing countries have generally fallen far short of expectations. In Africa, the Caribbean, and the Pacific, for example, the oldest regional economic communities have been in existence for more than 30 years. Their main aim was to encourage and strengthen trade among member countries, especially for food and other agricultural products.

BOX 8.3 Examples of Regional Integration in Agriculture in Africa

Significant progress has been made in Africa over the past few years toward regional integration in agriculture through the creation of common agricultural policies. The most recent example is that of the West African Common Agricultural Policy (ECOWAAP), adopted in January 2005 by the conference of West African heads of state and government. ECOWAAP is a wide-ranging initiative that seeks to harmonize procedures across the participating countries with regard to land access, natural resource management, assistance for farmers, and access to credit.

The improvement of regional infrastructures is another crucial element toward the integration of African agriculture. In East Africa, for example, the African Development Fund estimates that the Mombasa–Nairobi–Addis Ababa Road Corridor Development Project will increase trade in the region by 500 percent.

However, according to the United Nations Economic Commission for Africa (UNECA), intraregional trade today accounts for only 9 percent of total trade in West Africa and just 4 percent in central Africa. Trade also remains weak within the Caribbean Community (CARICOM), since many of the islands produce similar products. By contrast, in the European Union more than half of all trade is conducted among member states. Nevertheless, some examples of significant progress toward regional integration in agriculture can be cited (box 8.3).

Strengthening of Agricultural and Nutritional Research

The exceptional growth in agricultural productivity over the past century was primarily a result of investments in agricultural research, agricultural extension, irrigation, and rural infrastructure, combined with private investment in agriculture, agricultural input supply, and processing. Research generates new knowledge and technologies, which may or may not benefit the poor and increase food security. In industrialized countries, agricultural research is increasingly conducted by private companies and has benefited farmers and consumers in those countries. By contrast, less research has been done in low-income countries, and what research has been done has focused on the staple crops grown by poor farmers and on techniques suited to nonirrigated, low-input, risk-prone agriculture on marginal lands. This has contributed, along with the other factors described above, to many poor farmers remaining poor.

The UN Millennium Project Task Force on Hunger recommends supporting a more active role for the public sector in agricultural and nutrition research in developing countries by increasing national investment in such research to at least 2 percent of agricultural GDP by 2015. Three-quarters of this should go to agricultural research—embracing sustainable crop, livestock, fish, and tree production systems and associated natural resource and ecosystem management—and the rest to nutrition research. This would much more than double the current funding for such research. Rural infrastructure and other rural services (such as finance and marketing) also need significantly increased investment.

In addition, developing country governments and donors should enter into a new partnership with private companies with deep pockets for research. Governments, donor agencies, and the international agricultural research centers coordinated by the Consultative Group on International Agricultural Research should increasingly facilitate the transfer of technology between developed and developing countries and between the private sector and the public domain.

International agricultural research can support the fight against malnutrition and hunger in numerous ways:

- Crop breeding is perhaps the most direct approach toward improving nutrition through increased agricultural production. This was shown by the Green Revolution, which succeeded in increasing farm productivity and output in South Asia, leading to price declines and increased human food energy intake.
- More recent work has focused on plant breeding to improve micronutrient status by biofortifying staple crops.
- Livestock farming can improve nutrition both by raising producer incomes and by increasing consumption of high-protein animal-source foods.
- Fish provides proteins and a wide range of vitamins and minerals. However, increasing fish production to improve nutrition has proved to be quite a complex undertaking, and success at integrating fish production and nutrition appears to be largely context and project specific. There have, however, been some notable successes, particularly in China.
- Postharvest activities can affect nutrient availability in many ways, such as by increasing the nutrient density of foods consumed by infants and increasing consumption of nutrient-rich foods.

To be sure, both the potential and the actual nutritional benefits of these types of interventions will depend largely on the context and on the specific project, as well as on the other factors that affect nutrition.

Actions by the International Community

The international community has committed itself on several occasions to fighting global malnutrition and hunger. The right of all people to adequate food and nutrition has been recognized in various international human rights instruments, both legally binding conventions and nonbinding declarations (table 8.2). In the Rome Declaration, described in box 8.1, heads of state reaffirmed "the right of everyone to have access to safe and nutritious food, consistent with the right to adequate food and the fundamental right of everyone to be free from hunger." Although nonbinding, declarations such as these exert a measure of moral suasion on the signatory governments.

Concrete targets were set at the UN Millennium Summit in 2000, where world leaders pledged to reduce hunger and extreme poverty by half. The nutrition target of the Millennium Development Goals (MDGs) is to reduce by half the prevalence of underweight among children under five between 1990 and 2015. The link with agriculture is also strong for the MDG of reducing poverty and hunger by half. Other MDGs also have direct or indirect links with agriculture.

International donors also made a strong financial commitment in the Monterrey Consensus of 2002, which urged rich countries to raise their annual overseas development assistance from 0.2 percent of their combined gross national product ($53 billion at the time) to 0.7 percent. Reaching the Monterrey target would require raising total assistance to $175 billion a year. Many scholars and various civil society groups have made a persuasive case for ending extreme poverty by 2025 by honoring the Monterrey Consensus and increasing assistance to sectors related directly to hunger reduction, such as agriculture, nutrition, water, and sanitation, and markets related to agriculture.

TABLE 8.2 Key International Conventions and Declarations Relating to Hunger and Food Security

1948	Universal Declaration of Human Rights
1974	Universal Declaration on the Eradication of Hunger and Malnutrition
1990	Convention on the Rights of the Child
1992	World Declaration and Plan of Action on Nutrition
1996	Rome Declaration on World Food Security and World Food Summit Plan of Action
2000	United Nations Millennium Declaration
2002	Monterrey Consensus on Financing for Development
2002	Johannesburg Declaration on Sustainable Development

Finally, international donor agencies must increase the effectiveness and coordination of their investments in agriculture, nutrition, and humanitarian food aid. Projects are often not as efficient as they could be because of their typically short horizon (three to five years), cumbersome procedures, inadequate monitoring and evaluation, and failure to address problems on a national scale. Suitable vehicles for donor coordination must be sought through sharing coordination mechanisms, adopting common monitoring procedures, and developing robust systems for sharing knowledge and results.

The World Bank's Role in Addressing Undernutrition and Hunger

The World Bank is the single largest source of funding for agriculture and rural development in developing countries. In financial year 2005, total World Bank lending to agriculture was $2.1 billion, and lending for all rural development activities was $8.7 billion. About 70 percent of Bank lending to agriculture supports production of food and cash crops, irrigation and drainage, and the development and distribution of technology.

The agricultural dimension of the World Bank's approach to malnutrition and hunger is outlined in its rural development strategy as presented in its 2003 publication *Reaching the Rural Poor*. That strategy is aligned with the Bank's focus on poverty reduction and therefore sets broad-based economic growth, and specifically, economic growth in rural areas, as one of its main objectives. At the country level, the Bank's support is mainly focused on policies that are agriculture-friendly, as well as projects and programs that pursue increased agricultural productivity and economic growth in other sectors. These projects and programs may contain nutrition components.

On the policy front, the World Bank works with client countries to create an appropriate overall macroeconomic and agricultural-rural policy and a supportive institutional framework. That includes, for example, the liberalization of agricultural markets by both industrial and developing countries. The Bank urges the industrial countries to remove trade barriers to developing countries' products and to phase out agricultural subsidies. A concrete example of Bank support related to greater openness to trade is its review of the role and effectiveness of state enterprises in food crop production (for example, in India and Indonesia) and in producing crops for export (for example, in Burkina Faso, Ghana, and India).

Improved agricultural productivity and growth are a central focus of the World Bank's rural development strategy, recognizing that, in many low-income countries, agriculture is the main source of rural economic growth and that agricultural growth is the cornerstone of reducing rural poverty. The Bank has supported numerous interventions aimed at increased agricultural productivity in countries throughout the developing world and continues to do so.

In the past few years, the World Bank and other donor agencies have increased their support to agricultural programs in low-income countries. However, more is needed because the level of investment in agriculture remains inadequate to achieve the MDG of reducing hunger and malnutrition by half by 2015. Increased and sustained investments in agriculture in collaboration with other sectors are required. If the global effects of malnutrition are not adequately addressed through increased investments, the consequences would be disastrous. The world's low-income countries, in partnership with the donor community, should work together to rid humanity of the scourge of malnutrition.

Note

1. Sen (1981, p. 1).

Selected Readings and Cited References

Barrett, Christopher B., and Daniel G. Maxwell. 2005. *Food Aid After Fifty Years: Recasting Its Role.* London: Routledge.

de Onis, Mercedes, Edward A. Frongillo, and Monika Blössner. 2000. "Is Malnutrition Declining? An Analysis of Changes in Levels of Child Malnutrition since 1980." *Bulletin of the World Health Organization* 78: 1222–33.

Food and Agriculture Organization of the United Nations. 2002. "World Agriculture: Towards 2015/2030. Summary Report." Rome.

_____. 2004. *FAO Statistics Yearbook 2004.* Rome.

_____. 2005. "The State of Food Insecurity in the World 2005." Rome.

Hoekman, Bernard M., Phillip English, and Aaditya Mattoo. 2002. *Development, Trade, and the WTO: A Handbook.* Washington, DC: World Bank.

Kennedy, Eileen, and Howarth Bouis. 1993. *Agriculture/Nutrition Linkages: Implications for Policy and Research.* Washington, DC: International Food Policy Research Institute.

Lomborg, Bjorn, ed. 2004. *Global Crises, Global Solutions.* Cambridge, United Kingdom: Cambridge University Press.

Newfarmer, Richard. 2005. *Trade, Doha, and Development: A Window into the Issues.* Washington, DC: World Bank.

Overseas Development Institute. 1997. "Global Hunger and Food Security After the World Food Summit." Briefing Paper 1997(1), Overseas Development Institute, London.

Rosegrant, Mark, Michael S. Paisner, and Siet Meijer. 2001. "Long Term Prospects for Agriculture and the Resource Base." Rural Strategy Background Paper 1, World Bank, Washington, DC.

Sachs, Jeffrey D. 2005. *The End of Poverty: Economic Possibilities for Our Time.* New York: Penguin Press.

Sen, Amartya. 1981. *Poverty and Famines.* Oxford, United Kingdom: Clarendon Press.

United Nations Millennium Project Task Force on Hunger. 2005. *Halving Hunger: It Can Be Done.* New York: United Nations.

World Health Organization. 2005. "Turning the Tide of Malnutrition. Responding to the Challenge of the 21st Century." Geneva.

World Bank. 2003. *Reaching the Rural Poor. A Renewed Strategy for Rural Development.* Washington, DC.

————. 2005. "Agriculture and Achieving the Millennium Development Goals." Washington, DC.

————. 2006. "Repositioning Nutrition as Central to Development. A Strategy for Large-Scale Action." Washington, DC.

Selected Web Links on Undernutrition and Agriculture Policy

Consultative Group on International Agricultural Research	http://www.cgiar.org
Food and Agriculture Organization of the United Nations	http://www.fao.org
International Food Policy Research Institute	http://www.ifpri.org
World Health Organization	http://www.who.int

PART TWO
Human Development

The world's population is expected to approach 11 billion sometime in the next century, nearly double what it is today. The challenge of developing and harnessing this human capacity for the greater good of the planet is a formidable one. At the same time the downside risks of human suffering that such growth could cause, especially through widespread hunger and disease, is all too easy to imagine. The chapters in this part of the book address these challenges and dangers head on and explore what the world community can do to address them. Large amounts of funds, knowledge, and national and international actions will be needed to prevent hunger, raise well-nourished children, avoid common diseases, and contain and eventually overcome disease pandemics. Global virtues of tolerance and respect for human rights within families and across nations will require fostering. This places education at the core of human development, aimed at promoting a global social environment in which all men and women can achieve their full human potential.

9

Diseases Without Borders: Coping with Communicable Disease

JAYSHREE BALACHANDER

The twentieth century was a period of steady progress in preventing and controlling a wide range of communicable diseases. Effective public health measures and the development and widespread use of vaccines and drugs have greatly reduced the death toll and disease burden from infectious diseases. Immunization saves an estimated 3 million children annually,[1] and the percentage of children who die before reaching the age of five has been cut in half since 1960. Smallpox, formerly a major killer in the developing world, has been eliminated, and polio has been declared eradicated in a number of countries. Many other serious conditions such as bacterial meningitis and pneumonia can now be satisfactorily treated with antibiotics. Medical advances have spread, improving health around the world.

Despite this remarkable progress, infectious diseases remain a leading cause of death worldwide, accounting for more than 10 million deaths every year according to the World Health Organization (WHO), including nearly two-thirds of all deaths among children under age five. The *big three* infectious diseases—HIV/AIDS, tuberculosis, and malaria—account for more than half of all deaths from communicable diseases. These diseases continue to be major public health threats, especially in developing countries, despite years of organized national and international efforts to control them. Vaccines that could effectively prevent these diseases have not yet been developed.

Virtually unknown 25 years ago, the human immunodeficiency virus (HIV) that causes AIDS has already infected more than 60 million people

This chapter draws on previous World Bank research and publications. Useful inputs and comments were provided by Olusoji Adeyi, Rama Lakshminarayanan, and Tawhid Nawaz.

worldwide, and more than 20 million have died, 3.1 million in 2005 alone. Over 8 million children under 15 years of age have been orphaned. Of the approximately 40 million people living with HIV/AIDS today, some 38 million live in developing countries. AIDS is now the leading cause of death in Sub-Saharan Africa and the fourth-largest killer globally. The epidemic has cut life expectancy by more than 10 years in South Africa and Botswana. Meanwhile, HIV continues to spread at varying but unknown rates in the Caribbean, China, India, and Russia. A series of new, potent antiviral drugs have been developed which, when used in combination, can retard the progress of HIV. However, these drugs cause a range of side effects and must be constantly reevaluated as HIV develops resistance to them, and they are expensive— indeed, unaffordable except in high-income countries (see box 9.1).

Another worldwide killer, tuberculosis, causes 8.8 million new cases each year (nearly 25,000 a day) and is responsible for an annual mortality of 1.7 million. The microbe that causes the disease, *Mycobacterium tuberculosis,* is resilient and highly adaptive. Efforts to control it are seriously hampered by drug resistance and by co-infection with HIV. About a third of the world's 40 million HIV-positive people also suffer from tuberculosis, and HIV infection increases the chance of developing tuberculosis 10-fold. More HIV-positive patients die from tuberculosis than from any other infection. Without treatment, 50 to 70 percent of those with infectious tuberculosis will die, and a single untreated person can, on average, infect between 10 and 15 people a year.

BOX 9.1 Can HIV/AIDS Treatment Be Made Affordable?

A *Washington Post* editorial by Donald M. Berwick, titled "We All Have AIDS," challenged the directors of drug companies to reduce to zero the cost of HIV treatment in poor countries. The editorial, which appeared on June 26, 2001, sparked off a spirited debate in which the chairman of GlaxoSmithKline said that his company offered its medicine to poor countries at preferential prices but had to cover costs so that the supply remains sustainable. However, manufacturers in countries such as India and Brazil have been able to sell the same drugs at a cost of $600 per patient per year, 40 percent less than the discounted price offered by the major manufacturers in the industrialized countries. The production of the drugs by these countries bypasses patents on the drugs by reverse engineering them—a practice recognized under current patent laws in India and Brazil but that would be phased out under the revised Trade-Related Aspects of Intellectual Property Rights Agreement being negotiated under the World Trade Organization. Affordable HIV treatment is still a pipedream in most of the countries staggering under the HIV/AIDS epidemic.

Source: Author.

Malaria is likewise widespread and deadly, especially in children or in its more severe cerebral form. More than a third of the world's population now live in areas where malaria is endemic. Up to 500 million new clinical cases of malaria occur each year, and the annual mortality from the disease is 1.2 million a year.

In addition to these three major diseases, new infectious diseases can arise from hitherto unknown microbes, many of them zoonotics,[2] which are capable of causing a pandemic. The pathogens move among humans, pigs, and bird species and can mutate during these transmissions, occasionally leading to highly contagious or more deadly forms. Their genetic variability seems designed to overcome the defenses of the hosts they infect. Zoonotics appear to be a growing threat to human health because of increased human activity in or alteration of ecosystems or habitats of certain insects and animals. Severe acute respiratory syndrome (SARS), for example, is a viral respiratory illness caused by a coronavirus believed to replicate in animal hosts. An outbreak of a virulent and superinfectious form of the virus, hitherto unknown in humans, occurred in 2003. A total of 8,098 people worldwide fell ill during the outbreak, and 774 died. WHO estimates the case fatality ratio of SARS to range up to 50 percent, depending on the average age of those affected. The outbreak was effectively contained, but a number of important questions about SARS and other zoonotics remain unanswered: How important are animals in transmission? What are the factors responsible for the *superspreader* phenomenon, in which one patient may infect several others through casual contact or environmental contamination? What is the nature of the infection that leads to transmission between humans and animals? Prevention and containment of pandemics will be extremely difficult unless microbiologists discover the answers to these questions.

The ongoing avian flu epidemic is caused by a type of influenza virus, H5N1, that is potentially deadlier and far more devastating than any other influenza virus to date. The virus occurs naturally in certain aquatic migratory bird species. It is harmless to these birds but is fatal to other birds such as chickens, domestic ducks, and swans. The migrating species pass the virus on to the local birds through their droppings, which the latter may ingest when pecking on the ground. For a decade, H5N1 was confined to a small pool of migratory birds, mostly inside China. In May 2005, however, a major outbreak occurred at Lake Qinghai in central China, killing 6,000 birds, including many species that had not been infected in the past. This was a turning point, since it signified that the virus had mutated and had become more contagious and deadlier to a larger number of species. The first human transmission followed shortly thereafter, and more than 90 of the 170 persons known to have been infected have died. So far the vast majority of those infected are believed to have caught the disease directly from infected chickens. If the microbe were to mutate further so as to spread easily from person to person, an influenza pandemic could be in the making.

Factors Driving the Spread of Communicable Diseases

Infectious diseases can be caused by a wide variety of organisms of different taxonomic lines, including viruses, bacteria, fungi, protozoa, and helminths. Many factors—social, economic, climatic, technological, and environmental—shape disease patterns and influence the emergence and spread of these diseases. The current global socioeconomic situation seems to influence and favor these factors. The Institute of Medicine committee on emerging infections in the United States identified six major factors that contribute to the emergence and reemergence of infectious disease:

- Changes in human demographics and behavior
- Advances in technology and changes in industry practices
- Economic development and changes in land-use patterns
- Dramatic increases in the volume and speed of international travel and commerce, including movements not only of people but of animals, foodstuffs, and other commodities
- Microbial adaptation and change
- Breakdown of the public health capacity required to combat infectious diseases at the local, state, national, and global levels.

Meanwhile, the challenge posed by communicable diseases has grown in scope and complexity. Some 30 previously unknown diseases, including, most importantly, HIV/AIDS but also others such as Ebola hemorrhagic fever, Rift Valley fever, and Lyme disease, have emerged. Still other diseases once viewed as declining in significance, such as tuberculosis, have resurged as the agents that cause these infections have developed resistance to the drugs used for treating them. An additional threat is the potential deployment of disease pathogens as weapons of war or instruments of terror. Several bacteria and viruses have been identified as potential biological warfare agents, including the pathogens responsible for causing anthrax and smallpox. After the eradication of smallpox by the late 1970s, the global vaccination program was phased out and the pathogens destroyed. The vaccine that protects against anthrax is also in relatively short supply because anthrax is such an uncommon disease. Thus the general population is particularly vulnerable to both smallpox and anthrax, which can be deadly when used as weapons.

These circumstances require that microbiologists, public health experts, and law enforcement officials work together to develop a broad-based, coordinated strategy for dealing effectively with the threat of bioterrorism.

Finally, war-torn states, those with weak enforcement of law and order, and those affected by natural calamities such as drought or flood pose special problems, because the impairment of access for disease control teams compounds the difficulties normally associated with controlling an epidemic. During an outbreak of the deadly Ebola virus in Kelle, the Democratic Republic of Congo (formerly Zaire), in 1993, four teachers who were engaged in epidemic control activities were branded as witches and killed. Polio vaccination efforts in the same country were hampered when an ongoing civil war kept vaccine supplies from being delivered to patients, resulting in 1995 in the largest outbreak of polio in modern times: more than 1,000 cases of paralytic poliomyelitis were recorded in the city of Kisangani. Typhoid, malaria, and gastrointestinal diseases are also serious threats in disaster-hit zones, where even clean drinking water can be unavailable for days or even weeks; this was the case after the "super cyclone" that killed over 20,000 people in the Indian state of Orissa in 1999.

What Makes Communicable Diseases a Global Issue?

Although the great majority of deaths from communicable diseases occur in developing countries, the threat they pose constitutes an important issue for the world as a whole, on several counts. First, the sheer magnitude of the problem makes it a substantial threat to people in all parts of the world and demands worldwide attention and action. Infectious diseases can be a substantial obstacle to countries' economic and social development. For example, the Roll Back Malaria program has estimated that malaria has led to a reduction in gross domestic product growth in Africa of about 1.3 percent a year. Similarly, the economic cost of AIDS is estimated to be between 0.3 and 1.5 percent annually, although recent research sponsored by the World Bank suggests that the long-term economic impact is likely to be much greater. Health care costs are growing rapidly in many countries, absorbing a rising share of income and forcing them to forgo other badly needed goods and services. Moreover, the heaviest burden of infectious diseases falls not only on developing countries but also on the poorest households within them. These households bear the largest share of the burden of infectious diseases, yet they have the least opportunity to adopt protective measures and the least access to affordable, good-quality care. Sickness further impoverishes the poor through health care costs and loss of wages.

Second, communicable diseases do not recognize international boundaries or sovereign states. With the rise in international traffic and commerce that accompanies globalization, diseases can be transmitted easily around the world—a disease can now emerge anywhere on the globe and spread quickly to other regions. Before 1999, for example, the West Nile virus, a well-recognized cause of disease in Africa, Europe, and the Middle East, had never been observed in the Western Hemisphere. Since then several thousand cases have been reported throughout the United States and in parts of Canada and Mexico. Severe acute respiratory syndrome (SARS) was first reported in Asia in February 2003, and within a few months the illness had spread to more than two dozen countries in Asia, Europe, North America, and South America before the outbreak was contained. Avian flu has already rapidly spread far and wide—Russia, Ukraine, Romania, Greece, Turkey, and all the other countries along the Black Sea—and Mediterranean bird migratory routes have been affected. The latest countries to join the list are Egypt, India, Israel, and Nigeria. Figures 9.1 and 9.2 trace the global transmission routes of the 2003 SARS outbreak and the 2005 avian flu along bird migratory routes.

Third, globalization has far-reaching impacts on public health and international economies. The shrinking of the world by technology and the growing interdependence of national economies allow diseases to spread rapidly through trade and travel. International air passengers carried SARS across the Atlantic within a matter of days of its outbreak. The increasingly global nature of food handling, processing, and sale is another means of rapid transmission of pathogens. HIV/AIDS, tuberculosis, cholera, and malaria are examples of infections that have spread from region to region through international commerce. The scale and scope of today's international economic transactions are unprecedented, and local outbreaks have global implications because of the disruption of travel and commerce that can occur. For example, India's brief outbreak of plague in 1994 is estimated to have cost over a billion dollars in economic damage from the travel restrictions and trade embargoes imposed by other countries.

Fourth, communicable diseases of global scope affect or are affected by other global issues discussed elsewhere in this volume, such as climate change, malnutrition, biodiversity, access to safe water, and migration. If climate change follows the trajectory projected by current global circulation models, it may have important and far-reaching effects on the spread of infectious diseases, especially those transmitted by organisms whose body temperature changes with the surroundings, such as mosquitoes and ticks. Most scientists agree that global climate change will influence the transmission dynamics of infectious disease, although the extent of the influence is uncertain. Infectious

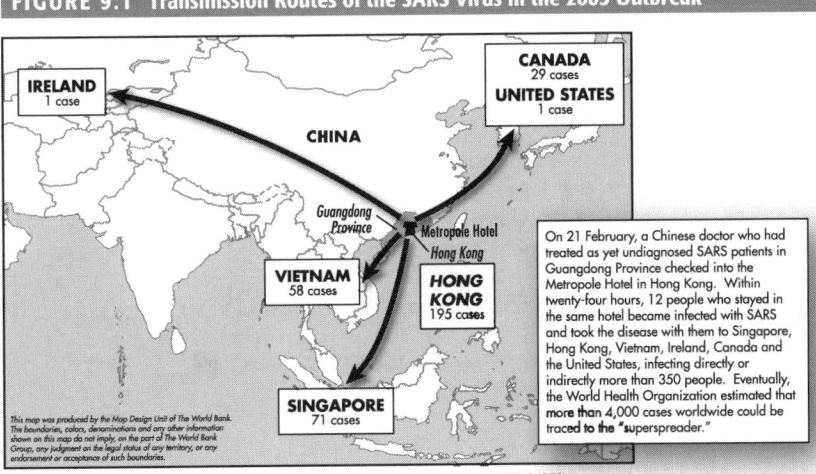

FIGURE 9.1 Transmission Routes of the SARS Virus in the 2003 Outbreak

Source: U.S. Centers for Disease Control and Prevention 2000.

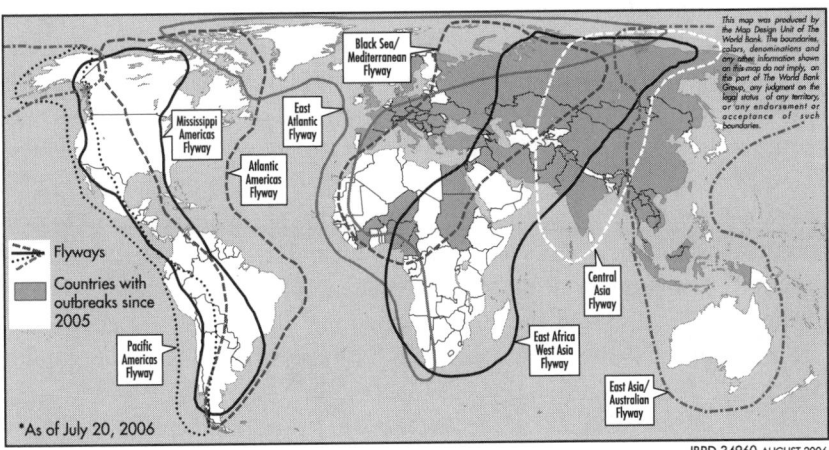

FIGURE 9.2 Avian Flu Outbreaks in 2005 and Major Flyways of Migratory Birds[a]

Sources: OIE World Organisation for Animal Health, Food and Agriculture Organization, Wetlands International, and national government sources.
a. As of August 30, 2005. Dots indicate districts with H5N1 virus outbreaks since January 2005.

BOX 9.2 The Relationship Between Biodiversity and Human Health

Traditionally, biodiversity has contributed to human health mainly as a source of important medicines. Ancient health systems, notably those of China and India, relied on several species of herbs, trees, and other plants for medicinal use. In recent years, these traditions are losing not only their practitioners and clients but also their raw material, through the loss of a rich diversity of plant and animal species as natural areas come under development. Moreover, human disturbance of ecosystems has resulted in hitherto unknown diseases emerging or existing diseases spreading to new areas. Jungle yellow fever, transmitted by a mosquito that resides solely in the forest canopy, high above human habitation, reached ground level by the felling of trees in the jungles of the Amazon. Lyme disease affected humans only after forest deer made human contact through land-use changes in the eastern United States.

Source: Author.

---

diseases in children are highly correlated with malnutrition, which is a major underlying factor in child mortality in many countries. The clearing of forests and the construction of dams can have unforeseen health consequences when natural habitats are affected, including a loss of valuable biodiversity (box 9.2). Unclean water is a major cause of ill health; indeed, even the most basic public health measures cannot be taken in the absence of safe water. The Agreement on Trade-Related Aspects of Intellectual Property Rights, negotiated in 1994 as part of the Uruguay Round of trade negotiations, will have far-reaching impacts on the production and distribution of pharmaceuticals, many of them critical in the treatment of infectious diseases. Another recent challenge has been to address the issue of health workers migrating from the poor developing countries that need them the most to rich countries, where they face better employment and income prospects. Nurses have migrated en masse from countries such as the Philippines and Malawi to the United States and the United Kingdom. This presents yet another challenge for the delivery of quality health care services in many developing countries.

Finally, the global nature of the threat posed by new and reemerging infectious diseases requires international cooperation in identifying, controlling, and preventing these diseases. New vaccines and drugs for some of these diseases are global public goods, whose development may be best facilitated and financed globally. Infectious diseases themselves, however, are global public "bads," generating negative health, economic, and security-related externalities that must be dealt with. Understanding and responding to infectious disease requires a global perspective, conceptually and geographically. The recognition that countries need to cooperate to tackle infectious diseases itself demonstrates that public health policy has been denationalized. An Institute of Medicine report concludes that distinctions between domestic and international health problems are losing their usefulness and often are misleading,[3] and that countries must increasingly come together to deal with infectious diseases through internationally coordinated public health actions.

International Cooperation Against Diseases Without Borders

Countries have cooperated to control infectious diseases for the past 150 years, first through international sanitary treaties, whose origins date back to 1851, following a cholera epidemic in Europe. After the formation of WHO, its member states adopted International Sanitary Regulations in 1951 (renamed International Health Regulations in 1969). The original purpose of these regulations was to outline measures that countries may take to protect themselves against epidemics of three diseases: cholera, plague, and yellow fever. The regulations required that countries report cases of these three diseases to WHO, which then made that information available to other countries to provide national authorities with a basis for applying protective measures. However, the regulations did not provide a framework for addressing epidemics within countries through international actions, nor did they obligate the international community to help the affected countries. This, together with noncompliance with the regulations in connection with reporting disease outbreaks, led to doubts about the effectiveness of the regulations. In 1995, WHO initiated an effort to revise the International Health Regulations to create a firmer legal footing and a stronger institutional commitment to outbreak surveillance and response. The World Health Assembly approved the revised regulations in May 2005, and full implementation is projected for May 2007.

Besides the International Health Regulations, various forms of voluntary cooperation have mushroomed in recent years, mostly in response to globalization, the growing recognition of greater global interdependence, and the inevitability of the rapid global spread of infectious disease outbreaks. In 1998, several organizations, including WHO, other United Nations (UN) organizations, and the World Bank, inaugurated campaigns to reduce the global burden of malaria by 50 percent (the Roll Back Malaria initiative) and to reduce the prevalence of and mortality from tuberculosis by 50 percent (the Stop TB campaign) by 2010. These commitments were later consolidated in the UN-sponsored Millennium Development Goals (MDGs), which also include the objective of halting and beginning to reverse the spread of HIV/AIDS by 2015.

Public health programs have also gone global through a number of other channels involving new actors, including public-private partnerships. There are estimated to be about 70 such global health initiatives. One of the largest is the Global Fund to Fight AIDS, Tuberculosis, and Malaria, set up through a commitment made at a UN special session on AIDS in June 2001, which was endorsed later that year by the Group of Eight at their summit in Genoa, Italy. The Global Fund has committed about $5 billion to date for programs covering these three diseases. The Bill and Melinda Gates Foundation, with an estimated endowment of $28 billion, is the largest private foundation working in the health domain. Global health is a major concern of the foundation, which funds projects to deal with AIDS, polio, and other communicable diseases. The foundation also finances other initiatives such as the Global Alliance for Vaccination and Immunization, whose goal is to ensure an adequate supply of vaccines in all developing countries, and an International AIDS Vaccine Initiative. The World Bank has funded a Multi-Country AIDS Program for Africa, and the United States has established an Emergency Plan for AIDS Relief. Worldwide funding available for malaria intervention in 2005 was estimated to be $570 million, and the commitment for HIV/AIDS prevention and treatment programs in that year was an estimated $6 billion. The plethora of funding actors has in fact led the Joint United Nations Programme on HIV/AIDS to formulate the "Three Ones" principle for AIDS programs in countries: programs should be implemented under one strategy, one implementing agency, and one monitoring and evaluation system. These initiatives have succeeded in raising global awareness, stimulating and funding new drug and vaccine research, and ensuring that the poor have access to health services.

It remains to be seen whether these initiatives will ensure that the MDGs for communicable diseases will be met. Although some other MDGs are on track (the reduction in the number of people living on less than a dollar a day, and the net primary enrollment goal), performance to date on the communicable diseases goals has not been encouraging. A 2004 review of progress on the health MDGs by the World Bank concluded that progress has varied across indicators and across regions. No region is on track to reduce the under-five mortality rate by two-thirds, with Sub-Saharan Africa the furthest away from the target. Although additional resources are needed, they will not be sufficient to reach the MDGs. Numerous policy and institutional weaknesses in the health system also need to be addressed, and the focus has to shift to households, not only as users of health services but as producers of good health themselves.

Key Elements of a Global Disease Response Plan

Both WHO and the U.S. Centers for Disease Control and Prevention (CDC) have developed response plans for global disease outbreaks. The WHO Global Disease Response Plan consists of three key strategies: strengthening global outbreak management, strengthening surveillance capacity within developing countries, and improving coordination and cooperation on surveillance at the national and the regional levels. The CDC's Emerging Infections Plan, articulated in 2000, has four goals: strengthening infectious disease surveillance and response to ensure timely detection and control of diseases and their agents; addressing the many research issues raised by new and emerging infectious diseases; strengthening public health systems, especially through training; and strengthening prevention and control programs locally, nationally, and globally. Some of the key elements of a global infectious diseases response plan are discussed below.

Outbreak Management

In April 2000, WHO inaugurated the Global Outbreak Alert and Response Network to help organize and coordinate an international response to any communicable disease outbreak. Various organizations have volunteered to participate, including national public health institutions such as CDC, as well as UN and nongovernmental organizations. The actual management of an outbreak will depend on the nature of the disease, but it is likely to involve isolation and quarantine of the persons or the area where the infection has been identified, culling of animals exposed to the pathogen, rapid laboratory testing of relevant samples from all suspected cases, training of staff, stockpiling of supplies, and establishment of standards and guidance in the management of the outbreak (box 9.3).

Disease Surveillance

Disease surveillance is the first line of defense in an epidemic, together with the ability to rapidly conduct an epidemiological investigation and the presence of trained staff and modern laboratory facilities to diagnose diseases accurately and rapidly. Surveillance systems in all countries suffer from a

---

BOX 9.3 The Successful Campaign to Contain the Ebola Virus

Ebola hemorrhagic fever is one of the most virulent viral diseases known to humankind, causing death in 50 to 90 percent of all clinical cases. The virus was first identified in 1976 after epidemics broke out in Sudan and the Democratic Republic of Congo (DRC). Several different species of the Ebola virus have since been identified. The virus is transmitted by direct contact with the body fluids or tissues of infected persons. Transmission has also occurred when people handled ill or dead infected chimpanzees. In February 2003, an outbreak in the town of Kelle in DRC was effectively handled by a WHO disease response team, which swung into action immediately after the outbreak was reported. An intensive media campaign was launched to warn people not to touch or eat the meat of animals found dead in the forest, particularly monkeys, gorillas, chimpanzees, and rats. On February 14, a statement was made in the National Assembly and on television news about the outbreak. On February 18, the WHO team arrived in Kelle and immediately set about securing the hospital and creating an isolation ward. Disinfection procedures were established and facilities provided in the security zone outside the isolation ward. Clinical management and safe burial protocols were likewise established, and a mobile team was organized to visit neighboring villages to carry out control and surveillance. By the end of June 2003, after 135 cases and 120 deaths had been recorded, the epidemic was declared to be under control.

Source: Author.

---

number of common constraints, such as weak links in the diagnostic and reporting chains. However, these constraints are most severe in the poorest countries, where expenditure per capita on health care is less than 1 percent of that in high-income countries, according to World Bank data. Surveillance in developing countries is often handicapped by shortages of human and material resources. Key positions in laboratories and clinics are often vacant or are filled by people who lack the necessary qualifications. According to WHO, staff in over 90 percent of developing country laboratories are not familiar with quality assurance practices, and more than 60 percent of laboratory equipment is outdated or not functioning. WHO-sponsored assessments of Sub-Saharan African health systems reported weaknesses in laboratory capacity, ranging from a lack of trained technicians and communications equipment to poor roads and crumbling buildings. Health care workers find it difficult to alert higher authorities about outbreaks or quickly transport specimens to laboratories. Even if they do succeed in contacting the authorities, they are unlikely to get much help, because higher management levels suffer from the same systemic handicaps. All this has resulted in a severe underreporting of routine infectious diseases as well as increased drug resistance and the emergence of new diseases.

The basic responsibility for disease surveillance and response lies with individual countries. However, the international community has recently launched a number of initiatives that may improve global surveillance. First, the commitments to meeting the MDGs for the three major diseases call for investments that will facilitate efforts to improve surveillance for these diseases. Second, the international community has launched more broadly targeted initiatives to upgrade laboratories, strengthen epidemiological capacity, and otherwise improve surveillance for infectious diseases as a group.

National and Local Public Health Services

The basic strategy for fighting communicable diseases in developing countries is to strengthen national and local public health services to the point where they can provide effective service. In too many countries, publicly provided health services still fall short of minimum standards and are especially failing the poor. Resources often fail to reach frontline providers in rural and poor urban areas altogether, and where poor people do receive services, the quality is often low. The situation would be several times worse during a pandemic, when facilities and resources even in the industrialized countries would likely be overwhelmed. The same issues of financing, governance, and technical and physical resources identified as weaknesses in surveillance affect the system as a whole. WHO dedicated the 2000 edition of its annual *World Health Report* to the issue of strengthening public health systems.

Health Providers

The MDGs are not achievable without an adequately trained, properly deployed, and well-supported health work force. Although many health service providers have the necessary qualifications and training, can deliver high-quality care, and are responsive to their patients even in difficult circumstances, the same is not true of many others, and very often even the best providers lack the necessary support systems or the equipment and supplies necessary to carry out their functions. As a result, health facilities are underutilized in many developing countries, and patients often receive care that is inappropriate to their needs, paid for out of very limited means. WHO's 2006 *World Health Report* is devoted to this important issue.

Research and Development

A program of research on infectious diseases in different parts of the world is another key part of the international response. Research is now under way to develop vaccines against malaria and HIV/AIDS as well as an improved antituberculosis vaccine. The existing vaccine against tuberculosis has been effective in preventing the disease in young children in many parts of the world but has proved less efficacious in adults, and it has not been effective in controlling the disease in most developing countries. Recent research efforts have focused on the genetics of the microorganisms responsible for the major infectious diseases, with large-scale projects to develop more-effective drugs and vaccines. Similar projects are under way to determine the full DNA sequences of a range of important human pathogens as a way of developing better diagnostic tests, vaccines, and drugs.

A Stronger International Legal and Regulatory Framework

Because of the need for international cooperation in the fight against diseases without borders, international regulation will certainly play a role in the global strategy for the control of infectious diseases. Recognizing this fact, WHO revised the International Health Regulations so as to be effective to "prevent, protect against, control and provide a public health response to the international spread of disease," and to "ensure the maximum protection of people against the international spread of diseases, while minimizing interference with world travel and trade."[4] Under the revised regulations, countries have much broader obligations to build national capacity for routine preventive measures, as well as to detect and respond to public health emergencies of international concern. Reporting requirements cover all "events of urgent international health importance." The regulations also define a "code of conduct" or set of core requirements for countries in the areas of surveillance, notification, and response.

Prevention and Control

Ultimately, the struggle against global diseases must move from a reactive, fire-fighting approach to a longer-term strategy of prevention and control in the context of a globalized and rapidly changing environment. Strong health care systems, along with improved communication strategies to educate and alert the public about the risks of and prevention strategies for infectious diseases, are the best long-term control measures. Although disturbances of ecosystems that will affect the geographic incidence of diseases seem inevitable, greater attention must be paid to the risks, and suitable mitigation measures must be taken. A new instrument, the Infectious Diseases Impact Statement, has been devised to make predictive assessments of changes in infectious diseases arising from human activities. The instrument is intended to be proactive, like an Environmental Impact Statement, providing a formal mechanism for answering specific questions about future changes in local health conditions. Among the questions posed are the following: Which populations are potentially susceptible? Which diseases are likely to increase in response to development? What, if any, control measures already exist? What disease vectors (such as insects or birds) are likely to be affected? and What are the risks of any diseases that could be transmitted as a result? The assessment has the potential to provide a rational basis and direction for development, surveillance, and prevention measures.

The Role of the World Bank

The World Bank developed its first Health, Nutrition, and Population Strategy in 1997 and is currently revising it. A briefing was provided to the Bank's Board of Directors in June 2006, and a revised strategy will be completed by December 2006. Broadly speaking, improving public health systems and ensuring adequate health services for the poor are central to the World Bank's mandate of poverty reduction: better health contributes to higher productivity and income; poor health both results from and exacerbates poverty. Some health activities are purely or partly public goods with substantial external spillover effects—an important criterion for public financing. The Bank is also a major player in health financing, which covers financing modalities and instruments for the implementation of health policies. The Bank has diverse instruments at its disposal, including investment lending; grants for pilot or research activities; and Poverty Reduction Strategy Credits, which support policy changes or investments in the health sector. Activities typically financed by the Bank include health policy reform, the strengthening of primary health care systems, human resources development and training, strengthening of surveillance systems, immunization and other preventive services, and pharmaceutical procurement and planning.

The World Bank is formally committed to achieving the MDGs, including those relating to communicable diseases, and indeed it is already one of the world's largest financers of programs to control and eradicate such diseases. It provides significant resources in the fight against malaria ($150 million since 2000) and tuberculosis ($560 million in current portfolio investments in 30 countries). By the end of June 2004, the Bank had committed nearly $2.5 billion for 106 freestanding AIDS projects and projects in the health, education, transport, and social protection sectors with AIDS components of more than $1 million each. These programs finance the strengthening of infrastructure; the scaling up of disease control strategies; the provision of services ranging from information and education campaigns to testing and counseling to condom distribution to vulnerable groups; and the development and testing of vaccines against AIDS and malaria, among other diseases. The Bank has also financed or managed several analytical studies on HIV/AIDS.

The World Bank also participates in the international response to new epidemics or outbreaks, providing support both internationally, in cooperation with WHO, and bilaterally to governments of the affected countries. During the SARS epidemic, for example, the Bank's East Asia Region worked with national governments in the region to restructure existing projects to allow the implementation of national strategies to fight SARS; it also made available some grant funding for cross-regional information exchanges. The Bank has set up an Avian Flu Task Force and a fund of up to $500 million. These resources will allow affected countries to access financing to strengthen their veterinarian and health services to deal with avian flu outbreaks, promote activities to minimize the risk of human transmission, and prepare for and respond to any potential human flu pandemic.

Strong partnerships with governments, beneficiaries, nongovernmental organizations, the private sector, other multilateral agencies, bilateral donors, and foundations have become central to the World Bank's work in health. These can take the form of commitments to international development goals such as the MDGs; partnership in global technical initiatives such as the Partnership for Maternal, Neonatal, and Child Health and Safe Injection Global Network, the Global Alliance for Improved Nutrition, and the Global Alliance for Vaccines and Immunization; or programs such as Roll Back Malaria and Stop TB. A critical goal of the partnerships is the coordination and harmonization of policies and financing for meeting global health targets.

The World Bank's work in health is also indirectly supported by its work in other sectors and on cross-cutting themes. Improved infrastructure services, for example, can reduce the burden of communicable diseases: the lack or high cost of transport is a major barrier to obtaining health care. Improved rural roads through Bank-financed road projects have been associated with a substantial increase in access to health care in Morocco and Tanzania. Slum upgrading projects have been successful in reducing the incidence of diseases in those areas, and access to clean water has been shown to reduce child mortality by up to 55 percent. Electrification projects allow for refrigeration for vaccine storage as well as lighting for clinical care. Thematic areas of the Bank's work that affect the performance of health systems include improved governance, transparency, and accountability of public institutions, including health services; decentralization to bring management and accountability closer to the level of service delivery; and participation to allow the beneficiaries, civil society, and the media to become engaged in improving health care. As an example, citizen report cards have been widely distributed in the state of Bangalore in India, allowing poor people to participate in their own health care while giving providers an incentive to improve their services. Human rights issues have surfaced in confronting AIDS, and the Bank supports reducing the stigma of HIV infection through information and education campaigns.

The World Bank has some comparative advantage in health through its established relationship with practically every sovereign state in the developing world; its country-specific knowledge; and its capacity to work across sectors and to convene diverse partners, national and international, in the private and the public sectors. The Bank regularly evaluates its projects, and these evaluations have identified some important success stories, including a significant reduction in infant mortality and malnutrition in the Brazilian state of Ceará, the reform of city health services in Johannesburg, and the reduction of the public health caseload through cash transfers to households in Mexico linked to participation in preventive health activities. A sectorwide evaluation carried out by the Bank concluded that Bank projects have been successful in expanding health care coverage, training health personnel, and supplying basic inputs.

The World Bank has also successfully used its lending to influence health policy in developing countries. However, the Bank has been less successful in bringing about sustained, systemic service quality improvements or institutional changes, which seem to be driven mainly by factors specific to each country. The Bank's sectorwide evaluation, mentioned above, recommended that projects focus more on what needs to be changed and how those changes might be effected in the country context and in the context of macroeconomic (especially fiscal policy) constraints.

Conclusion

The influenza epidemic of 1918, which killed an estimated 20 million to 40 million people all over the globe in a matter of 6 months, is a grim reminder of the destructive power of diseases without borders. The Nobel laureate Joshua Lederberg, in a 1999 briefing to the U.S. Congress,[5] predicted that although the world is better equipped to contain epidemics than in the past, a major pandemic will occur sometime during the 21st century. Despite the risk, global travel and commerce will continue, as will the evolution and transmission of microbes. The large-scale movement of people, goods, and services, accompanied by significant changes in the physical environment, is a potent combination for the rise of unanticipated diseases and their spread

---

TABLE 9.1 Elements of an Effort to Deal with Infectious Diseases

The essential elements needed to deal with infectious diseases include the following:
- Worldwide surveillance to map the global movement and evolution of microbes
- Research and development to understand the complexities of the genetic mutations of microbes and their modes of transmission
- Adequate and steady financing, on a global scale but especially for low-income countries, to strengthen health systems and implement disease control programs
- National capacity to take difficult and, if necessary, locally unpopular action to contain any outbreaks
- Committed health care staff with the technical skills and physical resources necessary to perform effectively
- Integration of knowledge and skills from many disciplines in the social, biological, and physical sciences.

Source: Author.

---

through many different channels. New infections will continue to emerge, and known infections will change in form, severity, and frequency. The list of essential components of an effort to deal with the challenges posed by diseases without borders, presented in table 9.1, is daunting in itself.

Despite the significant efforts made to date, more is needed. James Hughes, director of the U.S. CDC, in a concluding address to the International Emerging Infectious Diseases Conference in Atlanta in 2000, summarized the challenge as follows:

> If we truly want to end the threat of infectious diseases, we must do even more together. We must inject into global gatherings—no matter where they are, no matter what the subject—the urgency of working together to defeat infectious disease. We must never let research into infectious disease become a forgotten stepchild. We must continue to invest in vaccine research and development and ensure that preventive vaccines are available, affordable, and effective everywhere. We must work with all our partners in the private sector to ensure that drugs, vaccines, and tests are available during an infectious disease emergency.... We must work together to deal with urban overcrowding, poverty, and poor sanitation, which are spreading infectious disease in many parts of the world. Finally, we must pool our greatest resources—our imagination and intellect—to fight this collective fight. For as Joshua Lederberg once noted, "Pitted against microbial genes, we have mainly our wits."[6]

Notes

1. Statistics cited in this section are from the World Bank's *World Development Indicators 2005*, the World Health Organization's *World Health Report 2004*, and the Center for Global Development (2004).
2. Zoonotics are diseases caused by infectious agents that can be transmitted or shared between animals and humans.
3. Institute of Medicine (2003).
4. World Health Organization press release, "World Health Assembly Adpopts New International Health Regulations," Geneva, May 23, 2005.
5. American Society for Microbiology Congressional Briefing, "Infectious Disease Threats As We Enter the New Century: What Can We Do?" Washington, DC, July 1999.
6. U.S. Centers for Disease Control and Prevention (2000).

Selected Readings and Cited References

Berwick, Donald M. 2001. "We All Have AIDS." *Washington Post*, June 26, p. A17.

Center for Global Development. 2004. *Millions Saved: Proven Successes in Global Health*. Washington, DC.

Food and Agriculture Organization of the United Nations.

Institute of Medicine. 2003. *Microbial Threats to Health: Emergence, Detection and Response*. Washington, DC.

OIE World Organisation for Animal Health.

U.S. Centers for Disease Control and Prevention. 2000. *Proceedings of the International Emerging Infectious Diseases Conference*. Atlanta.

Wetlands International.

World Bank. 1999. *Investing in Health: Development Effectiveness in the Health, Nutrition, Population Sector*. Washington, DC.

————. 2004. *The Millennium Development Goals for Health: Rising to the Challenges*. Washington, DC.

————. 2005. *World Development Indicators 2005*. Washington, DC.

World Health Organization. 2000. *World Health Report*.

————. 2004. *World Health Report 2004: Changing History*. Geneva.

————. 2006. *World Health Report*.

Selected Web Links on Communicable Diseases

Bill and Melinda Gates Foundation	http://www.gatesfoundation.org
Center for Global Development	http://www.cgdev.org
Global Fund to Fight AIDS, Tuberculosis and Malaria	http://www.theglobalfund.org
Roll Back Malaria	http://www.rbm.who.int
Stop TB	http://www.stoptb.org
U.S. Centers for Disease Control and Prevention	http://www.cdc.gov
World Bank page on Health	http://www.worldbank.org/hnp
World Health Organization	http://www.who.int

10

Securing the Future Through Education: A Tide to Lift All Boats

RUTH KAGIA

Formal education is an organized effort by society to impart to its members the skills and knowledge considered essential for them to function in society—as productive workers, as informed citizens, and in many other ways. Education is thus a critical tool for economic and social development. Indeed, it is widely recognized as one of the most powerful instruments not only for promoting sustained economic growth but also for reducing poverty and inequality: as the 19th-century American educator Horace Mann said, "Education, then, beyond all other devices of human origin, is a great equalizer of the conditions of men."[1]

Education is fundamental, in particular, for the construction of societies that are democratic and economies that are knowledge-based and globally competitive. The history of civilization itself reflects the transformative power of education: the invention of the printing press in the 15th century led to popular demand for literacy and the freedom to choose what to read, and from there to a hunger for other freedoms. This, in turn, precipitated major religious and political changes in Europe. More recently, the quality of human capital—the accumulated skills of educated workers—was found to be the most important predictor of economic success in the East Asian miracle economies, explaining 38 percent of their economic growth during the 1980s.

But never before today has the economic and social fate of nations depended so heavily on the acquisition of education, knowledge, and skills. No longer does a nation's prosperity depend on its access to natural resources, but rather on how effectively it uses its human resources to raise productivity and nurture innovation. As global economies become more knowledge driven, the level of education attained by a country's labor force, and the quality of that education, become key determinants of that country's economic competitiveness. Technology and globalization have made it possible for firms to hire the best minds and tap into the most creative ideas from anywhere in the world. One reason that India, for example, has succeeded in capturing a large share of the global outsourcing market is that it has a large pool of well-educated and trainable workers, connected by modern communications to the world economy. These same forces are also increasingly allowing the world's best and most creative young minds to travel anywhere in the world to develop their talents: 34 percent of doctoral degrees in natural sciences and 56 percent of those in engineering in the United States are awarded to foreign-born students.

What all this means is that, for workers and countries seeking to compete in a global economy, a primary education—mastering the "three R's"—is just not enough. A global, digitized, knowledge society increasingly needs a more sophisticated labor force, equipped with competencies, knowledge, and workplace skills that can only be developed through secondary and tertiary education. Secondary schooling is essential to developing certain key mid-level skills, but about 80 percent of the fastest-growing jobs of the future will require some postsecondary education. Countries wishing to participate in the evolving knowledge economy must therefore invest in dynamic, holistic education systems that begin with early childhood development and basic education but then continue through to secondary and tertiary education, and on to lifelong learning opportunities.

Left to market forces alone, however, the benefits of education would reach only a few people, and the challenges of building societies that can participate effectively in the 21st century would be too great for many poor nations, many of which are unable to provide even basic education for their children. If current trends are maintained, more than 60 countries will not achieve the Millennium Development Goal of universal primary education by 2015. In a world that is increasingly interconnected, helping these countries close the education gap is a global concern. Galvanizing international action to strengthen education in all countries, especially the poorest ones, is not just morally right; it is also good business, good policy, and good politics, for several reasons. Education enables these countries to contribute to and benefit from the global economy; it reduces inequality both within and between countries; it widens the pool of available skills and innovative capacity; it broadens opportunities for employment, thereby stemming the flow of economic refugees; it helps to create free and open societies; and it is a wise investment for global peace and stability.

A broad range of national and international actions is required to create educated and productive societies that can compete in a global economy.

They include supporting and strengthening countries' capacity to provide strong national leadership and vision; providing a stable and enabling macro-economic framework to bolster the investment climate and expand job opportunities; and creating capacity to deliver quality services to all, to generate resources and allocate and utilize them efficiently, and to monitor and measure outcomes. Quite often, it is not enough to focus on the education sector alone; complementary actions are required in other sectors to boost the impact of education investments (figure 10.1). For example, recent studies show positive correlations between nutritional status and cognitive development: every 100-gram increase in birthweight is associated with an increase in mean IQ at age 7 of 0.5 point for boys and 0.1 point for girls. Education benefits from having these problems addressed, and it, in turn, is a means to address these problems: education helps to prevent HIV infections, and

FIGURE 10.1   A Virtuous Cycle of Education and Development

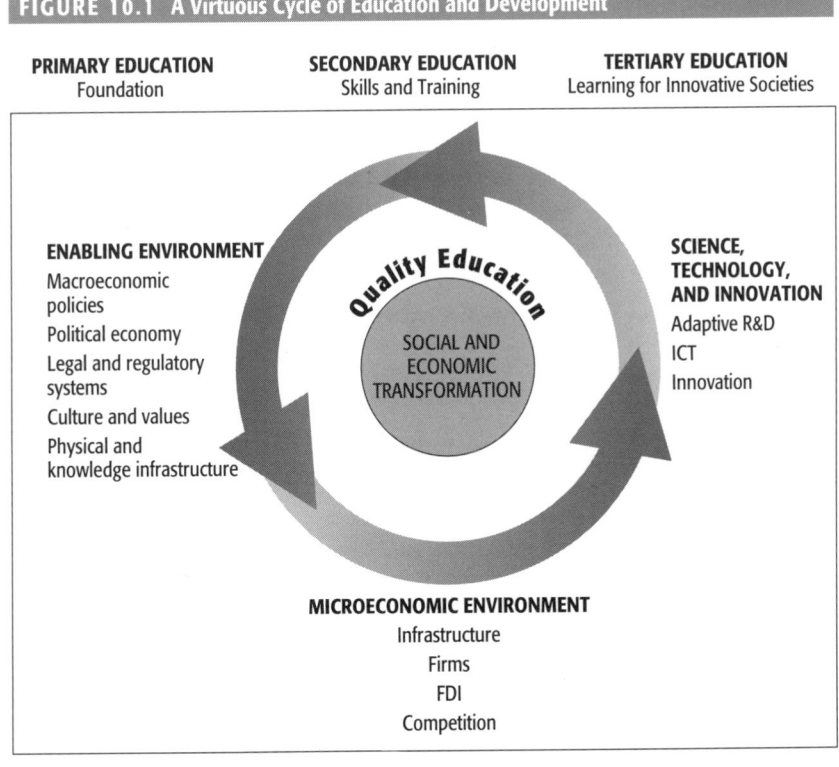

PRIMARY EDUCATION	SECONDARY EDUCATION	TERTIARY EDUCATION
Foundation	Skills and Training	Learning for Innovative Societies

ENABLING ENVIRONMENT
Macroeconomic policies
Political economy
Legal and regulatory systems
Culture and values
Physical and knowledge infrastructure

Quality Education

SOCIAL AND ECONOMIC TRANSFORMATION

SCIENCE, TECHNOLOGY, AND INNOVATION
Adaptive R&D
ICT
Innovation

MICROECONOMIC ENVIRONMENT
Infrastructure
Firms
FDI
Competition

Source:
FDI = Foreign Direct Investment
ICT = Information and communication technologies
R&D = research and development

female education helps to improve mother and child health. It is against this backdrop that the World Bank has been supporting education development in poor nations since 1963, within a broad development framework of strengthening the investment climate for growth and investing in and empowering the poor.

Education as a Tool for Development

As figure 10.2 shows, knowledge matters as much to a country's economic growth as does the accumulation of physical and human capital—if not more. Higher education and technical education are necessary for the effective generation, dissemination, and application of that knowledge and for preparing an entrepreneurial labor force that can adapt flexibly to a constant stream of technological advances and change in a globalized world economy. Therefore, to ensure their full participation in knowledge-driven development, countries need to both build their human capital and adapt their entire education system to the new challenges of the "learning" economy. (It should, however, be noted that the share of the difference in growth between the Republic of Korea and Ghana attributed to accumulation of knowledge in figure 10.2 also includes other important factors, such as sound political governance.)

Global poverty cannot be reduced unless the knowledge and skill gaps across and within countries are narrowed dramatically. This implies

FIGURE 10.2 Accounting for the Difference in the Growth of Gross Domestic Product Between Ghana and the Republic of Korea, 1960–2000
GDP per capita (*thousands of 1995 dollars*)

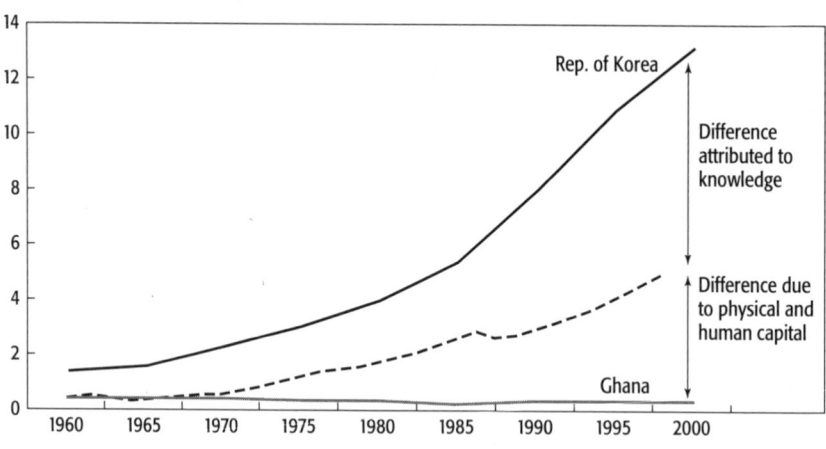

Source: World Bank (1999).

providing, in all countries, a full curriculum of quality primary education as the foundation for further learning and training, secondary and tertiary education to provide skills and training, and lifelong learning opportunities to harness new knowledge as it emerges and create innovative societies that seek out new learning. Research on the impact of education on economic growth in different countries demonstrates that education, skills, and technology—or the lack of them—interact in important ways to create either a virtuous or a vicious cycle. Low levels of human capital accumulation in a country that also lacks other key assets necessary for economic growth lead to technological stagnation and a slow-growing economy, which generate little demand for higher-level skills and insufficient revenue to expand education opportunities. India in recent years provides a good example of a virtuous cycle: India's economic growth averaged 6.2 percent a year between 1994 and 2004. Since 1992, the net primary enrollment rate has increased from 68 percent to 82 percent, with more than 14 million additional pupils attending school. Building on this progress, India has recently decided to extend, by 2015, the universalization of education from those 6–11 years of age up to those 16 years of age.

In some countries, families remain trapped at a low level of income and skill from generation to generation. Education is key to breaking this intergenerational transmission of poverty because it increases the productivity of individual workers, which then increases their income and labor market opportunities, which, in turn, allow them to afford to educate their own children and so give them hope for a better life than their own. Each year of schooling increases an individual's earnings by a worldwide average of approximately 10 percent, and by up to 20 percent in the poorest countries. In the United States, a high school graduate can expect to earn about $275,000 more over the course of his or her lifetime than a student who does not finish high school; a college graduate with a bachelor's degree can expect to earn about $1 million more.

The case for education goes beyond its ability to stimulate and sustain economic growth. Education gives people the power to reflect, make reasoned choices, and improve their lives—what Nobel laureate Amartya Sen describes as *human capabilities*. Such capabilities promote greater social and civic participation, which empowers citizens to seek good governance and greater accountability from their leaders. It is in this sense that education is regarded as the cornerstone of democracy.

Less often recognized are the synergistic impacts of education on a wide range of development objectives, such as better adult and child health, reduced incidence of HIV/AIDS, and protection of the environment. Education is one of the most effective preventive weapons against HIV/AIDS, which infects an additional nine people worldwide every minute and kills a child below the age of 15 every six minutes. In one study covering 17 African and 4 Latin American countries, educated girls were found to have a significantly lower risk of HIV infection than uneducated girls. Research also demonstrates that education, particularly functional literacy, increases environmental awareness and contributes to the environmental sustainability of development programs.

Female education is perhaps the wisest investment of all. Apart from the simple fact that one cannot have an equitable society when half of the population lacks educational opportunities, the old adage also holds true that, "When you educate a boy, you educate an individual, but when you educate a girl, you educate a nation." Mothers' education has strong and well-documented impacts, including improved health and family welfare and reduced fertility. Better-educated women are more likely to send their children to school and keep them there. Research also indicates that mothers are more likely than fathers to use a higher proportion of their income to improve family welfare.

Why, Then, Does the Promise of Education Remain Elusive for So Many?

Despite the known benefits of education, there remain large gaps in education between rich and poor nations. A 5-year-old in Finland and a 5-year-old in the United Kingdom can each expect to attain about 20 years of education, whereas their counterparts in Cambodia, Mali, and Mozambique can expect to complete no more than five or six years of school. Out of every 100 girls who enroll in primary school in Mali, only 30 actually finish, compared with 100 percent of girls in Denmark, Germany, the Netherlands, and Slovenia. These geographical disparities widen as one goes up the education ladder: 83 percent of the eligible age cohort are enrolled in tertiary education in the United States, compared with 16 percent in Indonesia, 0.9 percent in Mozambique, and 9 percent in the Republic of Yemen.

Poor Access to Education

Worldwide, more than 100 million primary school–age children are not currently enrolled, and two-thirds of adults who cannot read or write are women. There are many interrelated reasons why children do not enroll or stay in school long enough to complete their primary education: inadequate supply of school infrastructure, weak demand for education (largely due to poverty), and the high cost (including the opportunity cost of income from work forgone) of attending school. Households in Cambodia, for example, devote 21 percent of their total spending to education; in contrast, children in the United States are guaranteed more than 10 years of free education. Financial constraints and cultural norms can intersect powerfully to limit households' ability to send their daughters to school (box 10.1). However, several strategies can be used to stimulate demand: one is to engage parents and communities in school activities; and another is to establish learning environments that are gender sensitive.

Inequality of Opportunity

Even though education is one of the shortest routes to reducing inequality, access to education is far from equally distributed, both within countries and across them. Low school participation rates translate into low educational attainment profiles for the adult population, which, in turn, translate into low earnings. In the developing world, a child from the richest 20 percent of the population is almost three times as likely to be enrolled in school as one from the poorest 20 percent. Indigenous peoples in Latin America have considerably less access to education than the nonindigenous: in Bolivia, for example, the difference between the two groups in average educational attainment is almost four years. Unequal access to education is important because low educational attainment leads to low incomes, with the result that the average adult in Cambodia or Mali earns less than $2 a day, about one-twentieth of the minimum wage in the United States. In Ecuador, each additional year of schooling reduces the probability of being poor by 4.8 percent.

Improvement of Educational Outcomes

Just as important as access to education is the quality of the education provided. Recent research indicates that educational quality has a consistent, stable, and strong influence on economic growth, and that quality matters as much as, if not more than, quantity. Nevertheless, almost every country in the world struggles with issues of educational quality. A survey of primary school graduates in Bangladesh revealed that 80 percent were reading at the third grade level. In Namibia and Zambia, fewer than 30 percent of sixth grade pupils met the specified minimum reading standards on the regional learning assessment. Only 23 percent and 16 percent of students in Morocco and Belize, respectively, reached the lower quarter benchmark for the Progress in Reading Literacy Study, a level that requires no more of students than to retrieve explicitly stated information from a grade-appropriate passage or to locate relevant information and use it to make inferences clearly suggested by the text.

But it is not just developing nations that are struggling to raise the quality of educational outcomes. In the United States, 25 percent of eighth graders could not identify, from a series of four drawings, which one showed the

BOX 10.1   What Works to Reduce the Gender Gap in Education?

When girls' access to education is broadened and the learning environment is conducive, girls tend to perform as well as, if not better than, boys and to complete the school cycle. The PROGRESA *conditional cash transfer* program in Mexico was directed at both boys and girls, but evidence from evaluations showed greater improvements in girls' attendance and rates of transition to junior secondary school. The Kenya Girls' Scholarship Program was dedicated to providing *scholarships for girls* to attend secondary school conditional on their examination performance. An evaluation of this program showed that its design worked to increase girls' attendance and their test scores. The attendance and test scores of boys and girls who were not eligible for the awards also increased, pointing to possible spillover effects. The program had different impacts in its two implementation areas, which were interpreted as suggesting that community support was important for improving learning outcomes for girls.

Countries that have been successful in reducing gender disparity at the primary and secondary levels use an integrated package of interventions by, for example:

- Addressing the *direct and opportunity costs* of girls' education by providing scholarships and stipends to girls and reducing fees
- Making schools *more accessible and safe* by bringing schools closer to the community and constructing sanitation facilities, which provide privacy and running water, especially for pubescent girls
- Targeting action to the rural poor, disabled, and socially underprivileged girls
- Improving the quality of education by providing instructional materials, teacher training, and school programs
- Making education more gender sensitive by increasing the number of female teachers (and requiring gender sensitization in teacher training) and promoting child- and girl-friendly teaching methodologies
- Increasing community involvement (and the involvement of mothers in particular) in the management of schools.

The World Bank is using these lessons to support broad-based, quality education focused on the disadvantaged; supporting programs to increase the participation of women, particularly in post-basic training programs in math, science, and technology; and targeting interventions such as stipends, scholarships, and collection of gender-disaggregated data. The Bank is also strengthening strategic partnerships with actors on the ground such as the Forum for African Women Educationalists (FAWE), who have used research evidence to push for policy changes; FAWE is also undertaking demonstration programs, including programs aimed at preventing early marriages and allowing reentry to school after teenage pregnancy. The Bank is funding FAWE through its Development Grant Facility.

direction in which a ball would fall if dropped from different locations on the Earth. Highschool math test scores in the United States have risen very little since the 1970s, and fewer than half of U.S. highschool graduates are adequately prepared for college-level math and science courses. (Box 10.2 excerpts a passage from a recent U.S. Department of Education publication on the growing mismatch in that country between job demands and available worker skills.) Norway, in spite of its top rank on other human development indicators, performs below average on international tests of mathematics given at the fourth and eighth grades, and ranks 20th out of 25 countries and 21st out of 46 countries, respectively, on fourth and eighth grade international science achievement measures.

Like other productive enterprises, educational institutions require well-defined performance standards and effective tools for measuring the quality of their output. As already emphasized, knowledge economies require skills and competencies that go beyond the "three R's." These include complex language and communication skills, the ability to work in teams, adaptability, and the ability to think creatively. Participation in international achievement tests and benchmarking have helped many countries improve the quality of their education systems and of those outcomes. Benchmarking with international assessments, such as the Progress in International Reading Literacy Study, the Program for International Student Assessment, and the Trends in Mathematics and Sciences Study, allows countries not only to compare their own results with those of other countries but also to use the data to analyze key investments and programs. Within the framework of a properly formulated system of accountability and quality assurance in education, these assessment instruments, together with national measures of learning outcomes, have been helpful in evaluating the extent to which national and transnational goals are being achieved. Although the use of those systems is limited at present to only a few countries, the international community, including the World Bank, is supporting the expansion of the geographical coverage of such systems and capacity building in assessments for low-income countries.

Delivering on the Promise of Education

We live in two worlds, one rich, the other poor. Education holds promise for closing the income gap between the rich and the poor, but that promise will be kept only if several conditions are met: access to basic education must be expanded to include children currently out of school, who tend to be female, poor, or marginalized; opportunities for education beyond basic education must be broadened; educational quality must be improved; emerging issues such as HIV/AIDS must be addressed; and complementary inputs such as water, sanitation, and basic infrastructure must be provided, all within a macroeconomic environment that is conducive to equitable economic growth.

Increasingly in the past 10 years, rich and poor nations alike have given greater attention to education as a key strategy for reducing poverty and strengthening their economic competitiveness. The result has been dramatic increases in enrollment at all levels of education. In the poorer countries, demand for education has outpaced the resources available from domestic budgets. It is estimated that low-income countries require a minimum of $5 billion a year from external sources to provide quality primary education to all children. Aid to education has increased significantly in the past five years: aid for basic education alone increased from $1.7 billion in 2002 to $3.4 billion in 2004. Issues, however, remain: aid is not sufficiently predictable or flexible to enable countries to make confident medium-term plans such as for teacher training; it is insufficiently coordinated, making transaction costs quite high for the recipient country; and many of the countries that need aid the most have quite low absorption capacity.

Several actions are under way to improve the effectiveness of aid. They include the Paris Declaration on Aid Effectiveness of 2005, which sets out a framework for donor harmonization, alignment, and coordination, and the Education for All–Fast Track Initiative (FTI; box 10.3). FTI was established in 2002 to help low-income countries achieve free, universal basic education

---

BOX 10.3 The Education for All–Fast Track Initiative

The Education for All–Fast Track Initiative (FTI) was launched as a global partnership to ensure accelerated progress toward good-quality universal primary education by 2015. This partnership includes 30 multilateral and bilateral development partners. All low-income countries that demonstrate serious commitment to achieving universal completion of primary education can receive support from FTI.

FTI is built on mutual commitments. Partner countries agree to put primary education at the forefront of their domestic efforts and to develop sound national education plans; donors agree to provide coordinated and increased financial and technical support in a transparent and predictable manner. By bringing donors, civil society, and developing country governments together around the same goal, FTI is improving the effectiveness of aid by strengthening donor collaboration, alignment, and harmonization. FTI has also evolved into a good model for country-driven implementation of a Millennium Development Goal—universal primary education—linked to a global initiative. It provides a framework and a platform whereby the country and its donors come to an agreement that follows key principles to which FTI partners agree. These include adequate domestic budget allocation to education and increased efficiency in the use of resources.

As of April 2006, 54 low-income countries were receiving financial or technical support from FTI, and 20 of these are fully endorsed partners. To date, FTI has received commitments of about $500 million for its two financing channels and has stimulated a doubling of Education for All funding through bilateral and multilateral channels. An additional 40 countries are expected to join FTI partnership over the next two years, requiring more resources to help some 70 million children achieve universal primary education by 2015.

---

by 2015; it was conceived in response to the Monterrey Consensus, which committed the world's rich nations to provide additional aid to those poor countries that implement sound policies.

But putting resources in schools will not by itself improve learning outcomes. It needs to be part of a package of reforms that include quality improvement measures, performance-based incentives for teachers and schools, increased levels of accountability, and a political economy that is meritocratic but equitable.

The World Bank and Education

The World Bank is one of the largest multilateral donors to education, with a current portfolio of $8.4 billion invested in 144 projects in 86 countries. As noted above, the Bank has supported education in developing countries since

1963, when it financed its first education project in Tunisia, and has transferred more than $39 billion in loans and credits for education since then.

World Bank lending in education has evolved continuously since that first loan to Tunisia. The early programs supported the training of mid-level staff, through expansion of general secondary and vocational education and building of education infrastructure. Later, primary education programs became the predominant focus, driven by evidence that the returns to primary education were highest for developing countries and exceeded the returns to vocational and tertiary education. In the 1990s, the World Bank put poverty reduction at the center of all its development efforts, while recognizing that institutions are important and that equity is essential for prosperity. Along these lines, the Bank's support for education in developing countries is intended to maximize the impact of education on economic growth and poverty reduction. The Bank's strategic thrust is to help countries integrate education into national economic strategies and policies and develop holistic and balanced education systems that are responsive to the socioeconomic needs of the country.

The World Bank's support for education extends beyond resource transfer, and it is increasingly integrated into a holistic program covering all levels of education. The Bank has a well-developed infrastructure for bringing together a menu of services for the benefit of client countries, including policy advice; finance; sharing of experiences across regions, countries, and sectors; and convening of a diverse range of stakeholders in formal and informal partnerships. In fiscal 2006, the World Bank transferred about $2 billion to developing countries to support the development of policies and strategies, strengthen institutions and service delivery, and help countries expand the qualitative and quantitative capacity of their education systems at all levels.

The World Bank recognizes that educational outcomes depend heavily on policies and factors beyond the education sector, which is why all its education programs are nested in the economic and policy environment of the client country. In addition, about a third of the Bank's lending for education is channeled through multisector programs such as public sector reform, infrastructure, and poverty reduction strategy credits. Examples of such multisector programs include school health programs (such as deworming), expansion of water and sanitation facilities, and school construction through community-driven programs.

An important element of World Bank work in education is knowledge generation and dissemination and capacity building. This includes research in all key areas of education, including teacher training, education quality, service delivery, labor market outcomes, private sector participation, girls' education, and the economics of education. Much of the research undertaken by the

Bank's Development Economics Group is of direct relevance to education. The most important is that associated with the annual *World Development Report*, in particular the 2004 report, *Making Services Work for Poor People;* the 2006 report, *Equity and Development;* and the forthcoming 2007 report, *Development and the Next Generation*. All of these have explored issues relevant to education in some depth. The World Bank Institute, the capacity development arm of the Bank, provides an education learning program to clients, consisting of more than 16 education courses that explore topics such as education reform, enhancing of education quality and equity, the economics and financing of education, and evaluation and performance monitoring. The World Bank increases its educational impact through more than 30 strategic partnerships.

Going Forward

The road ahead for education in developing countries is riddled with challenges but also replete with possibilities. Dramatic improvements are within reach where the political will is strong, effective reforms are being adopted, and international support is adequate. The past 10 years have demonstrated that it is indeed possible to make quantum leaps in education development. Countries such as Brazil, Eritrea, the Gambia, Guatemala, and Uganda demonstrate that gains of more than 10 percentage points in primary school completion rates can be achieved in less than a decade. The central challenges are to scale up the successes and to sustain the gains through secondary and tertiary education and into the labor market. More and more countries need to accelerate progress in education; to increase access, particularly for those most disadvantaged; and to improve quality and relevance, so that all people—children and adults—enjoy healthier, more productive, and more peaceful lives.

But broadened access to education is not enough. Education must produce demonstrable results in terms of learning outcomes, it must be responsive to the country's social and economic needs, it must produce workers who are sufficiently flexible and agile to respond to fast-evolving labor market demands in an increasingly globalized world, and it must empower individuals to make the personal and social choices that are in their own and society's interest. There is still much to do to achieve this ideal globally, and especially in low-income countries. But it can be done with strong political will and leadership; sustained international cooperation in education and development more generally; and more effective sharing of knowledge, enhanced by information technology. In addition, at the country level it will be important to strengthen accountability mechanisms for service delivery and institutional capacity for developing, managing, and monitoring education systems.

Note

1. Mann (1848).

Selected Readings and Cited References

Mann, Horace. 1848. "Education and Social Welfare." In *The Life and Works of Horace Mann*, ed. M. T. P. Mann and others (1891).

Organisation for Economic Co-operation and Development. 2005. *Education at a Glance: OECD Indicators 2005*. Paris.

United Nations Educational, Scientific, and Cultural Organization. 2005. *Education for All: The Quality Imperative. EFA Global Monitoring Report*. Paris: UNESCO Publishing.

U.S. Department of Education. 2006. *Meeting the Challenge of a Changing World: Strengthening Education for the 21st Century*. Washington, DC.

World Bank. 1999. *World Development Report 1998/99: Knowledge for Development*. Washington, DC.

_____. 2003. *Lifelong Learning in the Global Knowledge Economy: Challenges for Developing Countries*. Washington, DC.

_____. 2004a. *World Development Report: Making Services Work for Poor People*. Washington, DC.

_____. 2004b. *Education and HIV/AIDS: A Sourcebook of HIV/AIDS Prevention Programs*. Washington, DC.

_____. 2005a. *Reshaping the Future: Education in Post Conflict Countries*. Washington, DC.

_____. 2005b. *Expanding Opportunities and Building Competencies for Young People: A New Agenda for Secondary Education*. Washington, DC.

_____. 2006. *World Development Report: Equity and Development*. Washington, DC.

_____. forthcoming. *World Development Report: Development and the Next Generation*. Washington, DC.

Selected Web Links on Education and Development

Education for All Fast–Track Initiative	http://www1.worldbank.org/education/efafti/
School Health: HIV/AIDS and Education	http://www.schoolsandhealth.org/HIV-AIDS&Education.htm
Joint United Nations Programme on HIV/AIDS Inter-Agency Task Team on Education	http://portal.unesco.org/en/ev.php
World Bank page on Education	http://web.worldbank.org/WBSITE/EXTERNAL/TOPICS/EXTEDUCATION/

11

Hunger, Malnutrition, and Human Development

MEERA SHEKAR AND YI-KYOUNG LEE

C hapter 8 analyzed the global problem of hunger and malnutrition from the point of view of food security and food supply: how weaknesses in the agricultural sector, and rural underdevelopment more generally, lead to food scarcity and lack of access to food in many developing countries. This chapter approaches the same problem from a different perspective, that of human development. It assesses the scope of the problem and explores why malnutrition occurs even in countries and households where food scarcity is not an issue. It lays bare some persistent myths about the efficacy and effectiveness of various approaches to improving nutrition and health. Finally, it describes what international institutions, including the World Bank, can do to meet the Millennium Development Goal (MDG) of cutting malnutrition by half. First, however, it is important to understand why adequate nutrition deserves to be seen as central to human development and the global development agenda.

The Impact of Malnutrition on Economic and Human Development

It has long been known that malnutrition undermines economic growth and perpetuates poverty. It does so through three distinct channels.

- First, undernourished children grow up to become stunted or underweight adults, lacking the physical strength that they would have enjoyed had they been well nourished during childhood. Not only lack of calories and protein but also micronutrient malnutrition can result in diminished physical strength: for example, iron deficiency causes anemia, which results in weakness and fatigue and can lead to more serious disorders and death. Especially in countries where many jobs involve hard physical work in agriculture or manufacturing, the result is diminished productivity and hence lower incomes.

- Second, malnutrition—whether it manifests itself as low weight for age (underweight), low height for age (stunting), or a lack of certain critical micronutrients—also leads to poor cognitive function, higher rates of dropping out of school, lower educational performance for those who stay in school, and hence lower productivity in later years. Iodine deficiency, for example, is a leading cause of mental retardation. Thus malnutrition can have a substantial impact on intellectual as well as physical productivity.

- Third, a malnourished body is less resistant than a healthy one to a variety of diseases—from diarrheal disease and other diseases of childhood, to the major scourges of the developing world, such as malaria, tuberculosis, and AIDS, to the diseases that can result from unhealthy lifestyles and *over*consumption of the wrong nutrients, such as cardiovascular heart disease and diabetes. A society with a large malnourished population is likely to experience higher health care costs per capita, which it must pay for out of incomes already reduced by the first two effects. And because malnutrition remains the single largest contributor to child mortality, it also causes the outright loss of the lives of many children who would otherwise grow up to become productive members of society.

How large are the economic costs of malnutrition? Research indicates that they are substantial. The average productivity loss to individuals has been estimated at more than 10 percent of lifetime earnings; at the country level, conservative estimates suggest that losses may run as high as 2 to 3 percent of gross domestic product. Improving nutrition is thus as much a matter of sound economics as it is of human well-being and human rights. As will be shown later, the returns to investing in better nutrition are high.

When poverty is broadly understood to include hunger and other forms of poverty other than income poverty, better nutrition addresses this dimension of poverty by definition. But malnutrition is also strongly statistically linked to poverty defined more narrowly, in terms of income alone. The prevalence of malnutrition is often two to three times higher among the poorest 20 percent of a country's population than among the richest 20 percent, and in some countries it is many times higher. That is one reason why the first of the MDGs speaks to *both* income poverty and hunger: it aims to reduce by half, by 2015, both the proportion of the world's population who live on less than one dollar a day and the proportion of people who suffer from hunger, as measured by the prevalence of underweight among young children.

The Scope of the Malnutrition Problem

How widespread is malnutrition in the world today? Chapter 8 presented some global statistics on the prevalence of stunting, or below-normal height for age. However, the MDG on hunger cited just above measures hunger, or undernutrition, in terms of the percentage of children under five years of age who are underweight. Therefore this chapter addresses progress on this key measure. Some statistics on micronutrient malnutrition, or the lack of certain critical vitamins or minerals, will also be presented. Overweight and its associated problems were discussed briefly in chapter 8.

Nearly one-third of all children under five years of age in the developing world today are underweight. The World Health Organization projects that proportion will fall by about one-third by 2015, which would be laudable progress but still well short of the 50 percent reduction called for under the MDGs. Moreover, this global projection masks large differences between developing regions—differences that are widening (figure 11.1). Asia as a whole is expected to achieve the MDG on hunger reduction, thanks largely to dramatic improvements in China. But in South Asia, which currently has the highest prevalence of undernutrition of any developing region, not a single country is projected to reach the goal. (Only Bangladesh may even come close.) The shocking fact that underweight rates in many large South Asian countries such as Afghanistan, Bangladesh, and India are nearly double those in Sub-Saharan Africa has not been acknowledged by the larger global development community. Combined with the large populations in these countries, this high prevalence means that South Asia has the largest absolute number of underweight children of any region in the world.

Furthermore, undernutrition is actually worsening in 26 countries around the world, most of them in Sub-Saharan Africa, where a vicious cycle between human immunodeficiency virus (HIV) infection and malnutrition is grimly at work. In East Africa, a region of the continent severely ravaged by HIV/AIDS, underweight prevalence is expected to be 25 percent *higher* in 2015 than in 1990.

Although the picture is brighter in East Asia, a few countries—including Cambodia, Indonesia, the Lao People's Democratic Republic, the Philippines, Timor-Leste, and Vietnam—continue to have serious problems with undernutrition (and with micronutrient malnutrition). Developing countries in the Western Hemisphere have generally relatively low rates of underweight, but some countries in Latin America, including Ecuador, Guatemala, Haiti, Honduras, and Peru, are notable exceptions. In another 57 countries, progress toward the hunger MDG is simply not known, because no trend data are

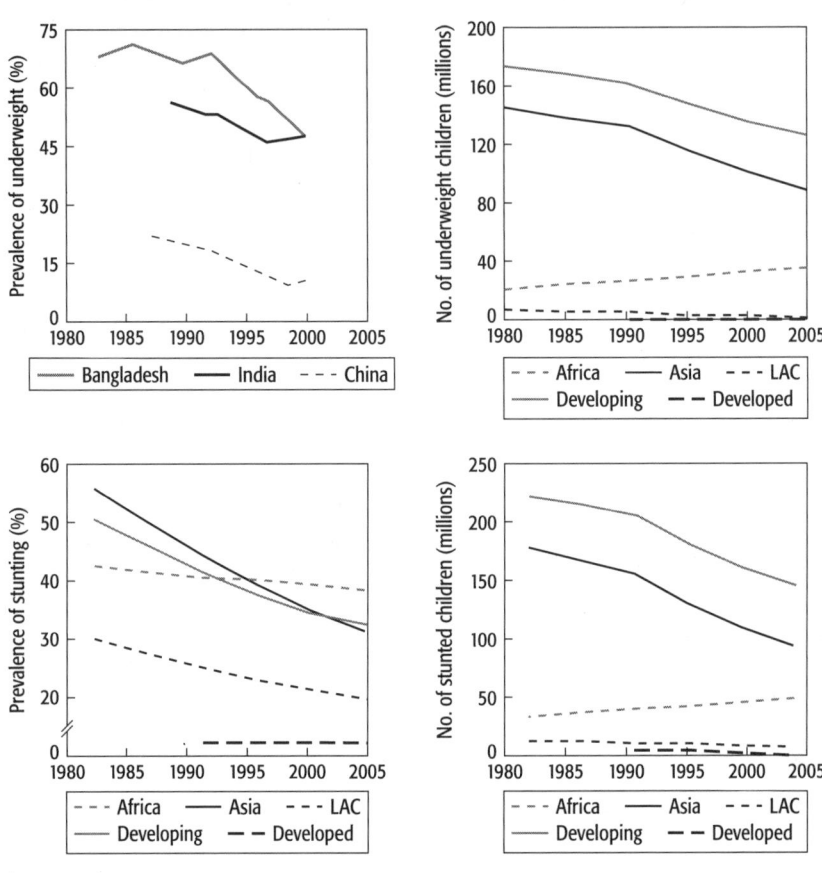

FIGURE 11.1 Indicators of Malnutrition Among Children Under Five in Selected Countries and Regions, 1980–2005

Source: De Onis and others 2004; United Nations Standing Committee on Nutrition 2004.
Note: Regions are as defined by the World Health Organization.
LAC = Latin America and the Caribbean.

available. In all, out of 143 developing countries in the world, only 34 are known to be on track to meet the MDG on hunger—this despite the fact that, by most assessments, most countries are on track to achieve the income poverty goal.

The MDGs do not specifically address micronutrient malnutrition, but it, too, is a serious problem. Recent reports find that 35 percent of people in the world lack adequate iodine in their diets, that 40 percent of people in the developing world suffer from iron deficiency, and that more than 40 percent of the world's children are vitamin A deficient. Micronutrient deficiencies such as these are especially tragic because they are relatively easy and inexpensive to address. It has been estimated that the cost of addressing *all* of Africa's micronutrient needs is a mere $235 million a year (although other estimates are higher). Salt iodization for those parts of the world that do not already have it could be provided for less than $1.5 billion a year, and twice-yearly vitamin A supplementation for all children under five in the developing world for about half that sum.

Because of micronutrients' low cost, investments in their provision typically have amazingly high benefit-cost ratios. Vitamin A supplementation for children under six produces benefits estimated to range from $4 to $43 for every dollar spent. The estimated payoff from iron fortification is even higher, ranging up to 200 to 1, and that from iodine supplementation for women may be as high as 520 to 1. The Copenhagen Consensus estimated that micronutrient interventions yield the highest social returns out of 17 types of development investments studied—higher than investments in trade liberalization, malaria control, or water and sanitation (table 11.1). Other types of nutrition interventions have similarly high benefit-cost ratios (table 11.2).

TABLE 11.1 Copenhagen Consensus Rankings of Development Investments by Social Return		
Rating	**Challenge**	**Opportunity**
Very good	1. Diseases	Controlling HIV/AIDS
	2. **Malnutrition and hunger**	**Providing micronutrients**
	3. Subsidies and trade	Liberalizing trade
	4. Diseases	Controlling malaria
Good	5. Malnutrition and hunger	Developing new agricultural technologies
	6. Sanitation and water	Developing small-scale water technologies
	7. Sanitation and water	Implementing community-managed systems
	8. Sanitation and water	Conducting research on water in agriculture
	9. Government	Lowering costs of new business
Fair	10. Migration	Lowering barriers to migration
	11. Malnutrition and hunger	Improving infant and child malnutrition
	12. Diseases	Scaling up basic health services
	13. Malnutrition and hunger	Reducing the prevalence of low birthweight
Poor	14–17. Climate/migration	Various

Source: Bhagwati and others 2004.

TABLE 11.2 Benefit-Cost Ratios for Selected Nutrition Programs	
Intervention program	**Range of benefit-cost ratios**
Breastfeeding promotion in hospitals	5–67
Integrated child care programs	9–16
Iodine supplementation (women)	15–520
Vitamin A supplementation (children under six years)	4–43
Iron fortification (per capita)	176–200
Iron supplementation for pregnant women	6–14

Source: Behrman, Alderman, and Hoddinott 2004.

When Does Malnutrition Occur?

It is now well established that undernutrition's most damaging effects occur during pregnancy and in the first two years of life. The effects of this early damage on health, brain development, intelligence, educability, and productivity are largely irreversible. Actions targeted to older children have little if any effect. Initial evidence suggests that the origins of obesity and noncommunicable diseases such as cardiovascular heart disease and diabetes may also lie in early childhood, or even during pregnancy. In countries where mean overweight rates among children under five are high, a large proportion of children are already overweight at birth. Governments with limited resources are therefore best advised to focus interventions on the narrow *window of opportunity,* from before conception to 24 months of age, although actions to control obesity may need to continue later.

Causes of Malnutrition in Food-Secure Households

Food scarcity and food insecurity can be important causes of malnutrition, as chapter 8 showed, but by no means the only ones. Many children in countries and in families where the food supply is ample, and many even in families that are not income-poor, grow up underweight or stunted or lacking key micronutrients. Moreover, in most parts of the world, underweight and overweight individuals often live in the same country, the same region within a country, and sometimes even the same household—a phenomenon that would be hard to explain if inadequate food supply were the only cause of undernutrition. This argument is further supported by the fact that undernutrition rates are sometimes the highest in regions where food production is high, such as the Iringa region in Tanzania and the Arsi region in Ethiopia. Despite major advances in agriculture in India during the Green Revolution, India today has the same aggregate levels of underweight as Ethiopia.

Why is malnutrition so common in countries and households where food supply is adequate? Research has shown that the two most important factors are, first, inadequate knowledge about the benefits of exclusive breastfeeding and complementary feeding practices and the role of micronutrients, and second, the lack of time that women have available for appropriate infant care practices and their own care during pregnancy. Poor hygienic conditions and inadequate access to health care services are also important.

It is now well established that breastfeeding is the best source of nutrients for infants and the best protection against many infectious and chronic diseases. Yet the more widespread availability of commercially processed infant formula has led many mothers to substitute it for their own milk, and many mothers introduce other foods to their infants too soon (or too late). The first milk that a mother produces after birth, called colostrum, is too often discarded, although it has been shown to be important in strengthening the newborn's immune system. Often colostrum is replaced by a mixture of sugar, local herbs, and unclean water that may lead to diarrhea.

Many poor mothers are simply too burdened with paid work or with household tasks, including the care of other children, to take the time to adequately nourish themselves or their infants. Pregnant and nursing women may consume too few calories and too little protein, have untreated infections such as sexually transmitted diseases that lead to low birthweight, or do not get enough rest. The disturbing truth is that some mothers and children do not get their appropriate share of whatever food is available to the household.

Sanitary conditions within the household can interfere with children's nutrition even when food supply is ample. Poor hygiene on the part of the mother or other caregivers may cause food to become contaminated with bacteria or parasites. Once infected, children may be too ill to keep food down, or their compromised digestive systems may be unable to absorb its nutrients. Caregivers may not know how to feed children properly when they are ill.

More broadly, parents often lack information about how best to feed and care for themselves and their children, and many pernicious myths about good nutrition persist (box 11.1). They and other caregivers may give children too little food, especially in the child's early years, or food that is not sufficiently energy-dense or that lacks critical micronutrients. Nor can the untrained

BOX 11.1 Three Myths About Nutrition

Poor nutrition is implicated in more than half of all child deaths worldwide—a proportion unmatched by any infectious disease since the Black Death of the Middle Ages. It is intimately linked with poor health and environmental factors. But planners, politicians, and economists often fail to recognize these connections. Among the more serious misapprehensions are the following:

Myth 1: Malnutrition is primarily a matter of inadequate food intake. Not so. Food is, of course, important. But most serious malnutrition is caused by bad sanitation and disease, leading to diarrhea, especially among young children. Women's status and women's education both play big parts in improving nutrition. Improving the care of young children is vital.

Myth 2: Improved nutrition is a by-product of other measures of poverty reduction and economic advance. It is not possible to jump-start the process. Again, untrue. Improving nutrition requires focused action by parents and communities, backed by local and national action in health and public services, especially water and sanitation. Thailand has shown that moderate and severe malnutrition can be reduced by 75 percent or more within a decade by such means.

Myth 3: Given scarce resources, broad-based action on nutrition is hardly feasible on a mass scale, especially in poor countries. Wrong again. In spite of severe economic setbacks, many developing countries have made impressive progress. More than two-thirds of all people in developing countries now eat iodized salt, combating the iodine deficiency and anemia that affect about 3.5 billion, especially women and children, in some 100 nations. About 450 million children a year now receive vitamin A capsules, tackling the deficiency that causes blindness and increases child mortality. New ways have been found to promote and support breastfeeding, and breastfeeding rates are being at least maintained in many countries and increased in some. Mass immunization and promotion of oral rehydration to reduce deaths from diarrhea have also done much to improve nutrition.

Source: Jolly 1996.

eye easily detect the early signs of malnutrition, especially micronutrient malnutrition, and in particular when such signs are so widespread in the community as to be mistaken for normal.

Because malnutrition is often caused by inappropriate care behaviors and poor sanitation, improving hygiene and the care given to young children is vital; without this, further increases in food supply are largely wasted. Raising the social status and educational attainment of women is another key factor in improving nutrition, because in most societies women remain the primary caregivers.

What Can Be Done to Improve Nutrition?

It is often assumed that once sustainable economic growth has been established and poverty reduced, nutrition will improve spontaneously; in this view, there is no need to intervene in nutrition directly to jump-start the process. In fact, whatever the state of the economy, improving child nutrition requires focused action on the part of families and communities, backed by action at the local and the national level to improve public services, and all these actions should occur simultaneously with other development initiatives. Economic growth is certainly an important factor in improving nutrition, but it (along with increased food production) is a *long route* to that destination compared with the *short routes* of nutrition education, micronutrient supplementation, and other essential, direct nutrition interventions. These shorter routes therefore should not be neglected during the long wait for incomes to rise; if they are, the MDGs will not be achieved.

What are some of the most effective short routes to better nutrition? Countries such as Bangladesh, Honduras, and Madagascar have successfully used public–private partnerships to mobilize communities to tackle malnutrition through community-based approaches. These approaches focus on promotion of the growth of young children through exclusive breastfeeding, adequate and timely complementary feeding, micronutrient supplementation, and improvement of mothers' capacities to make informed decisions about the health and well-being of their young children. Experience in Mexico has shown that, at least in a middle-income-country setting, cash transfers made conditional on the recipients regularly using health and nutrition services, coupled on the supply side with improved health and nutrition service delivery, can induce poor people to seek out these services and thereby improve child growth.

What Has Been Done to Date to Address Malnutrition?

Many developing countries have made impressive progress against malnutrition despite low income per capita, and indeed despite severe economic setbacks. Already more than two-thirds of the developing world's population, including many in some of the poorest countries, consume iodized salt and are thus protected against iodine deficiency. Some 450 million children a year worldwide now receive vitamin A capsules. Simply through the encouragement of breastfeeding, millions of children receive better nutrition than before. Mass immunization, together with the promotion of oral rehydration methods for diarrheal disease, has worked in synergy with better nutrition to improve the health and well-being of millions more. In countries that have done less to improve nutrition, weak government commitment and weak capacity to plan, design, and implement programs have proved a greater barrier to progress than lack of government funds.

In situations where both undernutrition and micronutrient malnutrition are prevalent, large-scale programs have already been shown to work in Asia (Bangladesh and Thailand), in Africa (Madagascar), and in Latin America and the Caribbean (Chile, Cuba, Honduras, and Mexico). In contrast, in addressing the problems of overweight, low birthweight, and the complex interactions between malnutrition and HIV/AIDS, tried and tested large-scale models are few. Here, therefore, action research is the priority. Such research needs to focus on the following areas where practical knowledge is lacking, so as to shorten the time lag between developing the science and scaling up interventions:

- Strengthening commitment and capacity, mainstreaming these nutritional initiatives within the broader development agenda, and documenting these experiences
- Strengthening and fine-tuning existing service delivery mechanisms
- Continuing to strengthen the evidence base that underlies these investments in nutrition.

Many countries have successfully implemented and scaled up individual nutrition programs even in the absence of a comprehensive nutrition policy; indeed, few countries yet have well-developed and well-resourced nutrition policies. But these policies are important. Without them, policies in other sectors—trade, foreign exchange, employment, gender, social welfare, health—can have haphazard and often adverse effects on nutrition, becoming in effect de facto nutrition policies themselves. Poverty and social impact analyses should be more widely used to assess the intentional and unintentional effects of countries' development policies on nutrition outcomes. Another important step is to develop, within a focal national institution such as the ministry of finance or the poverty monitoring office, the capacity to advise policy makers about the nutritional implications of other policies. If, as argued above, countries themselves need to take the lead in improving the nutrition of their people, a comprehensive nutrition policy is ultimately what is needed for that to happen.

What More Can Countries and the International Community Do?

The international community and the governments of most developing countries have not done enough to reduce malnutrition over the past several decades. This failure is all the more distressing because, as has been shown, well-tested and cost-effective means of tackling the problem already exist and have been shown to work at scale in some countries. As a result, malnutrition remains the world's most serious health problem, and most developing countries will not meet the MDG of reducing hunger and malnutrition by half by 2015 if current trends continue. The choice now is whether to continue to fail—and so jeopardize several of the other MDGs as well, in maternal and child health, education, HIV/AIDS reduction, and gender equity—or finally to give nutrition the place it deserves at the center of the development agenda. (table 11.3 shows how good nutrition can contribute to the success of each of the MDGs.)

Countries themselves should be taking the lead in improving the nutrition of their people. Good nutrition, after all, has some of the characteristics of a public as well as a private good: this chapter has already noted the effects of a healthy work force on a country's productivity, and communicable diseases are less likely to spread through a healthy population than an undernourished one. In these ways and others, better nutrition for each individual benefits both that individual *and* everyone else in the society.

Although some national governments are taking the lead, in others weak capacity to plan and implement nutrition programs and a lack of sustained government commitment to better nutrition have led to failure to scale up action to the level needed and, consequently, to low demand for outside assistance. When this is the case, the role of the international community must extend beyond merely responding when governments get around to asking for help. International institutions, developed country governments, and global nongovernmental organizations must pool their specialized resources of analysis, advocacy, and capacity building to encourage and influence developing country governments to move nutrition higher on the agenda.

Beyond the widespread myths and misconceptions, other informational and organizational barriers often impede efforts to improve nutrition. Malnutrition can easily go unrecognized in a community, and even when it is recognized, the poor typically have too little voice in society to get their needs attended to. Both they and society at large may fail to realize the full economic and social costs of poor nutrition. Governments and other health care providers may not know what interventions are available or which ones best suit their

212   *Global Issues for Global Citizens*

Goal	Nutrition effect
Goal 1: Eradicate extreme poverty and hunger.	Malnutrition erodes human capital through irreversible and intergenerational effects on cognitive and physical development.
Goal 2: Achieve universal primary education.	Malnutrition affects the chances that a child will go to school, stay in school, and perform well.
Goal 3: Promote gender equality and empower women.	Antifemale biases in access to food, health, and care resources may result in malnutrition, possibly reducing women's access to assets. Addressing malnutrition empowers women more than men.
Goal 4: Reduce child mortality.	Malnutrition is directly or indirectly associated with most child deaths, and it is the main contributor to the burden of disease in the developing world.
Goal 5: Improve maternal health.	Maternal health is compromised by malnutrition, which is associated with most major risk factors for maternal mortality. Maternal stunting and iron and iodine deficiencies in particular pose serious problems.
Goal 6: Combat HIV/AIDS, malaria, and other diseases.	Malnutrition may increase the risk of HIV transmission, compromise antiretroviral therapy, and hasten the onset of full-blown AIDS and premature death. It increases the chances of tuberculosis infection and reduces malarial survival rates.

TABLE 11.3 How Investing in Nutrition is Critical to Achieving the MDGs

Source: Adapted from Gillespie and Haddad 2003.

people's needs. The presence of many different stakeholders, and the division of responsibility for nutrition across different agencies or ministries, can allow the poor and the malnourished to fall between the organizational cracks, and the organizations that implement nutrition programs often suffer from weak governance, poor accountability, and inadequate resources. For all these reasons, officials responsible for public health may have insufficient incentive to address nutrition problems with vigor and urgency.

There is much that the international community can do, but, first, its members must agree on a common view of the problem and of the broad strategies needed to address it, and then they must speak with a common voice. This will involve, first, setting a strategic agenda for scaling up undernutrition and micronutrient interventions in priority countries and making them more effective and, second, engaging in action research (learning by doing) in the areas where less is known. Much of the agenda setting has already been proposed in a 2006 World Bank document. The messages in that document have been widely disseminated and have resonated at both the global and the country level.

Setting a strategic agenda involves addressing three widespread operational challenges: building global and national commitment and capacity to invest in nutrition; mainstreaming nutrition in country development strategies; and reorienting large-scale nutrition programs that have proved ineffective, so as to maximize their potential effect. But setting a common strategic agenda does not mean imposing a one-size-fits-all global approach. Rather, countries and their development partners need to work together to develop a common strategy tailored to the particular needs of each country, but with special attention paid to certain well-established recommendations. These include the following:

- Focus strategies and action on the poor, in a way that addresses the non-income aspects of poverty reduction, which are closely linked to human development and human capital formation.
- Focus nutritional interventions on the window of opportunity—pre-pregnancy and the first two years of an infant's life—because that is when irreparable damage can occur. This will entail a focus on improving maternal and child care practices such as exclusive breastfeeding for infants and appropriate and timely complementary feeding.
- Scale up micronutrient programs. This should be a high priority, given the widespread prevalence of micronutrient deficiencies, their impact on productivity in adulthood, and the affordability and hence extremely high benefit-cost ratios of these programs.
- Build on capacities developed through these micronutrient programs to extend public intervention into the area of community-based nutrition programs.
- Strengthen investments in the short route interventions to improve nutrition, discussed above, while maintaining balance between these and long route interventions.
- Integrate appropriately designed and balanced nutrition interventions into country assistance strategies, sectorwide approaches, multicountry AIDS projects, and Poverty Reduction Strategy Papers.
- Complement public health-oriented nutrition programs with appropriate actions in agriculture and rural development (see chapter 8), water supply and sanitation, social protection, education, gender equity, and community-driven development.

At the global level, the international development community needs to work together to recognize and communicate to others the importance of malnutrition as an underlying cause of slow economic growth, poverty, mortality, and morbidity. Agreement must be reached to coordinate efforts to strengthen commitment to and funding for nutrition, to pursue a broad set of strategic priorities for the next decade, to focus on an agreed-on set of priority countries, and to make a collective effort to shift from small-scale projects to large-scale programs.

Selected Readings and Cited References

Allen, Lindsay H., and Stuart R. Gillespie. 2001. *What Works? A Review of the Efficacy and Effectiveness of Nutrition Interventions.* Geneva: United Nations Administrative Committee on Coordination Subcommittee on Nutrition, Asian Development Bank, and International Food Policy Research Institute.

Behrman, Jere R., Harold Alderman, and John Hoddinott. 2004. "Nutrition and Hunger." In *Global Crises, Global Solutions,* ed. Bjorn Lomborg. Cambridge, United Kingdom: Cambridge University Press.

Bhagwati, Jagdish, and others. 2004. "Ranking the Opportunities." In *Global Crises, Global Solutions,* ed. Bjorn Lomborg. Cambridge, United Kingdom: Cambridge University Press.

Bryce, Jennifer, Cynthia Boschi-Pinto, Kenji Shibuya, Robert E. Black, and the World Health Organization Child Health Epidemiology Reference Group. 2005. "WHO Estimates of the Causes of Death in children." *Lancet* 365: 1147–52.

Caballero, Benjamin. 2005. "A Nutrition Paradox—Underweight and Obesity in Developing Countries." *New England Journal of Medicine* 352(15): 1514–16.

Caulfield, Laura E., Mercedes de Onis, Monika Blössner, and Robert E. Black. 2004. "Undernutrition as an Underlying Cause of Child Deaths Associated with Diarrhea, Pneumonia, Malaria, and Measles." *American Journal of Clinical Nutrition* 80: 193–98.

De Onis, Mercedes, Monika Blössner, Elaine Borghi, Edward Frongillo, and Richard Morris. 2004. "Estimates of Global Prevalence of Childhood Underweight in 1990 and 2015." *Journal of the American Medical Association* 291(21): 2600–06.

Gillespie, Stuart R., and Lawrence Haddad. 2003. "The Relationship between Nutrition and the Millennium Development Goals: A Strategic Review of the Scope for DFID's Influencing Role." London: U.K. Department for International Development.

Heaver, Richard. 2002. "Improving Nutrition: Issues in Management and Capacity Development." Health, Nutrition, and Population Discussion Paper, World Bank, Washington, DC.

Jolly, Richard. 1996. "Kenya: Our Planet: Poverty, Health, and the Environment." http://www.ourplanet.com/imgversn/122/jolly.html.

United Nations Standing Committee on Nutrition. 2004. *Fifth Report on the World Nutrition Situation: Nutrition for Improved Development Outcomes.* Geneva.

United Nations Children's Fund and Micronutrient Initiative. 2004. *Vitamin and Mineral Deficiency: A Global Damage Assessment Report.* http://www.unicef.org/media/files/davos_micronutrient.pdf.

World Bank. 2006. "Repositioning Nutrition as Central to Development: A Strategy for Large-Scale Action. Overview." Directions in Development Series. Washington, DC.

Selected Web Links on Hunger and Malnutrition

World Bank page on health, nutrition, and population	http://www.worldbank.org/hnp
World Health Organization	http://www.who.int
United Nations Children's Fund	http://www.unicef.org
The Micronutrient Initiative	http://www.micronutrient.org
Food and Agriculture Organization of the United Nations	http://www.fao.org
International Food Policy Research Institute	http://www.ifpri.org

PART THREE
Environment and Natural Resources

The global commons—humankind's vast inheritance of shared natural resources—is increasingly under stress. In the absence of effective global institutions and policies to husband these resources, a growing world population has made ever deeper incursions into them, placing some at risk of exhaustion or collapse. Fossil fuel reserves, sources of fresh water, the oceans' fisheries, and the continents' forests are all global resources on which the well-being of billions depends, and all are seriously threatened. At the same time, global climate change, the result of a growing world economy that remains dependent on fossil fuels, proceeds inexorably toward a possibly catastrophic outcome. The chapters in this part of the book probe the various challenges that we have created for ourselves through our own lack of foresight in using our planet's resources. However, they also offer hope that, cooperatively, the nations of the world can devise and sustain remedies adequate to those challenges.

12

Confronting Climate Change

IAN NOBLE AND ROBERT T. WATSON

Climate change is now recognized as a real and important global phenomenon, whose impacts are already being felt. Also well established is that recent climate change is mostly driven by human activity, primarily but by no means exclusively through the release of carbon dioxide into the Earth's atmosphere from the combustion of fossil fuels. Increased atmospheric concentrations of carbon dioxide and certain other gases give rise to the so-called greenhouse effect, whereby heat from solar radiation is trapped in the atmosphere, warming the Earth's surface. In the absence of any serious effort to reduce net emissions of these greenhouse gases, the effects of climate change on ecological, social, and economic systems during the rest of this century will be dramatic—threatening, among other things, the sustainable development of today's low- and middle-income countries and their elimination of poverty.

Fortunately, it is also within the technological and organizational capability of humankind to slow and ultimately halt the accumulation of greenhouse gases in the atmosphere, and to adapt to the effects already irreversibly set in motion by the uncontrolled emissions of past decades. Moreover, all this can be done, if done in the right way, at modest cost: it is possible both to mitigate the degree of climate change and to adapt to the effects without drastically reducing global economic growth or perpetuating poverty in the developing world. But mitigation and adaptation will require dedicated and concerted effort on the part of governments, private firms, international agencies, civil society, and individual consumers. Although there is no room for free riders, the United Nations Framework on Climate Change and its Kyoto Protocol does recognize the principle of differentiated responsibilities among

This chapter is adapted from Noble and others (2005).

countries. The response to climate change will have to be as global as climate change itself.

The Drivers of Climate Change

The standard of living that much of the world, especially the developed countries, enjoys today is possible only through the consumption of large amounts of energy. Since the start of the modern industrial era in the middle of the eighteenth century, the energy available for human use has vastly expanded—indeed, it is advancements in energy technologies such as the steam engine, electricity, and the internal combustion engine that one thinks of as the milestones of the industrial age. Besides enormously increasing potential economic output, and thus the incomes of people fortunate enough to live in today's industrial economies, these technologies also made possible an unprecedented expansion of those populations, which in turn further multiplied human energy consumption. Later, these same technologies spread to the developing world, where the same cycle of growth in energy use, growth in population, and still more growth in energy use is evident today.

With some relatively minor exceptions such as nuclear, biomass, solar and wind energy, and hydroelectricity, all modern energy technologies are based, directly or indirectly, on the same source, namely, fossil fuels: coal, petroleum, and natural gas. The combustion of these fuels—the reaction of the carbon they contain with oxygen in the air—creates carbon dioxide: hence industrialization implies a massive increase in carbon dioxide emissions. Worldwide, as for fossil-fuel emissions, about 6.4 gigatons of carbon (Gt, or billions of tons of carbon) were released into the atmosphere in 2000 alone.

Although real-time scientific measurements have been taken for only the past century or so, other methods have verified that atmospheric concentrations of carbon dioxide and certain other greenhouse gases have been rising—indeed, accelerating—since the late 18th century (figure 12.1). The concentration of carbon dioxide has risen from about 280 parts per million (ppm) to about 370 ppm; that of methane, the second most important greenhouse gas, from 750 parts per billion (ppb) to nearly 1,750 ppb; and that of nitrous oxides from about 265 ppb to about 312 ppb. Industrialization also led initially to increased atmospheric amounts of sulfate aerosols, which tend to cool the Earth, but regulation in many countries to combat local and regional air pollution has more recently led to a decrease in these emissions, at least in developed countries.

These increases in greenhouse gas concentrations have already been followed by a measurable rise in the Earth's surface temperature, as greenhouse

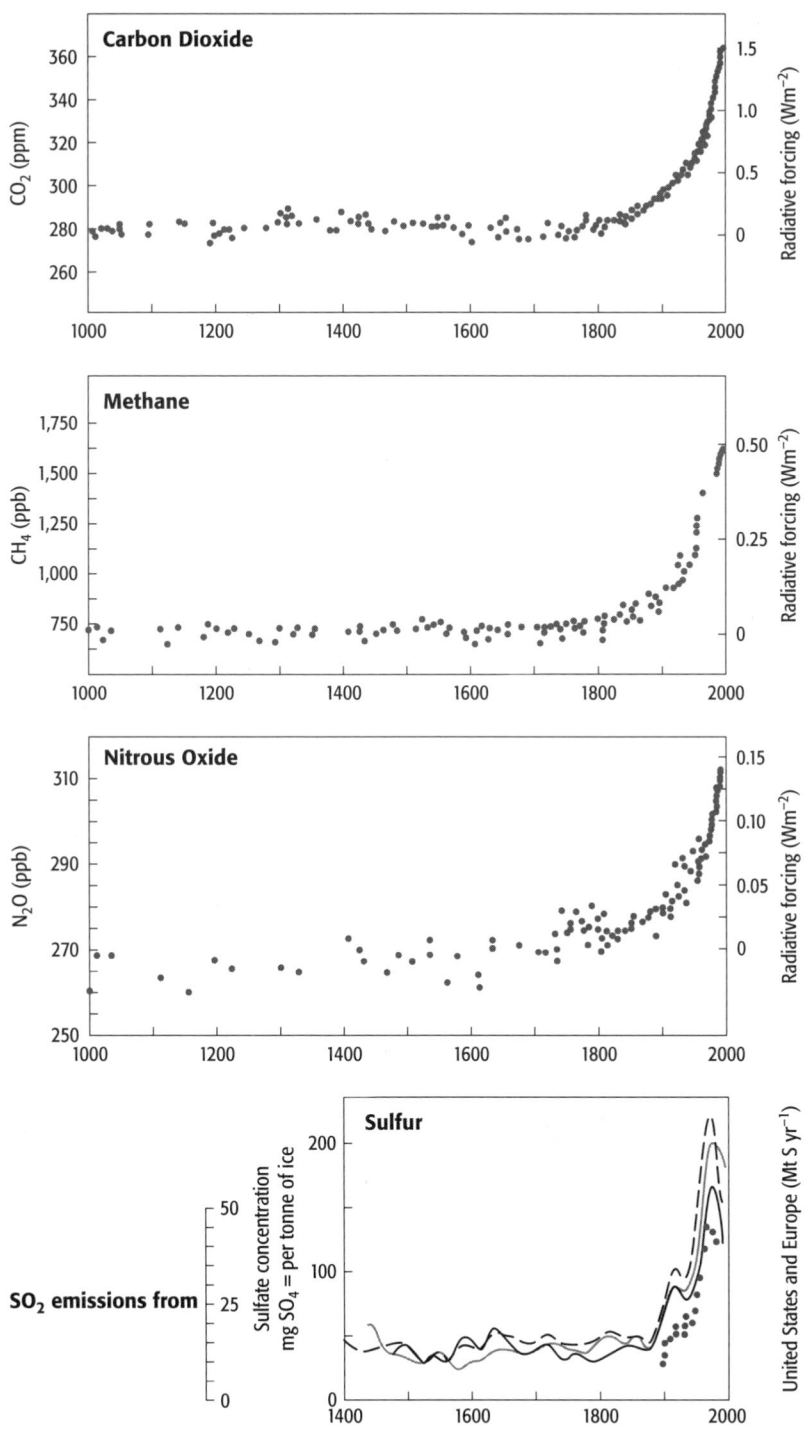

FIGURE 12.1 Global Atmospheric Concentrations of Major Greenhouse Gases since 1000 A.D.

Source: Watson 2006.
CO₂ = Carbon Dioxide   SO₄ = Sulfur
CH₄ = Methane   N₂O = Nitrous Oxide
Mt S yr⁻¹ = [AQ: Add]   Wm⁻² = [AQ: Add]

theory would predict. The increase in mean surface temperature over the past 100 years has been about 0.6°C, or about 1.1° F, and the decade of the 1990s was the warmest for the Earth as a whole since records first began to be kept in the 1860s. Other effects consistent with a warming planet have been observed, including a rise in sea levels, bleaching of coral reefs, thinning of sea ice, retreating of glaciers, changes in precipitation patterns and growing seasons, changes in the frequency of pest and disease outbreaks, changes in the populations and geographical range of certain animal species, and changes in the cultivable ranges of certain crops.

Of course, correlation does not necessarily imply causation—it is known, for example, that fluctuations in solar radiation intensity and other natural phenomena can also cause global surface temperatures to rise or fall, often for long periods. But mathematical climate models that take account of such *natural forcing* have shown that they cannot account for the observed rise in temperature. Only a model that includes both natural and anthropogenic (that is, human) influences tracks the actual temperature data closely at the continental and global scale. The connection between human energy use and climate change has become extremely difficult to deny.

Consequences of a Warming World

As the effects of climate change manifest themselves ever more starkly, and as the scientific understanding of climate dynamics grows, estimates of the warming still to come under unchanged policies become increasingly better understood, and the contours of a warming planet become increasingly clear. The picture that emerges is a sobering one.

Estimation of Temperature Change Under Current Policies

The Intergovernmental Panel on Climate Change (IPCC) is the principal international body charged with assessing the risks associated with human-induced climate change. IPCC constructs various scenarios involving different plausible future concentrations of greenhouse gases in the atmosphere, derived from alternative projections of world population and economic growth and energy use patterns. Using models that combine these results with quantitative estimates of climate sensitivity and other inputs, IPCC then projects how much warming should occur under each scenario, globally and in different parts of the world, and with what effects.

In its most recent comprehensive analysis, published in 2001, IPCC projected that world population would grow from 5.3 billion in 1990 to somewhere between 7 billion and 15 billion in 2100, and that the world economy (as measured by gross world product) would expand from $21 trillion to somewhere in a range of $200 trillion to $550 trillion over the same period. World energy demand would increase as a consequence from 351 exajoules a year to between 515 and 2,740 exajoules a year, in the absence of a concerted international effort to mitigate climate change. (An exajoule is 1 quintillion joules, roughly equivalent to 1 quadrillion British thermal units.) If energy consumption is at the upper end of that range, IPCC further projects that related carbon emissions could rise as high as 36.8 Gt a year in 2100, from 6.0 Gt in 1990. (At the lower end, emissions could actually decline under some scenarios, to as low as 3.3 Gt.) The atmospheric concentration of carbon dioxide would then rise as high as 970 ppm (or to as little as 540 ppm for the lower end of the emissions range), from 370 ppm in 1990. (Annual methane emissions would go from 310 megatons in 1990 to between 236 and 1,039 megatons, and its atmospheric concentration from 1,750 ppb to between 1,600 and 3,760 ppb.) The resulting global mean temperature increase from the 1990 level would be between 1.4°C and 5.8°C, or approximately between 2.5°F and 10.4°F.

Predicted Effects of Rising Temperatures

What impacts would such a rise in global temperature have on natural ecosystems and human societies? Here it is difficult to be precise, both because the estimated range itself is so broad and because the linkages from temperature change to its many possible effects are not completely known and are in many cases interrelated, with possible feedbacks both positive and negative. (The estimated temperature range is broad for two reasons. One is uncertainty about the *climate sensitivity factor,* which can be thought of as the coefficient that translates a given increase in greenhouse gas concentration into a predicted amount of warming. The other is the breadth of the estimated range in emissions from which the concentrations are calculated. The two reasons happen to contribute in roughly equal amounts to the total uncertainty.) However, a number of effects have been identified as likely to result, at least to some degree, from an increase in global mean temperature anywhere within that range, and these can be described qualitatively, if not always quantitatively.

The first and most obvious is that it will be hotter. Specifically, most parts of the world will experience both warmer maximum and warmer minimum temperatures, as well as more hot days and fewer cold days (and fewer days with frost). But the increases will not be uniform: higher latitudes (those nearer the poles) will see a larger absolute average temperature rise than the

---

FIGURE 12.2 Geographic Distribution of Projected Global Temperature Increases

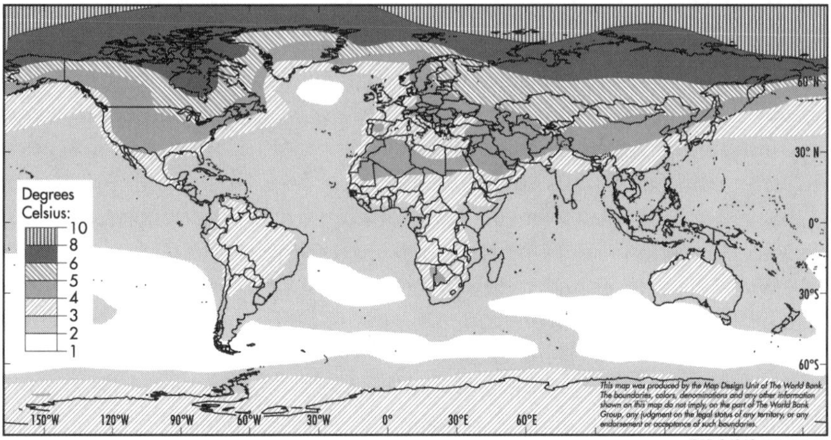

IBRD 34962 AUGUST 2006

Source: Watson 2006.

tropics and subtropics, and land areas in general will experience a larger rise than the seas. As an example, if the average global temperature rise turns out to be 3.1°C (near the middle of the projected range), then temperatures in parts of northern Alaska, Canada, and Siberia are projected to rise by 6°C or more, while oceans throughout most of the world should experience a rise in surface temperature of less than 3°C (figure 12.2). Temperatures on land will also tend to vary within a narrower range over the course of the day and night than before the change.

One of the most certain effects of climate change is rising sea levels, brought about both by thermal expansion of seawater and by partial melting of the vast sheets of ice at the Earth's poles. Already the mean global sea level has risen by between 10 and 25 centimeters; IPCC forecasts an additional rise of between 8 and 88 centimeters by 2100. A rising ocean threatens the very existence of some small island states, such as Maldives, as well as low-lying alluvial regions, such as the heavily populated delta of the Ganges and Brahmaputra Rivers. Many of the world's largest cities, including many of the developing world's most important, are built on coastlines; these cities face the choice of building costly protective infrastructure or being submerged. Finally, the rise in sea levels also endangers a variety of biologically rich and economically important ecosystems such as coral reefs, mangrove forests, and other wetlands.

FIGURE 12.3 Geographic Distribution of Projected Global Precipitation Change

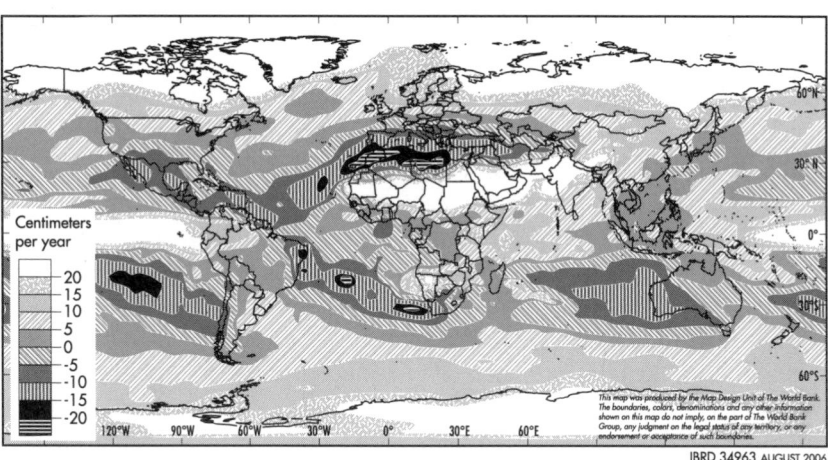

Source: Watson 2006.

Global precipitation is expected to rise with climate change, as warmer temperatures cause more rapid evaporation from the oceans. But, as with the rise in temperature itself, there will be significant variation across latitudes, with the upper latitudes receiving much more rainfall and snowfall while some areas in and around the tropics actually see rainfall diminish: the Mediterranean, Mexico and Central America, central Chile, northeastern Brazil, Mesopotamia, South Africa, and western Australia are among the areas likely to be affected the worst (figure 12.3). These include some important agricultural areas. In addition, heavy precipitation events are expected to increase and light precipitation events to decline, resulting in an increase in severe floods and, at the other extreme, severe droughts. Accompanying these changes in precipitation will be an increased incidence of extreme weather events in most parts of the world, including more and more-intense hurricanes and cyclones.

Reduced precipitation, in those parts of the world where it is projected to occur, will have one almost certain consequence, namely, reduced agricultural productivity. Since many of the likely affected areas lie in developing countries—often in places where agriculture is already a marginally remunerative activity—the impact will be concentrated among people who are already poor and have few resources and little technological or social capacity to deal with such a change. At the same time, the reduction in precipitation will lessen the potential for hydroelectric generation and make less biomass available for fuel. This could well induce a shift in these areas toward greater use of fossil fuels, tending to worsen the problem in the long run. And, to the extent that climate change shifts the world's productive agricultural regions poleward, it could lead to wholesale human migration in the same direction, leading to competition for agricultural land, leading, in turn, to social and political tensions and possibly violent conflict.

Nor would human beings be the only would-be migrants. Many species of plants and animals would also find their supporting ecosystems degraded and themselves stressed by rising temperatures, changes in precipitation, and other greenhouse effects. These changes, moreover, would occur much more rapidly than similar changes in the prehistoric past that stemmed from natural causes, allowing less time for adaptation. Some species would succeed in reestablishing themselves in less hostile areas, but others would encounter gaps in their potential migration routes, or human infrastructure blocking the way. For example, although some wetlands and their native flora and fauna could simply rise in elevation along with the sea level (if the change is gradual enough), others will be trapped between the rising sea and human settlements on the higher ground. Ecosystems that overlie permafrost in the northern latitudes of Asia and North America could find their total habitat reduced to a fraction of its former size. Thus it is probable that many species worldwide will become extinct—one study of a sample of some 1,100 animal and plant species estimates that between 15 and 52 percent of them may face extinction as a result of climate change. With the loss of so many species, many ecosystems would suffer a devastating loss of biodiversity.

Even as many larger species dwindle and disappear, some of the microorganisms responsible for infectious diseases and infestations may thrive in a warmer global climate. Higher average temperatures will likely expand the territorial range of malaria-carrying mosquitoes and other pests; reduced precipitation in some tropical and subtropical areas, by concentrating the sources from which humans and animals get their water, may encourage the spread of water-borne diseases like cholera. Thus the incidence of some of the world's most feared diseases may increase. Already the World Health Organization attributes more than 150,000 deaths a year worldwide to causes related to climate change.

Finally, all of the effects of climate change thus far described are expected to occur more or less in proportion to the degree of climate change itself, more or less gradually, and are reversible, at least over some reasonable time horizon. This allows some degree of confidence that their impacts can be managed. But other possible consequences of climate change are subject to major, unpredictable, and probably irreversible threshold effects. Of those identified so far, the most disruptive would be the shutdown of the thermohaline conveyor that drives the major currents of the oceans. The Gulf Stream carries warm water from the Gulf of Mexico to the North Atlantic, giving Western Europe a warmer climate than it would otherwise have, given its latitude. A shutdown of the Gulf Stream, due to changes in the saltiness of the North Atlantic resulting from ice melt, would thus significantly lower temperatures in that major industrial region and population center. One study puts the likelihood of a thermohaline collapse during the next 100 years at 30 percent.

The aggregate costs of the damage that all these effects of climate change might entail are even more difficult to gauge than the physical effects themselves, both because of the many uncertainties involved and because some of the damages, for example to the health of ecosystems and of people, are difficult to quantify in economic terms. Many ecosystem *goods,* such as flood control, soil formation, biodiversity, and aesthetic value, are not traded in any marketplace and so cannot easily be priced—nor can the value of a long and healthy human life—but an attempt needs to be made and to be set against a reasonable estimate of the costs of prevention, mitigation, and adaptation, to determine hard-headedly whether the endeavor is a paying one, or whether the more economically prudent course is to suffer and make do.

In 1996, IPCC estimated the economic costs associated with a doubling of carbon dioxide at between 1.5 and 2.0 percent of world gross domestic product (GDP) (1.0 to 1.5 percent in developed countries and 2 to 9 percent in developing countries). A group of experts led by the economist William Nordhaus reported a mean estimate of 3.6 percent of world GDP for the economic costs of warming by 3°C by 2090, although the cost rose to 21 percent of GDP in some scenarios.

Strategies for Responding to Climate Change

Given what is known today about the dynamics of climate systems and the responses of ecological and socioeconomic systems, and what can be guessed about the costs that would be imposed, how should the world community respond to the changes in climate that IPCC has projected? In answering this question, it is important to take into account that the thresholds at which damages to ecosystems and critical resources become unacceptable are a matter of judgment as much as of science, and therefore cannot be stated precisely. Moreover, some countries and regions, and some industries and populations within them, are more sensitive than others to the effects of climate change—some, such as many high-latitude farmers, may even benefit.

With these caveats, and given current understanding of the climate system and the response of different ecological and socioeconomic systems, if significant global adverse changes to ecosystems are to be avoided, the best guidance available today suggests that efforts should be made to limit the increase in global mean surface temperature to less than 2°C above the pre-industrial level, while also limiting the *rate* of change in temperature to less than 0.2°C per decade. Meeting those targets would require limiting the atmospheric concentration of carbon dioxide to about 450 ppm or lower, compared with 370 ppm about 1990, and stabilizing or reducing current concentrations of the other greenhouse gases. Maintaining climate change within those parameters would give reasonable assurance that significant global adverse changes in ecosystems can be avoided: a recent meeting of climate scientists concluded that a concentration of 450 ppm of carbon dioxide would have a "medium likelihood" of keeping the change in global surface temperature below 2°C. It has also been estimated that setting a less stringent target would likely cross an important threshold, from a world in which climate change has adverse impacts on only certain regions to one in which nearly all of the world would be worse off. Meeting the above targets would also result in a low probability of large-scale catastrophic events such as thermohaline shutdown or a collapse of the major polar ice sheets.

Given that some adverse effects of climate change are already evident, as described above, it is obvious that setting a target for carbon dioxide concentration that is more than 20 percent above today's level implies that some further damage is inevitable. This means that strategies to deal with the problem will have to include not only measures to *mitigate* the rise in greenhouse gas concentration but also to *adapt* to some degree of unavoidable rise in temperature and its effects.

Mitigation

The goal of stabilizing greenhouse gas emissions at or below the target level is more likely to be met if pursued across a wide range of activities simultaneously. These fall into three categories: developing energy resources in ways that reduce emissions; increasing the efficiency with which energy is used; and making changes in land-use practices. Many of these efforts will have the added benefit of reducing local and regional pollution, for example, from airborne particulate matter and from ozone and sulfur dioxide.

What is absolutely necessary for mitigation to succeed, however, is the participation of countries in all regions of the world and at all income levels, while acknowledging the principle of differentiated responsibilities mentioned above. The industrial countries alone, despite their greater resources

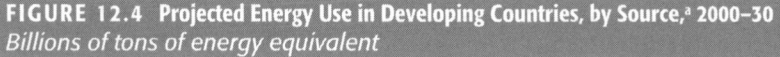

FIGURE 12.4 Projected Energy Use in Developing Countries, by Source,ᵃ 2000–30
Billions of tons of energy equivalent

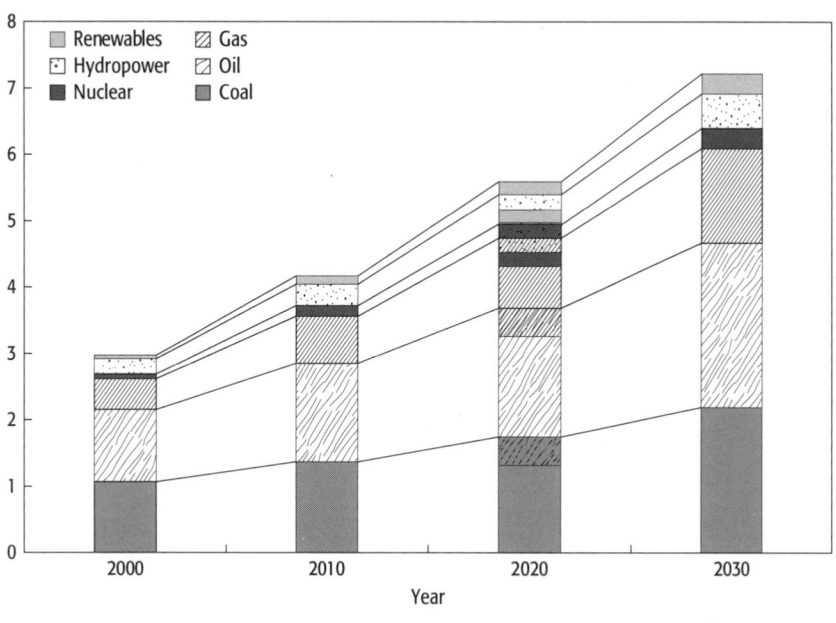

Source: Watson and Noble 2004.
a. Under the International Energy Agency's business-as-usual scenario.

and more advanced technology, cannot reduce their emissions by enough to stabilize atmospheric concentrations, because today's developing countries are industrializing and will soon become major contributors to emissions themselves. As figure 12.4 shows, developing countries will more than double their total energy consumption between 2000 and 2030, under unchanged policies, and fossil fuels will continue to provide about 85 percent of the total. For their part, although developing countries have the opportunity to build energy-efficient, reduced-emissions economies from the ground up rather than engage in expensive retrofitting, it is unlikely that these countries will accept—nor should they—a larger share of the mitigation burden than the rich industrial countries bear. Cooperation on a global scale will be needed, including transfers of finance and technology from the industrial world to the developing world where the opportunities for low-cost mitigation are greater.

Numerous options exist within the energy sector itself to reduce greenhouse gas emissions. Some of these involve changes in the ways in which energy is extracted from fossil fuels, others in how that energy is distributed, and still others exploit opportunities to replace fossil fuels with other sources of energy that do not emit carbon dioxide or other climate-unfriendly gases.

Improving Fossil-Fuel Technologies

Within the fossil-fuel domain, several avenues appear promising:

- Some fossil fuels, such as coal, emit more carbon dioxide in combustion for a given amount of energy than do others, such as natural gas. Substitution of natural gas for coal can therefore reduce emissions, where transmission of the gas is feasible, for a given energy output. Natural gas–fired combined-cycle power plants are relatively inexpensive and highly efficient and reduce local and regional pollution as well.
- Fuel cell technologies offer significant potential for cogeneration (production of both electricity and heat for living spaces) at smaller scales, for example at the level of a single commercial building. This avoids the need to transport the heated air over long distances from a few large-scale generating plants.
- The different types of fossil fuel are fungible, capable of being converted from one form into another that is more climate friendly. For example, coal can be gasified through partial oxidation to produce synthetic gas (primarily carbon monoxide and hydrogen). Superclean fuels derived from synthetic gas in polygeneration facilities may soon be economically competitive.
- Technologies to capture and store emitted carbon dioxide at the site of production would allow the continued use of fossil fuels, with little or no emission of carbon into the atmosphere. The carbon dioxide could be injected into depleted oil and gas wells or other geological formations, or into the deep ocean (although the latter option would be less permanent and entails environmental risks of its own). An alternative would be to store the carbon in the form of stable solid carbonates, although this would be more costly and the technology has not been proven on a large scale.

Developing Noncarbon Energy Technologies

Nuclear energy and various forms of renewable energy—small- and large-scale hydropower, wind, solar, biomass, and others—have been around for decades, and in some cases centuries, yet today they supply a relatively small fraction of the world's energy needs (about 6 percent in the case of nuclear, and about 14 percent for all forms of renewables combined, with large-scale hydropower being the dominant one). New technologies that lower the cost or improve the efficiency of these non-carbon-emitting forms of energy could allow them to substitute for a large share of the energy now provided by fossil fuels:

- Nuclear energy is already a major source of energy in some industrial countries. However, several drawbacks limit its potential. Like fossil fuels, its source (uranium) exists in finite supply; it is widely perceived by the public as unsafe; and management of its waste products remains a contentious issue, complicated by the danger of nuclear weapons proliferation.
- Biomass energy—from fuelwood to crop wastes to animal dung—is today mostly devoted to traditional small-scale uses such as household cooking and heating. Although combustion of biomass also emits carbon, if growing plants create equal amounts of new biomass simultaneously, the net climate impact is neutral. The development of lower-cost biomass sources on a large scale—cheaper ethanol, for example—would transform the biomass sector, but its potential remains constrained because suitable agricultural land is limited, so that conversion of land to growing biomass could displace food crops. If uncultivated land is converted instead, biodiversity could be lost. On the other hand, siting of bioenergy plantations on degraded land or abandoned farmland could actually improve biodiversity. In addition, there are questions regarding the economic viability of expanded biomass production without significant subsidies.
- Harnessing the kinetic energy of running water provides a clean and perpetual source of power. However, geographic formations suitable for developing hydropower also are finite; most unexploited sites today are in the developing world. Construction of dams for hydropower raises issues of displacement of communities as well as ecological concerns. *Run-of-the-river* hydropower projects avoid the need to construct dams and in general are less disruptive of ecosystems.
- "New" renewable energy sources, such as wind, solar, and geothermal energy, today contribute very small fractions of the world's energy supply (less than 4 percent). Thus, even if new capacity could be installed at a prodigious rate of increase, they would remain a minor factor in solving the challenge of climate change for decades to come. All three continue to face differing degrees of technological barriers to their wide-scale adoption as affordable sources of energy, except in certain off-grid situations.

Increasing Energy Efficiency

Literally hundreds of opportunities exist, in all sectors of the economy, to improve the efficiency with which energy is used. It is estimated that, on a worldwide basis over the next 20 years, the amount of primary energy needed to perform a given amount of work could be reduced by 25 to 40 percent, cost-effectively, even at current energy prices. Structural changes in the economy that shift it toward less-energy-intensive outputs could further reduce the average amount of energy used to produce a unit of GDP. In the long run, the efficiency of the global energy system could be improved by an order of magnitude before theoretical limits are reached. Industrial uses, commercial and residential buildings, and transport systems together account for well over 90 percent of all consumption of energy, and enormous scope for improvements in efficiency exists in all three areas. Many of these are *no regrets* options: their adoption would more than pay for itself even before any consideration of the benefits from reduced harm from climate change.

Industry accounted for about 43 percent of energy-related carbon emissions globally in 1995, but the rate of increase in its emissions has slowed dramatically since 1990, to about 0.4 percent a year, in large part because of the collapse of the notoriously energy-inefficient heavy industries of the former Soviet bloc. Even so, improvements in the energy efficiency of industrial processes offer great opportunities for reducing emissions, especially in developing countries, and often with net negative costs.

Buildings—their heating and cooling and other operations—contributed about 31 percent of energy-related carbon emissions in 1995, with an average growth rate from 1971 to the present of about 1.8 percent a year. Both residential and commercial buildings can be made more energy-efficient through improvements in windows, insulation, lighting, heating and cooling systems, and appliances, as well as more energy-efficient architectural design.

Transportation contributed only 22 percent of energy-related carbon emissions in 1995, but since then it has turned in the highest growth rate in emissions: 2.5 percent a year. Opportunities to increase transport efficiency can be exploited in the redesign of automobiles—from more efficient engines and lighter materials in conventional models to hybrid gasoline-electric and fuel cell–powered vehicles—and in expanded mass transit systems. Changes in land use and in work practices (for example, telecommuting) could also help reduce the sector's fossil-fuel consumption.

Adding Land-Use Changes

Reducing carbon emissions due to human activity is not the only way to stabilize atmospheric concentrations of carbon. Another approach is to store

more carbon in soils and vegetation. The world's forests and some other terrestrial ecosystems act as carbon absorbers or *sinks;* already these sinks take
up and release 60 Gt a year. To the extent that rising carbon dioxide levels,
higher temperatures, and increased precipitation stimulate additional plant
growth, this could provide a natural feedback mechanism that partly blunts
climate change.

Human efforts can augment this natural process in several ways. The most
effective and immediate would be to reduce the deforestation that today
continues apace in parts of the developing world—the clearing of land for
agricultural and pastoral use results in over 1 Gt of carbon being released into
the atmosphere each year. Beyond that, positive efforts can be made to grow
new forests or restore forests that have been cut down. IPCC has estimated
that such afforestation and reforestation, together with improved management of existing forests to prevent their degradation, could allow several
hundred megatons of carbon to be sequestered annually. Better management
of agricultural land and rangeland could contribute a similar amount, even
though such land carries far less biomass per hectare than do forests. Reduced
tillage of cropland, for example, can contribute significantly to reducing
carbon concentrations, while also improving soil conditions.

Adaptation

As was emphasized above, the leading edge of climate change is already being
felt around the world, and more is in the climatological pipeline. Therefore
no amount of effort today at mitigation, however rigorous, can prevent
climate change altogether. Indeed, if the recommended strategy is adopted of
limiting the change in global mean surface temperature to 2°C, it will ensure
that still more climate change will have to be tolerated. Adaptation is thus an
essential component of the global response.

Taken broadly, adaptation includes any adjustment in human or natural
systems in response to actual or expected climate change, intended either to
moderate harm or to exploit beneficial opportunities. Some adaptation will
occur autonomously, as a natural response on the part of ecosystems or as a
rational economic or social response on the part of human populations. But
the natural adaptive responses will occur only after climate change has begun
to make itself felt, and by then it may be too late. The same may be true for
some human responses; some more-timely responses, even if rational from
the individual's perspective, may be less than adequate or even counterpro-
ductive from a broader social viewpoint. Many people will lack sufficient
resources to adapt, or they may not know how to adapt, to the new threat;
some, acting in their self-interest, may take actions that worsen the impact on

all. All of this argues for well-planned policy intervention to ensure that the adverse effects of climate change are minimized for as many of the Earth's inhabitants as possible.

Helping Ecosystems Adapt

For ecosystems that are already intensively managed, such as farmlands, the options for adaptation are straightforward, if not always cheap. Farmers and other managers of land have coped with transient variations in their weather and climate for millennia, and the early effects of climate change will often mimic these changes. In regions where climate change is relatively slight, altering planting times or shifting to different crop varieties or different types of livestock may suffice. Where the change in climate is greater, farmers may need to change to altogether different crops or different livestock management techniques, or they may have to undertake further changes in land use, for example, switching from crop production to grazing. Emigration and abandonment of the land should be necessary only in the most extreme situations.

Other ecosystems, such as forests and rangelands, are less intensively managed but do provide goods and services to human communities. Here the decisions are more complex. Should resource managers try to keep the composition and functioning of the ecosystem largely unchanged? This might be achieved by inhibiting the direct drivers of change, for example by preventing forest from being burned off, controlling invasive species, or setting limits on what may be harvested. Or should they accept and try to facilitate change, possibly by fostering a shift to different outputs? To date, attempts to comprehensively reconfigure such systems in response to climate change have been few; however, ecosystems have been deliberately replaced following major disturbances such as fire or prolonged drought. Damaged forests have been cleared and converted to farmland or tree cropping, for example.

A third set of ecosystems are forest and other reserves set aside for the protection of endangered species or general biodiversity. Management of such areas should take into account the shifts in species distribution expected with climate change (mainly toward the poles and to higher elevations). Greater attention will have to be paid to preventing disturbances, or sequences of disturbances (such as drought followed by fire), that will become more frequent in an altered climate. Beyond these considerations, the management approach will depend on the primary goal of the reserve, whether it be to protect certain species or to maintain an entire ecosystem intact. Of course, many such areas have multiple goals, making careful planning indispensable.

Helping People Adapt

Human adaptation to climate change is largely a matter of managing risks, both to societies as a whole and to individuals. Broadly speaking, these risks can be managed in three ways: by decreasing the probability of adverse climate-related events occurring (for example, by building coastal barriers against floods, or expanding irrigation systems in the face of expected drought); by limiting the expected damage from such events when they do occur (for example, by putting buildings on stilts in flood-prone coastal areas, or resettling communities on higher ground); or by providing services that enhance individuals' ability to cope with such damage (for example, by setting up early-warning systems against storms or making flood insurance available).

The capacity to adapt to climate change varies greatly both across countries and societies and within them. The Netherlands and Bangladesh, for example, both occupy low-lying river deltas, but the Netherlands has both more installed infrastructure to deal with floods and more financial resources to augment that infrastructure to cope with rising sea levels. Within developing countries, the poorest are often not only the least equipped to adapt to climate change but face the greatest threat from it as well: they are more likely to live on the most marginal land, or in cities with inadequate and failing infrastructure; to depend on a single crop or other source of livelihood, which may be precisely the one most threatened by climate change; to lack information about coping strategies and available resources; and to lack robust social networks to support them in time of need.

Traditional coping mechanisms are often the starting point for successful adaptation in developing countries: as noted earlier in the case of farmlands, the initial effects of climate change fall within the range of most societies' past experience. Strengthening these mechanisms can add to their resilience. But when the traditional mechanisms fail, as climate change persists and intensifies, they need to be superseded by, or incorporated into, wider regional and national planning initiatives.

Here the key word is *mainstreaming,* that is, integrating those policies and measures aimed at responding to climate change into already-existing development initiatives and programs, from food security to water and sanitation to education to health care. There is a danger of adaptation becoming *projectized*—broken up into a series of discrete and disconnected projects that risk becoming embroiled in institutional turf rivalries. Worse, it is all too easy to imagine climate adaptation and development efforts working at cross-purposes: the engineers designing the new reservoir may work in a different department than the environmental scientists fretting over the coming decline in rainfall. Coordinating their activities is essential. Yet studies have found that although some 40 percent of development projects and loans face some element of climate risk, only 2 percent integrate that risk into their project design. Adaptation has to become more firmly rooted in the broader development strategy—and be prepared to learn from its experience.

Getting Incentives Right

Although, as described above, many of the necessary human responses to climate change will occur autonomously, as individuals pursue their own self-interest to avoid being made worse off, other responses will not. Intervention by governments and other institutions, from the local to the international, will then be needed. Some of these actions, such as the provision or adaptation of large-scale infrastructure in most cases, will be direct. Others, and possibly the more important in the aggregate, will involve aligning the incentives facing individuals, businesses, and other organizations with the broader social need to address climate change, so that appropriate actions are taken. This section focuses on those indirect interventions.

Pricing Strategies

One sure way to decrease the consumption of any good or service, including fossil fuels, is to raise its price. In principle, the simplest way for a government to raise the price of such fuels is to tax them. When a carbon tax or other price intervention is set "just right," the full price of the fossil fuel covers the full cost of consuming the fuel, including the environmental cost, which would otherwise go unpaid by the consumer and instead be shifted to society at large, or to future generations. Economists describe this as *internalizing an externality.*

An added benefit of a carbon tax is that it raises revenue that can be put to other uses, including other climate-change initiatives; or an equivalent amount of other, more economically distortive taxes can be cut. Ideally, the tax would be set at just the level that induces the desired reduction in use, but this can be difficult to determine. Substituting a carbon tax for another tax, such as an income tax, could also undesirably shift the overall burden of taxation from the relatively well off to the poor. And the response of consumers to a given rise in fossil-fuel prices—that is, the price elasticity of fossil-fuel demand—is likely to be small, because energy is such an essential commodity for modern economies. Achieving the desired environmental result through taxation alone might require an oppressively high tax rate.

If a price-based strategy to reduce fossil-fuel consumption is undertaken, the logical place to begin is with fuels that are already underpriced. All too often, countries retain subsidies on gasoline and other fuels as a way of assisting the poor, supporting economic activity generally, or pacifying otherwise politically irritable urban populations. There are better ways to achieve all these ends, especially when the hidden environmental costs loom so large. And subsidies to producers to search for still more fossil-fuel deposits make scarcely any better sense in a warming world than do fuel subsidies to consumers.

Emissions Regulation and Emissions Trading

Governments have the power, of course, simply to outlaw fossil-fuel consumption or other practices that they view as promoting climate change or as otherwise environmentally harmful. Or they can regulate the use of fossil fuels, for example, by setting vehicle emissions standards or mandating the adoption of climate-friendly technologies or practices by power plants. These *command-and-control* approaches obviously create a powerful incentive for the regulated producers to behave as the government wishes—the alternative is a heavy fine or other sanction. However, these approaches may achieve the objective in a less than efficient way: different producers' equipment and processes, and thus their cost functions, will differ, so that if the same regulation or mandate applies to all producers equally, some producers will have a high cost of complying, while others could go beyond what the regulation calls for at little or no cost but will not do so because they lack the incentive.

This inefficiency can be avoided by issuing a fixed number of emissions permits to producers and allowing the permits to be freely traded among them. Those producers that can reduce emissions most cheaply will do so, because it leaves them with unused permits that they can then sell to other producers whose costs are higher. Under a well-enforced tradable permits scheme, the amount of emissions that will occur is known at the outset (and can be set at whatever level the government deems optimal), and the emissions reduction is achieved at the lowest possible cost. Tradable permit regimes have already proved successful, for example at reducing air pollution in the United States, and have been introduced for reduction of greenhouse gas emissions as well (box 12.1).

> **BOX 12.1 Emissions Trading in the European Union**
>
> In 2003, the European Union established a trading system in which each country receives a fixed number of carbon dioxide emissions allowances for its companies in energy-intensive industries such as electric power generation, refining, paper, steel, glass, and cement. Countries achieving reductions that leave them with surplus allowances can trade the allowances to other European Union (EU) and, in some cases, non-EU countries. Penalties for noncompliance are set at €40 per ton of carbon dioxide in the trading period ending in 2007, increasing to €100 in the 2008–12 period.
>
> In mid 2004, a "Linking Directive" was issued, which allows extra flexibility. This is expected to reduce costs by about 20 percent. The directive also established a formal link to the Kyoto process for the first time, but the EU system will still not allow the full range of credits that Kyoto does: nuclear power is excluded and hydropower projects are to be closely monitored. Reductions achieved through creation or expansion of carbon sinks are also excluded.
>
> *Source:* Adapted from Nobel and others (2005).

Promotion of New Technologies

A still more proactive form of public intervention is to conduct research into climate-friendly technologies or to subsidize such research by private sector or other organizations. Typically, the best division of this labor assigns basic research to the public sector, and more-applied research and development of actual products to the private sector. Again, this kind of subsidization internalizes an externality: the expected benefits of such research to society far exceed what the private firm conducting the research would realize in profits, especially when the risk of failure is taken into account. Therefore the firm would undertake less research than is socially optimal, were it not for the subsidy.

Possibly just as important as the research subsidy that midwifes the new technology is public support for its deployment in the market. The "buy-down" phase of product development, where production is ramped up to a scale that lowers unit costs to an affordable level, is critical yet often neglected. Much risk remains at this phase: incremental investment costs must be financed, projected costs may be underestimated, and expected demand may not materialize. Governments can reduce these risks and so bridge the gap by mandating certain performance standards, or by providing a market itself through its own acquisitions, for example, of hybrid or natural gas–powered or other fuel-efficient vehicles.

Finally, governments can promote the adoption of new technologies by disseminating information about their benefits and training people in their use. An example of the former is the Energy Star program in the United States, which, since 1992, has certified qualifying household appliances—and, more recently, homes and commercial buildings—as energy-efficient.

The Cost of Coping with Climate Change—and a Tentative Bottom Line

Estimates of the costs of dealing with climate change vary widely, reflecting differences in modeling methodologies and in the set of policies assumed to be adopted. IPCC has estimated that, with well-designed policies, fully half of the projected increase in carbon emissions between now and 2020 could be eliminated *at negative cost*—that is, the ancillary benefits of such action, wholly aside from the primary benefit in terms of reduced climate change, would more than defray the cost. (Some of the ancillary benefits were described above; they include the elimination of subsidies and other market and institutional inefficiencies; local and regional air quality improvements leading to improved health; and use of revenue from a carbon tax to reduce other, more distortionary taxes.) The other half could be eliminated at a cost of about $100 per ton of carbon.

IPCC has also estimated the costs to industrial countries of complying with the Kyoto Protocol: these range from 0.2 to 2.0 percent of GDP in the absence of international carbon permit trading, and from 0.1 to 1.0 percent of GDP if such trading is instituted. These costs could be reduced further by expanding the stock of carbon sinks through afforestation, reforestation, and avoiding deforestation, and through improved forest, cropland, and grassland management; by implementing project-based emissions swapping between industrial and developing countries through the Clean Development Mechanism (discussed below); and by reducing emissions of the other greenhouse gases, including methane and halocarbons.

The cost of stabilizing carbon dioxide concentrations steepens as one proceeds from less ambitious to more ambitious targets. For example, according to the Millenniun Ecosystem Assessment, the mitigation cost of keeping the concentration of carbon dioxide at or below 650 ppm is about $4 trillion (in present value using 1990 dollers) in the highest-cost model. Lowering the acceptable concentration from 650 ppm to 550 ppm. (These figures are net present values in 1990 dollars using a discount rate of 5 percent a year. They include neither the cost of adapting to the climate change that would occur, as discussed above, with a target carbon dioxide concentration of 450 ppm, nor the offsetting costs of economic damages avoided.)

Recall that the estimated global cost of the change in climate caused by a doubling of atmospheric carbon dioxide concentration (according to IPCC) ranged from 1.5 to 2.0 percent of world GDP (1.0 to 1.5 percent in developed countries and 2 to 9 percent in developing countries), and the group of experts led by Nordhaus reported a mean estimate of the economic costs of a 3°C warming by 2090 of about 3.6 percent of world GDP. Thus, unless the cost of mitigating climate change turns out to lie at or near the high end of the higher set of estimates (for a scenario that does not allow for international carbon emissions trading), *and* the cost of business as usual falls at or very near the low end of a very wide range of estimates, taking action to deal with climate change is very much a paying proposition. Despite the myriad uncertainties, the appropriate course of action seems clear.

What the International Community Is Doing Now

Serious global efforts to address climate change began with the Earth Summit (formally known as the United Nations Conference on Environment and Development) in Rio de Janeiro in 1992. That conference produced the United Nations Framework Convention on Climate Change (UNFCCC), a treaty aimed explicitly at limiting climate change by reducing emissions of greenhouse gases. The UNFCCC, however, did not establish mandatory emissions ceilings or enforcement provisions. Instead, it provided for the signing of protocols under the treaty's auspices that would contain such mandates. The Kyoto Protocol is by far the best known of these protocols.

The Kyoto Protocol

The Kyoto Protocol of the UNFCCC was negotiated at Kyoto, Japan, in late 1997 but did not enter into force until early 2005, after it had been ratified by the requisite number of countries. As of this writing, 163 countries have ratified the protocol; the only major countries still abstaining are Australia and the United States. The United States has so far declined to participate because, in its view, the costs of compliance are excessive, the exclusion of developing countries will render the undertaking ineffective, and the scientific uncertainties surrounding climate change remain too significant to warrant the actions taken.

Under the Kyoto Protocol, most of the world's developed countries agree to reduce their emissions of greenhouse gases by an average of about 5 percent from 1990 levels between 2008 and 2012; the negotiated emissions limits vary by country and range from a reduction of 8 percent to an increase not to exceed 10 percent. Developing countries are not subject to such firm commitments under the protocol. Core elements of the protocol include rules for compliance; land-use, land-use change, and forestry (LULUCF) provisions; and mechanisms aimed at giving countries greater flexibility in achieving the reductions to which they have committed.

The Kyoto Protocol recognizes that LULUCF activities, which essentially involve the development and preservation of carbon sinks, can play an important role in meeting the ultimate objective of stabilizing carbon dioxide concentrations. However, the rules of the protocol constrain the entry of LULUCF sequestration into the compliance system to only about 100 megatons of carbon a year. This falls far short of the 100 Gt that IPCC estimates to be technically feasible, but it is likely that not even the 100 megatons will be achieved during the first commitment period.

Several flexibility mechanisms are provided for under the protocol. The most straightforward of these simply allows one country in good standing under the agreement to sell emissions credits to another. Since emissions limits for some countries are set well above their actual emissions, there is considerable scope for such exchanges. As discussed above, this trading in emissions allowances rewards those countries that meet and exceed their commitment, while giving other countries a financial incentive to do the same.

The second mechanism, called Joint Implementation (JI), allows legal entities in one country that has an emissions commitment to earn credit toward that commitment by undertaking emissions reductions projects in another such country. Countries facing relatively high costs for emissions reductions can reduce their costs of compliance by earning such credits in countries where the costs are lower. The amount of emissions eliminated is the same as it would be without the exchange.

The third mechanism, called the Clean Development Mechanism (CDM), is important because it brings developing countries into the process. Under CDM, as under JI, developed countries may accrue emissions credits toward their reduction commitment by sponsoring projects in developing countries that reduce carbon emissions. Not only does this give the developed country an opportunity to meet its commitment at lower cost than otherwise, but it also promotes sustainable development in the developing country and encourages the transfer of technology. Under both JI and CDM, the emissions reductions undertaken must be additional to what would have occurred in their absence. Demonstrating this additionality is a major challenge in practice.

After 2012

Without a strong likelihood for a regulatory framework beyond 2012, the carbon emissions market will remain soft, and the private sector is unlikely to become involved in any significant way. Because of the recognition of common yet differentiated responsibilities in the UNFCCC, and because the industrialized countries are responsible for most of the anthropogenic greenhouse gases currently in the atmosphere, developing countries are not expected to bear the additional costs of a low-carbon economy. There are only three sources of funding for mitigating greenhouse gas emissions: voluntary action, international grants, and trade. Although all are potentially important, carbon trade is likely to confer the biggest flow of funds (between \$20 billion and \$120 billion a year). An efficient trading system will require a long-term, stable, and predictable framework and accompanying regulatory system, which could be based upon targets, policies, and other measures. Therefore, one question facing governments is whether to go ahead with a second commitment period (covering 2013–17), or to develop instead a long-term framework, with intermediate goals and targets, incorporating the principle of differentiated responsibilities.

The Role of the World Bank in Mitigation and Adaptation

The World Bank participates in global efforts to mitigate and adapt to climate change mainly through two initiatives: the Global Environment Facility and the Carbon Finance Portfolio.

The Global Environment Facility

The World Bank acts as an implementing agency for the Global Environment Facility (GEF), which was established in 1991 to provide grants for projects to support biodiversity, climate change, international waters, land degradation, the ozone layer, and persistent organic pollutants. Through GEF the Bank disburses about \$250 million a year for projects related to energy efficiency, renewable energy, and sustainable transportation. GEF has a small pilot portfolio on adaptation and has managed two special funds related to adaptation. Here the Bank's major role is in piloting projects that link adaptation to more general development finance, although at this stage annual disbursements amount to only a few million dollars a year. During the first commitment period of the Kyoto Protocol, the Adaptation Fund, based on a 2 percent levy on CDM credits, will significantly increase the resources available for adaptation—probably to hundreds of millions of dollars a year.

Carbon Finance Portfolio

The Bank was a pioneer in facilitating carbon trading under the CDM and JI flexibility mechanisms of the Kyoto Protocol. The Prototype Carbon Fund was launched in 1999 with a target of $180 million, and by 2006 the Bank was managing nine funds with available funds approaching $2 billion. Approximately 850 project proposals covering a wide range of energy sources, reductions of greenhouse gases other than carbon dioxide, and LULUCF activities have been reviewed by the technical specialists within the Carbon Finance Unit, and about 40 contracts for the delivery of carbon credits have already been signed.

The challenge for the Bank is to support the delivery of the energy needed for development at low cost and with equitable access. This energy has to be clean, both in terms of its impact on local and regional air quality and in terms of greenhouse gases emitted. The challenge is to mobilize all available sources of funding for these activities.

Whatever success is achieved in reducing greenhouse gas emissions, the impact of climate change will be felt. The Bank must play a leading role in mainstreaming climate risks into the development planning process so that the poorest and most vulnerable are not trapped in poverty through recurring climate-related losses.

Selected Readings and Cited References

Claussen, Eileen, and Lisa McNeilly. 1998. "Equity and Global Climate Change: The Complex Elements of Global Fairness." Pew Center on Global Climate Change, Arlington, VA. http://www.pewclimate.org/report2.html.

Cline, William R. 2004. "Meeting the Challenge of Global Warming." Paper prepared for the Copenhagen Consensus Program of the National Environmental Assessment Institute. http://www.copenhagenconsensus.com/files/filer/cc/papers/sammendrag/accepted_climate_change_300404.pdf.

Intergovernmental Panel on Climate Change. 2001. *Climate Change 2001: Synthesis Report,* edited by Robert T. Watson. Cambridge, United Kingdom: Cambridge University Press.

Lackner, Klaus S., and Jeffrey D. Sachs. 2005. "A Robust Strategy for Sustainable Energy." *Brookings Papers on Economic Activity* 2:2005, pp. 215–69.

Meyer, Aubrey. 2000. *Contraction and Convergence: The Global Solution to Climate Change.* Totnes, United Kingdom: Green Books.

Noble, Ian, and others. 2005. "Climate Change." In *Ecosystems and Human Well-Being. Policy Responses.* Washington, DC: Island Press.

Nordhaus, William D. 1994. "Expert Opinion on Climate Change." *American Scientist* 82: 45–51.

Pershing, Jonathan, and Fernando Tudela. 2003. "A Long-Term Target: Framing the Climate Effort." In *Beyond Kyoto: Advancing the International Effort Against Climate Change.* Pew Center Report, Pew Center on Global Climate Change, Washington, DC.

Smith, Joel B., Richard J. T. Klein, and Saleemul Huq. 2003. *Climate Change, Adaptive Capacity and Development.* London: Imperial College Press.

Victor, David G. 2001. *The Collapse of the Kyoto Protocol and the Struggle to Slow Global Warming.* Princeton, NJ: Princeton University Press.

Watson, Robert T. 2006. "Climate Change: Current State of Scientific Understanding." PowerPoint presentation. http://siteresources.worldbank.org/EXTABOUTUS/resources/ClimateChange.ppt.

Watson, Robert T., and Ian R. Noble. 2004. *The Global Imperative and Policy for Carbon Sequestration: The Carbon Balance of Forest Biomes.* London: Garland Science/BIOS Scientific Publishers.

Selected Web Links on Climate Change

Carbon Finance Portfolio (World Bank)	http://carbonfinance.org
Earth Institute at Columbia University	http://www.earthinstitute.columbia.edu
Global Environment Facility	http://www.gefweb.org
Intergovernmental Panel on Climate Change	http://www.ipcc.ch
Millennium Ecosystem Assessment	http://www.millenniumassessment.org
United Nations Environment Programme	http://www.unep.org

13

Toward a Sustainable Energy Future

JAMAL SAGHIR AND KYRAN O'SULLIVAN

The global community today is working toward a potential *double divi-dend*: meeting the essential needs of economic growth and fighting poverty, while at the same time leaving a smaller environmental footprint. Strategies to support clean energy and a low-carbon economy are vital to fulfilling this promise.

Affordable and reliable energy services matter today more than ever in the fight against poverty. Most economic activity, even the village and household enterprises in developing countries that are the main source of income for the poor in those countries, would be impossible without energy. The services that hydrocarbons and electricity provide—motive power for industry and agriculture, transportation of people and goods, heating and cooling of workplaces, power for appliances—increase productivity and economic output. Thus economic growth that creates jobs and raises incomes depends on greater access to and more efficient use of energy services and their constituent energy resources. Figure 13.1 illustrates the strong correlation between commercial energy consumption and national income: countries with higher income per capita also tend to be those with higher energy consumption per capita.

Figure 13.2 shows a similarly strong correlation across countries between commercial energy consumption and the Human Development Index (HDI). This standard measure, reported annually by the United Nations (UN) Development Programme, is derived from indicators that reflect countries' progress in providing the most basic human needs: a long and healthy life (life expectancy), possession of knowledge (literacy and educational achievement),

This chapter draws on earlier publications, which are included in the selected readings at the end of this chapter.

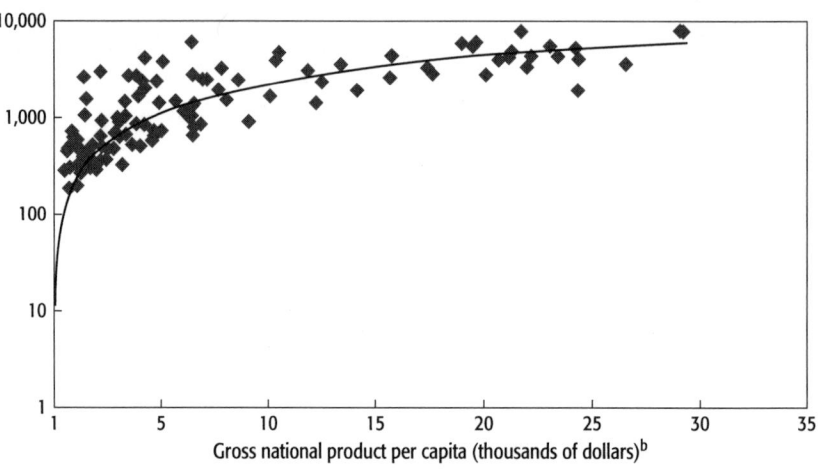

FIGURE 13.1 Energy Consumption and Economic Growth
Kilograms of oil-equivalent per capita[a]

Source: World Bank, World Development Indicators database.
a. Energy is commercially supplied energy only. Each symbol represents one country. Logarithmic scale is used.
b. Adjusted for international differences in the purchasing power of a dollar.

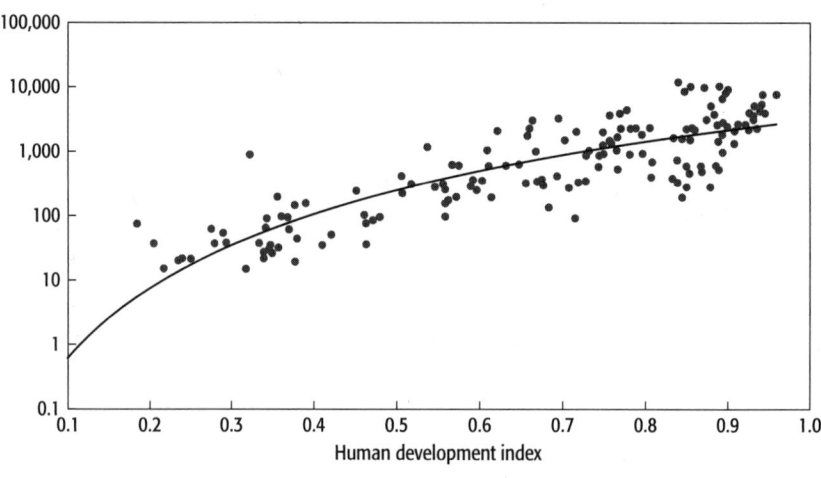

FIGURE 13.2 Energy Consumption and Human Development
Kilograms of oil-equivalent per capita[a]

Source: UN Development Programme and World Bank Energy Sector Management Assistance Programme 2005.
a. Energy is commercially supplied energy only. Each symbol represents one country. Logarithmic scale is used.

and a decent standard of living (income, measured in dollars adjusted for international differences in purchasing power).

Yet the reality today in many of the world's least developed countries is that the poor often cannot afford to purchase sufficient fuel and electricity to meet their basic cooking and lighting needs, and energy services are often only intermittently available to industry and social services. This lack of reliable energy services constrains the delivery of social services and imposes a huge cost on industry and commercial firms, undermining their competitiveness and therefore their ability to expand and provide employment. The poor performance of the energy sector in many countries is evidenced by poor resource utilization, low asset yields, and commercial and technical inefficiency, leading to much energy being wasted, as well as financial losses.

The good news is that much can be done at the national and local levels of government to promote the development of sustainable energy. Governments can remove institutional and regulatory barriers that prevent energy companies from delivering modern fuels and electricity to firms and households. They can also help mobilize financial resources for investments in energy infrastructure and services. At the same time, they can and should regulate the environmental performance of energy production and use. Legislators and other policy makers can take the lead in linking energy planning to national plans for economic and social development and can play a critical role in sustaining political commitment to sound energy sector management and governance.

However, action at the national and lower levels alone is not enough to ensure sustainable energy development. There are also global aspects to the challenge, and these will require international consensus building, coordination, and action. This chapter provides a brief introduction to these aspects from a number of points of view:

- Energy security
- Energy and poverty reduction
- Energy and the environment
- Investment for energy development
- Development and deployment of clean-energy technology
- International trade in energy.

Energy Security

For developed and developing countries alike, energy security means a reliable and affordable supply of energy that makes further economic development possible and supports a high and growing quality of life. For the international community, including the World Bank, energy security means ensuring that countries can sustainably produce and use energy at reasonable cost in order to facilitate economic growth (and, through this, poverty reduction) and directly improve the quality of peoples' lives by broadening access to modern energy services.

Today, world energy demand is growing rapidly. The latest forecast of the International Energy Agency (IEA) shows global energy demand, under current policies, increasing by more than 60 percent from 2004 to 2030 (although vigorous new policies to reduce energy use could reduce this figure sharply). IEA concludes that the world's primary energy resources are adequate to meet this projected increase in demand: proven reserves of gas, oil, and coal far exceed cumulative projected consumption, and more reserves will be added during the projection period. But developing these resources and ensuring that demand is met will require a huge amount of investment at every point in the energy supply chain. If that investment is not forthcoming or is delayed, shortages, price increases, and price volatility may impede economic growth in both developed and developing countries.

IEA's projections imply increasing interdependence between energy-producing and energy-consuming countries, because a pronounced shift in the geographical sources of incremental oil and natural gas supplies will occur over the next several decades, and because growth in energy demand will be increasingly concentrated in developing countries. International trade in primary energy will have to expand to accommodate the growing mismatch between the location of demand and that of production. As energy markets become increasingly global, integrated, and interdependent, an enhanced policy dialogue between the governments of importing and exporting countries will be essential in addressing long-term energy security risks. All countries—energy producers and consumers, rich and poor—have a vital common interest in ensuring a sustainable supply of the energy needed for a growing global economy.

The attention of the international community toward the issue of energy security has been greatly heightened by the increase in oil prices to record levels in nominal terms since 2002 (figure 13.3). This poses a risk to all countries, but especially the poorer oil-importing countries, which are the least able to cope. The direct effect on an economy is felt through the worsening of the balance of payments and the subsequent contraction of the economy required to restore balance-of-payments equilibrium. The impact of the shock is proportional to the percentage rise in oil prices times the ratio of net imports of oil and oil products to gross domestic product (GDP).[1] The increase in the oil bill has been particularly severe for a number of countries that combine high energy intensity

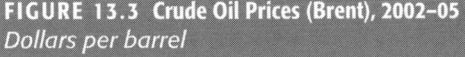

FIGURE 13.3 Crude Oil Prices (Brent), 2002–05
Dollars per barrel

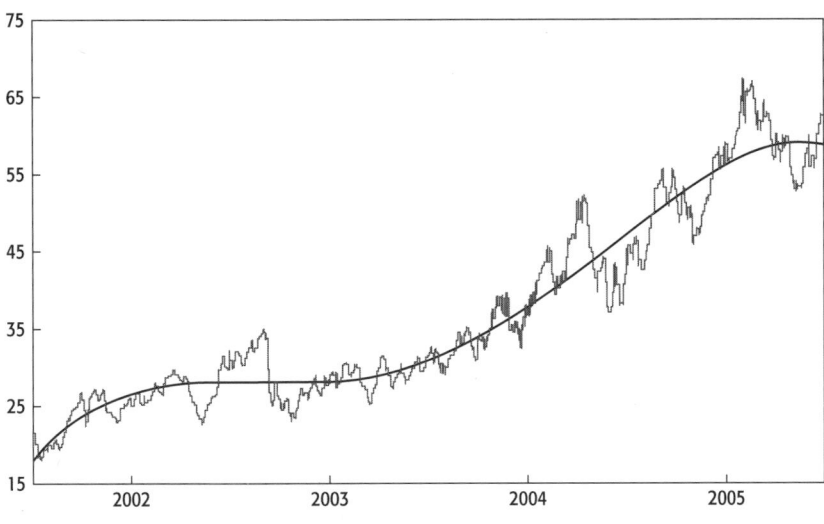

Source: Platts.

(that is, high consumption of energy per unit of GDP produced) with a heavy reliance on imported oil. For these countries, even the relatively modest hike in oil prices between 2003 and 2004 implied an increase in their oil bills of between 1.5 and 5 percent of GDP. A sustained price increase of $10 per barrel would deliver an economic shock equivalent to a 1.5 percent loss of GDP, on average, for the world's poorest countries (those with GDP per capita of less than $300). With a sustained price increase of $20 a barrel relative to 2003, the GDP loss for these countries would be 3 percent. The lowest-income countries experience the largest proportionate loss of GDP, as they are the most dependent on oil imports. Countries have limited options for dealing with high oil prices, especially in the short run. Policies that reduce dependence on oil as a primary fuel and that reduce energy intensity take time to have an effect, but in the long run they can reduce the vulnerability of the economy to oil price shocks.

Energy and Poverty Reduction

Improved energy services will be critical for strategies aimed at achieving the Millennium Development Goals (MDGs). Worldwide, nearly 2.4 billion people use traditional biomass fuels—wood, agricultural residues, and dung—for cooking and heating, and nearly 1.6 billion lack access to electricity. Four out of five people without access to electricity live in rural areas. The average resident of a poor country consumes only 5 percent of the modern energy services (fossil fuels, electricity, and renewables) that his or her counterparts in the developed countries consume. Modern energy services provide lighting, cooking, heating, refrigeration, transportation, motive power, and telecommunications that are indispensable to increasing productivity, creating enterprises, raising employment and incomes, and providing safe water and sanitation as well as health and education services. Without access to these services, the poor are deprived of opportunities for economic development and improved living standards.

Low-income households are affected most by increases in world oil prices. Households experience the effect of high oil prices directly when they purchase petroleum products (such as kerosene, liquefied petroleum gas, and gasoline) and indirectly when they purchase other goods or services, including transport and water services, whose costs are raised by higher oil prices. Higher oil prices reduce the expenditure of households at all income levels in oil-importing countries, and the poorest may have to cut their spending the most. (Box 13.1 reports some dismaying statistics that illustrate the scale of energy deprivation currently faced by the world's poor.)

Policy makers have many options for improving the focus of current energy policies on poverty reduction. Among the more important options to consider are the following:

- *Designing scaled-up programs for energy access.* Scaling up implies the need for programs that will achieve ambitious rates of access within 10 to 15 years. Three types of access usually need to be addressed: access to cleaner cooking systems, access to electricity, and access to mechanical power. With respect to the first of these, the goal is to increase the use of modern cooking fuels, as well as the adoption of improved cook stoves and an increase in sustainable biomass production. Increasing access to mechanical power plays a critical role in meeting the MDGs though agroprocessing and water pumping. Mechanical agroprocessing increases food production and reduces the labor that women must devote to producing food. Water pumping improves health and nutrition and enables irrigation.
- *Maximizing the development impact of electricity scale-up programs.* Here the implication is that implementation should be driven by considerations of poverty reduction, including the enhancement of productive enterprises and income generation and delivery of health

---

BOX 13.1 Energy and the Poor: A Fact Sheet

- Some 1.6 billion people worldwide lack access to network electricity. In the absence of vigorous new policies, 1.4 billion people will still lack electricity access in 2030—only 200 million fewer than today.

- Four out of five people without electricity live in rural areas of the developing world, mainly in South Asia and Sub-Saharan Africa.

- Some 2.4 billion people rely on traditional biomass—wood, agricultural residues, and dung—for cooking and heating. This will increase to 2.6 billion by 2030 with no change in policies.

- Poor people in developing countries spend up to a quarter of their cash income on energy.

- In 2004, the richest 20 percent of the world's population consumed 58 percent of total energy usage, whereas the poorest 20 percent consumed less than 4 percent.

- The world's 1 billion poorest people use only 0.2 ton of oil-equivalent energy per capita annually, whereas the 1 billion richest—those earning on average over $20,000 a year—use nearly 25 times as much.

- High transaction costs and high unit costs of investment constrain electricity service provision in poor rural areas because of low demand and dispersed populations. The cost of connections can range from $400 to $1,000 for households who may only consume $4 worth of electricity a month.

- Indoor air pollution from solid fuel use is responsible for 1.5 million deaths a year worldwide. These deaths occur disproportionately among women and children.

- Low-grade fuels and poor environmental controls in transport and industry are a leading cause of severe urban air pollution in the fast-growing cities of developing countries. More than 80 percent of all deaths in developing countries attributable to air pollution–induced lung infections are among children under five.

and education. Scaling up also implies implementing the electrification of homes and institutions as quickly as possible, for the largest number of people feasible, while balancing affordability to end users with that to the government in terms of the capital subsidies required. Large gains in electrification rates among households and among health, education, and other public institutions are feasible through grid extension. Many of those unserved today live in urban or periurban areas within reach of the grid and can be connected through phased programs of grid extension. In other areas, where grid extension is not cost-effective, independent small grids and solar photovoltaic systems will be necessary for remote institutions and households that can afford such systems. Modern lighting systems for basic needs can be marketed to very poor households. For example, LED (light-emitting diode) lamps manufactured locally and sold by local private operators can provide good-quality lighting at a lower operating cost than kerosene lamps.

- *Ensuring that service providers are capable of delivering ambitious electrification targets.* Successful implementation requires that service providers, including incumbent national utilities, be fully capable of undertaking the necessary planning and execution functions and that they exercise commercial discipline in their operations. Scaling up electricity access implies an expansion in electric power generation. In Sub-Saharan Africa and elsewhere, economies of scale can be achieved by developing large generation and transmission projects that will serve regional needs; small *island* systems are prone to high costs as well as to heightened risk of service interruption.

- *Establishing effective regulatory frameworks and policies for rural and off-grid areas for various types of providers of energy services.* Sound regulatory frameworks would stimulate local community participation, remove barriers and develop the roles of local entrepreneurs in providing energy services under new business models, and mobilize women's groups to find locally tailored solutions for meeting energy needs.

- *Focusing subsidies on the public good component of energy services.* The transfer mechanisms used should be targeted to the poor, predictable, transparent, and fully funded. The prices charged for energy supply and services—supported by appropriate regulatory and tax policies—should remove market distortions that favor highly polluting forms of energy, by taking both the economic and the environmental costs and benefits into account. Many governments subsidize petroleum products, holding prices to consumers below international prices. When such subsidy schemes remain in place for a long time, the drain on the public finances can become very large, to the point where it limits spending on desirable social programs. In addition, such subsidies distort the economy: low prices provide little incentive for efforts to increase energy efficiency and substitute for oil. Removing subsidies on oil products has proved politically difficult in many countries, especially when oil prices are rising rapidly. It is easiest to reduce subsidies when international oil prices are falling, by reducing the domestic price by less than the reduction in the international price until the two prices are at parity.

Country-specific energy strategies to help achieve the MDGs will be vital. It will also be important to work *upstream,* for example, by supporting evaluations of energy-poverty linkages in country poverty assessments, so that long-term national poverty reduction strategies incorporate energy strategies and plans. In this regard, actions in the energy sector should be linked with complementary activities in other areas such as agriculture, health, education, finance, enterprise development, and institution building.

International support for energy programs, both through bilateral development assistance and from the international financial institutions, will continue to be critical. Often this support will be best applied when it leverages the complementary roles of public and private investments (both local and international) and when it draws on the comparative strengths of different stakeholders to manage different risks through public-private partnerships. Such partnerships make possible a coordinated effort to expand energy services to the poor. Mobilizing and coordinating long-term commitments from development partners to scale up energy investments, transfer knowledge, and deploy financing instruments for leveraging private capital and resources will be key, particularly for countries with the largest concentration of the energy-poor, such as those in Sub-Saharan Africa and South Asia.

Energy and the Environment

The links between energy and the environment are many and profound, and the environmental impacts of energy use are felt both locally, from indoor pollution from cooking fires to urban air pollution, and globally, through emissions of greenhouse gases by power plants, factories, and automobiles.

Climate Change

Climate change presents an urgent challenge. The Earth's climate is already changing because of human activities, primarily the combustion of fossil fuels, deforestation, and other land management practices, and it is projected to continue to change in the coming decades (see chapter 12). The Earth has already warmed by about 0.6°C over the past 100 years, and it is projected to warm by as much as another 5.8°C during the next 100 years in the absence of effective, internationally agreed-upon policies to address climate change.

For governments today, climate change poses one of the greatest challenges of the new millennium, namely, how to achieve and sustain economic growth, with its promise of prosperity for all, while reducing the threat of climate change to human health and ecological systems. In fact, the two are linked: sustaining global prosperity becomes increasingly difficult with a global climate that continues to become warmer and more unstable. But economies cannot grow without increasing energy consumption, and, today, energy production is primarily dependent on the carbon-emitting fuels that result in global warming. How these energy and environmental challenges are addressed in the next two decades will, to a large degree, determine whether future generations enjoy sustainable growth, environmental quality, and national security.

Developing countries and the poor people who live in them are the most vulnerable to climate change. Warmer temperatures, more-variable precipitation, and an increased incidence of extreme climatic events will become more common and, when coupled with rising sea levels, will threaten agriculture, water resources, human settlements, human health, and ecological systems, undermining economic development and the achievement of many of the MDGs. Dealing with climate change will require the development and implementation of climate-friendly technologies.

Air Pollution and Its Impacts

Most of the industrialized countries have managed to clean the once heavily polluted air in their cities, despite continued high energy use per capita. In many developing countries, however, local air pollution from energy use remains a major environmental and public health hazard. Exposure to smoke and soot has been estimated to cause as many as 4 million premature deaths each year, as well as 40 million new cases of chronic bronchitis and widespread cases of other respiratory illnesses. Small particulates (airborne particles less than 10 microns in diameter) from fuel combustion are particularly dangerous and are a leading cause of cardiovascular disease, chronic bronchitis, and upper and lower respiratory tract infections.

Lead exposure is another widespread public health hazard in regions that still use leaded fuels. Lead is a treacherous poison: at lower levels of exposure, no obvious symptoms may occur, but children exposed to lead become less able to learn, putting them at a lifelong disadvantage.

In addition to its effects on human health, air pollution from energy use damages ecological systems. Emissions of sulfur dioxide and nitrous oxide react with other chemicals in the atmosphere to form sulfuric acid and nitric acid, which fall back to earth in rainfall. This acid rain has been found to damage crops, forests, rivers, and lakes, sometimes thousands of kilometers from the original source.

The first step in addressing local pollution is to identify and implement those solutions that provide environmental benefits at no additional cost. These win-win opportunities include improvements in energy efficiency at the user level and a switch from highly polluting to less polluting energy fuels. Energy sector reform that introduces competition between alternative energy forms and between suppliers, and that allows market prices to send the right signals to producers and consumers alike, will promote the shift from polluting to clean energy use.

Reducing local air pollution beyond what can be achieved through these win-win strategies, however, comes at an additional cost. Even so, the financial cost of abatement (for example, to meet improved emission standards in power generation) is usually small compared with the value of the health and environmental damage thereby avoided. It is therefore important for policy makers to take account of these external effects.

There is considerable scope for international action on air pollution issues. The phasing out of lead additives from gasoline is an example: regionwide harmonization of fuel specifications and fuel pricing can help eliminate fuel smuggling and fuel adulteration. Regional agreement on the timetable for revised fuel specifications permits suppliers to make informed investment decisions about the refinery reconfiguration that will be necessary to supply fuels with the new specifications.

Energy Sector Investment

Converting the world's resources into available supplies on a scale that meets projected demand will require massive investment. IEA estimates that total capital investment of $8.1 trillion, equivalent to an average of $300 billion a year (in 2005 dollars), is needed from 2003 to 2030 to meet the energy needs of the world's developing and transition economies. Of this investment, roughly 73 percent will be for electricity, 12 percent for oil, 12 percent for natural gas, and 3 percent for coal. Financing will come from three sources: internal cash generation, private financing, and public funding. Developing countries will face great challenges in raising these funds from domestic and international capital markets (public funding is limited and usually cannot be diverted from priority social spending), because their needs are larger relative to the present size of their economies and because the investment risks are bigger. The extent to which the huge investment gap, especially in the electricity sector, can be funded in the future will depend on the pace of policy and regulatory reform, including the measures needed to attract private sector investment in these countries.

Although many of the barriers to increased investment in developing countries relate to their overall investment climate, others are specific to the sector. A survey of international investors revealed that the most significant barriers to investment in the electric power industry in developing countries are weak legal protection for investors, absence of multilateral guarantees, and weak payment discipline on the part of consumers.[2] The study pointed to several priorities for governments seeking to attract and retain international (and domestic) investment in the industry:

- *Ensure adequate cash flow.* Among the highest priorities identified by investors were the need to set prices adequate to cover costs and the need for discipline in payment collection. Investors are unlikely to consider a proposed investment if these conditions are not present.
- *Maintain the stability and enforceability of laws and contracts.* A clear and enforceable legal framework is always important to investors. The rules of the game should not be altered at the government's convenience once investment decisions have been made on the basis of those rules. A government's willingness and ability to honor its commitments are key.
- *Be more responsive to the needs of investors.* Investors identified government unresponsiveness to their needs and time frames as the most important factor in the failure of investments. They considered the administrative efficiency of the host government one of the top criteria in deciding whether to invest in a country. Better preparation of the proposed transaction before inviting investors to participate can help reduce processing delays and investors' opportunity costs.
- *Minimize government interference.* Investors are most satisfied with their investment experience when they are free to realize returns from their investments without government interference. Investors pointed to their ability to exercise effective operational and management control of their investments as a key factor in successful operations. Investors also give much weight to the independence of regulatory processes from government interference.

Energy Technology Development and Deployment

Achieving a truly sustainable global energy system will require technological breakthroughs that will radically alter how energy is produced and used. Which new technologies and which new forms of energy will transform today's energy systems remains uncertain. Absent some immediate and unforeseen technological breakthrough, fossil fuels are expected to remain the backbone of primary energy supply for the next several decades. This underscores the need for high-performance technologies that permit the continued use of existing fossil fuels together with abatement of the resulting greenhouse gas emissions, particularly in electric power generation. Government action can promote faster deployment of the enhanced energy technologies that are available today. The resulting gain in market share will, in turn, make these technologies still more cost effective.

An extensive array of technologies and practices in both energy supply and end use are already available to enhance access to energy; improve energy security; and promote environmental protection at the local, regional, and global levels. No single energy production or end-use technology promises to alter the energy development path of any country. Instead, a broad portfolio of technologies, supported by appropriate policies, will be required to address the challenge of reducing the emissions that cause local and regional air pollution.

These technologies are also required for the transition to a low-carbon economy. The same technologies employed to reduce greenhouse gas emissions normally reduce the emissions of local and regional pollutants as well. A clean-energy, low-carbon economy can be realized through a balanced portfolio of energy production and distribution technologies. On the supply side, the technologies needed include new thermal power plants based on combined-cycle and supercritical boilers; natural gas as a bridging fuel in the transition period until renewable energy technologies become commercially viable; new renewable energy technologies (solar, wind, small and large hydropower, biomass and biofuels, and geothermal sources); and improved nuclear fission technologies. Energy supply technologies are complemented by end-use efficiency technologies in the transportation sector (including efficient gasoline and diesel engines), the buildings sector (insulation, advanced windows, new lighting technology, and efficient space cooling and heating), the industrial sector (cogeneration, waste heat recovery, preheating, new efficient process technologies, efficient motors and drives, and improved control systems), and the agricultural sector (efficient irrigation pumps), as well as in municipal and urban systems (district heating systems and combined heat and power).

Renewable forms of energy today still satisfy only about 3 percent of the world's primary energy demand. Hydropower is the largest renewable source; *new* renewables, such as solar and wind power, each account for only a small fraction of global energy demand. Several European governments currently favor using renewables to reduce carbon dioxide emissions, and they have set national targets for increasing their use. Several developing countries, such as China and Brazil, also have programs to promote renewables. Renewables are, on average, more expensive per unit of energy than fossil fuels in supplying large, grid-connected power systems, but as their deployment becomes more widespread, their unit costs will fall. Therefore new government policies that push for faster deployment of renewables will be important if renewables are to meet a much larger share of world demand than the 4 percent currently forecast by 2030.[3] Several renewable energy technologies are potentially lowest-cost options for mini-grid applications (village- and district-level networks with loads between 5 and 500 kilowatts that are not connected to a national grid).

Energy Trade

Like trade generally, trade in energy can be mutually beneficial to both suppliers and customers. In various regions of the world, neighboring countries are seeking to develop their energy trade for a number of reasons:

- *Energy trade can advance regional economic integration.* Regional trade in electric power helps build institutions and relationships that, as part of a wider network of institutions, can help integrate a region economically and politically. Joint development of energy projects can help build closer ties between countries through closer collaboration and increased economic interdependence.
- *Trade can underpin energy security.* Trade can increase the reliability of energy supply by making one country's lower-cost supplies available to other countries. Also, cross-border energy supply often contributes to the diversification of energy sources—a key component of energy security. Stable long-term agreements between countries are necessary for such trade to flourish, however.
- *Trade can exploit economies of scale.* Many national markets, especially in Africa, are too small to justify the investment needed to develop the energy supply opportunities available to them. Merging national markets can provide the needed economies of scale in such cases. As markets mature and competition is introduced, the integration of small neighboring markets can provide the scale necessary for competition to be effective.

The interconnection of contiguous electric power networks can capture significant economies of scale. The price of electric power generation in grid-based systems can vary enormously from one country to another, depending on the availability of hydroelectric resources, the cost of fuel, and many other factors. Interconnecting transmission networks and integrating power system operations can thus bring significant benefits. In a regionally integrated power system, the direct benefits accruing to each national power sector include reduced operating costs, increased efficiency, lower energy costs, and increased system reliability. Operating costs are lower in an interconnected network because they allow development of the least-cost regional energy resources. Also, by aggregating the demand of contiguous national systems, regional integration creates sufficient demand to justify large investments that would not have been economically feasible at the national level.

International Organizations Active in Promoting Sustainable Energy

A number of international organizations have initiated programs and activities aimed at ensuring sustainable energy. This section discusses a few of the more prominent.

Food and Agriculture Organization

The work of the Food and Agriculture Organization (FAO) in the energy sector focuses on bioenergy, agro-energy, wood energy, and climate change. Providing multiple energy services for cooking and heating as well as power for electricity, industry and transportation, and bioenergy can contribute significantly to increased labor productivity and diversification of economic activities in rural areas. FAO works to ensure the delivery of sustainable, equitable, and accessible bioenergy sources and services irrespective of gender, wealth, location, or culture, for sustainable development, energy security, and climate change mitigation.

International Atomic Energy Agency

The mandate of the International Atomic Energy Agency (IAEA) is to build national capabilities in overall energy planning and, in particular, nuclear power for peaceful purposes. IAEA's Major Programme 1 on Nuclear Power, Fuel Cycle, and Nuclear Science provides three major services: support of power programs for additional uses of power reactors, catalyzing of innovation, and energy analysis and building of planning capabilities.

International Energy Agency

IEA is an intergovernmental body committed to advancing the security of energy supply, economic growth, and environmental sustainability through cooperation on energy policy. IEA acts as energy policy adviser for its

26 member countries in their efforts to ensure reliable, affordable, and clean energy for their citizens. Founded during the oil crisis of 1973–74, IEA had as its initial role the coordination of national measures in times of oil supply emergencies. But in recent decades, as energy markets have changed, so has IEA. Its purview now extends well beyond oil crisis management to broader energy issues, including climate change policies, market reform, collaboration on energy technology, and outreach to the rest of the world.

United Nations Development Programme

The efforts of the UN Development Programme (UNDP) in energy are focused on supporting the achievement of the MDGs, especially the goal of halving, by 2015, the proportion of people living in poverty. Increasing access to sustainable energy services is one of six priority areas in UNDP's energy and environment practice and one of 30 service lines in its development support worldwide. In support of energy-related work, UNDP aims to strengthen national policy frameworks to support energy for poverty reduction and sustainable development; increase access to energy services to support growth and equity; promote clean energy technologies for sustainable development; and augment access to investment financing for sustainable energy.

United Nations Environment Programme

The energy program of the UN Environment Programme (UNEP) focuses on building human and economic capacity—the technical skills, institutions, and markets to create sustainable development that avoids the huge environmental burdens of past development. Underpinning all UNEP energy activities is the integration of environmental and social factors into energy-related decisions, bringing a longer-term, more comprehensive approach to the sector.

United Nations Framework Convention for Climate Change

The Climate Change Secretariat in Bonn, Germany, is the secretariat to both the United Nations Framework Convention on Climate Change (UNFCCC) and the Kyoto Protocol. A total of 189 parties have ratified the UNFCCC, and 161 parties have ratified the protocol. The UNFCCC entered into force in 1994 and the protocol in 2005. The ultimate objective of both the UNFCCC and the protocol is the stabilization of greenhouse gas concentrations in the atmosphere at a level that would prevent dangerous anthropogenic interference with the climate system. That level should be achieved within a timeframe sufficient to allow ecosystems to adapt naturally to climate change, ensure that food production is not threatened, and enable economic development to proceed in a sustainable manner.

World Energy Council

The work of the World Energy Council (WEC) spans the entire energy spectrum—coal, oil, natural gas, nuclear, hydropower, and new renewables—and focuses on market restructuring; energy efficiency; energy and the environment; financing of energy systems; energy pricing and subsidies; energy poverty; ethics; benchmarking and standards; use of new technologies; and energy issues in developed, transitional, and developing countries. Every three years, WEC holds a World Energy Congress, which features a major energy exhibition, keynote addresses, roundtables, and technical presentations by energy experts.

World Health Organization

The World Health Organization (WHO) provides information on the many linkages between climate variability and health and reviews the threats to health posed by human-induced climate change. WHO provides regular updates on the linkages between household energy, indoor air pollution, and health, and it implements projects and programs to tackle this preventable disease burden and evaluates the impacts of technical solutions on health, socioeconomic conditions, and the environment.

United Nations Department of Economic and Social Affairs

The Department of Economic and Social Affairs of the United Nations Secretariat works in three main interconnected areas:

- To compile, generate, and analyze a wide range of economic, social, and environmental data and information upon which member states of the United Nations can draw to review common problems and take stock of policy options
- To facilitate the negotiations of member states in many intergovernmental bodies on joint courses of action to address ongoing or emerging global challenges
- To advise on ways and means of translating policy frameworks developed in UN conferences and summits into programs at the country level and, through technical assistance, help build national capacities.

The World Bank Group and Sustainable Energy Development

The World Bank Group supports government efforts at sustainable energy development in developing countries through financing, advice, and knowledge transfer (box 13.2). The International Finance Corporation issues loans

---

BOX 13.2 Selected World Bank Group Energy Projects in 2005

- In China, the Renewable Energy Scale-up Project supports that country's commitment to increase the share of renewable energy in electric power generation to 15 percent by 2020, compared with 7 percent in 2005.

- In the Lao People's Democratic Republic, the Nam Theun 2 Project will enable the country to export electricity to Thailand. The resulting income can be spent on improving living standards.

- In Nigeria, the National Energy Development Project supports the government's energy sector reform and facilitates the transition of the energy sector to the new market and institutional structure. Investments will be made to upgrade and improve the power transmission system and to reduce losses and improve the reliability of electricity service as well as customer service. The project will increase access to electricity in rural areas and will promote the use of renewable energy.

- In Bulgaria, the Energy Efficiency Project supports a large increase in energy-efficiency-promoting investments through the development of self-sustaining, market-based financing mechanisms. The project has a credit enhancement facility to mitigate investment risk, supports a Bulgaria Energy Efficiency Fund, and provides capacity building and information dissemination services.

- In Peru, the Community Development Carbon Facility supports the 4.1-megawatt Santa Rosa Hydro Project, the first small-scale clean-development mechanism project in the country. The Peru Rural Electrification project will make investments to supply electricity services to about 160,000 currently unserved rural households, businesses, and public facilities (such as schools and health clinics that serve about 800,000 people), using both conventional grid extension and renewable energy sources.

---

and equity, and the Multilateral Investment Guarantee Agency issues guarantees, to support private investment in energy. The International Bank for Reconstruction and Development (IBRD) and the International Development Association (IDA) can issue partial risk guarantees, with sovereign counterguarantees, to support such investment, particularly where the key risk of a project relates to concerns about government performance or policy reversal. Similarly, IBRD or IDA partial credit guarantees with sovereign counterguarantees can help catalyze long-term private financing for projects that improve public services. IBRD loans and IDA credits to countries with sovereign guarantees can also be used when private financing cannot be catalyzed.

The World Bank Group works with member countries and multiple other partners on urgent energy development issues, including increasing access to clean fuels and electricity, securing reliable energy supply that underpins economic growth, catalyzing investments in the sector, reducing the sector's demand on public finances, and improving governance in the sector. In the context of the Group of Eight's Gleneagles Communiqué on Climate Change, Clean Energy and Sustainable Development of July 2005, the World Bank Group is preparing an investment framework for clean energy and development, which will complement ongoing Bank activities in energy sector reform, energy investment, implementation of projects of the Global Environment Fund, development of carbon markets, and development and application of methodologies to address climate variability and change. The Development Committee of the World Bank and the International Monetary Fund, which facilitates intergovernmental consensus building on development issues, endorsed the approach in an April 2006 communiqué and noted that the goal of securing affordable and cost-effective energy supplies to underpin economic growth and poverty reduction need not conflict with the goal of preserving the environment. The Development Committee called on the Bank to review its existing financial instruments and to explore the potential value of new financial instruments to accelerate investment in clean, sustainable, cost-effective, and efficient energy.

Notes

1. Bacon (2005).
2. Lamech and Saeed (2003).
3. International Energy Agency (2004).

Selected Readings and Cited References

Bacon, Robert. 2005. "The Impact of Higher Oil Prices on Low Income Countries and the Poor: Impacts and Policies." Energy Sector Management Assistance Program Knowledge Exchange Series 1, World Bank, Washington, DC.

Deloitte Touche Tohmatsu. 2004. "Sustainable Power Sector Reform in Emerging Markets—Financial Issues and Options." Joint World Bank/U.S. Agency for International Development Policy Paper. Washington, DC.

Her Majesty's Treasury. 2006. "Stern Review on the Economics of Climate Change." London.

International Energy Agency. 2004. *World Energy Outlook 2004*. Paris.

———. 2005. *Mobilising Energy Technology*. Paris.

Lamech, Ranjit, and Kazim Saeed. 2003. "What International Investors Look for When Investing in Developing Countries. Results from a Survey of International Investors in the Power Sector." Discussion Paper 6, World Bank, Washington, DC.

Saghir, Jamal. 2005. "Energy and Poverty: Myths, Links, and Policy Issues." Energy Working Note 4, World Bank, Washington, DC.

Toyo Engineering Corporation and others. 2005. "Technical and Economic Assessment: Off Grid, Mini-Grid and Grid Electrification Technologies." Discussion Paper, Energy Unit, Energy and Water Department, World Bank, Washington, DC.

United Nations. 2005. "The Energy Challenge for Achieving the Millennium Development Goals." New York.

United Nations Development Programme and World Bank Energy Sector Management Assistance Program. 2005. "The Impact of Higher Oil Prices on Low Income Countries and on the Poor." Energy Sector Management Assistance Program and World Bank, Washington, DC.

United Nations Millennium Project, United Nations Development Programme, World Bank, and Energy Sector Management Assistance Program. 2006. "Energy Services for the Millennium Development Goals." New York.

World Bank. 2000. "Fuel for Thought: An Environmental Strategy for the Energy Sector." Washington, DC.

————. 2006. "Clean Energy and Development: Towards an Investment Framework." Washington, DC.

Selected Web Links on Sustainable Energy

International Atomic Energy Agency	http://www.iaea.org
International Energy Agency	http://www.iea.org
UN Department of Economic and Social Affairs	http://www.un.org/esa/desa
UN Development Programme page on energy and environment	http://www.undp.org/energyandenvironment
UN Environment Programme page on sustainable energy	http://www.unep.org/themes/energy
UN Framework Convention on Climate Change	http://www.unfccc.int
World Bank energy page	http://www.worldbank.org/energy
World Health Organization	http://www.who.int

14

Calming Global Waters: Managing a Finite Resource in a Growing World

CLAUDIA SADOFF, KARIN KEMPER, AND DAVID GREY

Water is unique in many ways, from the vast range of its uses to its profound symbolic significance in many cultures. It is a source of great productive opportunities in agriculture, industry, energy, and transport, and it is vital for the health of both people and ecosystems. However, water is also a source of tremendous risk and vulnerability, both through its potential for catastrophe from drought, flood, landslide, and epidemic, as well as more insidiously through erosion, inundation, desertification, contamination, and disease. Because of its enormous power for both good and ill, water must be responsibly managed, to fully capture the opportunities while limiting the risks.

In today's the opportunities created by water have an increasingly global impact. Responsible, sustainable investment in water resources holds great promise for increased human productivity, more abundant food, cleaner energy, and more efficient trade and transport. Improvements in water management offer great potential to leverage economic growth and human well-being and to bind countries together in mutually beneficial cooperation.

But the vulnerabilities, too, have growing global reach. The loss of water-dependent ecosystems and biodiversity, the spread of waterborne disease, the tragedy of large-scale natural disasters such as drought and flood, and the insecurity and even violence that arise from perceived injustices over contested waters can all reach across borders.

This paper draws heavily on earlier World Bank publications. Acknowledgment for their contributions is due, in particular, to John Briscoe, Meike van Ginneken, and Rafik Hirji.

265

Achieving basic water security—a situation where water's productive potential is harnessed and its destructive impacts are limited—has been a struggle for humankind throughout history. Security against climatic variability, against unpredictable flood and drought, was the primary reason why the industrialized countries made early investments in major water infrastructure projects such as dams and interbasin transfer schemes. For many other countries the struggle to achieve this basic security continues. Millions in the developing still suffer from inadequate and unreliable basic water services—many developing countries today have as little as 1/100th as much water infrastructure as do developed countries with comparable climatic variability. And many people still die from water-borne diseases because they drink unsafe water or lack adequate sanitation or hygiene (figure 14.1). Yet, at the same time, people in developing countries are disproportionately affected by water-related disasters: losses associated with these disasters are estimated to be about five times higher per unit of gross domestic product than losses from equivalent disasters in rich countries, according to the second *World Water Development Report.*[1] Meanwhile, the number of such disasters appears to be on a rising trend, as figure 14.2 indicates.

The ever-increasing demand for safe water and the increased frequency of water-related disasters, combined with continued growth in the populations affected by both, call for greater effort than ever before in water resources

FIGURE 14.1 Deaths from Unsafe Water and Poor Sanitation and Hygiene, 2001

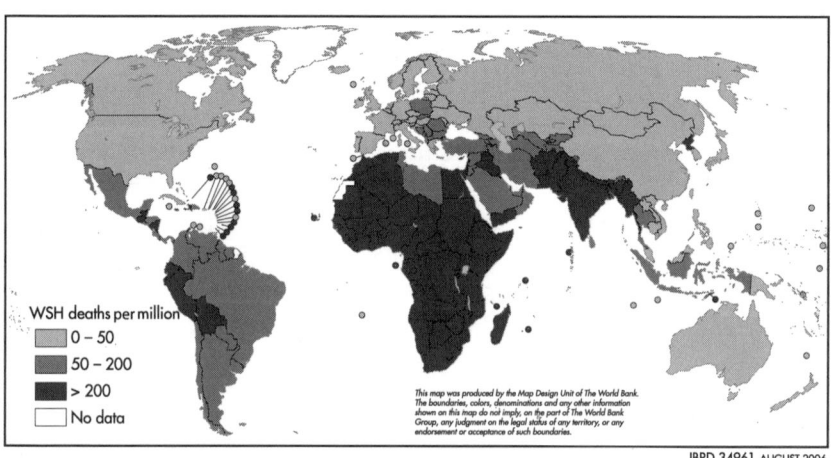

WSH deaths per million
- 0 – 50
- 50 – 200
- > 200
- No data

This map was produced by the Map Design Unit of The World Bank. The boundaries, colors, denominations and any other information shown on this map do not imply, on the part of The World Bank Group, any judgment on the legal status of any territory, or any endorsement or acceptance of such boundaries.

IBRD 34961 AUGUST 2006

Source: World Health Organization 2002.

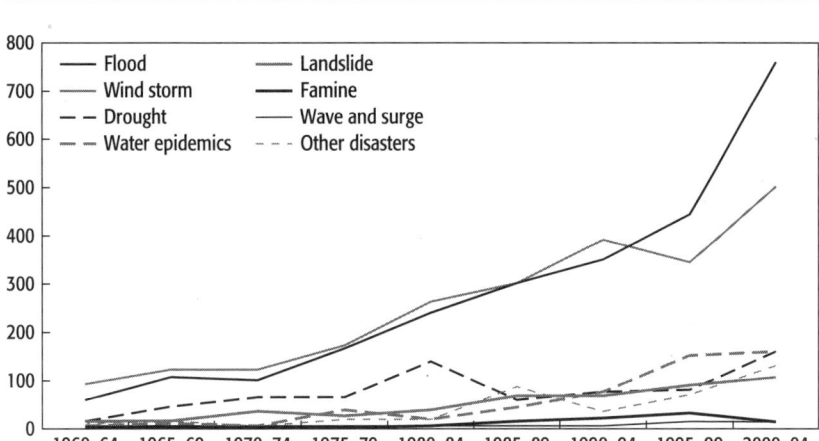

FIGURE 14.2 Incidence of Water-Related Disasters by Type, 1960–2004
Number of disasters

Source: International Centre for Water Hazard and Risk Management, Tsukuba, Japan.
Note: Data from the Center for Epidemiology of Disasters, Louvain, Belgium; analysis by the Public Works Research Institute, Tsukuba, Japan, 2005.

management. Providing basic water security in the developing world will require expertise, technology, and in some cases finance from the developed world to ensure that water resources are developed in responsible ways, ensuring environmental sustainability and promoting social development. This fact alone ensures that water is and will continue to be a global issue.

Throughout history, water has also been a source of dispute and at times even violent conflict, both at the local level and internationally. As water becomes ever scarcer relative to demand, the danger grows that waters shared by two or more countries will become a source of dispute between them. Meanwhile, as populations and economies grow and climate change makes rainfall even more erratic, pressures will mount on this finite global resource, adding to the challenge. Fortunately, however, there is also an emerging record of fruitful cooperation on transboundary waters, supporting regional integration as a driver of growth.

Approaches to Improved Water Management

If the potential of water as a driver of sustainable, responsible growth is to be successfully harnessed, two things are indispensable: sound infrastructure and sound institutions, where the latter includes adequate management capacity and a commitment to good governance. Investment in both infrastructure and institutions in all water-related sectors—water resources management, water supply and sanitation, irrigation and drainage, hydropower, and environmental conservation—is critical.

Most developing countries need to take action both in managing their existing water resources infrastructure and in further developing that infrastructure. But the challenges need to be approached without preconceptions. Not all problems can be solved with infrastructure, nor, in countries where existing infrastructure is minimal, can all problems be addressed through better institutions and management. Instead, an appropriate balance of investments in institutions (from local to basin-wide to national to international) and investments in infrastructure (from small-scale to large-scale) will always need to be considered, reflecting each country's unique circumstances.

The main management challenge is not to construct a vision of integrated water resources management, but rather to adopt a *pragmatic and principled* approach that respects efficiency, equity, and sustainability, while recognizing that water resources management is intensely political and that reform requires the articulation of prioritized, sequenced, practical, and patient interventions. In both design and implementation, more explicit attention needs to be paid to the political economy of water management reform. This will mean recognizing that solutions have to be tailored to specific, widely varying circumstances, and that broader reforms outside the water sector (often relating to overall economic liberalization and fiscal and political reform) may be necessary preconditions.

In many developing countries today, water management is at a crossroads, where business as usual means the unsustainable use of increasingly inadequate physical and financial resources, which in turn means forgone growth opportunities and increasing social tensions. Policy changes and the adoption of new practices are needed in many areas, often simultaneously: in providing adequate water supply and sanitation services to the urban and rural poor; in harnessing the energy potential of the available water resources; in factoring environmental and ecosystem needs into water management decisions; and in managing irrigated or rain-fed agriculture to feed a growing population.

In each area, reforms should be designed with regard to how they affect the incentives facing those involved: water users (both commercial and household), government officials, water service providers, and investors. An effective incentive structure is needed to improve the performance of water services managers, to encourage conservation on the part of users, to attract investment, and to achieve better returns on existing investments. Several key factors influence these incentives: the degree of transparency in decision-making processes, the degree of involvement of stakeholders, the prices that users have to pay, their perception of their rights to water resources and to water services, and the strength of enforcement of regulations and laws. When these various building blocks are in place, a virtuous cycle can be started that enables countries to tackle their water challenges effectively.

Examples from many countries show that *transparency* matters. When members of civil society receive information about issues that affect them, and when their views are solicited, government decision making becomes more responsive to the needs of different stakeholder groups, including the poor, as well as the needs of the environment.

Most improvements in the water sector will fail to be effective if governments do not develop socially acceptable and, to the extent possible, self-financing *pricing and tariff policies*. Water and water services have historically been underpriced, resulting in inefficient use. Underpricing has also led to a lack of financial resources in the water sector, which then often operates unsustainably, dependent on subsidies. When instead prices that accurately reflect water's scarcity value are applied to resources or services that were formerly provided free, two beneficial things happen. First, users now have information on the value of the resource or service, leading them to use it more sparingly. Second, the income thereby derived can be used to maintain existing infrastructure and build new facilities. Increased investment in the water sector, whether from public or from private sources, must be accompanied by the recognition that water pricing is essential both to ensure the sustainability of the resource, in part by maintaining effective water resources management, and to expand services, including both operation and maintenance. Subsidies, appropriately designed and targeted, may be needed to ensure the poor have access.

Finally, clear definition of *water use rights and obligations* is critical. Realizing the full potential of a country's water resources will require significant effort across a range of activities, including harnessing the water resource, putting efficient and equitable allocation mechanisms in place, building water distribution structures, motivating good performance of water utilities and irrigation districts, and providing for effective drought and flood management. All these are interconnected and require adequate management capacity, investment, and information. The assignment of water use rights (which, as the name implies, constitutes a right to use water, not a right to own water) promotes efficient and sustainable water allocation and facilitates voluntary reallocation. These rights may encompass both individual and collective rights, depending on the cultural context.

Once established, such rights give rise to a series of fundamental and healthy changes. First, those who require additional resources (such as growing cities) may be able to meet their needs by acquiring rights from those who are using water for low-value purposes. Second, the establishment of water use rights gives rise to strong pressures to improve the data required to manage the resource. Third, those who have rights have a powerful interest in sustainability. However, it is not a simple task to introduce rights-based systems for a fugitive resource with deep cultural associations in administratively weak environments.

Uses and Users of Water

Globally, by far the largest share of freshwater resources goes to agricultural production, as figure 14.3 shows. Water is essential, however, across all productive sectors and is a key component of almost all environmental systems.

Water Supply and Sanitation

Improving access to water supply and sanitation is essential for socioeconomic development and poverty reduction—and for human dignity. These services contribute both directly and indirectly to income generation, health,

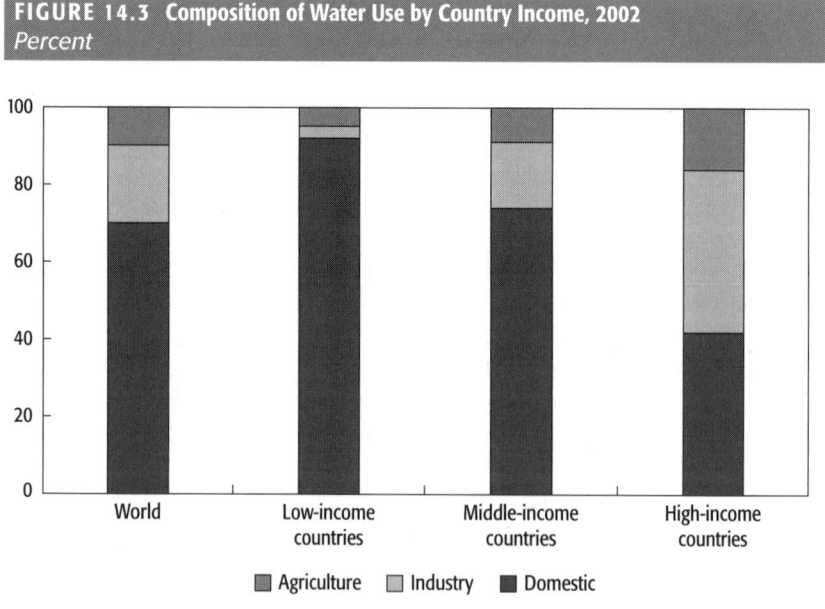

FIGURE 14.3 Composition of Water Use by Country Income, 2002
Percent

■ Agriculture   ☐ Industry   ■ Domestic

Source: World Bank 2002.

and education. Significant investments have been made in water supply and sanitation in developing countries: over the past two decades alone, more than 2 billion people have gained access to water supply for the first time. Yet over 1 billion still lack access to improved water services, and hygiene and sanitation continue to lag far behind, with some 2.4 billion people worldwide still living without improved sanitation.

The challenge is to mobilize all stakeholders to expand, improve, and sustain affordable water supply and sanitation services. The following are some considerations to be kept in mind as part of this effort:

- *The very poor often pay much higher prices for lower-quality water than do the better off.* The poor are typically the last to receive water supply and sanitation services, and often it is women and children who are forced to travel long distances to fetch water.
- *Water supply and sanitation sector priorities can only be achieved if they are integrated into the government's strategic objectives,* and resources are allocated accordingly, often at the local government level.
- *It is the service, not the provider, that matters.* The debate is not about whether provision should be public or private but about sustainable access to safe and affordable water supply, provided in the most effective way.
- *Water sector institutions must be accountable to the communities they serve, either directly or through their representatives.* The traditional, top-down approach to service delivery has generally not worked.
- *Water supply is always paid for by someone, and inevitably it is either the consumer or the taxpayer who pays.* Only service providers that generate sufficient cash can ensure continued operation and maintenance of water supply systems and attract investment funding to expand their services.
- *Investments in service expansion need to be supported by policy and institutional reforms and by increased professional capacity in order to achieve lasting results.* Necessary reforms include the introduction of sound policies, responsive institutions, and capacity at all levels—reforms are only as effective as the people who implement them.
- *The poor in medium-size and smaller towns also need to be served.* Significant numbers of poor people are not benefiting from either expansion of community-based services in rural areas or reform of municipal utilities, because they live neither on farms nor in cities but in emerging and rapidly growing towns.
- *Sanitation and hygiene affect everyone.* Improved sanitation (sewerage, wastewater treatment, and drainage) benefits mainly the households

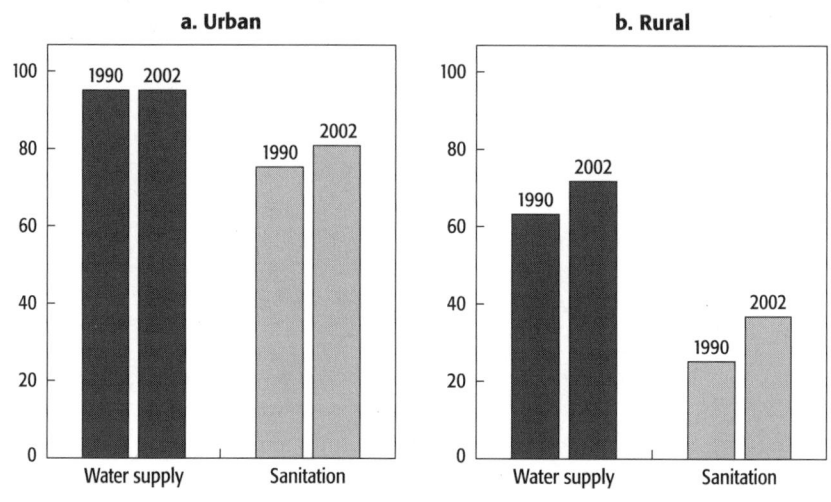

FIGURE 14.4 Access of Urban and Rural Residents to Water Supply and Sanitation, 1990 and 2002
Percentage of population

Source: Joint Monitoring Programme for Water Supply and Sanitation, World Health Organization and UNICEF.

that receive these services, but it also improves living conditions for others living in the same neighborhood, the same city, and further downstream, by reducing the prevalence of disease.

- *Behavioral change is essential for improved sanitation to meet its full potential.* An important tool in this effort is hygiene education in the schools.
- *The greatest sanitation challenge lies in the rapid growth of high-density slums.* Given the scale of the problem in urban areas (figure 14.4), sanitation must be placed firmly within the urban development agenda.

Irrigation and Drainage

Improvements in irrigation and drainage have succeeded in boosting food production, reducing poverty, and spurring regional development in many parts of the developing world. Land currently under irrigation—about 250 million hectares—produces 40 percent of global food supply on just 17 percent of the world's agricultural land. Irrigation accounts for two-thirds of all water consumption, and even more than that in some developing countries.

But today a new and conflicting set of challenges has arisen: global food security must be achieved against a backdrop of growing populations, increasing water scarcity, and rising environmental concerns. Reforms are needed to promote the intensification of irrigated agriculture, through greater participation by farmers in irrigation management and in investments to modernize and rehabilitate existing infrastructure. In the next 25 years, 90 percent of the increase in food production will have to come from land already under cultivation. Meanwhile, the need for new water supply for urban and industrial uses and for environmental protection will increasingly take both water and land away from irrigated areas. All of this means that the productivity of the remaining irrigated land will have to double through the following:

- *Modernization and rehabilitation of irrigation and drainage systems and improved operation and management are key* to diminishing waterlogging and salinity, increasing the efficiency of water use, raising agricultural productivity, reducing poverty, and minimizing the negative impacts of irrigation and drainage systems on water ecosystems.
- *The roles and responsibilities of governments, users, civil society, and the private sector* need to be reflected in the institutional framework for irrigation and drainage services.
- *Improved financial mechanisms* are needed so that farmers and farmers' organizations share in the costs of infrastructure improvement.
- *An efficient system of water use rights and volumetric delivery* can give users an incentive to increase efficiency, encouraging less efficient users to transfer water, temporarily or permanently, to more efficient users or higher-value uses.
- *Where irrigation systems are not viable, because of insuperable financial or environmental obstacles, those systems should be restructured.* However, such restructuring may need to be delayed for a time to avoid high social and economic costs from resettlements that are inadequately planned and implemented.

The Environment

Water resources—watersheds, rivers, wetlands, lakes, aquifers, and floodplains—are essential for the sustenance and health of all species. They also sustain the integrity of ecosystems that serve important "natural infrastructure" functions, such as storing water, regulating flows, and absorbing wastewater discharges. Unsustainable use and management practices due to poor environmental, social, or economic policies and actions are increasing the stress on the world's water resources. Threats arise from the degradation of water resources at all levels—local, basin-wide, national, and international—and from global climate variability and change. The hydrological, ecological, and economic consequences are significant:

- *Understanding the importance of the functions provided by aquatic ecosystems and managing the environmental dimension of water are essential* to sustaining development, economic growth, and poverty reduction.
- *Environmental objectives cannot be managed separately from consumption objectives* and must take priority in important watersheds, recharge areas, and wetlands.
- *The downstream impact of drainage and sanitation projects* is often underestimated.
- *Invasive weeds, fish, and other species can impose high costs on communities*, particularly the poor.
- *Preventive action is needed to avoid costly remediation of degraded water quality in vital water bodies such as lakes, wetlands, and groundwater systems*. Particular attention needs to be paid to groundwater, where impacts are slow to appear and remediation is difficult and costly.
- *Water managers need to incorporate the impacts of climate change and variability into water resources planning and management*, including through adaptive planning, predictive and forecasting capability, and strategic drought and flood management strategies.

Energy

Today, 1.6 billion people worldwide remain deprived of the opportunities provided by basic electricity services: in some countries as few as 3 percent of the population have access to the electric power grid. Hydropower has great potential to make electricity more widely available. Already it provides about 2,650 terawatt-hours a year worldwide, or 20 percent of all of the world's electricity (and 92 percent of all electricity from renewable sources), and bringing on line the world's remaining economically exploitable hydropower sites could almost triple that figure. Ninety percent of that additional electricity would come from sites in developing countries, which, to date, have developed only about 20 percent of their hydropower potential (the figure in Africa is only about 5 percent, compared with about 70 percent in the industrial world). New, well-designed hydropower facilities are therefore probably the single most important option, renewable or otherwise, for expanding electricity generation and service coverage in Africa, Asia, and South America. It is arguably the only proven, mature, renewable, and clean technology available at the necessary scale:

- *Developing hydropower resources is instrumental for energy and water security.* When implemented well, hydropower can serve a wide range of beneficiaries while respecting environmental and social values.
- *Planning and operation of hydropower infrastructure need to be undertaken within an integrated water resources management perspective* that considers other users of the water resource, such as farmers who depend on downstream flows, as well as the environment.
- *Hydropower development can support the financing of other improvements in water management.* Hydropower can provide the backbone of a broader water resources management system, providing water storage and river flow regulation for multiple purposes, including water supply, irrigation, and drought and flood management.
- *The future development of hydropower in most developing countries will be very limited if left entirely to the private sector.* In the private power boom of the 1990s, hydropower accounted for only 2.5 percent of new capacity developed. The necessary investments are so large that they generally require public-private partnerships.
- *There is not yet—and there may never be—a universally accepted code of practice for developing hydropower.* Rather, the practical application of sustainable hydropower, both small-scale and large-scale, will draw on evolving good practice, including the recommendations of the World Commission on Dams and the International Hydropower Association and the environmental and social safeguards of the World Bank.

Forces Shaping the Challenges of Water Management

Growing populations and growing economies are putting water resources under increasing pressure, especially in developing countries. At the same time, the ecosystems that sustain life on Earth and provide valuable services to all humankind also need sufficient water to function.

Economic Growth and Demographics

A growing world population requires more water services and water infrastructure for economic activity, notably to provide safe water and sanitation, meet increasing food needs, and secure inputs for industrial processes, as well as to reduce the impacts of water-related shocks on society. As world population has tripled since World War II, the amount of fresh water available for the average person has fallen accordingly, by about two-thirds.

But population growth is not the only cause of decreased water availability. Pollution, which degrades water's usefulness, has also reduced the amount of usable, safe water that is available, and economic growth, by increasing the demand for water per person, has put further pressure on the supply. Figures on average water availability, moreover, obscure sharp differences between countries and regions. Developing countries, with their more rapidly growing populations and economies and typically weaker environmental regulation, are expected to suffer a disproportionate share of the growing imbalance between supply and demand for safe water over the next 30 years.

Global Climate Change and Adaptation

Climate change will add further to the global challenge of water management. On the one hand, it will dramatically affect the demand for water. Irrigation, which today accounts for some 70 percent of global water use, is the most climate-sensitive water user, and the shifting pattern of irrigated crops in response to climate change is likely to have major effects on the spatial and temporal pattern of water demand, as well as on the need for water storage. Industrial and municipal demand will likewise be affected. The effect on cities will be further accentuated through the migration of people from increasingly water-scarce to water-plentiful regions.

Climate change will also affect water management from the supply side. Although total global precipitation is likely to increase during the next century, this increase will not be uniform across the world. Broadly speaking, the wet countries will get wetter and the dry countries dryer: global warming will likely reduce water availability in those countries where water is already scarce, while also increasing the variability of rainfall and runoff. Water will likely be less available in Central Asia, in the area around the Mediterranean, in Sub-Saharan Africa, and in Australia in winter. South Asia and Southeast Asia, in contrast, will likely have more water during the summer, possibly leading to increased snowmelt and more frequent and severe flooding in the countries downstream of the Himalayas. The high-latitude countries of the Northern Hemisphere are likely to have more precipitation in both summer and winter.

In poor countries, which today generally lack adequate institutions and infrastructure to manage, store, and deliver their water resources, these changes will be superimposed on existing, and in some cases extreme, vulnerabilities. In many of the poorest countries, particularly in Sub-Saharan Africa, variations in weather from year to year or decade to decade are already many times greater than their predicted climate change. Thus, even as many developed countries are focusing on mitigating climate change, these developing countries remain more concerned with adapting to their current variability. In all countries, however, adaptive capacity—both social and physical—will need to be increased to protect the poorest and most vulnerable populations.

Scarcities at All Levels

The growing scarcity of water can be seen as not only a challenge of physical resource scarcity, but one of economic and institutional scarcity as well. In many of the world's poorest countries, physical water resources may be adequate to the need, but there is inadequate investment in the infrastructure required to capture, store, and deliver this water—a situation described as *economic water scarcity*. Similarly, *institutional water scarcity* exists when both physical and infrastructural resources are sufficient, but because of unresolved issues of rights, governance, or social structures, not all members of society have adequate access to water.

Water scarcity afflicts different groups of people in different ways, not only within societies (urban residents versus rural residents, rich versus poor) but also between societies that share a common water resource. Worldwide, about 260 river basins are shared by two or more nations; together these nations make up perhaps 90 percent of the world's population. As demand for water grows across the world, and as poorer countries sharing these river basins seek to realize the growth opportunities they offer, real threats to regional security and peace are in the offing. However, if all parties understand the benefits that cooperation in managing the resource can bring, benefit-sharing arrangements can be reached that often bring substantial gains for each nation (or states and provinces within nations): more water, more food, more power, less risk from flood and drought, and better-conserved ecosystems. Regional tensions over water can give way to economic cooperation and integration.

Creation of More from Less

Alarming as current trends in water scarcity may appear, it is important to recognize that only a very small share of the world's fresh water is currently used for basic needs, and that there is enormous scope for using the bulk of the Earth's water resources more wisely. Evolving management policies, practices, and technologies can make water use much more efficient and more equitable.

Efficiency can be dramatically improved in the many water supply systems around the world where nearly half of the water resource goes unaccounted for, lost to leaks or illegal connections. In agriculture and industry, better management, governance, and technologies could increase efficiency by enough to cut global water use by perhaps 50 percent, without diminishing production.

Water infrastructure can be designed and operated in ways that capture multiple benefits, while paying greater attention to river ecosystems and the livelihoods of affected communities. For example, only about 25 percent of the world's existing dams are used to generate hydropower.

Policies that promote international trade in water-intensive products, such as most agricultural goods, can lead to more efficient global patterns of water use by encouraging their production in water-rich countries or regions, which can then sell those goods in countries and regions where water is scarcer. This makes much more economic sense than managing water through huge investments in water transfer and storage infrastructure. Similar water efficiency gains may be possible if water use patterns are considered on a basin-wide scale, whether within a single country or shared by several. Then, for example, agriculture or hydropower can be sited where the hydrology is most favorable.

Finally, technological advances—for example, in desalination, aquifer storage and recovery, and wastewater reuse—offer effective ways to enhance the world's water resource base. Although today many of these technologies are too expensive for the world's poorest countries, they hold great promise for the future as their costs diminish and global incomes rise.

Choices and Controversies

The fact that water is so central to the opportunities and the vulnerabilities of so many people, to basic social values, and to the health of the environment makes water use and management particularly prone to controversy. Among the issues currently being debated are the privatization of water, water as a human right, and the development of large-scale infrastructure.

Public Versus Private

The first water supply services in some industrial countries were initiated by private companies or cooperatives. Today, however, urban water supply and sanitation services are typically provided by state-owned water utilities, often (especially in smaller countries) run by the national government. Many of these public utilities have been unable to finance or manage improvements in service or even the expansion of connections. In the 1980s and 1990s, as part of a general move to greater efficiency and accountability of services, a new paradigm emerged to transform water utilities into more modern service delivery organizations, emphasizing operational and financial sustainability.

As a consequence, private sector involvement is one important option for the improvement and expansion of water and sanitation services.

It is invariably the case, however, that among those who lack access to safe water are the poorest in society. People without access to piped water generally rely on unsafe, expensive, inconvenient services from water vendors or obtain water themselves from unprotected sources. As noted above, the latter burden usually falls on women and children. Given the importance of access to clean water for all, every potential option for immediate delivery of services to those currently without water should be considered.

The private sector has played an increasingly important but still limited role in managing and financing water and sanitation services in the last decade. To date, private financing has accounted for less than 10 percent of total investment in water supply and sanitation in developing countries, and that share has decreased in the past few years. Public resources will likely remain the most important source of financing for many years to come.

All investment and management in water and sanitation, whether public or private, should be complemented by robust regulatory and monitoring frameworks, designed with the active participation of water users and civil society. The structure of financing, regulation, and management relations will affect the performance of the utility. A range of models combining public and private financing, and public and private management relationships, are available, but the choice of any public-private partnership structure must be driven by social objectives, efficiency, and cost-effectiveness—not by dogma. Ultimately, the chosen approach must be tailored to the circumstances of the country and its water sector, in line with the country's long-term poverty reduction objectives. The central question, then, is not public versus private, but rather which solution works best and gets water to people—especially the poor—in the most reliable and affordable manner.

Water as a Human Right

The International Covenant on Economic, Social and Cultural Rights by the United Nations (UN) calls for recognition of water as a human right. The importance of this declaration is that it obliges the 145 countries that have ratified the covenant progressively to ensure access to clean water, equitably and without discrimination. It therefore has the potential both to strengthen efforts to deliver water services to the poor and to increase transparency in this process. However, the challenge remains to implement sound political decisions, reforms, and investments in an accountable and sustainable manner.

Debate has arisen because many have read the UN covenant as a call for free water for all, and thus to argue against measures seeking cost recovery for water services. The text of the covenant, however, merely adds access to water to an existing list of "rights emanating from, and indispensable for, the realization of the right to an adequate standard of living"—a list that already included "adequate food, clothing and housing." It therefore no more implies free provision of water than it implies free provision of any of those other necessities.

The bottom line is that, although water supply and sanitation services are vital, they are also costly, and someone—whether consumers or taxpayers—is certain to end up with the bill. To ensure long-term and sustainable access to safe water supply and sanitation services for all, appropriate cost recovery mechanisms are needed. These must take into account environmental and social considerations and, where appropriate, provide well-targeted subsidies to the truly needy.

The Role of Infrastructure

In the late 19th and early 20th centuries, all of the industrialized countries invested heavily in water infrastructure and institutions, and these investments contributed to the remarkable economic growth that followed. However, in hindsight it has become apparent that many of the inevitable trade-offs in water infrastructure development could have been better addressed, and many projects have been poorly implemented, to the detriment of affected communities and local environments. In recent years, a great deal of controversy has grown up around water infrastructure development, and particularly around large-scale projects such as dams and reservoirs in developing countries. The perception has become fairly widespread that the development of water resources infrastructure is *intrinsically* bad for the poor, for others directly affected, and for the environment. This perception has become a barrier to obtaining finance for water development, more so in countries with limited infrastructure (which are generally poorer) than in countries with mature infrastructure platforms (generally richer).

But, in fact, there is no fundamental constraint to designing water development investments to ensure that local communities and the environment share real and early benefits from these investments, while still allowing the economy and society at large to benefit from the growth that they make possible. Moreover, without these investments it is generally the poor who will remain vulnerable to the destructive impacts of water, and whose limited access to water services does not allow them to exploit the production opportunities that water can provide. This suggests that a lack of investment in water infrastructure may, in fact, be intrinsically anti-poor. Past experience, both good and bad, with large-scale water projects offers insights for all countries on how to strengthen institutions and management capacity, ensure better design of new (or operation of existing) water resource infrastructure, and strive for equity in the sharing of benefits. This knowledge, often gained at great environmental and social cost, must be used to help guide future policies, reforms, and investments so as to achieve growth in a more equitable and sustainable—and responsible—manner.

International Initiatives on Water

During and after the Rio Earth Summit (the United Nations Conference on Environment and Development, held in Rio de Janeiro in 1992), a global consensus was forged that modern water resources management should be based on four fundamental principles, which have become known as the Dublin Principles:

- Fresh water is a finite and vulnerable resource, essential to sustaining life, development, and the environment.
- Water development and management should be based on a participatory approach, involving users, planners, and policy makers at all levels.
- Women play a central part in the provision, management, and safeguarding of water.
- Water has economic value in all its competing uses and should be recognized as an economic good.

More than a decade later, experience with implementing the Dublin Principles continues to accumulate. A major review by the Organisation for Economic Co-operation and Development of implementation by the industrialized countries concluded that progress has been difficult, slow, and uneven and that even the most advanced countries are far from full compliance. The situation in developing countries should be seen in this light, and expectations need to be adjusted in a pragmatic manner that helps developing countries move forward.

The Millennium Development Goals

The seventh of the Millennium Development Goals (MDGs) adopted at the United Nations Millennium Summit includes an explicit target to "reduce by half the proportion of people without sustainable access to safe drinking

water." Several of the other MDGs call for a range of global actions and investments to which water will be central:

- Eradicating extreme poverty and hunger (MDG 1)
- Promoting gender equality and empowering women (MDG 3)
- Reducing child mortality (MDG 4)
- Combating HIV/AIDS, malaria, and other diseases (MDG 6)
- Ensuring environmental sustainability (MDG 7).

In a 2005 progress report on the MDGs, UN Secretary General Kofi Annan
summarized efforts to date as follows: ". . . the report shows us how much
progress has been made in some areas, and how large an effort is needed to meet
the Millennium Development Goals in others. If current trends persist, there is
a risk that many of the poorest countries will not be able to meet many of them"
(United Nations 2005, 3).[2] In this regard, one issue now being highlighted is
the linkage between water resources management and water supply services.
Focusing only on drinking water supply will not provide the desired results, if
the underlying water resources are not adequately managed and developed.

Ongoing International Dialogue

Many organizations are engaged in promoting greater understanding and
exchanging views and information on the challenges of water. Several global
nongovernmental organizations (NGOs) focus exclusively on water, including the Global Water Partnership, the World Water Council, the Stockholm
International Water Institute, the International Water Management Institute,
the Water Supply and Sanitation Collaborative Council, and the Arab
Water Council. A number of other international NGOs, such as IUCN—The
World Conservation Union and the World Wildlife Fund, address water
issues as part of a larger portfolio of interests. Targeted capacity-building
organizations include the UN Educational, Scientific, and Cultural
Organization–Integrating the Healthcare Enterprise Institute for Water Education and Cap-Net (the International Network for Capacity Building for
Integrated Water Resources Management). The multilateral development
banks as well as several UN agencies and most major bilateral donors are all
active in water policy discussions. A number of meetings and forums on water
issues are held on a regular basis and offer important opportunities for
exchange. Among these are the World Water Forum, held every three years
and sponsored by the World Water Council and rotating host governments;
the Stockholm World Water Week, held every August by the Stockholm
International Water Institute; and the "Water Weeks" held regularly at the
multilateral development banks.

In addition, the international community occasionally launches specialized, cooperative undertakings. Important recent examples include the World Commission on Dams (1997–2000), which examined the development impact of large dams; the World Panel on Financing Water Infrastructure (the Camdessus Panel 2001–03) and its current follow-up by the Gurria Task Force; and the ongoing activities of the UN Secretary General's Advisory Board on Water, which is mandated to mobilize resources and action for water and sanitation toward achievement of the MDGs.

The World Bank and Water

The World Bank Group has historically invested about $3 billion a year in water-related sectors, accounting for about 5 percent of its investment in developing countries. Lending for water accounted for about 16 percent of World Bank lending over the past decade, and the major water services components (irrigation, hydropower, and water supply and sanitation) as well as water resources each accounted for about 4 percent.

Given the formidable challenges that remain to improving the technical, financial, social, and environmental performance of water management worldwide, the World Bank Group is committed to using its knowledge, its convening power, its ability to link water issues to other sectors through economy-wide engagement and a multidisciplinary perspective, its relations with almost all riparian countries, its financial resources, and its engagement at all scales (local, watershed, city, irrigation district, river basin and aquifer, country, and regional) to integrate interventions across these various dimensions.

The World Bank Group will continue to be a partner in bringing about both investment and reform in a sequenced and prioritized manner aimed at achieving sustainable, integrated water resources management and water services, and thus responsible growth and poverty reduction in developing countries. Depending on the needs of individual developing countries, the Bank will support the development of water infrastructure, including hydropower at a range of scales, depending on national and local needs and opportunities.

Notes

1. United Nations Educational, Scientific, and Cultural Organization World Water Assessment Program (2006).
2. United Nations. 2005. "The Millennium Development Goals Report 2005." New York.

Selected Readings and Cited References

Dubreuil, Celine. 2006. "The Right to Water: From Concept to Implementation."
Marseilles: World Water Council.

Grey, David, and Claudia W. Sadoff. 2006. "Water for Growth and Development." In
Thematic Documents of the IV World Water Forum. Mexico City: Comisión
Nacional del Agua.

International Center for Water Hazard and Risk Management.

Komives, Kristin, Vivien Foster, Jonathan Halparn, and Quentin Wodon. 2005.
Water, Electricity, and the Poor: Who Benefits from Utility Subsidies? Washington,
DC: World Bank.

United Nations Educational, Scientific, and Cultural Organization World Water
Assessment Program. 2006. *Water, A Shared Responsibility: The 2nd United Nations
World Water Development Report*. Paris: Berghahn Books.

United Nations Office of the High Commissioner on Human Rights. 2002. "General
Comment 15. The Right to Water." Comment on articles 11 and 12 of the International
Covenant on Economic, Social and Cultural Rights. U.N. document
E/C.12/2002/11 (Twenty-ninth session). New York.

World Bank. 2002. *World Development Indicators 2002*. Washington, DC: World
Bank.

World Commission on Dams. 2000. *Dams and Development: A New Framework for
Decision-Making*. London: EarthScan Publications.

World Health Organization. 2002. *The World Health Report 2002: Reducing Risks,
Promoting Healthy Life*. Geneva.

Selected Web Links on Water and Sanitation

Global Water Partnership	http://www.gwpforum.org/servlet/PSP
UN Environment Programme GEMS	http://www.gemswater.org
UN Educational, Scientific, and Cultural Organization World Water Assessment	http://www.unesco.org/water/wwap
World Bank site for river basin management	http://www.worldbank.org/riverbasinmanagement
World Bank site for water resources	http://www.worldbank.org/water
World Bank site for water and sanitation	http://www.worldbank.org/watsan
World Resources Institute Earth Trends	http://earthtrends.wri.org

15

Toward Sustainable Management of World Fisheries and Aquaculture

KIERAN KELLEHER AND MICHAEL L. WEBER

The continuing depletion of the world's marine fisheries is a key indicator of a critical decline in ocean health and a global issue of increasing concern. Fish is an important food for billions of people and provides a livelihood for an estimated 200 million people worldwide. The living marine resources of the planet are also an important part of the Earth's diversity of life, providing a range of ecological services and supporting recreation, scientific research, and tourism. Yet, in the last half century, the growth of human populations and economies, the spread of new technologies such as fishing nets made from synthetic materials, and the motorization of fishing fleets have led to overfishing and contributed to the decline of many fisheries, jeopardizing ecological and economic sustainability for coastal communities around the world.

The task of making fisheries sustainable has local, regional, and global dimensions. Fish and fishers move from sheltered bays and estuaries to the open ocean, and from sea to sea. Small-scale fishers from Senegal and Ghana fish in the waters of many other countries in West Africa and in the Gulf of Guinea; European and Asian industrial tuna fleets operate throughout the Atlantic, Indian, and Pacific Oceans. The rapid expansion in the global fish trade means that fish products from even the most remote fisheries are gradually entering world trade.

The depletion of fish stocks and loss of critical marine habitats due to overfishing can be traced to the inherent nature of wild fisheries as a common property to which all have access (see figure 15.1). For example, in

FIGURE 15.1 Growth of an Ungoverned Open Access Fishery

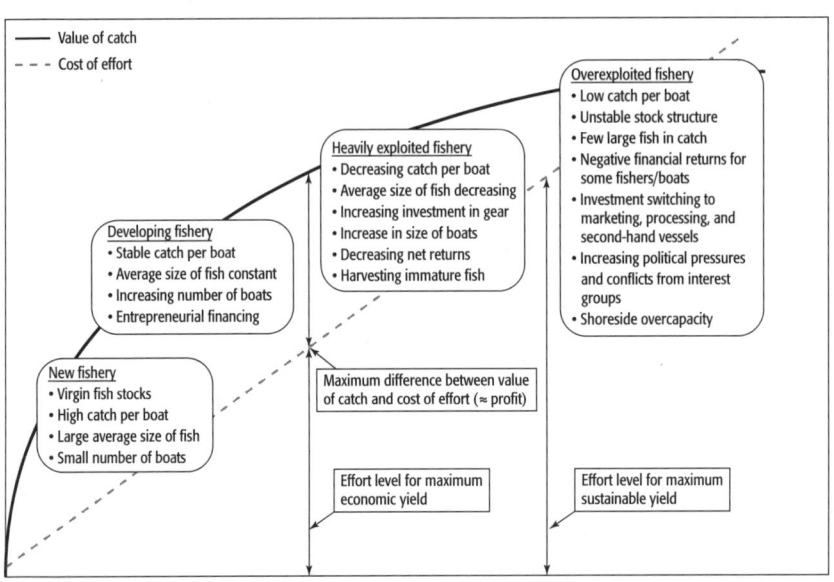

Source: Kelleher 1996.

many small-scale fisheries there are no restrictions on who may fish; as a result, a growing number of fishers, having few alternative economic options available, compete for limited fish resources. Since individual fishers have no incentive to restrict their fishing so as to preserve the common resource, an effective form of governance is needed, either to provide such an incentive or to enforce restrictions to ensure the sustainable use of the resource.

The problem is the same at the international level. Nations may act like individual fishers, each seeking its own individual benefit. Thus, without effective international regulation, fisheries accessible to more than one country, including those on the high seas, may suffer this *tragedy of the commons.* Yet efforts to provide such regulation have been beset with problems. Many existing international instruments designed to regulate high-seas and trans-boundary fishing are weak. Subsidized international fisheries access agreements may benefit fishers from industrial countries at the expense of fishers from developing countries. Regional fisheries management organizations have limited powers of enforcement, and their consensus decisions often reflect an ineffective compromise at the lowest common denominator. The existing Law of the Sea Convention and its subsidiary instruments have important gaps, and effective enforcement of measures for responsible high-seas fishing has proved elusive. Vessels flying flags of convenience transgress national and international law with impunity, and subsidies provide inequitable support to maintain overcapacity in industrial fleets.

At the heart of the matter lies a lack of political commitment to resolve a difficult problem, one that requires long-term national, regional, and international efforts to build awareness and consensus. The short-term political costs of fisheries reform may be high, yet the techniques and applications required to reduce risks and secure the potential long-term benefits often require investment and testing as well as sensitivity to the social costs of change.

The Global Importance of Fisheries

For some 2.6 billion people around the world, fish provides at least 20 percent of average per capita intake of animal protein. Fish is a particularly important part of the diet in developing countries, where total protein-intake levels may be low. In Bangladesh, Cambodia, the Republic of Congo, Equatorial Guinea, and Sri Lanka, and in some small island states, fish may account for 50 percent of total animal protein. (For comparison, the average share in industrial countries is only 8 percent.) Declines in fishery resources caused by overfishing or a significant increase in the price of food fish can thus seriously affect the nutritional status of major population groups.

In 2002, about 76 percent of estimated world fish production was used for direct human consumption; much of the remainder was used in the manufacture of fishmeal and oil. These products are generally manufactured from small pelagic fish (fish that live in surface waters). These species, such as anchovies and sardines, made up 37 percent of total marine catches in 2002.

Worldwide, 38 million people are full-time fishers or fish farmers, and fishing, aquaculture, and related activities such as fish processing employ roughly 150 million people in developing countries. The Food and Agriculture Organization of the United Nations (FAO) estimates that, since 1990, the number of full-time fishers has been growing at an average rate of 2.5 percent a year; the total increase since 1950 is about 400 percent. Most of this growth has been in small-scale fisheries in the developing world, particularly Africa and

Asia, where poverty among coastal communities is often high and fishing is often the livelihood of last resort. In 2004, the global fishing fleet comprised roughly 1.3 million decked fishing vessels and 2.8 million open, or undecked, fishing vessels, of which 65 percent were without engines.

Trends

FAO, which monitors trends in the world's fisheries, reports that total world production of fish products by freshwater and marine fisheries and by aquaculture increased steadily from 19 million metric tons in 1950 to 100 million tons in 1989 and nearly 140 million tons in 2004 (figure 15.2). Since 1985, developing countries have accounted for more than half of this production.

Marine fishery catches increased to about 80 million tons by the end of the 1980s and have since then remained at about that level, accounting for about 60 percent of global production in 2003. However, the relatively stable level of catches in recent years obscures some problematic changes in the world's fisheries. In many areas, catch levels have been maintained only through increasing effort and investment in more and better-equipped

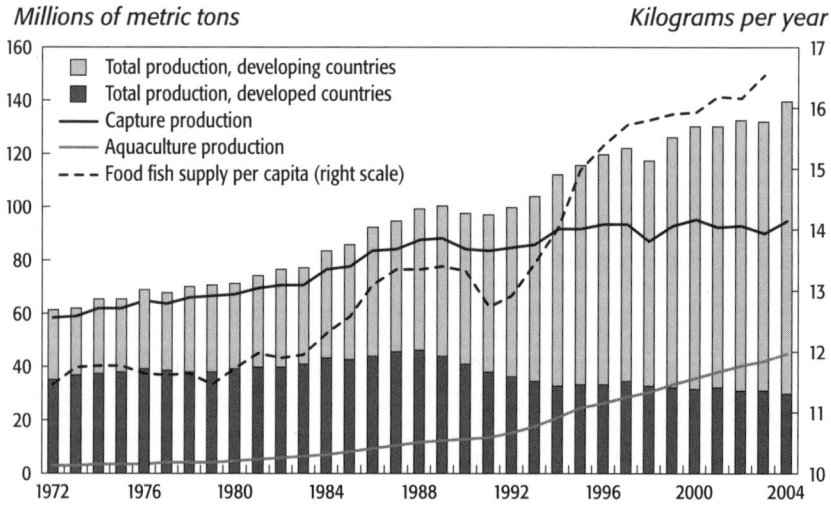

FIGURE 15.2 Production from Capture Fisheries and Aquaculture by Developed and Developing Countries, and Food Fish Supply per Capita, 1972–2004ª

Source: Food and Agriculture Organization of the United Nations fishstat.
a. Excludes aquatic plants.

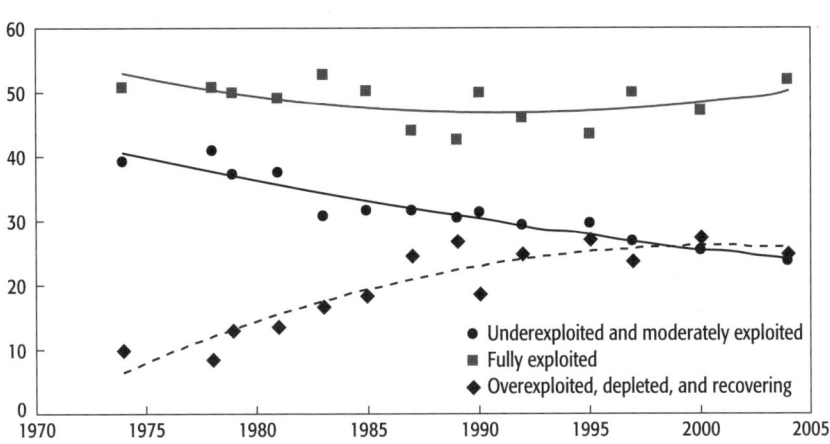

FIGURE 15.3 State of Exploitation of Global Fish Stocks, 1974–2004
Percentage of total

Source: Food and Agriculture Organization of the United Nations 2005.

vessels with increasingly efficient gear. Analysis of global fisheries data shows that the mean size of individual fish caught has declined, previously discarded fish are being retained, and, in many cases, the net value of the catch has also decreased.

Today, a quarter of the world's marine fish stocks are being fished at an unsustainable level (figure 15.3). Half of all stocks are fully exploited, with no scope for further increases in catches. Seven of the top ten marine fisheries are fully exploited or overexploited. It is unknown whether these overexploited stocks can recover in the face of continued fishing and other pressures such as pollution, disease, climate change, and habitat loss. Besides the impoverishment of the Earth's natural heritage, damage to marine ecosystems can have long-term impacts on coastal communities.

Overfishing already has led to fewer jobs, higher fish prices, and reduced income for coastal, regional, and national economies in both developing and developed countries. The impacts are particularly troublesome in the developing world, where fishing has played a particularly significant role in providing food and income to many of the poorest people.

More generally, fishing can dramatically affect the rich diversity of life in the oceans and the ecosystems of which they are a part. Fishing activities that use certain kinds of gear, or that use them improperly, may do serious harm to populations of marine wildlife other than those the fishers are seeking.

According to FAO, 7.3 million tons of fish and shellfish are caught and then discarded because there is no market for them or, at times, fishers must comply with quota or size regulations. Some types of fishing gear, such as trawls, can also damage important fish habitats, such as reefs and seagrass beds. In March 2005, the Millennium Ecosystem Assessment, the first global assessment of the state of the world's ecological health, identified fisheries as one of five global systems in critical condition.

Trade

Not only are many species of fish themselves highly migratory, passing easily across national borders, but fish (including fish raised by aquaculture) is the most heavily traded food commodity worldwide and the fastest-growing agricultural commodity on international markets. In 2003, the top five fish-importing countries by value—Japan, the United States, Spain, France, and Italy—accounted for nearly 54 percent of the total value of global imports of fish products. Between 1985 and 2003, the export value of fish and fishery products (including from aquaculture) rose from $14.5 billion to $63.5 billion. In 2003, the top five fish-exporting countries—China, Thailand, Norway, the United States, and Canada—accounted for one-third of the global export value of fish products.

Exports from developing countries rose from $6.7 billion to $30.3 billion between 1985 and 2003, and net foreign exchange earnings of developing countries from exports of fish products amounted to $17.4 billion—more than the value of their combined net exports of rice, coffee, sugar, and tea. This represents an enormous shift since 1985, when developing countries were net importers of fish products. Fish products now represent more than 10 percent of the total merchandise exports of at least 20 countries, most of them developing. Although the expanding global fish trade creates opportunities for developing countries, it can also foster overfishing and can place fish beyond the purchasing power of the poor.

Climate Change

Climate change, by affecting ocean temperature and chemistry, may have a profound effect on both inland and coastal fisheries. With rising temperatures, the amount of oxygen in the water may decline, while salinity levels and sea levels may rise. Loss of coral reefs and wetlands may reduce critical habitat and alter the availability of food for some fish species. These changes will have a disproportionate impact on the lakes and coastal areas of some developing countries, which lack the resources to adapt to or mitigate these changes. Among these countries are many small island developing states, which have contributed little to the greenhouse gas emissions to which global warming is largely attributed. Fisheries on the high seas are likely to be less affected by global warming, although it may alter the distribution of some species, such as tuna, that are of critical economic importance to many developing countries.

The Forces and Dynamics Affecting Global Fisheries

Four major forces have contributed to the decline of marine and inland fisheries: lack of effective governance, growing demand for seafood, more-effective fishing technologies, and subsidies to fishing operations.

Governance

In most societies, fish are traditionally a common resource to which all have free access. Unlike crops and livestock, fish resources are freely mobile and hidden beneath the waves, making them difficult to measure or control. This complicates the identification of ownership and tenure, which are the usual bases for assigning responsibilities for stewardship of natural resources. Numerous other factors complicate fisheries governance: the interaction between industrial and small-scale fishing; climatic factors that influence the abundance and distribution of fish; the fact that the by-catch of one fishery may be the target species of another; and the poor selectivity of many types of fishing gear.

Additional management challenges are presented by the geographical distribution and movement of fish populations between different jurisdictions—between federal and state waters, between countries' exclusive economic zones (EEZs, or waters within 200 nautical miles of a country's coast, where it may claim exclusive rights to fish), or to and from the high seas. Solutions are typically an outcome of protracted negotiations among fishers, governments, and other stakeholders and are often superseded by the volatile nature of the fisheries themselves. Even with an agreed management system in place, difficulties in enforcing regulations remain. In many countries, fishers consider penalties for illegal fishing as simply a cost of doing business, because the benefits of breaking the law far outweigh the risk of detection and punishment. Meanwhile, developing countries lack cost-effective means of deterring the incursions of foreign vessels into their EEZs.

In many countries, the basic regulatory framework for fisheries management is weak or nonfunctional. Efforts to improve fisheries management can also be hindered by disagreements among the different subsectors of a fishery (for example, between small-scale and industrial fishers targeting the same resource), between fisheries, or between or within governments. For example, attempts to maximize revenue from foreign exchange earnings or from the sale of access privileges to foreign fishing fleets can conflict with efforts to manage fisheries sustainably by setting lower catch limits.

Ineffective governance also undermines the development of sustainable forms of aquaculture, leading to water pollution, destruction of important fish habitats, and declines in wild fish populations. In many countries, aquaculture has expanded dramatically without careful planning and consideration of the trade-offs between increased production and sustainability. As a result, valuable habitats such as mangrove swamps have been destroyed in some areas, and wild fish populations have been exposed to disease and parasites.

The Maldives tuna fishery, which contributed about 9 percent of the country's gross domestic product in 2004, provides an example of the risks involved. Maldives exports about two-thirds of its catch, earning $75.6 million in 2003, or about half the country's exports by value. The fisheries sector accounts for about 20 percent of Maldives' total employment. In recent years, the tuna fleet has been modernizing, replacing traditional wooden vessels with larger vessels fitted with more powerful engines. Now concerns are growing about fleet overcapacity, economic overfishing,[1] and possible declines in some fish stocks.

Demand

As the human population grows and countries around the world become more affluent, the demand for fisheries products increases as well. Globally, annual consumption of food fish products per capita has increased from 10.5 kilograms to 16.2 kilograms over the past three decades (figure 15.2). Most of that increase occurred in China, India, and Southeast Asia. However, excluding China, fish supply per capita was 13.2 kilograms in 2002, the same as it was in 1992. In some countries, such as Ghana, Liberia, and Malawi, the average diet contained less fish protein in the 1990s than it did in the 1970s.

Global demand for fish products is predicted to reach about 20 kilograms per person per year by 2020. Developing countries' share of worldwide fish consumption rose from 45 percent in 1973 to 70 percent in 1997. The growth in aquaculture activities worldwide has also resulted in increasing demand for fishmeal. The share of global fishmeal production used by aquaculture rose from 10 percent in 1988 to over 50 percent in 2003.

The projected gap between supply and demand is of particular concern in some regions. For example, the International Food Policy Research Institute and the WorldFish Center project that, by 2020, the gap between supply and

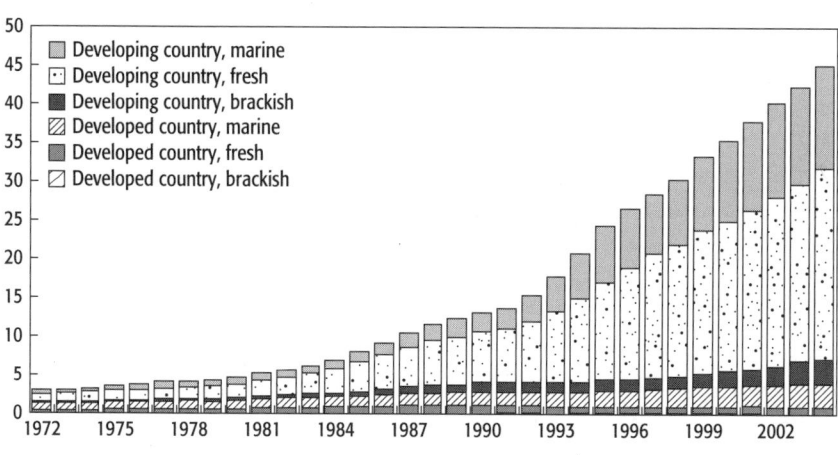

FIGURE 15.4 World Aquaculture Production by Type and Location, 1972–2004
Millions of metric tons

Legend:
- Developing country, marine
- Developing country, fresh
- Developing country, brackish
- Developed country, marine
- Developed country, fresh
- Developed country, brackish

Source: FAO Fishstat.

demand in Africa will still be growing, even if existing harvests of wild-caught fish can be maintained and aquaculture continues to progress at the current rate.

Aquaculture is the most dynamic and rapidly growing sector of the global agricultural economy (figure 15.4), and it remains the leading hope for bridging the widening gap between supply and demand for fish products. However, if pursued without adequate consideration for the wider social and environmental impacts, commercial aquaculture developments may damage aquatic ecosystems and social relationships in coastal communities.

Technology

Although the number of vessels in the global fishing fleet of large (industrial) vessels has remained relatively stable over the past several decades, the catching capacity of much of the fleet has increased enormously, because of ever-larger vessels and increasing sophistication and availability of the technology for locating and catching fish. It has been estimated that average fishing power per vessel has increased by 270 percent since 1965. Little reliable information is available on the global fleet of small vessels, but there is ample evidence that their number has multiplied in many developing countries. In the Republic of Yemen, for example, it is estimated that the small-scale fleet has increased threefold in the past decade, while the number of fishers has quadrupled.

In the past, practical limitations on the size and power of fishing vessels and the technology to detect and catch fish often limited fishing activities to near-shore areas or other shallow waters. The open ocean and the deep sea provided natural refuges for fish. Today, in contrast, global positioning systems (GPS), echo sounders, and monofilament nets all greatly enhance the efficiency of fishing operations. For example, in the Pacific island countries, outboard motors have allowed small-scale fishers to exploit remote fishing grounds previously accessible only to local communities, and canoe fishers equipped with handheld GPS units can now locate seamounts in the open ocean.

Subsidies

Governments often subsidize fishing, along with many other activities, for what are presumed to be socially beneficial reasons. Subsidies are not inherently perverse: although they may distort markets and incentives, they do not necessarily foster environmentally damaging activities. However, it is clear that the billions of dollars in subsidies that governments provide to the fisheries sector do undermine efforts to manage fisheries for ecological and economic sustainability. A number of studies by the World Bank and other international organizations estimate fisheries sector subsidies worldwide at between $12 billion and $20 billion a year. Up to half of these subsidies promote excess capacity and overcapitalization in fishing fleets, leading to overexploitation.[2] The remaining subsidies are directed toward fisheries management, research, conservation, and programs designed to reduce fishing fleets.

Some Controversies Surrounding Fisheries and Aquaculture

The diversity and changing nature of fisheries and the difficulties involved in regulating mobile resources and fishers make fisheries and aquaculture management a challenging task. Some of the controversies that have arisen alongside efforts to make the global fishing industry sustainable are briefly described below.

Allocation of Resources

The allocation of fish resources between small-scale or artisan fisheries and industrial fisheries has been a recurring source of argument and conflict. Table 15.1 reports some selected indicators relating to large- and small-scale fishing; although the data are from 1980, they illustrate the relative

TABLE 15.1 Selected Global Indicators on Large-Scale and Small-Scale Fishing, 1980		
Indicator	**Large-scale fishers**	**Small-scale fishers**
Total employment	500,000	12 million
Annual catch of marine fish for human consumption	29 million metric tons	24 million metric tons
Capital cost per person employed on vessel	$30,000 to $300,000	$250 to $2,500
Fishers employed per $1 million invested	5 to 30	500 to 4,000
Fish discarded at sea per year[b]	8 million tons[c]	

Source: Adapted from Thompson (1980) and FAO sources.
Note: Data are approximate.
a. Data are from recent FAO sources.
b. Figure is for all fishers, of which small-scale fishers account for only a small proportion.

distributional impacts and capital and environmental costs of the two subsectors. Large-scale fishers claim, with some justification, that they are over-regulated and complain about the lack of control over small-scale fisheries; the latter, for their part, point to the destruction of artisan gears and fishing grounds by industrial vessels.

International fisheries access agreements are a special case of the allocation controversy. Under such agreements, one country compensates another for access to its surplus fish resources. However, these access payments are normally paid to the national treasury and thus provide little direct benefit to domestic fishers. The manner in which the surplus is determined can also result in controversy: the quotas sold to the foreign fleets are measured as a biological surplus, which does not necessarily correspond with allocations for local fleets if measured in terms of what can be harvested economically by the domestic fleet.

Scientific Advice

Independent scientific advice is vital when decisions are being made about the sustainability of fisheries. However, the results of scientific investigations are subject to considerable uncertainty, resulting in disputes over their interpretation and over the efficiency or equity of proposed management measures. Although controversy still surrounds the details, the collapse of the Canadian cod fishery provides a classic example. Uncertainty over the state of the stocks delayed management measures, and over a decade later the cod fishery has still not recovered. A precautionary approach is now strongly advocated: the absence of adequate scientific information should not be used as a reason for postponing fundamental conservation and management measures.

Deepwater Trawling

Deepwater trawling is a high-cost, high-risk operation and highly destructive of deepwater coral reefs and other habitats, which can take decades to recover. However, declining coastal fish stocks push fishers to exploit the deeper waters, often in areas outside national control. There is widespread support for a global ban on deepwater trawling, particularly on the seamounts of the high seas. Enforcement of such a ban presents numerous jurisdictional problems, however, as reflagging of noncompliant vessels and use of ports with weak controls often allow these activities to continue. More-rigorous controls in ports and by the states under whose flags these trawlers operate are needed.

Impacts on Endangered Species

Fishing affects numerous endangered species including marine mammals, sharks, seabirds, and turtles. This has led to controversy between environmentalists, who seek bans or other limitations on fishing to protect the endangered animals, and the fishers themselves, who naturally view the potential loss to their livelihood as outweighing the benefit of such protections. Trade sanctions to enforce measures that mitigate the impact of fishing on endangered species have resulted in disputes being arbitrated within the World Trade Organization. The best known of these cases is the tuna-dolphin dispute between the United States and Mexico (and the European Union) and a dispute between the United States and several Asian countries with regard to the use of turtle excluder devices in shrimp trawl nets. In both instances, the United States placed restrictions on imports of seafood captured by fishers that were not employing gear or fishing practices that reduced or eliminated the incidental drowning of dolphins or turtles.

The United Nations Fish Stocks Agreement

Fewer than 60 countries are party to the United Nations Fish Stocks Agreement, the primary international instrument governing fishing on the high seas, and this lack of universal participation undermines its effectiveness and global utility. Some countries are dissatisfied with certain provisions of the agreement, but the contracting parties are reluctant to open the agreement for renegotiation. Increased accession to the agreement would greatly assist global efforts to address illegal fishing, limit the use of flags of convenience, and help enforce international management measures.

Aquaculture and the Environment

Finally, controversy surrounds the expansion of some types of aquaculture, principally those for shrimp and for carnivorous fish such as salmon and cod. Shrimp aquaculture has contributed to the destruction of large areas of mangrove forest, which serve as a very productive habitat for fish and other wildlife, a source of livelihood for subsistence users, and a coastal barrier to the effects of typhoons. Many types of aquaculture also rely on large quantities of fishmeal and fish oil produced from wild fish and may contribute to the spread of disease to wild populations and the displacement of wild species. Codes and best practices such as the technical guidelines prepared to apply FAO's Code of Conduct, and those prepared with World Bank assistance for marine shrimp aquaculture, provide guidance for environmentally sustainable aquaculture.

The Consequences of Failure to Manage Fisheries Sustainably

Resolving the controversies just described is an important task for the international community, because failure to place the exploitation of marine and freshwater fisheries and aquaculture on a truly sustainable foundation will have significant consequences, particularly for coastal and lake communities in developing countries:

- *Economic consequences:* Continued declines in fisheries will result in the sector becoming a net economic burden rather than a benefit, with calls for increasing public support for unprofitable fishing based on a depleting resource. The economic consequences of inaction can be large and long-lasting: for example, some 15 years after the collapse of Canada's Atlantic cod fishery the coastal communities of eastern Canada are still recovering. Similarly unsustainable aquaculture development has jeopardized important fish habitats and wild fisheries and resulted in local economic collapse due to disease and environmental degradation.
- *Social consequences:* The collapse of fisheries in developing countries, by reducing the well-being of dependent communities, will encourage increased emigration with all its attendant social tensions and difficulties. Concentration and intensification of aquaculture may aggravate disparities in income and in economic and political power.
- *Security consequences:* Failure to maintain or increase the availability of fish in the local markets in developing countries may lead to social

unrest. Incursions by fishers into the waters of neighboring states continue to be a source of international incidents. Similarly, the failure of fisheries will increase poverty and dislocation, possibly contributing in some circumstances to failed states.

- *Health consequences:* In developing countries, fish from capture fisheries and sustainable aquaculture can be an important source of protein and micronutrients essential for the good health of the population. Unsustainable fishing and aquaculture development will compromise this supply.
- *Environmental consequences:* Poorly managed fisheries will undermine ocean, coastal, and lake ecosystems, reducing the rich biological diversity of these areas and the many benefits that derive from healthy ecosystems. Similarly, imprudent aquaculture practices will degrade water quality in coasts, lakes, and rivers; damage or destroy critical coastal and freshwater habitats; and threaten wild fisheries.

Steps Already Taken Toward Improved Global Fisheries Management

The mobility of fish and fishers, the difficulties in assessing the state of diverse fish stocks, and the various impacts of overfishing and environmental change pose substantial challenges to fisheries management. Similarly, aquaculture uses public goods including freshwater resources, marine spaces, and common-property wetlands and intertidal areas and can have an adverse impact on critical habitats, biodiversity, and genetic heritage.

Addressing these issues requires establishing good fisheries governance. Good governance, in turn, means protection of the inshore and coastal fisheries on which poor subsistence fishers and small-scale commercial fishers depend, while clearly defining the important role of industrial fisheries. Good governance also recognizes the important links among aquaculture development; healthy wild fisheries; and the responsible management of water basins, wetlands, and coastal zones. Good governance involves transparent and participatory decision making that is accountable to both today's stakeholders and future generations.

Explicit policy frameworks that identify clear, realistic goals and how and when they may be reached are an important instrument for realizing sustainable fisheries management. These frameworks, attuned to the needs of each country, include a legal framework and an effective means of applying fishery regulations, means of engaging stakeholders, provisions for conflict resolution and mediation, arrangements for cooperation and participation, financing of independent scientific advice, extension and outreach institutions, and the use of nongovernmental organizations for monitoring and independent oversight.

Fisheries management also has a vital economic dimension, since economic measures must complement measures targeted on the biological state of the fishery. A profitable fishery can be considered a source of infinite positive cash flow, and thereby an important contributor to an economy.

Several important international conventions provide a framework for management of fisheries at the national and the international levels. These include the following:

- The United Nations Convention on the Law of the Sea, the principal international instrument in this domain
- The United Nations Fish Stocks Agreement, made pursuant to the Law of the Sea Convention, which addresses management of highly migratory species of fish and populations of fish that straddle international boundaries
- The FAO Compliance Agreement, which further defines the international obligations of states with respect to their fishing vessels
- Conventions establishing regional fisheries management organizations, such as the International Convention for the Conservation for Atlantic Tunas, charged with the management of the Atlantic tuna fisheries
- A range of nonfisheries agreements and conventions, such as the Convention on Biological Diversity and the Convention on International Trade in Endangered Species, as well as conventions on rivers, lakes, regional seas, pollution, safety at sea, labor standards, and other relevant matters.

The international community also has adopted a number of nonbinding instruments, including the following:

- The FAO Code of Conduct for Responsible Fisheries, which sets out principles and international standards of behavior regarding capture fisheries and aquaculture development
- International plans of action on illicit fishing, fleet capacity, and the protection of sharks and seabirds
- Regional instruments integrating the FAO Code of Conduct into regional fisheries policy and practice, such as the South African Development Community Protocol on Fisheries and various policies and regulations of the European Union

- Numerous United Nations General Assembly resolutions
- Specific deadlines on five issues agreed on as part of a plan of action at the 2002 World Summit on Sustainable Development (WSSD) in Johannesburg, South Africa: illegal, unrecorded, and unregistered fishing (often referred to as IUU fishing); fishing capacity; application of an ecosystem approach; restoration of depleted stocks; and establishment of *representative networks* of marine protected areas.

Management of fisheries has become increasingly sophisticated in the past two decades, partly in response to the failure of past approaches to maintain fisheries at sustainable levels. In line with the WSSD Plan of Action, several promising tools can be highlighted:

- *Monitoring and enforcement:* Cost-effective monitoring, control, and surveillance are fundamental to enforcement of fishery regulations. Current technology can track and detect fishing vessels worldwide, including those engaged in IUU fishing.
- *Buybacks:* In many fisheries, it is necessary to reduce the current fishing fleet or fishing capacity in order to achieve sustainable fishing levels. Buybacks are a means of removing fishing vessels from the fleet by decommissioning them (scrapping the vessels or transferring them to other uses), or by compensating fishers for the reduction in the number of fishing licenses.
- *Rights-based management:* Different forms of community or private property rights can be created with respect to fisheries previously considered to be public, open-access resources. Experience shows that property rights systems can improve sustainable use and profitability, but they may also undesirably concentrate wealth. The application of property rights requires analysis of opportunities and challenges on a case-by-case basis and must meet equity objectives, in terms of both access to resources and distribution of benefits.
- *Co-management and decentralized decision making:* Co-management is an arrangement whereby government and users of a resource share responsibility for its management. This allows fishers to influence the decisions made, while governments can ensure that long-term management objectives are met. Participation in decision making gains the support of the fishers, confers legitimacy on the regulations, and fosters compliance, which may also reduce the costs of monitoring and surveillance.
- *Ecosystem approach to fisheries:* In previous decades, fisheries management generally focused on the main target species in a fishery.

However, fishing activities also affect species other than the target species and may alter overall ecosystem functions such as predator-prey interactions, species composition, nutrient flows, and habitat quality. Sustainable fisheries management requires consideration and management of the entire marine ecosystem that supports the fishery—not just the target species. The *ecosystem* approach to fisheries is an evolving body of best practice that incorporates ecosystem considerations into fisheries management.

- *Marine protected areas:* A marine protected area (MPA) can offer a range of protection, from complete prohibition against removal of any living creature to seasonal closure or restrictions on the removal of certain designated species. It has been shown that MPAs contribute to sustainable fisheries. The long-term benefits to fishers can outweigh the short-term loss that they may experience when the MPA is first established. MPAs require careful design not only in their spatial configuration but also with respect to stakeholder involvement and institutional sustainability.
- *Certification programs for fish products:* Certification programs can promote sustainable fishing and poverty reduction by creating market mechanisms that encourage fisheries to be managed in compliance with a suite of criteria, such as stock condition and ecosystem impact. The Marine Stewardship Council is one example of a fisheries certification program. The council links suppliers (fishers) with consumers through a chain of sustainable production by certifying fisheries as sustainable, and recruiting distributors, such as major retail chains, to market sustainable products to discerning consumers, often at premium prices.

The Role of the World Bank in Maintaining Sustainable Fisheries

The fisheries and aquaculture loan portfolio of the World Bank has evolved considerably in recent decades. Before 1980, about 60 percent of all World Bank fisheries loans were for large-scale fisheries development, such as the building of industrial vessels and fishery service facilities. By the 1980s, the Bank had reduced its support for increased production from capture fisheries and shifted its emphasis toward aquaculture, resource assessment, and fisheries research. In the 1990s, the Bank further reduced its investments in capture fisheries and increased its investments in aquaculture to roughly half of its total direct investment in the sector.

The World Bank has responded to the growing concerns of its member countries over the sustainability of increased harvesting of wild fish stocks and the impact on aquatic ecosystems of rapidly expanding aquaculture production. The Bank has acknowledged that, to ensure the sustainability of capture fisheries and aquaculture, long-term investments are required at many political and societal levels: in planning, ecosystems-based resource management, and postharvest operations; in human resources and applied science and extension institutions; and in public–private partnerships. The Bank's current efforts concentrate on improved governance, coastal management, inland fisheries, and smallholder aquaculture operations, mostly in Africa and in South and East Asia.

The World Bank will broaden its support for sustainable fisheries at the country, regional, and global levels and has established a new Global Program on Fisheries (PROFISH). In implementing this program the Bank is focusing on policy reforms guided by the FAO Code of Conduct for Responsible Fisheries and is working with global partners, including the FAO, the IUCN—The World Conservation Union, the WorldFish Center, and regional organizations. PROFISH will focus on good governance, sustainable fisheries policies, and promoting effective fisheries strategies. In cooperation with the Global Environment Facility (GEF), the Bank is participating in regional fisheries initiatives, such as the Strategic Partnership for a Sustainable Fisheries Investment Fund in the Large Marine Ecosystems of Sub-Saharan Africa, while also building on the GEF's large marine ecosystem projects.

The rationale for greater involvement by the Bank and the international community in fisheries issues follows directly from the agreements at the WSSD and the Millennium Development Goals. These initiatives identified an imperative to reduce poverty among 30 million small-scale fishers and their dependents, many of whom now face declining incomes. These initiatives also speak to the urgent need to address the looming ecological crisis associated with overfishing and degraded aquatic ecosystems.

Working with its client countries and the international donor community, the World Bank has the capacity to combine policy dialogue at the highest levels with specific investments. The Bank plans to help mount a global effort to revitalize fisheries as follows:

- Strengthening the institutions dealing with the governance of fishing in the developing world
- Assisting countries to include a fisheries component in national development and poverty alleviation strategies

- Helping countries develop the legal and regulatory frameworks needed for sustainable fisheries
- Supporting the establishment of market-based incentives for sustainable fishing, and curtailing open access to fisheries through rights-based fishery management regimes
- Raising awareness within industrial countries of the need for reform in areas such as subsidies
- Providing support and training for human capacity building, including development of effective negotiating skills and strategies
- Supporting the further provision of services to marginalized rural fishing communities, and assisting coastal communities in managing their fisheries in a sustainable manner
- Promoting the establishment and implementation of marine reserves and protected areas
- Providing technical support for the development of sustainable aquaculture.

The World Bank recognizes that it is time for a proactive, international approach to improving the fisheries sector worldwide. The challenge in moving toward a sustainable fishing industry is to maintain economic growth and development by enhancing productivity and the wealth of fisheries, while avoiding the overfishing and ecological degradation observed today. The Bank is committed to helping establish institutions, values, and practices that will safeguard the future of fish resources and the health and livelihood of communities that depend on these resources for their income, nutrition, and quality of life.

Notes

1. Economic overfishing can occur when the fish catch is sustainable but large enough to drive prices down, so that total income is less than it would be with a smaller catch. Economists describe this as a *dissipation of resource rents*.
2. Excess capacity has both short-term and long-term dimensions. In the short term, excess capacity is capacity that exceeds that required to capture and handle the allowable catch. In the long term, it refers to capacity that exceeds the level required to ensure the sustainability of the stock and the fishery at the desired level.

Selected Readings and Cited References

Food and Agriculture Organization of the United Nations. 1995. *Code of Conduct for Responsible Fisheries*. Rome.

_____. 2004. *State of the World's Fisheries and Aquaculture*. Rome.

_____. 2005. "Review of the State of World Marine Fisheries Resources." *Fisheries Technical Paper 457*, Food and Agriculture Organization of the United Nations, Rome.

Kelleher, M. Kieran. 1996. "Approaches to Practical Fisheries Management." Discussion paper presented at the Round Table on Fisheries Management and Regulation in the Area Covered by the Sub-Regional Fisheries Commission, Dakar, July. GCP/RAF/302/EEC.

Millennium Ecosystem Assessment. 2005. "Ecosystems and Human Well-Being: Current State and Trends, Findings of the Condition and Trends Working Group, Millennium Ecosystem Assessment Series." http://www.millenniumassessment. org//en/Products.Global.Condition.aspx.

Thompson. 1980. "Conflict Within the Fishing Industry." *ICLARM Newsletter* 3: 3–4.

World Bank. 2004. "Saving Fish and Fishers: Toward Sustainable and Equitable Governance of the Global Fisheries Sector." Washington, DC.

Selected Web Links on Fisheries Management

Fisheries Department of the Food and Agriculture Organization of the United Nations	http://www.fao.org/fi/default.asp
IUCN—The World Conservation Union Marine Program	http://www.iucn.org/places/wescana/programs/marine.html
Marine Stewardship Council	http://www.msc.org
Millennium Ecosystem Assessment	http://www.millenniumassessment.org/en/index.aspx
United Nations Law of the Sea	http://www.un.org/depts/los/index.htm
World Bank Fisheries and Aquaculture page	http://www.worldbank.org/fish
WorldFish Center	http://www.worldfishcenter.org/cms/default.aspx

16

Sustaining the World's Forests: Managing Competing Demands for a Vital Resource

WORLD BANK ENVIRONMENTALLY AND SOCIALLY SUSTAINABLE DEVELOPMENT FORESTS TEAM

Forests cover about 25 to 30 percent of the Earth's land surface, or between 3.3 billion and 3.9 billion hectares, depending on the definitions used. Each year forests covering an area the size of Portugal (approximately 92,000 square kilometers) are cut down. The Food and Agriculture Organization (FAO) of the United Nations estimates that, during the 1990s, the world suffered a net loss of 95 million hectares of forests—an area larger than República Bolivariana de Venezuela—with most of the losses occurring in the tropics. The loss of 161 million hectares of natural forests to deforestation was somewhat offset by 15 million hectares of afforestation (deliberate creation of forest where none existed before), 36 million hectares of natural expansion of forests, and 15 million hectares of reforestation.

These losses are serious because forests provide a complex array of vital ecological, social, and economic goods and services. About 60 million people (mainly indigenous and tribal groups) are almost wholly dependent on forests, and another 350 million people who live within or adjacent to dense forests depend on them to a high degree for subsistence and income. In developing countries, about 1.2 billion people (including more than 400 million in Africa; see box 16.1) rely on open woodlands or agroforestry systems that help to sustain agricultural productivity and generate income. Some 1 billion

---

BOX 16.1   Why Forests Matter to Africa

Forests are vital for the welfare of millions in Africa, especially the poor and marginalized. Used wisely, they could improve livelihoods and people's quality of life. The following statistics give a sense of forests' importance to the continent:

- Over two-thirds of Africa's 600 million people rely directly or indirectly on forests for their livelihood, including food security.
- Wood is the primary energy source for at least 70 percent of African households.
- Forest-related activities account for 10 percent of gross domestic product in at least 19 African countries, and more than 10 percent of national trade in 10 others.
- Africa is home to 25 percent of the world's remaining tropical rainforests and contains 20 percent of the world's biodiversity hotspots.

The end of violent conflicts in countries such as Angola, the Central African Republic, the Democratic Republic of the Congo, Liberia, Mozambique, Sierra Leone, and Sudan presents new opportunities to support sustainable forest management. African countries can also take advantage of a growing national and global demand for forest goods and services.

Source: Adapted from Centre for International Forestry Research 2005, 2.

---

people worldwide depend on medicines derived from forest plants or rely on common-pool forest resources for meeting essential fuel wood, grazing, and other needs.

At the global level, forests make an important contribution to economic development. Wood and manufactured forest products add more than $450 billion to the world market economy each year, and the annual value of internationally traded forest products has been running between $150 billion and $200 billion. The International Labour Organization estimates global forest-based employment (including both industrial and nonindustrial forest harvesting and industrialized forest products manufacture) at approximately 47 million; forest-based employment in developing countries accounts for about 32 million of those jobs, or almost 70 percent. FAO estimates that, out of roughly 3.5 billion hectares of global forest area, 1.2 billion hectares is available for industrial wood supply.

Besides providing wood and other products, forests are the repository of the great bulk of terrestrial biodiversity, with all that that implies for gene pools, pharmaceuticals, and other unique and valuable goods and services. Forests also contain large amounts of sequestered carbon, and their destruction or degradation (especially by burning) is estimated to contribute between 10 and 30 percent of all carbon gas emissions into the atmosphere.

Deforestation is thus a considerable factor in global warming. In addition, forests help maintain the fertility of agricultural land, protect water sources, and reduce the risks of natural disasters such as landslides and flooding. Mismanagement of woodlands in humid tropical and subtropical countries contributes significantly to soil losses equivalent to 10 percent of agricultural output in those countries each year. In some countries in the Asia-Pacific region, forest destruction is responsible for global biodiversity losses on the order of 2 to 5 percent per decade, resulting in inestimable harm to ecosystem stability and human well-being.

Sustainable management of forests is crucial for poverty reduction in many developing countries. Many of the rural poor rely on forests for both subsistence and income. Small-scale forest product processing and trade are often important activities in rural economies. The forest products sector in most developing countries continues to be dominated by small and medium-size enterprises. Forest harvesting and primary processing are characterized by low entry costs, enabling the rural poor to engage in these activities. For countries with large forest endowments, and even for others that have limited forests, if forest issues are not fully incorporated into broad national government and assistance strategies, the overarching goals of poverty reduction are unlikely to be achieved.

The Forces and Dynamics Affecting the World's Forests

The forest sector represents one of the most challenging areas in the development of community and global public policy. Despite significant resource flows, international concern, and political pressure, a combination of market and institutional failures has led to forests failing to realize their potential to reduce poverty, promote economic growth, and be valued for their contributions to the local and global environment.

Forest Law Enforcement and Governance

Many countries with substantial forest resources have been subject to corruption and serious inadequacies in how forests have been allocated, administered, and monitored. Despite their great economic value, forests are one of developing countries' most mismanaged resources, with both political and business elites sharing the blame. Illegal logging and associated trade and corruption at high political levels flourish because timber rights provide an extremely valuable reward for services to political elites. Besides channeling potential timber revenue away from national development efforts, particularly from the people living in and near the forests, the low prices at which these concessions are often granted encourage waste, unsustainable management, plundering for short-term gain, and replacement by less valuable and less sustainable activities. Such loss and degradation have come at the expense not only of national economies but also of the rural people who depend on forest resources for their livelihood. This mismanagement translates into enormous national costs. For example, failure to collect appropriate royalties and taxes from legal forest operations costs governments around $5 billion annually. Illegal logging results in additional losses of forest resources from public lands of at least $10 billion to $15 billion a year. Improvements in forest law enforcement and governance are critical to capturing the full economic potential of forests in a sustainable manner.

Given forests' significant commercial value, the private sector is the principal source of finance in forest production in most countries. Indeed, the level of activity and influence of the private sector in forests dwarfs that of the international community—and sometimes of the national government. Official development assistance accounted for only a fraction of the funds available for forestry in the mid 1990s, and it has declined sharply since then. Meanwhile private sector investment—from both domestic and foreign sources—has been on the upswing, and direct public sector investment has dropped only slightly. Given this trend, legal and regulatory frameworks that support sustainable forest practices must be developed to promote responsible private sector investment and eliminate corruption.

Local communities are playing an increasingly important role in forest management. Studies of the ownership and administration of forests project a near doubling of forest area under recognized community ownership and a doubling of the area reserved for community administration (figure 16.1). Community participation in decision making and implementation is considered to be essential for good governance, equitable distribution of benefits, and sustainable resource management.

Forests in Poverty Reduction Strategies

Many of the world's poor depend on forests for their livelihoods. Forests can therefore play a significant role in realizing the Millennium Development Goal of halving the number of people living in absolute poverty by 2015. Unfortunately, rural development strategies often have neglected forests, because forests have been mistakenly viewed as being outside the mainstream of agricultural development. However, conservation and production must coexist if the full potential of forests for poverty reduction is to be realized. Although large areas of the world's forests must be preserved intact for their ecological and cultural value, much of what remains will inevitably be used

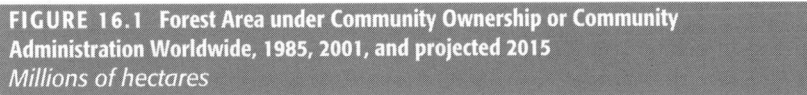

FIGURE 16.1 Forest Area under Community Ownership or Community Administration Worldwide, 1985, 2001, and projected 2015
Millions of hectares

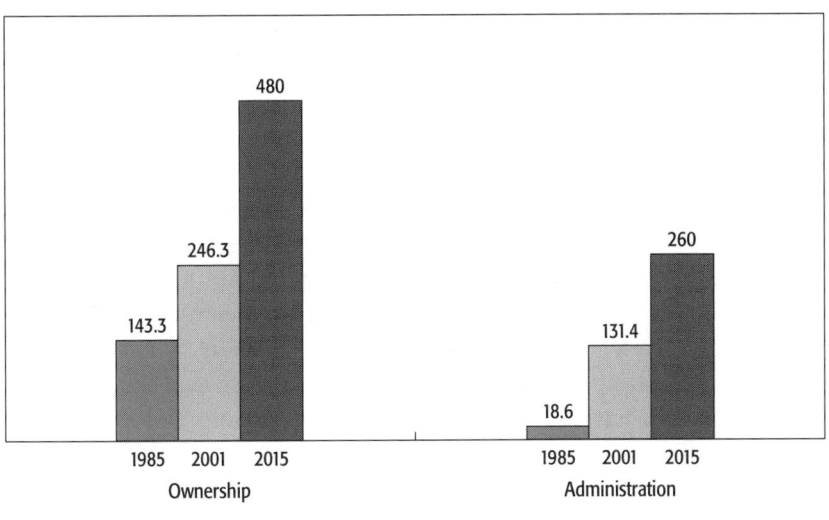

Source: Forest Trends.

for productive purposes. In addition to the lumber and wood products industry, the gathering and marketing of hundreds of forest products, such as forest fruits, fuel wood, and medicinal products, constitute an economic activity of enormous scale. Consequently, a dual approach covering both protection and productive use is needed. Efforts to improve sustainable use and management in the productive sector must accompany continued efforts toward protection and conservation.

Using forests for poverty reduction also requires a strong institutional framework and an effective legal and regulatory environment in which the rights of specific groups among the poor are recognized and protected. Additionally, opportunities to develop sustainable forest businesses must be provided to these and other groups. Therefore, development organizations need an approach that focuses on participation and conflict resolution and not just on the technical and economic aspects of forestry.

Global Values from Forests

Forests play a critical role in balancing the global climate through carbon sequestration, and they serve as the repository for most of the planet's terrestrial biodiversity. In both these roles, forests constitute global public goods (see chapter 1), which, to be maintained, must be both protected and managed sustainably. Although biodiversity and key environmental services have traditionally been sustained through the establishment of protected areas, the wide range of competing uses of forests by diverse groups imposes constraints on how much can be achieved by protection alone. Improving forest management practices in production forests (forests where productive use is permitted) is an essential component of any strategy to protect vital local environmental services, in addition to efforts aimed at bolstering the effectiveness of management within protected areas.

Although some forest products, primarily lumber and fuel wood, are delivered through markets, the economic value of many of the other contributions of forests to the environment, to biodiversity, and to the stability of the global climate go unrecognized by the market. Creative new mechanisms are needed to ensure that the costs of any loss of forests' environmental services are paid for by those responsible. It is highly unlikely, however, that governments will be able to significantly scale down lumber extraction to preserve forests for their environmental services, unless the costs in terms of forgone revenue can be offset in some way. Moreover, very few countries would be prepared to borrow funds—from the World Bank or other sources—to finance forest protection as a substitute for forest production. Innovative financing options and markets for forests' environmental services, such as ecotourism, carbon offsets, and watershed management, will all have important roles to play. As carbon credits grow in value under a future global carbon-trading system, there will be increasing incentives to invest in the establishment of new forested areas for their carbon benefits.

Demand

As human populations grow and countries around the world become more affluent, the demand for wood forest products—solid wood, pulp, and paper—will increase as well. In 2005, removals of roundwood (wood in its natural state, as felled or harvested) were forecast to be valued at around $64 billion, an increase of about 11 percent over the previous 15 years. The demand for nonwood forest products has also increased slightly since 1990, with removals estimated at $4.7 billion. Furthermore, with growing populations there is an increase in the clearing of forests for agriculture (figure 16.2). FAO estimates that each year farmers permanently convert 13 million hectares of forest to agriculture, mainly in the tropics. Spillovers from poor policies in other sectors can also contribute to rapid rates of deforestation. This has been particularly evident in recent decades, for example, in the conversion of forest areas to oil palm plantations in Indonesia. Pressures on

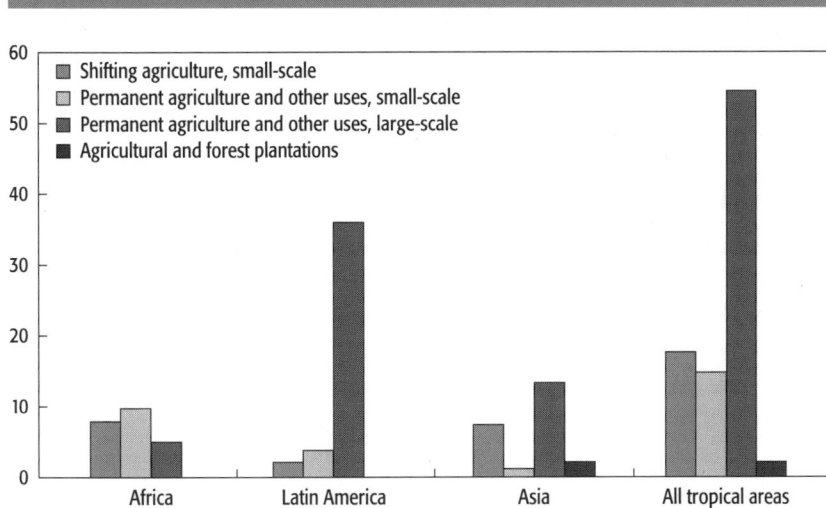

FIGURE 16.2 Main Causes of Deforestation by World Region, 1990–2000
Millions of hectares

- Shifting agriculture, small-scale
- Permanent agriculture and other uses, small-scale
- Permanent agriculture and other uses, large-scale
- Agricultural and forest plantations

Source: Food and Agriculture Organization of the United Nations.

forests from poorly aligned strategies in agriculture, transportation, energy, and industry, as well as unsound macroeconomic policies, are major causes of forest loss and degradation. Cross-sectoral cooperation to coordinate policies is essential to avoid forest degradation and to ensure that forests are managed in a sustainable manner.

Some Controversies Surrounding Forests

Forests and Poverty Reduction

Forests can be used to help alleviate poverty, but views differ on how this should be done. The poor are not a homogeneous group with respect to their use of forests. Among the poor are some who depend heavily on forests for their subsistence and livelihoods, whereas others have a higher level of industrial or artisanal skills and access to markets and therefore different forest needs. If too much emphasis is placed on building the poor's participation in market-based use of forests, those groups who need to use the forests communally for subsistence may be excluded. It is therefore essential to ensure that market opportunities are assessed realistically and that group is not set against group in a limited market. Appropriate collective control and management are also needed in community forest management systems, to ensure that liberalization of markets and privatization of state forest and other enterprises benefit the poor. Additionally, such controls should be incorporated into any program or initiative targeted at poverty reduction, including payment for environmental services schemes, to ensure that the funds reach the intended beneficiaries.

Governance Issues

Another area of potential conflict is that between state ownership of forests and the interests of communal and smallholder producers, who frequently are poor. These groups are often excluded, whether deliberately by policy or through failures in sector governance, from adequate participation in the commercial use of forests. Additionally, many of the world's indigenous peoples live within or near forests and are among the poorest, most vulnerable, and most powerless groups in developing countries. Their tenure rights, in forest areas in particular, tend to be insecure. It is clear that policies and institutional reforms, and legal reforms that establish and protect the rights of indigenous peoples—in a number of areas including forest use—are needed in many countries.

Devolution of management of forests to lower levels of government or local community groups is widely considered essential for good governance, equitable distribution of benefits, and sustainable resource management. However, the implementation of these schemes has often resulted in capture by local elites and created conflict in local communities. The result has been unsustainable forest management and social disruption. Issues of gender equality in access to forest resources have often not been adequately addressed when forest management has been decentralized. Such matters need to be taken on board in any decentralization or devolution process to ensure that systems for equitable benefit sharing and sustainable management are put in place.

Protection of Global Environmental Services

One of the problems inherent in protecting forests is that forests are in high demand for a range of often mutually exclusive uses by competing groups within society. Some conservation groups and policy makers mistakenly assume that the interests of the forest-dependent poor, on the one hand, and the global interest in protecting and preserving forests for their biodiversity and other global values, on the other, will always converge. Although in most cases the poor do share an interest in protecting an environment that will enable them to maintain their livelihoods, this does not necessarily imply a complete congruence of interests: the poor may prefer to change the existing forest landscape in ways that may not meet the interests of global stakeholders. The development of incentives, such as payment for environmental services, that will balance local and global demands thus needs careful consideration and further development.

Actions of the International Community Toward Sustainable Forest Management

In the past 15 years, the legal and international framework that governs forest issues has advanced and broadened. The main agreements that affect the forest sector are the conventions and processes arising from the 1992 United Nations Conference on Environment and Development held in Rio de Janeiro (the Rio Earth Summit) and from subsequent United Nations forums that focus on forests, specifically the Convention on Biological Diversity; the Convention to Combat Desertification; the United Nations Framework Convention on Climate Change (UNFCCC) and its Kyoto Protocol; and the international dialogue on forests, which has culminated in the United Nations Forum on Forests (UNFF). The Convention on International Trade in Endangered Species also addresses some aspects of forest management. Additionally, innovations by nongovernmental organizations (NGOs) and civil society, such as the development of forest certification schemes, have made important contributions to global sustainable forest management.

The Rio Earth Summit

At the 1992 Rio Earth Summit, forests posed some of the most controversial issues, which tended to polarize developing and developed countries. Intense negotiations among governments resulted in an authoritative but non-legally binding statement of Principles for a Global Consensus on Management, Conservation, and Sustainable Development of All Types of Forests. This declaration affirmed that states have sovereign rights over their natural resources but also recognized that forests are a global public good that provides ecosystem services of global value and significance, such as biodiversity preservation, carbon sequestration, and nutrient and hydrological cycling. Ultimately, agreements emerging from the Rio Summit had as their objective to enhance the scope and effectiveness of national institutions in developed and developing countries related to management, conservation, and sustainable development of forests. Lending organizations such as the World Bank are obliged to assist their clients in meeting the commitments and international conventions arising from the Rio Summit.

The Kyoto Protocol

The negotiation of the 1997 Kyoto Protocol to the UNFCCC established global commitments to mitigate climate change and created three flexible mechanisms to achieve this objective. Two of these relate directly to the forest sector. The first allows parties from developed countries and countries in transition from socialism to transfer or acquire emissions reduction units from any other party. This mechanism, called Joint Implementation, could play an important role in supporting sustainable forest management in transition countries. The second mechanism, the Clean Development Mechanism (CDM), regulates greenhouse gas emissions trading between industrial countries and developing countries. Forests could play a role in CDM by integrating forest management and conservation through reforestation and afforestation. Such integration could mobilize substantial resource flows to developing countries. The third mechanism is emissions trading, wherein a market for emissions reductions is created.

The first commitment period under the Kyoto Protocol is through 2012, and negotiations are under way to establish parameters for the next commitment period. Recently, the question of how to reduce greenhouse gas emissions from deforestation has received considerable attention, and the new concept of *avoided deforestation* as a means of compliance has been put on the negotiating table. If accepted, it could have major implications for the forest sector and the means of financing forest conservation.

The United Nations Forum on Forests

Significant progress has been made in the international dialogue on forests since the Rio Summit. During that time, the main focus within the United Nations has been to continue to develop coherent policies to promote the management, conservation, and sustainable development of all types of forests. The Intergovernmental Panel on Forests (IPF), from 1995 to 1997, and the Intergovernmental Forum on Forests (IFF), from 1997 to 2000, both under the auspices of the United Nations Commission on Sustainable Development, were the main intergovernmental forums for international forest policy development during this period. In October 2000, through the Economic and Social Council of the United Nations, the international community created UNFF, a new international body that will build on the work of IPF and IFF in providing a platform for high-level policy discussion and cooperation to strengthen long-term political commitment to the sustainable management of forests.

Independent Forest Certification

Since the 1990s, independent forest certification has become a powerful agent for broader participation by civil society in identifying and promoting improved forest management practices. Independent certification is a process under which a third party audits the performance of forest management to determine whether it meets broadly accepted environmental, social, and economic standards. Independent certification provides an opportunity to send clear and transparent signals about forest management to stakeholders, whether they are consumers, governments, investors, or local communities. Initially, the Forest Stewardship Council was the main body promoting independent third-party assessment of forest operations and the performance of forestry companies. However, a number of competing schemes have now emerged, reflecting a growing international recognition that centralized control and management of forest resources by weak government forest services had failed to stem escalating deforestation or ensure sustainable forest management.

Designation of Protected Areas

The definition of protected areas has evolved within such large conservation organizations as the World Wildlife Fund (WWF) and IUCN—The World Conservation Society to recognize possibilities for combining conservation with sustainable human use. Accordingly, governments in more countries today recognize the importance of establishing and maintaining protected area systems for protection of biodiversity. For example, in Latin America during the past decade, the average share of total land area covered by protected area designation rose from 5 percent to 12 percent. A study by Conservation International has demonstrated that tropical parks have been effective in protecting ecosystems and species within their borders, even as people continue to live within 70 percent of these parks. Protected areas have been particularly effective in preventing land clearing, which is the most serious threat to forests and biodiversity.

Additionally, the private sector has shown some interest in buying conservation concession rights to large blocks of forest. These concession rights are leased at quasi-market rates (estimates of what the market price would be if a market existed) and provide a direct incentive for conservation and provision of ecosystem services. The funds are used for social development and poverty alleviation in the areas surrounding the protected areas. For example, the Nature Conservancy has generated $700 million to acquire and protect habitats in the United States and elsewhere. Ecologically friendly enterprises such as ecotourism companies also attempt to combine the protection of forests and biodiversity with sustainable development.

Consequences of Failure to Manage Forests Sustainably

Failure to manage forests sustainably would have a variety of adverse consequences—economic, social, and environmental. At the national level, forests have an important role to play in sustaining economic growth and alleviating poverty. National economies could benefit much more than they do now from their forests. Destruction and mismanagement of forests lead to a decrease in export earnings, which in turn lowers government revenue, reduces employment, and limits the options for a diversified economy.

Over a billion people depend on forests as a direct source of income or livelihood, including maintenance of soil fertility and water resources. Approximately the same number depend largely on fuel wood for their cooking and heat. A billion people also depend almost entirely on medicines derived from forest plants for their medicinal needs. An estimated 60 million people depend on benefits from downstream forest industries such as sawmills, carpentry, and handicrafts. In addition to the tremendous loss of cultural value from the loss of forests, the number of extreme poor could increase significantly if forests are not well managed and new forest resources are not developed. With fewer opportunities open to these mostly rural poor, this would lead to increased rural-to-urban migration.

At least two-thirds of Earth's terrestrial species are primarily found in forests. The maintenance of significant areas of plant diversity ensures a sufficiently wide range of tree species to buffer forests and helps ensure their function in regulating the landscape and preventing disruption by pests, disease, and normal climate variations. Loss of the world's forests would also have a tremendous impact on global climate change, and the biotic diversity of forests is the base for selection and breeding of plants and animals for a range of environments and human uses. This genetic bank is the source of higher-yielding and more pest-resistant food crops and of materials of medicinal, pharmaceutical, and industrial value. Failure to manage forests sustainably would thus have tremendous environmental consequences at both the local and the global levels.

The World Bank's Engagement in Sustainable Forest Management

The World Bank's engagement in the forest sectors of developing countries inevitably addresses the balance between production and conservation. It also involves questions of the fair distribution of the benefits and responsibilities of forest use and protection among interested economic and social groups, as well as consideration of the longer-term issues of forest sustainability and environmental health. Managing these trade-offs is not only technically difficult but politically complex as well.

The World Bank's Forests Strategy

Recognizing these challenges, in 2002 the World Bank revised its overall forest strategy, and today the Bank uses its various instruments in innovative ways to further enable sustainable forest management. Beginning with its 1991 forestry strategy and its 1993 operational policy, the activities of the Bank in the forest sector were guided by a *do no harm* principle that focused largely on environmental issues and on pure protection options. Although the 1991 strategy recognized the role that forests could play in poverty reduction and the importance of policy reforms in containing deforestation, its hallmark was a strong commitment not to finance commercial logging in primary tropical moist forests. (Primary forests are forests that have not been previously felled.) The past decade has demonstrated that this strategy and operational policy constrained the Bank from adequately engaging in the sector, and to a large extent prevented the Bank from participating in international and national dialogues on this issue. Most important, the 1993 policy resulted in many missed opportunities for the Bank to harness the potential of well-managed forests, open woodlands, and on-farm woodlots to make a significant contribution to poverty reduction and to the protection of environmental services of global importance. Meanwhile, the loss of forests has continued at historically high rates, and successful efforts to reduce destructive and unsustainable logging and unwarranted forest clearing have been few and far between.

Starting in 1998, the World Bank reviewed its forest strategy. The new strategy approved in 2002 was based on findings from a review by the independent Operations Evaluation Department and a two-year process of analysis and consultation, which gathered information and viewpoints from development partners and other stakeholders around the world. The revised forest strategy is built on three equally important and interdependent pillars:

- Harnessing the potential of forests to reduce poverty
- Integrating forests into sustainable economic development
- Protecting vital local and global environmental services and values.

Harnessing the Potential of Forests to Reduce Poverty

The new strategy focuses on creating economic opportunity, empowerment, and security for people in rural areas, especially poor and indigenous groups. This is to be achieved mainly through strengthening of policies and institutions to ensure that the rural poor have sufficient access to, and are able to manage, forest resources for their own benefit. The World Bank will also help build the capacity of governments to support and regulate community use of forests, open woodlands, plantations, and on-farm woodlots. The Bank relies on its partners—particularly civil society—and on pilot operations supported by others to demonstrate feasible approaches that can then be scaled up. In collaboration with its client countries and partners, the Bank's primary objectives are to

- Work with client countries to strengthen policy, institutional, and legal frameworks to ensure the rights of people and communities living in and near forest areas
- Ensure that women, the poor, and other marginalized groups in society are able to take a more active role in formulating and implementing forest policies and programs
- Support the scaling up of collaborative and community forest management so that local people can manage their own resources, freely market forest products, and benefit from security of tenure
- Work with local groups, NGOs, and other partners to integrate forestry, agroforestry, and small enterprise activities in rural development strategies.

The Mexico Community Forestry Project, discussed in box 16.2, is an example of an investment loan that used a community-driven development approach.

Integrating Forests into Sustainable Economic Development

Under the second pillar, the Bank focuses on helping governments improve their policy, economic management, and governance in the forest sector, including forest concessions and other allocation policies, as well as addressing

BOX 16.2 Mexico: Second Community Forestry Project

Mexico's Second Community Forestry Project assists communities in developing and marketing forest and nonforest resources in order to increase their income. It exemplifies several good practices such as preparation of a detailed social and cultural analysis of the project site, recognition of the importance of forest resources and diversification of income, and the strengthening of the private sector for efficient service delivery.

Although other projects have addressed the social and cultural background of the project site, this project goes further to conduct a detailed analysis of the targeted communities, including an analysis of the social relationships among different groups and of intercultural conflicts. Understanding the social and cultural background of the project site helps in several ways: by identifying potential sources of conflict, by allowing a design of the project that suits the social and cultural context, and by allowing the necessary resources to be used in the most effective and appropriate manner in the local context.

The project recognizes that forest resources are, for many indigenous communities, their most marketable natural resource as well as a good way to diversify income and so reduce risk. Special attention has been given to the development of freshwater supplies (through water bottling projects), conservation of protected areas, conservation of biodiversity, and the development of ecotourism.

The project provides the following assistance to enable the diversification of forest and nonforest products:

- Studies to identify opportunities to diversify production and assist communities in decision making
- Specialized consulting services to carry out land-use zoning in accordance with community goals and available resources
- Studies of and recommendations for strengthening community enterprises
- Feasibility studies for non-timber product marketing
- Studies and recommendations for conflict management within and among communities.

The project is also actively engaged in building capacity in the private sector, to ensure efficient services for community development activities. The project will first identify a pool of potential providers. It will then seek to build their capacity to work with community and tribal organizations, as well as to develop skills in environmental planning and forest management, biological analysis of specific non-timber species, and economic and market analysis.

the potential impacts of economy-wide adjustment on forests. The Bank also supports government efforts to bring about ecologically, economically, and socially sound management of production forests (box 16.3). To this end, in addition to the Bank's standard implementation and safeguard procedures,

---

BOX 16.3 Forest Law Enforcement and Governance

As an integral part of its strategic approach, the World Bank has actively supported international and regional initiatives on forest governance. Since 2001,
the Bank has engaged in high-profile efforts to halt illegal logging and other
forest crimes, in partnership with producer and consumer country governments,
NGOs, and responsible members of the private sector.

An important aspect of this work has been the establishment of the Forest Law
Enforcement and Governance (FLEG) ministerial process. The approach of the FLEG
program has been to convene a regional preparatory conference followed by a high-
level ministerial conference. This approach has allowed for multistakeholder technical
meetings where experiences with FLEG issues are shared; intergovernmental negotiations for the drafting of a declaration or action plan for commitments to improve governance and combat illegal logging, corruption, and associated trade; and other
stakeholder discussions and development of statements for consideration by the negotiators. National-level actions with multistakeholder participation have assisted in
preparing inputs for the conferences and developing follow-up action plans. The
processes aim to create the high-level political commitment and the political *space* at
the national and regional levels needed to address these complex and politically sensitive issues, in partnership with major stakeholders from civil society and the private
sector.

Regional FLEG ministerial processes were conducted in East Asia in 2001 and in
Africa in 2003. Both were co-hosted by forest producer and consumer countries and
the World Bank. A similar process for Europe and North Asia culminated in a ministerial meeting and declaration in November 2005.

---

independent monitoring and certification of forest operations are encouraged.
These formal, market-based certification systems bring in an independent
third party to verify compliance with nationally or internationally agreed standards for forest management. Such certification is most useful when the bulk
of production goes to environmentally discriminating domestic or international markets.

In support of the second pillar, the Bank's objectives are to

- Analyze and coordinate policies and projects to ensure a cross-sectoral
  approach to planning and implementation of sustainable forest management, conservation, and development
- Support improved governance by reforming inappropriate policies
  on timber concessions and subsidies, and by encouraging multistakeholder involvement in the development and implementation
  of forest policy and practices

- Help governments contain corruption and other illegal activities through improved forest laws, regulations, and enforcement and through consumer-driven demand for forest products from legal sources
- Address financial, fiscal, and trade issues related to the forest sector and forest products, to enable governments to capture a larger portion of forest revenue for sustainable social and economic development
- Promote catalytic investments in the full range of goods and environmental services available from well-managed forests, including sustainable timber harvesting and management—but only outside critical forest conservation areas, in situations that can be independently monitored through a system of verification or certification that meets nationally agreed and internationally acceptable standards.

Protecting Vital Local and Global Environmental Services and Values

The revised forest strategy adopts a more inclusive, twofold approach of protection and productive use in all types of forests. This shift allows the World Bank to proactively engage with clients and partners to manage forests effectively for all uses. It also allows the Bank to engage in sustainable forest management operations in the temperate forests of Russia and other republics of the former Soviet Union. The Bank's primary objectives in implementing this third pillar are to

- Help governments in all client countries proactively identify and conserve critical forest conservation areas in all forest types
- Help governments promote the wide-scale adoption of responsible forest management practices in production forests outside critical forest conservation areas
- Develop options to build markets and obtain financing for global public goods such as biodiversity and carbon sequestration
- Help governments develop measures to mitigate and adapt to the anticipated impacts of climate change and reduce the vulnerability of the poorest to its effects
- Help governments design, implement, and finance national markets for the local environmental services provided by forests
- Help governments strengthen forest investments, policies, and institutions to ensure that any adverse indirect and cross-sectoral impacts on conservation activities and protected areas are minimized

---

BOX 16.4   Amazon Regional Protected Areas

The World Bank–WWF Forest Alliance has provided seed funding for the Amazon Regional Protected Areas (ARPA) project in Brazil. This engagement has been a flagship activity of the alliance ever since. This 10-year program will protect 12 percent of the Brazilian Amazon basin and establish a $220 million trust fund to support the ongoing management of that protected areas network. ARPA is the largest joint initiative for tropical forests in history, seeking to encompass 50 million hectares of new protected areas, including representative samples from all of Brazil's 23 ecoregions. This will triple the extent of Brazil's protected areas by 2012, to an area equivalent to that of Spain.

ARPA has already added new protected areas totaling more than 17 million hectares to the system of Amazonian protected areas in Brazil. This project has mobilized significant resources, including $30 million from the Global Environment Facility and $50 million from the WWF, the German development bank KfW, the government of Brazil, and other partners.

- Ensure that Bank investments and programs in the forest sector and other sectors that might harm protected forests and natural habitats are implemented according to the Bank's operational policies and safeguards.

The impact of the World Bank–WWF Forest Alliance illustrates how these partnerships have promoted sustainable forest management. In addition to providing seed money for innovative projects such as the Amazon Regional Protected Areas project (box 16.4), the alliance has been instrumental in developing a tool for identifying and conserving high-conservation-value forests in productive settings.

Are International Interventions Relevant?

The World Bank, in partnership with governments, donors, NGOs, universities, and other key stakeholders, plays an important role in advancing sustainable forest management. Without such interventions, the social, economic, and environmental benefits that forests provide would continue to be seriously undervalued, resulting in widespread mismanagement and poor governance and leading to billions of dollars of lost revenue. The spillover of poor policies in other sectors would also continue to contribute to the rapid rate of deforestation seen in recent decades.

The Global Vision for Forests 2050 project, which brought together leading experts, NGOs, industry representatives, and donor institutions, yielded

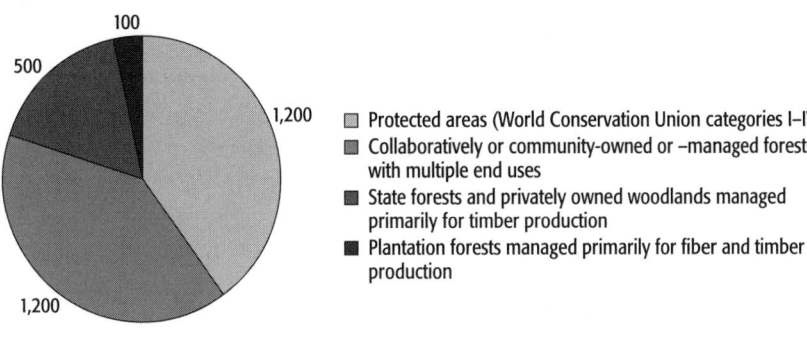

Protected areas (World Conservation Union categories I–IV)
Collaboratively or community-owned or –managed forests with multiple end uses
State forests and privately owned woodlands managed primarily for timber production
Plantation forests managed primarily for fiber and timber production

Source: Global Vision for Forests 2050 project.

the scenario depicted in figure 16.3 for a global closed-forest area of 3 billion hectares in 2050. This would result in an increase in community-owned and -managed forests and a significant increase in protected areas as defined by the World Conservation Union. The area of state and private production forests under intensive management would remain roughly the same as at present, and industrial plantation forests would increase slightly, from 95 million hectares to 100 million hectares.

Conclusion

The forest sector is complex, facing multiple demands and pressures while fulfilling diverse roles. Its resources are valued from a variety of perspectives and for a variety of purposes. Forests are important because of their contribution to the livelihood of the poor, the potential they offer for sustainable economic development, and the essential global environmental services they provide. Challenges for forest-rich countries and the international community include addressing complex institutional, governance, and land tenure issues such as community ownership and smallholder involvement; applying landscape-based approaches in improving rural livelihoods and addressing deforestation; and mainstreaming biodiversity conservation in productive landscapes. Addressing these issues is critical for maximizing beneficial forest outcomes for the poor, promoting economic development, and preserving the environment. The World Bank is committed to working in partnership with client countries and other stakeholders to maintain and enhance the delivery of the services that forests provide to all countries and peoples.

Selected Readings and Cited References

Centre for International Forestry Research. 2005. "Contributing to Africa's Development through Forests: Strategy for Engagement in Sub-Saharan Africa." Bogor, Indonesia.

International Monetary Fund. 2003. "Picture This: The World's Forests." *Finance and Development* 40(4): 40–41.

World Bank. 2003. "Sustaining Forests: A Development Strategy." Washington, DC siteresources.worldbank.org/INTFORESTS/Resources/SustainingForests.pdf.

Useful Web Links on Forestry Conservation and Management

Centre for International Forestry Research	http://www.cifor.cgiar.org
Collaborative Partnership on Forests	http://www.fao.org/forestry/foris/ webview/cpf/index.jsp?siteId= 1220&langId=1
Food and Agriculture Organization of the United Nations page on forestry	http://www.fao.org/forestry/index.jsp
Forest Trends	http://www.forest-trends.org
International Union of Forest Research Organizations	http://www.iufro.org
International Tropical Timber Organization	http://www.itto.or.jp/live/index.jsp
IUCN—The World Conservation Union	http://www.iucn.org
Program on Forests	http://www.profor.info
St. Petersburg Ministerial Declaration	http://web.worldbank.org/enafleg
United Nations Forest Forum	http://www.un.org/esa/forests
World Bank page on Carbon Finance	http://www.carbonfinance.org
World Bank page on Forestry	http://www.worldbank.org/forests
World Bank page on Forest Law Enforcement and Governance	http://www.worldbank.org/enafleg
World Bank–World Wildlife Fund Alliance	http://www.forest-alliance.org
World Resources Institute Global Forest Watch	http://www.globalforestwatch.org/ english/index.htm
World Wildlife Fund	http://www.wwf.org

PART FOUR
Global Governance

L ike globalization itself, the development of global institutions to build a more peaceful and prosperous world has not followed a straight upward path. Rather its history has been largely one of false starts, setbacks, and disappointments. The decades since World War II, and especially since the end of the Cold War, have been more successful in achieving meaningful global cooperation. But that success still lags behind globalization's own breakneck pace, while at the same time engendering a vocal opposition to both globalization and its current mode of governance. This part of the book first explores two of the main challenges to effective global governance, namely, the plague of violent conflict and the cancer of corruption. It then explores the various mechanisms thus far developed to manage a ceaselessly turbulent global economy and society: the United Nations system, the international financial institutions, and the historic series of global compacts that includes most prominently the Millennium Development Goals. The lesson derived is that such institutions and agreements may offer humankind's last and best hope for sustained peace and prosperity—but that they are also very much works in progress.

17

Development in the Crossfire: Conflict Prevention and Postconflict Reconstruction

KAZUHIDE KURODA

onflict is inherent in all societies—and between them. Differences in interests and opinions between different groups are natural and have existed throughout history. It is how such differences are expressed and managed that determines whether conflict manifests and resolves itself primarily in nonviolent ways or through violence.

The post–Cold War period has seen many deadly conflicts in which an unprepared international community called on the United Nations to mount peacekeeping operations of unprecedented scope and size, whose outcomes often left much room for improvement. Reconstruction operations undertaken in the wake of these conflicts have provided much insight, not only into how best to carry out such efforts but also into the broader relationship between conflict and development. The link between the two has begun to be seen as an indirect one, in which development can make crucial contributions toward minimizing the risk of conflict. Although principally aimed at reducing poverty, development efforts also strengthen the capacity for conflict management by, for example, making institutions more transparent,

This chapter is based on the pioneering work of David Hamburg and Paul Collier. Acknowledgments are due also to Ian Bannon, Bernard Harborne, and Laura Bailey of the World Bank for their contributions.

FIGURE 17.1 Active Conflicts by Type, 1946–2004
Number of conflicts

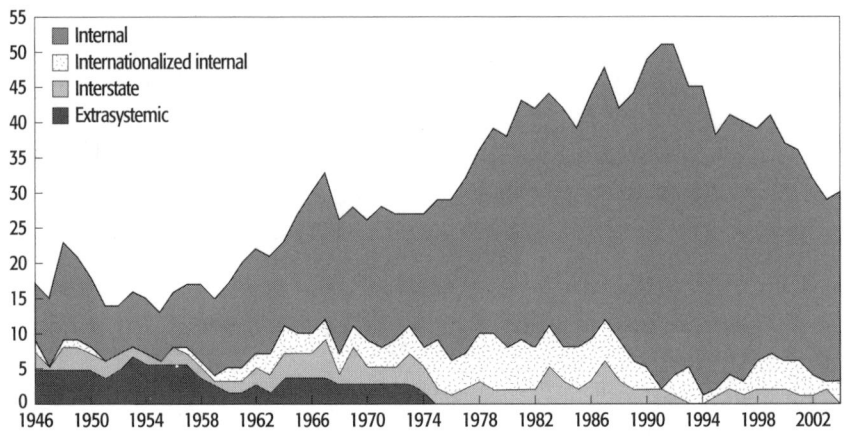

Source: Uppsala Conflict Data Program. Reprinted with permission.

ensuring accountability, and building more inclusive and participatory societies.

The majority of violent conflicts today are internal to countries—that is, they are intrastate, or civil, rather than interstate—and the prevalence of both kinds of conflict is declining (figure 17.1). A recent report by the Human Security Centre finds that the number of armed conflicts worldwide has dropped by 40 percent since 1992, and outright wars, defined as conflicts with 1,000 or more battle deaths per year, have fallen in number by 80 percent.[1] Yet many countries continue to be afflicted, especially the poorest: most of the world's conflicts now occur in low-income countries, particularly in Africa.

In addition, with globalization, the persistence of conflict anywhere has ripple effects that range far and wide, affecting people everywhere. Neighboring countries, in particular, suffer reduced income and increased incidence of disease, and often they must absorb large numbers of refugees fleeing the conflict. Civil conflicts frequently result in large territories lying outside the control of any recognized government, which may then become epicenters of crime and disease. In the post-September 11 world, these areas are also often linked to terrorism, making them a truly global concern.

Armed conflict almost inevitably increases public spending on the military in the countries involved, which, among other things, crowds out important public spending in areas such as health and education, which in many countries were already desperately short of funds. At the global level, military expenditure exceeds spending on international development assistance many times over. Worldwide defense spending in 2003 was almost $1 trillion, compared with total spending for development assistance of only $69 billion in that year (but which rose to a record high of $106 billion in 2005).[2] Conflict also generates the need for increased spending on the part of the international community to control it and, later, to repair the damage. A 1997 Carnegie Commission study estimated that the international community spent about $200 billion on seven major interventions in the 1990s: Bosnia and Herzegovina, Cambodia, El Salvador, Haiti, the Persian Gulf, Rwanda, and Somalia. The study also calculated that a successful preventive approach would have cost the international community almost $130 billion less. A similar, more recent calculation found that such an approach would have saved $54 billion in one low-income country alone.[3] Although these figures and their implications need not be taken at face value, it is clear that, the difficulties notwithstanding, efforts at conflict prevention are of pressing importance from a development perspective alone, not to mention the obvious humanitarian imperative.

The Changing Nature of Conflict and the Evolving Development Agenda

The post–Cold War period has seen a dramatic shift in the character of the United Nations (UN) and other multilateral peacekeeping activities, as the UN Security Council has authorized a greater number of more complex peacekeeping missions, often to help implement comprehensive peace agreements (which have included important nonmilitary components). These missions have met with some success in Cambodia, El Salvador, Mozambique, and Timor-Leste but were less successful in Bosnia and Herzegovina, Rwanda, and Somalia. Lakhdar Brahimi, a senior UN official, undertook a review of these operations and made several recommendations for future efforts: all such operations, he argued, should have a clear mandate, the consent of the parties in conflict, and resources adequate to the task. His report has greatly influenced the thinking and actions of UN peacekeeping operations since then,[4] and his call for local ownership and a demand-driven approach in post-conflict reconstruction has been taken to heart by all stakeholders.

During this period, the international community's attention was also drawn to efforts to prevent conflicts from occurring in the first place. In 1997, the Carnegie Commission on Preventing Deadly Conflict completed its multiyear project. Among its innovations, it applied a medical concept of prevention to conflict and introduced a new concept of operational and structural prevention. The former refers to measures taken in response to an immediate and pressing crisis, such as preventive diplomacy, and the latter to long-term structural preventive measures to keep crises from arising or, having arisen, to keep them from recurring. Often this involves a long-term commitment to helping vulnerable and poor countries develop their resources through increased development assistance. In the words of UN Secretary General Kofi Annan, speaking at the World Bank to endorse then-Bank president James Wolfensohn's call for integrating conflict prevention into development operations, "If war is the worst enemy of development, healthy and balanced development is the best form of conflict prevention."[5] The two leaders' joint stance on the issue prompted development agencies to begin reviewing their policies and activities in conflict-prone countries in order to align their actions so as to contribute to conflict prevention. The development community has come a long way since the time when the phrase "conflict and development agenda" implied that conflict and development was an either-or proposition, and that development could occur or resume only after the conflict was over.

Soon thereafter, a research project led by Paul Collier (then at the World Bank) on the economics of civil wars, crime, and violence produced findings with important implications for development policy. Among them were the following[6]:

- Some 1.1 billion people around the world are either currently affected by conflict or at extremely high risk of being affected in the foreseeable future. Most of them are very poor. Conflict and poverty are reciprocally linked, such that each can either cause or be caused by the other (figure 17.2).
- Conflicts are increasingly concentrated in low-income countries: 80 percent of the world's poorest countries have suffered a major civil war in the past 15 years. These countries have failed to sustain the policies, governance, and institutions that might give them a chance of achieving reasonable growth and diversifying out of dependence on primary commodities. Countries that have suffered conflict in the recent past are also likely to see conflict return: the risk that a country will fall back into conflict within the first five years of the end of a conflict is nearly 50 percent.
- Dependence on primary commodity exports increases a country's risk of conflict by at least four mechanisms: they provide a source of

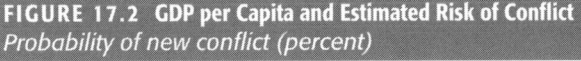

FIGURE 17.2 GDP per Capita and Estimated Risk of Conflict
Probability of new conflict (percent)

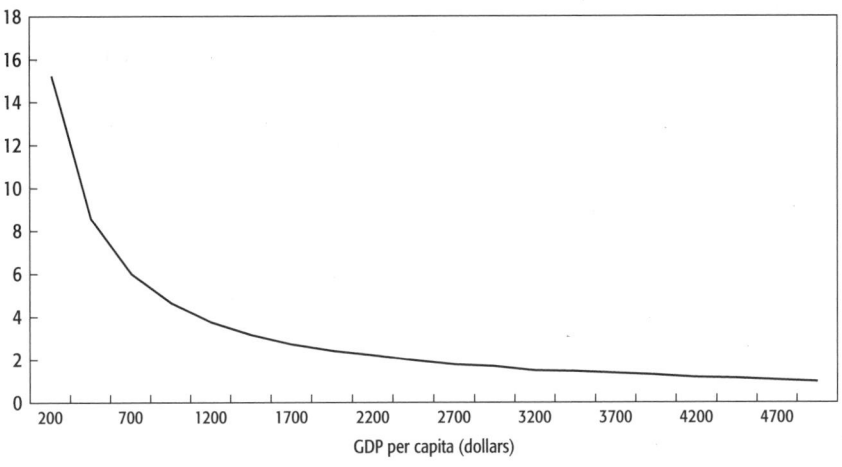

GDP per capita (dollars)

Source: Humphreys and Varshney 2004. Reprinted with permission.
GDP = gross domestic product

financing to potential rebels; they tend to worsen the corruption in governance that often leads to popular frustration with government and so to rebellion; they give commodity-rich regions of a country an incentive to try to secede; and dependence on such commodities increases a country's exposure to unfavorable trade shocks, which can deepen economic distress and poverty and thus provide tinder for conflict. Several practical approaches have been suggested to reduce this vulnerability. These include improving the transparency of government revenue flows from the extraction of oil and gas and other resources, and reducing rents from the illegal trade in commodities that have strong links to conflict.

- An abundance of poor, jobless young men in a society provides both motive and means for conflict and rebellion. Not surprisingly, a high rate of unemployment among youth is highly correlated with the onset of conflict.

Although research continues, policy makers and practitioners have already noted the relevance of these findings and have begun to view development issues through a "conflict lens," approaching programs and projects with greater sensitivity to the potential for conflict.

With violent conflicts still causing havoc in parts of the world despite the international community's increasing efforts at conflict prevention and post-conflict reconstruction, there has also been a rethinking of the concept of security. "National security" alone as traditionally conceived has proved insufficient to protect people in countries engaged in civil conflict. The emerging understanding is that, when a government fails in its responsibility to protect its people, the international community must step in to play this role by providing protection and assistance. Such thinking led Sadako Ogata, the former UN High Commissioner for Refugees, and Amartya Sen, the Nobel Prize–winning economist, to articulate a new concept of security to complement the traditional notion of national security. What they call "human security" emphasizes not the security of states as such, but rather the security of individuals.[7] Whereas traditional national security focuses on the protection of territory and sovereignty through national defense, human security focuses on achieving people's freedom from fear and want. Organizations engaged in conflict prevention and management are now exploring the policy implications of this concept and how to put it into practice.

Moving beyond the policy discussion, one observes that development activities are nowadays increasingly being carried out in a variety of insecure environments, in countries where organized armed conflict may be over but insecurity persists, in countries where isolated pockets of fighting still occur, and in failed states. Positive results on the ground suggest strongly that development activities should be carried out wherever they are possible and appropriate and should not wait until security is fully restored. Each reconstruction or development initiative, however, needs to take carefully into account, before being implemented, the different factors contributing to the conflict situation. Only in this way can one, at a minimum, avoid inadvertently worsening a fragile situation. In fact, given the specific context of each situation, it is becoming more common for development actors to carry out such an analysis.

In many postconflict countries, open conflict may have been replaced by a generalized insecurity, often with criminal elements exploiting weak security institutions such as the police and the judiciary. These countries may find themselves in a "security trap" from which they cannot easily escape on their own: without security, the development process cannot take root; yet without development, insecurity persists. In response, more development organizations are becoming involved in the reform of the security sector,[8] and are examining the development implications of the proliferation of small arms, other light weapons, and landmines, and the needs of ex-combatants, for example, in disarmament, demobilization, and reintegration programs.

Actions at the Global Level to Promote Peace and Development

As the conflict and development agenda evolves to encompass the political, military, and economic dimensions, all concerned stakeholders are trying to cooperate in finding the most appropriate way to meet the challenges. To move toward action following several comprehensive reviews of UN peace-keeping operations and other critical issues confronting the world community, the UN convened a World Summit in September 2005. On the peace and security agenda, following a recommendation by Secretary General Annan in his report, *In Larger Freedom: Towards Security, Development and Human Rights for All,*[9] the UN approved the establishment of a UN Peacebuilding Commission. This achievement recognizes the ongoing need of postconflict countries to be provided with assistance in a concerted manner after the departure of peacekeepers. The inaugural meeting of the Peacebuilding Commission was held on June 23, 2006. The international community, and in particular the people living in postconflict countries, are eager to see how the commission will improve on current practice so as to contribute more effectively to peace and sustainable development.

Even as the political momentum was gathering for the creation of the Peacebuilding Commission, an important attempt was already being made to get the UN, the international financial institutions, civil society organizations, the private sector, and academic institutions to address jointly the challenges of conflict prevention and postconflict reconstruction. For example, several UN departments and agencies and the World Bank, working with recipient governments, were making great progress in the areas of joint postconflict needs assessment and priority programs. Meanwhile, several development agencies have jointly produced a new conflict analysis instrument and are increasingly applying it to better understand the roots of conflict in an effort to design conflict-sensitive assistance programs. The impacts of these programs will be analyzed with much interest.

At the intergovernmental level, at the Organisation for Economic Co-operation and Development, the Development Assistance Committee Network on Conflict, Peace, and Development Cooperation is bringing together experts in conflict prevention and peace-building from a range of bilateral and multilateral development agencies, including the UN system, the European Commission, the International Monetary Fund, and the World Bank, to define and develop common approaches in support of peace. The group has so far issued guidelines on "Security Sector Reform and Governance" and "Helping to Prevent Violent Conflict," underscoring the importance of conflict prevention as an integral part of poverty reduction efforts.[9] An increasing number of donor governments and development agencies are now using these guidelines.

Other global actions are also taking place, bringing in still other stakeholders. One such innovative action is the Extractive Industries Transparency Initiative (EITI). Launched by the prime minister of the United Kingdom at the World Summit on Sustainable Development in 2002, EITI is intended to increase transparency in transactions between governments and companies in mining, petroleum, and other extractive industries. A similar effort is being undertaken by the Publish What You Pay (PWYP) coalition of over 280 nongovernmental organizations worldwide, which calls for the mandatory disclosure of all payments made by oil, gas, and mining companies to governments for the extraction of natural resources. As was noted above, revenues from primary commodity exports have often been misused to finance arms purchases. EITI and PWYP are making such diversion of funds more difficult, while also helping to reduce corruption.

Other noteworthy contributions have come from academic and research organizations, often working with governments and sometimes with the private sector. These organizations provide background analyses that inform both experts in the field and the general public, whose aggregate voice then propels governments to take action at the global level.

The Role and Programs of the World Bank in Conflict Prevention and Postconflict Reconstruction

The World Bank's role in postconflict reconstruction goes back to its origins: the Bank's very first loans supported the reconstruction of Western Europe after World War II. For most of the period since then, the Bank has focused more on traditional development projects in infrastructure and later on structural adjustment lending to developing countries. In the 1990s, however, the Bank became once again much involved in postconflict reconstruction, first in the West Bank and Gaza and then in Bosnia and Herzegovina, where it was asked, along with the European Union, to manage the postconflict recovery. Other such reconstruction efforts followed, for example, in El Salvador and Mozambique. In recent years, the Bank has been working closely with the UN and others in Afghanistan, the Democratic Republic of Congo, Haiti, Iraq, Kosovo, Liberia, Sudan, and Timor-Leste.

Drawing on the lessons learned from the reconstruction initiatives of the 1990s, the World Bank in 2001 established an operational policy on conflict and development cooperation. This has made the Bank's approach to conflict-affected and conflict-prone countries more systematic and more consistent. Financing instruments and support arrangements have been established to help Bank country teams provide timely and appropriate assistance to these countries.

The Post-Conflict Fund

Innovative work in uncertain and fragile conflict-affected societies often cannot be accomplished through normal sources of World Bank funding. In these cases, the Bank's Post-Conflict Fund (PCF) supports the planning, piloting, and analysis of groundbreaking activities through funding of governments and partner organizations at the forefront of this work. The emphasis is on achieving speed and flexibility without sacrificing quality. PCF was established in 1997 to enhance the Bank's ability to support countries in transition from conflict to sustainable peace and economic growth. The fund makes grants to a wide range of partners—institutions, nongovernmental organizations, UN agencies, transitional authorities, governments, and civil society institutions—to provide broad Bank assistance to conflict-affected countries sooner than would be possible otherwise. Grants are focused on restoring the lives and livelihoods of the war-affected population, with a premium placed on innovative approaches to conflict, partnerships with donors and executing agencies, and leveraging of resources through a variety of funding arrangements. During the Bank's fiscal year from July 2004 to June 2005, PCF approved $6.1 million through 12 grants. As of June 30, 2005, PCF had approved a total of $70 million for 157 grants, of which $64 million has been disbursed.

Assistance to Fragile States

The international development community had already been debating—and seriously questioning—the effectiveness of traditional aid mechanisms, especially in states seen as fragile or in danger of failing, when the September 11 attacks pushed the question to the top of the agenda. This discussion led to the establishment of the Low Income Countries Under Stress (LICUS) Task Force, whose recommendations included the establishment of a central unit within the World Bank as well as a LICUS Implementation Trust Fund to support the Bank's effort to reengage, and stay engaged, in fragile states. With an initial allocation of $25 million in 2003 out of the Bank's net income, replenished in January 2006 with another $25 million, this fund is designed specifically to provide support to and ensure the Bank's engagement in the poorest and most vulnerable fragile countries. Because many such countries are in arrears to the Bank, and therefore not able to benefit from regular Bank programs, the LICUS trust fund is a particularly important source of finan-cial assistance to these countries. Many postconflict countries are eligible for help under the LICUS initiative and through access to the trust fund. The trust fund will support domestic reform efforts to find a path out of crisis. The trust fund has already committed support to a number of integrated engagement strategies, including programs in the Central African Republic, Comoros, Haiti, Liberia, Somalia, and Sudan, totaling over $24 million.

New Financing Arrangements

In the past several years, besides PCF and the LICUS initiative, the World Bank has established other new financial instruments intended to improve its abil-ity to finance reconstruction and work more closely with its partners. These instruments are designed as quick-disbursing grants rather than loan arrange-ments, which require more time to ensure that certain conditions are met:

- *Multidonor trust funds* have been used successfully in the Afghanistan, Bosnia and Herzegovina, Iraq, Timor-Leste, and West Bank and Gaza, and in Africa for the Great Lakes' multicountry demobilization and reintegration program.
- Through the *Heavily Indebted Poor Countries Initiative* and other modalities, the Bank works with the International Monetary Fund to help low-income countries with large external debts, including post-conflict countries, obtain access to debt relief.
- The Bank has also recently improved its allocation system in a way that makes it easier for postconflict countries to receive resources from its concessional arm, the *International Development Association* (IDA), which administers grants and interest-free loans for the world's poorest countries.[10]

Integration of Conflict-Sensitive Development into World Bank Operations

Conflict prevention is central to poverty reduction and sustainable develop-ment, and the Conflict Analysis Framework (CAF) is one of the tools the World Bank uses to ensure that a conflict prevention perspective is integrated into its assistance programs. With CAF, the Bank and its partners are better able to identify the sources and consequences of conflict and other conflict-related factors so that strategies can be designed to address them; to examine a country's resilience to an outbreak of violence and its ability to de-escalate the conflict; and to determine how this resilience can be strengthened through development assistance. CAF identifies six categories to be analyzed: social and ethnic relations; governance and political institutions; human rights and security; economic structure and performance; environment and natural resources; and external forces. Many stakeholders are now benefiting from the conflict analyses that have been completed for Burundi, Nigeria, Somalia, and Sri Lanka.

Support of conflict sensitivity in Poverty Reduction Strategy Papers (PRSPs) is key to ensuring that reducing the potential for conflict is integrated into the World Bank's development efforts. More than 60 low-income countries are engaged in the PRSP process; of these, some have experienced violent conflict during the past 10 years, and many others have social and economic conditions that put them at risk of conflicts escalating into large-scale violence. The Bank, in collaboration with its partners, has embarked on a working program aimed at achieving effective poverty reduction in conflict-affected countries. The program will also produce a report deriving lessons from the program's experience.

Collaboration with Other Stakeholders

Recognizing that cooperation is essential in providing assistance in conflict settings, the World Bank has been strengthening its partnership with other stakeholders in the postconflict countries in which it is involved. In particular, support for reconstruction in postconflict countries has benefited from closer collaboration and coordination with UN entities, recipient and donor governments, and civil society organizations. The Bank has jointly led needs assessment missions in such countries as Afghanistan, Haiti, Iraq, Liberia, Sudan, and Timor-Leste, and it has co-hosted several international reconstruction conferences seeking agreement on reconstruction strategies and to raise financial resources. The Bank continuously maintains dialogues with the UN, donor countries, and intergovernmental organizations through a variety of fora to coordinate policy and address emerging issues.

Continuation of Work in Conflict Settings

Guided by Bank operational policy on conflict and development cooperation, World Bank country teams can continue to work even on projects that remain active in the midst of conflict, provided certain security conditions are met. For example, a project in Colombia is working in high-intensity conflict areas to support community-based activities and the reintegration of displaced populations; a project in Indonesia is working in six conflict-affected provinces to support conflict prevention and address the marginalization of youth; and a project in Nepal is attempting to redirect development efforts toward excluded populations such as women, minority indigenous groups, and *dalits* (the group formerly known as *untouchables*), whose exclusion provides the ostensible rationale for the Maoist insurgency in that country. Despite severe constraints, promising and tangible results have been achieved, and it will be worthwhile to learn what contributions the projects are making in reducing conflict intensity or preventing its escalation.

Consolidation of Peace

In addition to reconstruction activities in economic management, basic services, infrastructure, and capacity building, one other activity is key to any process aimed at restoring lasting peace to countries formerly in conflict, namely, disarmament, demobilization, and reintegration of the former combatants. The success or failure of such a process often determines whether the postconflict country achieves the transition from war to peace and advances toward stable nationhood. The challenge is twofold: to ensure that the necessary means are in place to achieve disarmament, and to enable ex-combatants to demobilize and reintegrate into society. This process has political, security, and economic dimensions, and no single entity has the capacity to handle all three. Close collaboration among stakeholders is therefore a must. The World Bank has provided assistance to some 16 countries in the design and financing of demobilization and reintegration programs. The Great Lakes program in Africa is among the most challenging, and there a regional approach has been found most useful, given the cross-border nature of the conflicts and the need for regionally coordinated international assistance.

Linking of Research to Policy, and Policy to Operations

Finally, it is important to stress that the World Bank's approach to conflict prevention and postconflict reconstruction is a holistic one. The Bank's research arm continues to deepen the development community's understanding of the developmental and economic aspects of conflict, providing both policy makers and development practitioners with recommendations for action. Thematic units discuss these recommendations to distill from them concrete policy suggestions and devise appropriate tools and instruments. Once completed, these are put at the disposal of country teams, which will apply them to project design and implementation and technical assistance. The intended outcome of this process is to advance and help shape the conflict and development agenda for the international community. More specifically, it is to offer a set of assistance packages to conflict-affected countries that both strengthens their capacity to manage conflict, to the extent possible, and, when peace returns, allows postconflict reconstruction activities to be undertaken more effectively.

Notes

1. The Human Security Centre's *Human Security Report 2005* uses the definitions in the Uppsala/PRIO data set, according to which a "conflict" is one that results in at least 25 battle-related deaths. Because that data set counted only state-based conflicts, data were also collected on non-state-based conflicts for 2002 and 2003. The result was that, in both those years, more non-state-based than state-based conflicts occurred, although the non-state-based conflicts involved fewer fatalities.
2. Stockholm International Peace Research Institute (2004). The development assistance figures are from the Organisation for Economic Co-operation and Development.
3. Collier and Hoefler (2004).
4. United Nations (2000).
5. Annan (1999).
6. World Bank (2003).
7. Commission on Human Security (2003).
8. The Organisation for Economic Co-operation and Development defines the security sector to encompass developing a clear institutional framework for the provision of security; integrating development and security policy; strengthening the governance of security institutions; and building professional security forces that are accountable to civil authorities.
9. United Nations (2005a).
10. Generally, IDA resources are allocated on the basis of policy performance: a country gets more resources, the better its implementation of economic and social policies that promote growth and poverty reduction. This policy often works against postconflict countries, however, since they typically have performed poorly in this regard at the very time they most need financial resources. The Bank has therefore devised a new set of indicators better tailored for these countries, including indicators that measure progress toward peace and good governance.

Selected Readings and Cited References

Annan, Kofi. 1999. *Towards a Culture of Prevention: Statements by the Secretary-General of the United Nations.* New York: Carnegie Commission on Preventing Deadly Conflict.

Carnegie Commission on Preventing Deadly Conflict. 1997. *Preventing Deadly Conflict: Final Report.* New York: Carnegie Commission on Preventing Deadly Conflict. http://www.wilsoncenter.org/subsites/ccpdc/frpub.htm.

Collier, Paul, and Anke Hoeffler. 2004. "The Challenge of Reducing the Global Incidence of Civil War." Oxford, United Kingdom: Oxford University Press. http://www.copenhagenconsensus.com/Files/Filer/CC/Papers/Conflicts_230404.pdf.

Commission on Human Security. 2003. *Human Security Now: Protecting and Empowering People.* New York.

Hamburg, David A. 2002. *No More Killing Fields: Preventing Deadly Conflict.* Lanham, MD.: Rowman & Littlefield.

Human Security Centre. 2005. *Human Security Report 2005.* Oxford, United Kingdom: Oxford University Press.

Humphreys, Macartan, and Ashutosh Varshney. 2004. "Violent Conflict and the Millennium Development Goals: Diagnosis and Recommendations." Working Paper 19, Center on Globalization and Sustainable Development and Earth Institute at Columbia University, New York.

Marshall, Monty G., and Ted Robert Gurr. 2005. "Peace and Conflict, 2005. A Global Survey of Armed Conflicts, Self-Determination Movements, and Democracy." http://www.cidcm.umd.edu/inscr/pc05print.pdf.

Organisation for Economic Co-operation and Development. 2001. "The DAC Guidelines: Helping Prevent Violent Conflict." Paris. http://www.oecd.org/document/32/0,2340,en_2649_34567_33800800_1_1_1,00.html.

Stockholm International Peace Research Institute. 2004. *Yearbook 2004: Armaments, Disarmament and International Security.* Oxford, United Kingdom: Oxford University Press.

United Nations. 2000. "The Report of the Panel on UN Peace Operations." Document A/55/305, S/2000/809. New York.

_____. 2005a. *In Larger Freedom: Towards Security, Development and Human Rights for All.* Report of the Secretary-General. New York.

_____. 2005b. "2005 World Summit Outcome." General Assembly document A/60/L.1, September 15. New York. http://daccessdds.un.org/doc/UNDOC/LTD/N05/511/30/PDF/N0551130.pdf?OpenElement.

United Nations Development Programme. 2005. "Violent Conflict—Bringing the Real Threat into Focus." In *Human Development Report 2005.* New York.

World Bank. 2003. *Breaking the Conflict Trap: Civil War and Development Policy.* Washington, DC: World Bank; New York: Oxford University Press.

_____. 2004. "The Role of the World Bank in Conflict and Development: An Evolving Agenda." In *The World Bank in Conflict and Development.* Washington, DC.

Selected Web Links on Conflict and Development

Carnegie Commission on Preventing Deadly Conflict	http://www.wilsoncenter.org/subsites/ccpdc
Commission on Human Security	http://www.humansecurity-chs.org
Low-Income Countries Under Stress Initiative	http://www.worldbank.org/licus
Post-Conflict Fund	http://lnweb18.worldbank.org/essd/essd.nsf/CPR/PCF-Homepage
Stockholm International Peace Research Institute	http://www.sipri.org
U.S. Institute of Peace	http://www.usip.org

18

Curing the Cancer of Corruption

VINAY BHARGAVA

T he World Bank defines corruption as the abuse of public office for private gain. In 1996, the then-President of the World Bank, James D. Wolfensohn, declared that, for developing countries to achieve growth and poverty reduction, "we need to deal with the cancer of corruption."[1] With that speech at the annual meetings of the Bank and the International Monetary Fund, Wolfensohn confronted head on a topic that the development community had long ignored. In the decade since then, fighting corruption has moved to the forefront of all national and international development dialogues. Several recent global public opinion polls indicate that corruption is seen as a major issue all around the world, affecting people's lives everywhere. For example:

- In a 2003 Global Poll by the World Bank covering 48 countries, corruption ranked fourth among the most important development issues facing the world—close behind economic growth, poverty reduction, and education.
- In a 2005 Transparency International Global Corruption Barometer survey covering 69 developed and developing countries, 75 percent of respondents said that corruption affects political life in their countries to a moderate or large extent; 65 percent said the same thing about the business sector; and 58 percent said that corruption affects them personally.

Corruption occurs in a variety of forms (box 18.1) and in almost all countries, as shown by worldwide research on corruption by Transparency International as well as other cross-country governance indicators published by the World Bank Institute (figure 18.1).

I would like to thank Sanjay Pradham and Randi Susan Ryterman of the World Bank for their helpful comments on earlier versions of this chapter.

BOX 18.1   The Types of Corruption

Corruption can occur in different forms, in different types of organizations, and at different levels within organizations. Because of these differences across several dimensions, the categories used to describe the types of corruption often overlap. Corrupt practices range from small amounts paid for frequent transactions (*petty corruption*) to bribes to escape taxes, regulations, or win relatively minor procurement contracts (*administrative corruption*) to massive and wholesale corruption. Corruption occurs within private corporations (*corporate corruption*) or, more famously, in the public sector, including the political arena (*political corruption*). When corruption is prevalent throughout all levels of society, it is seen as *systemic,* and when it involves senior officials, ministers, or heads of state serving the interests of a narrow group of businesspeople, politicians, or criminal elements, it is aptly called *grand* corruption.

FIGURE 18.1   Corruption Perceptions Index for Selected Countries, 2005
Score (0 = perceived most corrupt)

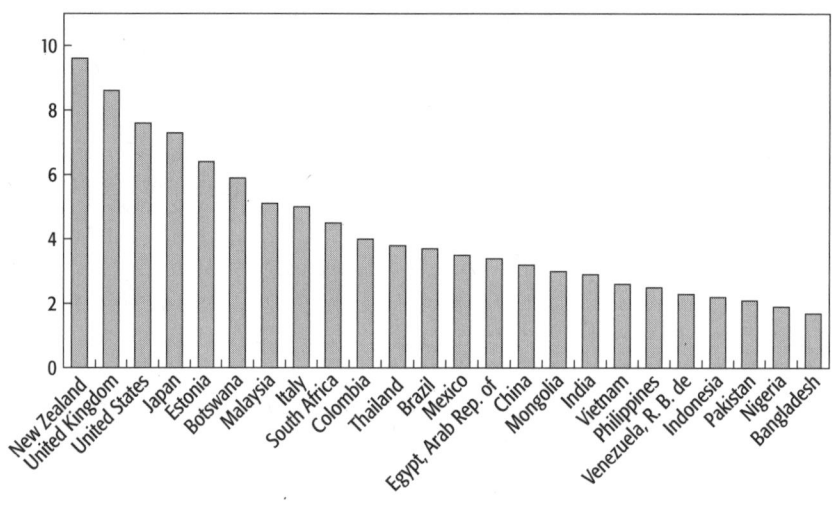

Source: Transparency International. Reprinted with permission.

Corruption as a Global Development Issue

Experience and evidence show that corruption has both national and international dimensions. Although fighting corruption is primarily a national matter, many types and instances of corruption at the national level also have an international aspect, which requires international action.

The Transnational Scope of Corruption

In 2004, the World Bank estimated that, worldwide, more than $1 trillion, or the equivalent of 3 percent of gross world product, is paid in bribes each year. This form of corruption takes place at both the national and the international level, but the latter, or transnational corruption, is one of its most detrimental forms. The victims are usually developing countries, whose precious foreign aid and investment are siphoned off from badly needed development projects and into the pockets of corrupt government officials, their family members or cronies, or corrupt brokers or middlemen. The following examples demonstrate the nature and scope of transnational corruption; they also show that international corruption usually requires a permissive international business environment and the complicity of international companies as bribe givers:

- *The Iraq Oil-for-Food Scandal.* Following Iraq's invasion of Kuwait in 1990, the United Nations imposed comprehensive economic sanctions on Iraq, including sanctions on Iraqi oil exports. In response, Iraq's then-president, Saddam Hussein, refused to allow the United Nations (UN) to feed Iraq's starving children, in the hope of getting the sanctions lifted. In 1996, Iraq agreed to the UN-supervised Oil-for-Food Programme, which allowed the Iraqi government to sell oil as long as it used the revenue to buy humanitarian goods for its citizens. When the program ended following the U.S.-led invasion in 2003, over $64 billion worth of oil had been sold, of which $39 billion had been used to purchase food. However, reports started surfacing that the Iraqi government had been imposing surcharges on the oil and collecting kickbacks from companies supplying the humanitarian goods. A UN investigation in 2005 found that $1.8 billion in illicit payments had been diverted from the program and that much of the purchased food was unfit for human consumption. More than 2,200 companies were involved (figure 18.2). Illicit kickbacks came from companies and individuals from 66 different countries, and illicit surcharges were paid by companies from around 40 countries.
- *The Enron debacle.* In 2001, Enron Corporation, the seventh-largest publicly owned company in the United States and one of the world's largest energy, commodities, and services companies, filed for bankruptcy, driven to insolvency by the corrupt practices of its officials as well as corrupt business dealings. At the time of its collapse, Enron's 21,000 employees and its $32 billion in assets were spread across 40 countries, including operations in Asia, Europe, Latin America, and the

After-sales-service fees
$1.02 billion

Surcharges
$229 million

Iraq ★
Baghdad

Oil surcharges

Inland transportation fees
$.53 billion

Humanitarian
kickbacks

Total illicit income: $1.8 billion

Source: Independent Inquiry Committee into the United Nations Oil-for-Food Programme 2005.

Middle East. Its fall, therefore, had both direct and indirect international consequences, and some of its international deals were among those that came under scrutiny for corruption. Among those directly affected were Enron's worldwide investors and employees, with many of the latter losing their pension accumulations as well as their jobs. The scandal's silver lining was that it led to stricter U.S. regulation of the accounting industry, better disclosure policies for corporations, and harsher penalties for corrupt executives. The U.S. Congress also passed campaign finance reform legislation, partly in response to the finding that Enron had been a major political donor and may have unfairly benefited from its political connections.

- *Kleptocracy on a grand scale.* In its *Global Corruption Report 2004,* Transparency International estimates that Suharto, president of Indonesia from 1967 to 1998, embezzled somewhere between $15 billion and $35 billion during his presidency. Philippine President Ferdinand Marcos embezzled anywhere from $5 billion to $10 billion, and President Mobuto Sese Seko of Zaire (now the Democratic Republic of Congo) up to $5 billion. These sordid achievements would not have been possible except in a global environment that enables multinational companies to enter into such deals and allows the domestic beneficiaries of these illegal payments to deposit funds in secret bank accounts or in dubious offshore companies. Frequently, when finally cornered, corrupt high officials have escaped prosecution by fleeing to developed country sanctuaries, taking their spoils with them. In recent years, however, some of the recipient banks have agreed to freeze and return such funds to the countries from which they were stolen.

- *Acres International.* In 2004, the World Bank imposed sanctions on a Canadian firm, Acres International, for bribing, through an intermediary, the chief executive in charge of the $8 billion Lesotho Highlands Water Project. The Bank declared Acres ineligible to receive any new Bank-financed contracts for a period of three years. This debarment followed the precedent-setting conviction of Acres for bribery by the High Court of Lesotho in 2002, a conviction upheld by the country's Court of Appeals in 2003. Masupha Ephraim Sole, the executive who had accepted bribes from Acres and several other major international infrastructure companies, was sentenced to 15 years in prison, on evidence obtained through a Swiss court order to disclose Sole's secret bank accounts. Following the Acres trial, a German company, Lahmeyer International, was also found guilty of bribery in 2003— in fact, it had used the same intermediary as Acres. A South African intermediary also pleaded guilty to bribery, and French and Italian companies were charged as well. These cases are significant in that they held both bribe givers and bribe takers to account, and for showing that a small and very poor country could take several major international construction companies to court and win. In addition, the World Bank's response in the Acres case set an example for other international financial organizations; perhaps most important, the cases increased companies' perceived risk of punishment for bribery committed anywhere in the world.

The Costs of Corruption

Why are people around the world so concerned about corruption? The short answer is that, thanks to ever-increasing information flows in an interconnected world, people are becoming more aware that corruption is impeding economic growth, perpetuating poverty, and feeding political instability by undermining faith in society's key institutions of governance.

Corruption reduces growth and undermines development by lowering incentives for, and the efficiency of, both domestic and foreign investment (figure 18.3). It also reduces growth by lowering the quality of public infrastructure and services, as funds intended for these public goods are diverted to private pockets.

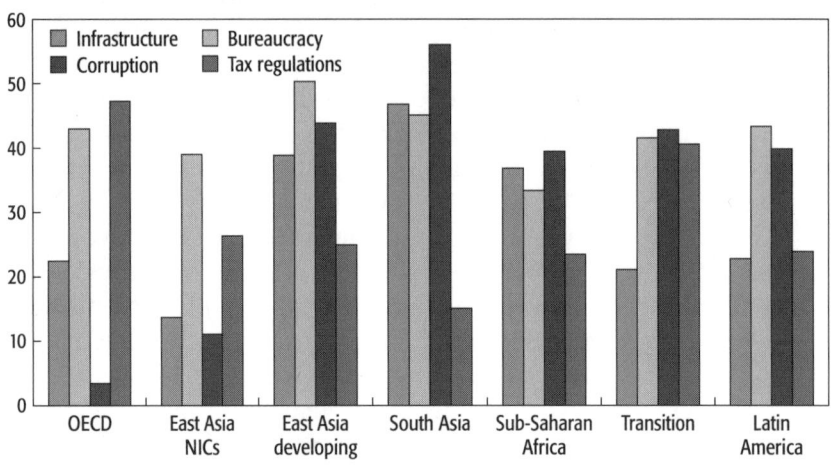

FIGURE 18.3 Key Constraints on Business as Reported by Firms, by World Region
Percentage of firms surveyed that reported indicated constraint as among top three[a]

Source: World Economic Forum 2005. Reprinted with permission.
a. Firms were asked to "Select among the above 14 constraints the five most problematic factors for doing business in your country."
NICs = newly industrializing countries
OECD = Organisation for Economic Co-operation and Development

The 2005–06 *Global Competitiveness Report* by the World Economic Forum discusses the links between corruption and growth, and between corruption and poverty reduction, as well as the payoffs from controlling corruption. The report cites econometric evidence showing that even a slight (one standard deviation) improvement in governance results in a threefold increase in income per capita in the long run. The research also shows that good governance substantially reduces infant mortality and illiteracy. A recent survey by Transparency International confirms that corruption not only lowers growth but also hurts the poor the most (table 18.1).

Another factor driving public concern about corruption is that it undermines key institutions of society and leads to political instability. Results published in Transparency International's *Global Corruption Barometer 2005* show that people in 69 countries believe that corruption affects all key governance-related sectors and key institutions in society (figure 18.4). As a consequence, public trust in governments, corporations, and global institutions is declining, as was reported by a survey reported at the 2005 World Economic Forum (figure 18.5).

TABLE 18.1   Personal Effect of Corruption on Respondents, by Household Income
Percentage of households surveyed

Reported extent of effect	Household income		
	Low	Middle	High
Not at all or small extent	54	59	62
Moderate or large extent	42	38	36
Do not know or no answer	3	3	2

Source: Transparency International.
Note: Percentages may not sum to 100 because of rounding.

FIGURE 18.4   Sectors and Institutions Most Affected by Corruption
Index (1 = not at all corrupt; 5 = extremely corrupt)

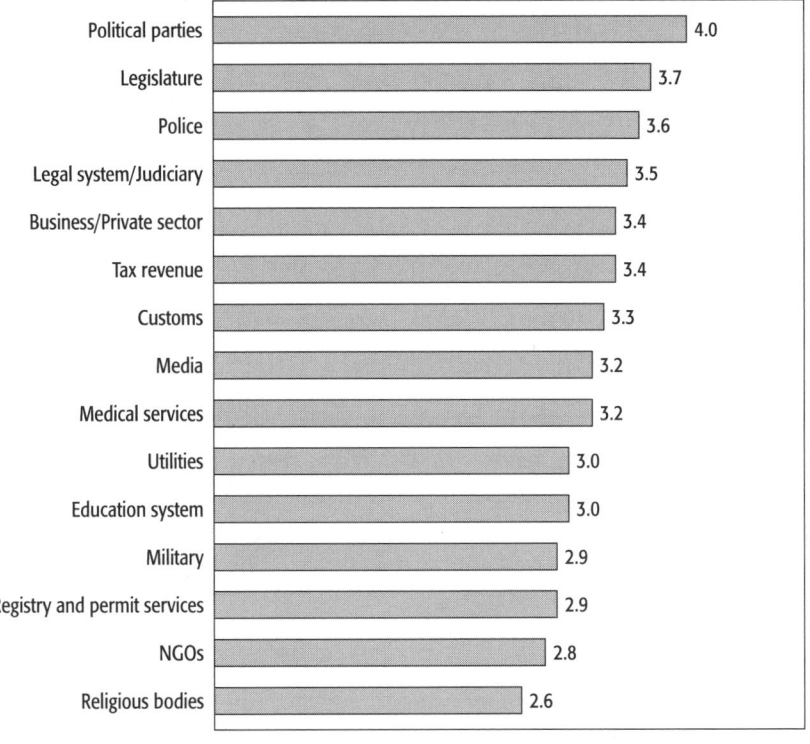

Political parties	4.0
Legislature	3.7
Police	3.6
Legal system/Judiciary	3.5
Business/Private sector	3.4
Tax revenue	3.4
Customs	3.3
Media	3.2
Medical services	3.2
Utilities	3.0
Education system	3.0
Military	2.9
Registry and permit services	2.9
NGOs	2.8
Religious bodies	2.6

Source: Transparency International *Global Corruption Barometer*. Reprinted with permission.
NGOs = nongovernmental organizations

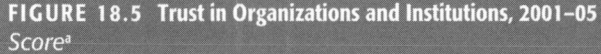

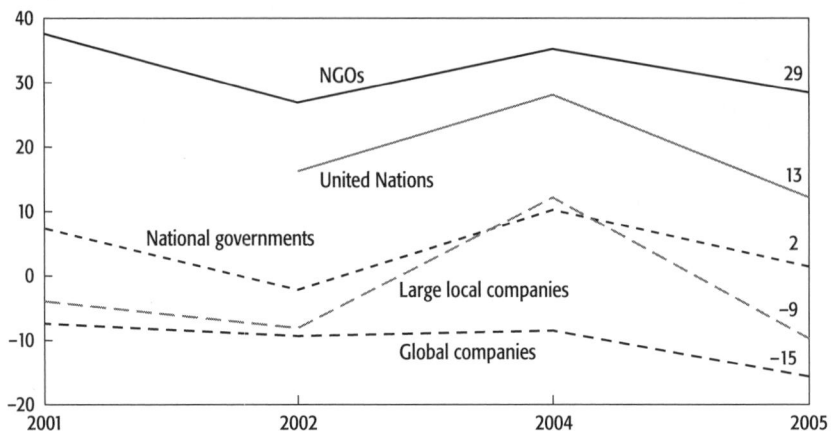

FIGURE 18.5 Trust in Organizations and Institutions, 2001–05
Score[a]

Source: World Economic Forum. Reprinted with permission.
a. Higher values indicate greater trust. Data are averages for 14 countries.
NGOs = nongovernmental organizations

Can Corruption Sometimes Be Tolerated?

Some argue that, although corruption is undeniably a bad thing, under some circumstances it may be tolerated. The following arguments for tolerance are frequently heard:

- Corruption is a Western concept, inconsistent with the culture and traditions in some non-Western countries.
- Corruption is rooted in the colonial practice of paying civil servants below-subsistence wages and expecting them to take bribes to survive; therefore, until civil service pay is raised so that it provides a living wage, some corruption may have to be accepted.
- Bribes serve the function of reintroducing an effective price mechanism in the presence of scarcities of certain public goods due to public sector inefficiency or distorted prices.
- Some countries such as Bangladesh, China, and Vietnam are growing rapidly and reducing poverty despite widespread corruption; therefore corruption may not be worth the trouble of eradicating.
- Denying development assistance to poor people in countries with corrupt governments will only make their suffering worse and cause them to feel victimized by the donor community as well as their own government.

- A policy of zero tolerance for corruption in development assistance will only create more failed states, which will be much more costly to deal with than corrupt but functioning states.
- Even if some foreign aid is lost to corruption and fraud, at least the bulk of the funds reaches the intended beneficiaries.

Most development experts and policy makers, however, agree that the cost and consequences of corruption to society on a global scale are simply too great to tolerate. Indeed, several recent global compacts articulate the importance of fighting corruption nationally as well as internationally:

- The UN's Millennium Declaration specifically includes (as part of Millennium Development Goal 8) "a commitment to good governance . . . nationally and internationally."[2] This pledge was reaffirmed by UN member countries as part of the Monterrey Consensus of 2002 and again at the 2005 World Summit.
- In 2001, a group of African leaders pledged to fight corruption as part of the New Partnership for Africa's Development, an integrated development framework designed to tackle the continent's chronic underdevelopment and marginalization.
- In 2002, the Group of Eight (G-8) leading industrial countries acknowledged the importance of the African leaders' commitment to good governance and promised to match this commitment with economic and other forms of support in the G-8 Africa Action Plan. The G-8 followed up on this promise at its 2003 economic summit with detailed proposals for combating Africa's pervasive corruption.
- A February 2006 joint statement of the European Parliament, the Council of Europe, and the European Commission, "The European Consensus on Development," repeatedly stressed the importance of good governance for development.[3] The statement identified good governance as one of the European Union's main objectives, as a key competency of the commission, as one of nine areas the European Union will actively address, and as one of the cross-cutting issues it intends to mainstream in its activities.

Forces Shaping the Evolution of Corruption as a Global Issue

In a dynamic world, many forces will shape the way the global community addresses the global aspects of the cancer of corruption. Broadly speaking, the key forces that national and international public policy makers can influence or control will be the evolution of demand for good governance, supply responses to that demand, and the strength and effectiveness of governance-related institutions. A fourth, underlying force is globalization itself, and in particular the continuing global integration of financial systems that makes money flows harder to monitor and the spread of instantaneous forms of communication that multiply the risks of corrupt behavior.

Demand for controlling corruption globally and nationally will, in turn, be shaped by policies that increase transparency in the public, corporate, and international financial arenas, and by the extent to which ongoing research contributes new remedies for corruption as well as credible information on its incidence, its causes and consequences, and the effectiveness of global advocacy efforts. The supply response will take the form of anticorruption measures across a broad range of areas that shape the governance landscape nationally and internationally. Whether strong and effective institutions emerge will depend on the speed with which such institutions mature at the national and the international level, and the extent to which they practice good governance themselves and act to apply checks and balances.

Stimulation of Demand for Control of Corruption

A steady flow of information from credible sources on the incidence and consequences of corruption, coupled with increased awareness of the involvement of international actors using international systems in this illicit behavior, is increasingly shaping public opinion and inspiring outrage, increasing the pressure on public officials to control corruption. The results of global and national opinion surveys and other research by international organizations such as Transparency International, the World Bank Institute, and the International Finance Corporation will be pivotal to strengthening the information arsenal in the fight against corruption.

In 1995, Transparency International published its first Corruption Perceptions Index, which compares levels of corruption across countries, and the *TI Source Book,* which introduced the concept of a "national integrity system" and reports on global best practice in fighting corruption.[4] These seminal tools were followed by annual reports documenting the organization's activities and thrusts; the Bribe Payers Index (starting in 1999), which measures the propensity of leading exporting countries to bribe abroad; and the *Global Corruption Report* (starting in 2001), which provides an overview of the 'state of corruption' around the globe. Transparency International's newest tool, the Global Corruption Barometer (based on Gallup International's Voice of the People survey) measures international attitudes, experiences, expectations, and priorities on corruption.

The World Bank Institute, using a rich base of sources from 1996 onward, keeps track of six governance indicators: voice and accountability, political stability and absence of violence, government effectiveness, regulatory quality, rule of law, and control of corruption. The institute publishes updates on these indicators every two years. Integrated into the indicators are measures of countries' ability to enforce their laws and guarantee the protection of property rights, measures of the degree of openness of their economic and political systems, and measures of other factors that may determine how much opportunity there is for corrupt behavior within their borders.

The World Bank and its affiliate the International Finance Corporation also maintain and publish databases of the costs of doing business and of the results of enterprise surveys in many countries. The surveys track such indicators as the number of days it takes to process a business license (the longer it takes, the more opportunity for corruption to occur), the amounts paid *unofficially* to obtain such licenses, the value of a gift expected to secure a government contract, and the severity of corruption as an obstacle to firms. These indicators reveal which countries have business environments conducive to bribery—that is, which ones lack clear rules, require *speed money* to cut through red tape and reduce costly delays, permit illegal activity in exchange for compensation, and give preferential treatment to those who can pay for it, among other common causes of corruption.

The international surveys mentioned above usually contain national data as well. However, some countries also collect and present data from their own national surveys. For example, in the Philippines, the Social Weather Stations, an independent social survey institute, has tracked public satisfaction with the government's anticorruption efforts for 20 years.

Although the availability of good-quality information on corruption has increased dramatically in recent years, efforts remain at an early stage. Much more research is needed on the causes and consequences of corruption and on preventive and remedial measures.

Another force increasing the demand for good governance is advocacy. Combined with increased information and instant communications (see box 18.2), growing global advocacy against corruption increases the risks that corrupt elements must face and helps shift the balance of power to constituencies among whom the political will to control corruption is growing. Domestic pressure for reform will be crucial for any anticorruption strategy to take root; nothing lasting can be accomplished if the public is indifferent. Outside actors can help by assisting civil society in the monitoring of

BOX 18.2 Disclosure: The Right to Know

"Access to information ebbs and flows in any country but the transformation has begun and it is no longer possible to tell citizens that they have no right to know."
–David Banisar, Electronic Privacy Information Center, May 2004

In this global Information Age, governments are increasingly judged, by their citizens and the world, according to the credibility and timeliness of information they provide as well as the ease and willingness with which they provide it. "Freedom of information (FOI)"—or the right of the public to access information held by authorities and, conversely, the obligation of governments to disclose information to citizens—is enshrined in the constitutions and laws of over 50 countries. In more than half of these countries, the laws were adopted within the past decade.

The extent to which disclosure policies have increased transparency in the public sector, however, is dependent on many factors. Many of the laws are obsolete, inadequate, or even dormant. In some countries, governments abuse exemptions. Campaigns such as the global war on terror have undercut some of the laws. In other instances, international organizations are active in countries but are not subject to national disclosure policies.

The implementation of FOI laws depends on the ability of governments to move from a culture of secrecy to one of openness. Civil society must continuously push for this transformation and test it by demanding information. This has not happened in some countries with FOI laws such as Zimbabwe and Serbia. The Public Information Act in Serbia actually restricted public information. In Albania and Bosnia and Herzegovina, the laws are mostly unused for lack of awareness or demand.

Implementation rules in many countries, such as Panama and Australia, make it very difficult or expensive to make use of FOI laws. National security is often invoked as a reason to withhold information from the public even when to do so would not actually put the state at risk. In the case of Mexico, after the information law was enacted in 2002, it was found that many official records had been destroyed or removed.

For national disclosure policies to more effectively increase transparency of government actions, therefore, constant pressure from civil society, the media, governance institutions, and the international community is needed.

Source: Banisar 2004.

governance reforms, supporting the mobilization of like-minded groups against capture by large vested interests, and backing responsible media. The international community can also exert direct pressure for reform, using both carrots (such as the promise of increased aid) and sticks (such as sanctions enshrined in international laws).

Increase in the Supply of Anticorruption Measures

Research is growing on the remedies for corruption. One important conclusion of this research is that combating corruption requires addressing broader governance and institutional issues. A multidimensional approach to the problem generally involves actions to improve legal, judicial, and prosecutorial systems; voice and participation by civil society; public-sector expenditure management; competition in the private sector; and political accountability. Frequent areas for action are inadequate public sector pay, a culture of corruption, opaque rules and regulations and broad discretionary powers, inadequate regulation of the private sector, state capture, political corruption, weak disclosure requirements in the public and the private sectors, lack of media freedom, and limited space for civil society organizations. Measures to increase the supply of reform include putting information about government services and performance in the public domain, arranging for inclusion and participation in the design and implementation of service delivery projects, promoting social accountability, increasing the access of the poor to justice and to productive assets, and promoting judicial independence and accountability.

One example of an international action to increase the supply of anti-corruption measures is the Asian Development Bank (ADB)/Organisation for Economic Co-operation and Development (OECD) Anti-Corruption Initiative for Asia-Pacific. In 2000, 36 member countries of ADB and OECD launched this initiative to address the damage that corruption was wreaking on their economies and societies. As of April 2005, 25 countries had endorsed the ADB/OECD Anticorruption Action Plan for Asia and the Pacific, which lays out legally nonbinding principles and standards for policy reform. The plan is organized around three pillars (see annex 18.1 for details):

- *Public service reform: developing effective and transparent systems for the public sector.* This pillar focuses on integrity in public services (codes of conduct and civil service fairness and efficiency) and accountability and transparency (legal frameworks, management practices, and auditing procedures).
- *Private sector reform: strengthening antibribery actions and promoting integrity in business operations.* Here, the focus is on effective prevention, investigation, and prosecution, and corporate responsibility and accountability.
- *Supporting active public involvement.* This third pillar focuses on public discussion of corruption, access to information, and public participation.

Under the Action Plan, the endorsing countries voluntarily commit to regional cooperation in fighting corruption and acknowledge the usefulness of regional and international anticorruption instruments such as those developed by the ADB, the Asia-Pacific Economic Cooperation forum, the Financial Action Task Force on Money Laundering, the OECD, the Pacific Basin Economic Council, the UN, and the World Trade Organization.

Anticorruption Institutions

Key institutions in the fight against corruption in any country are the judiciary, the regulatory agencies, an anticorruption commission or agency, a public ombudsman, public prosecutors, a vigilance commission, the media (including investigative journalists), and citizen groups and other nongovernmental organizations. Some of these, such as the judiciary and the media, are—or should be—independent of the executive branch, while others are part of it. All require long-term support to become effective and must demonstrate best-practice governance in their own operation.

These institutions must also function in an integrated manner. Otherwise they will most likely be ineffective, even if each functions well in isolation. As noted above, Transparency International has explicitly called for such an integrated approach, in the form of a national integrity system, whose aim should be to uphold national integrity and allow the country to develop in a sustainable manner, live by the rule of law, and enhance the quality of life of its citizens. Dependence on only a few of these institutions without the others, or on just one—a benign dictator, for example—would leave the system vulnerable to collapse. Beyond this, the efficacy of each institution depends on a number of factors, including clear mandates, rules, powers, and duties prescribed in the constitution or in law, or embedded in tradition; independence from influences that might compromise the integrity of the institution or of its authorities; transparency and accountability to key stakeholders, often including the general public; and adequate resources to fulfill its mandate, including competent staff, updated knowledge on international standards, and the ability to share information and experiences with relevant groups.

Finally, the past failure of many of these institutions, especially in developing but also in developed countries, makes it abundantly clear that institutions alone are not enough—governance matters, too. Many of these institutions are designed to work in an environment of good governance and have proved ineffective where corruption is pervasive and endemic. However, where leadership is strong—sometimes with international or bilateral support—there have been instances of success in even the most corrupt of environments.

International Actions to Combat Corruption

International initiatives against corruption are presently working along five major fronts:

- *Ensuring that loans and grants to developing countries are used effectively.* All international financial institutions and bilateral donors have adopted measures to prevent fraud and corruption in the projects they finance. Yet half of opinion leaders in developing countries surveyed in a global poll commissioned by the World Bank in 2002 still believed that most foreign assistance is wasted because of corruption.
- *Bolstering donor support for reform.* Bilateral donors are being encouraged to support reform measures, on both the supply side and the demand side, as are national and international organizations and institutions that promote accountability.
- *Reducing the incentives for multinational businesses to pay bribes.* Such measures may include criminalizing bribery, eliminating the tax deductibility of bribery as a business expense, and increasing the transparency and integrity of public procurement.
- *Promoting international programs to control organized crime and the flow of illicit funds.* It is very hard for outside organizations to reduce corruption linked to organized crime, such as money laundering, if such corruption has already become systemic.
- *Improving the institutional framework for resolving international disputes.* A stronger framework is needed to impose and enforce sanctions when nations fail to comply with agreed rules and treaties. The World Court, the International Centre for Settlement of Investment Disputes (a World Bank affiliate), and the World Trade Organization are among the institutions available to serve this purpose, although their jurisdiction is not entirely clear in all cases.

Beyond these five major areas, worthwhile measures can include linking aid and trade to good governance; improving corporate governance and corporate social responsibility; strengthening the capacity of global governance institutions, including civil society institutions, in fighting corruption; and increasing access to information.

A number of international initiatives have been undertaken recently to combat and prevent corruption. Most of these are voluntary agreements and thus do not have the force of law.

United Nations Convention Against Corruption

The UN Convention Against Corruption (UNCAC) is the first truly global anticorruption convention. It is unique not only in its global coverage but also in the extent and detail of its provisions. The convention takes a comprehensive approach, aimed at both preventing and combating corruption. It obliges the signatories to implement a wide range of detailed anticorruption measures, affecting their laws, institutions, and official practices. These measures aim to promote the prevention, detection, and punishment of corruption, as well as to strengthen international cooperation among the signatories on these matters. UNCAC was initially signed by 111 countries in Mérida, Mexico, in December 2003; by September 2005, the number of signatories had risen to 133. The 30 ratifications required for the convention's entry into force were reached on September 15, 2005.

UNCAC focuses on four key aspects in the fight against corruption: preventive measures, criminalization and law enforcement, international cooperation, and asset recovery. The convention also contains provisions promoting technical assistance and information exchange, and specific provisions on mechanisms for implementation of the convention.

UNCAC aims to fight corruption in both the private and the public sectors. Its prescribed preventive measures include the establishment of anticorruption bodies, enhanced transparency in campaign and political party financing, safeguards to ensure efficient and transparent delivery of public goods and services, codes of conduct and financial disclosure for public servants, and transparency and accountability in public finance transactions and in critical areas such as procurement and the judiciary. The convention also encourages participation by civil society and the general public in efforts to prevent and fight corruption.

UNCAC goes beyond previous instruments of its kind in that it does not criminalize bribery and embezzlement only. Its provisions also cover trading in influence and the concealment of any gains from corrupt acts, as well as any support of corruption, money laundering, or obstruction of justice in the prosecution of such crimes. The convention also emphasizes cross-border cooperation in gathering and transferring evidence for use in court and requires signatories to support the tracing, freezing, seizure, and confiscation of the proceeds of corruption.[5]

Finally, the asset recovery provisions of the convention were a major break-through. Inclusion of the provisions will allow developing countries to recover much-needed development resources illegally taken from their coffers.

The OECD Antibribery Convention

The OECD Antibribery Convention (formally known as the OECD Convention on Combating Bribery of Foreign Public Officials in International Transactions) went into effect on February 15, 1999. This convention makes it a crime in OECD member countries to offer, promise, or give a bribe to a foreign public official in order to obtain or retain an international business deal. OECD actively promotes adoption of the convention in all parts of the world, with the aim of "leveling the competitive playing field for companies doing trans-border business" by raising international norms through its framework for fighting global bribery.[6] By 2005, all 30 OECD members and 6 nonmembers had enacted laws in compliance with the convention, making it a punishable offense for one of their multinational companies to bribe an official in a host country.

Members' compliance with the convention is managed by the OECD Working Group on Bribery and is based on a peer-review system in which examinations are conducted in two phases: first, a country's antibribery laws are assessed for their conformity with the convention, and then an intensive assessment is undertaken of how effective these laws are in practice. The second assessment is held in the country under examination and includes leaders from government, business, trade unions, and civil society, with representatives of two member countries in the Working Group leading the assessment.

The review process for each country ends with the release of reports from the Working Group on how the country can improve its compliance with the convention. Many countries have responded to these reports by amending their legislation according to the Working Group's recommendations. As of March 2006, 36 member countries had completed the first examination phase. By February 2006, 22 members, including all of the Group of Seven, had received assessment reports.

The Financial Action Task Force on Money Laundering

The Financial Action Task Force on Money Laundering (FATF) is an intergovernmental body whose purpose is the development and promotion of national and international policies to combat money laundering and terrorist financing. Created in 1989, FATF works to generate the necessary political will to bring about legislative and regulatory reform in these areas. It focuses on three principal areas: setting standards for national anti–money laundering efforts and programs to counter terrorist financing; evaluating the degree to which countries have implemented measures that meet those standards; and identifying and studying money laundering and terrorist financing methods and trends. FATF has published 49 recommendations (40 basic and 9 special), which have been updated periodically, to meet this objective.

As of 2006, 30 countries as well as the Hong Kong Special Administrative Region of China, the European Commission, and the Gulf Cooperation Council (composed of six Middle Eastern countries) were members of FATF. China has observer status and is being considered for membership, along with India. FATF observer status has also been granted to several FATF-styled regional organizations and to international organizations that have specific anti–money laundering functions. The former include such organizations as the Asia-Pacific Group on Money Laundering and the financial action task forces of the Caribbean, South America, and the Middle East and North Africa; the latter include the regional development banks, multilateral organizations, international police organizations, and others.

FATF is working to broaden its jurisdiction and to respond to emerging threats. The latest special recommendation was adopted in October 2004, for example, to deal with problems that may arise with cash couriers. The organization also maintains a list of Non-Cooperative Countries and Territories, that is, those found to have deficient anti–money laundering systems. At present, of the original 47 countries and territories examined, only Myanmar, the Republic of Nauru, and Nigeria remain on this list. All the others have made legislative reforms and put in place measures to comply with international anti–money laundering standards.

Civil Society Initiatives

A number of civil society organizations are also at the forefront of the international fight against corruption. Among the best known are Transparency International, discussed above, and the Extractive Industries Transparency Initiative (EITI). Other important organizations include Global Witness and the Global Organisation of Parliamentarians Against Corruption.

EITI supports improved governance in resource-rich countries through the full publication and verification of company payments and government revenue from oil, gas, and mining. Studies have shown that, when governance is good, the revenue from these resources can foster economic growth and reduce poverty, but that weak governance may instead cause poverty, corruption, and conflict—the so-called resource curse. EITI aims to defeat this curse by improving transparency and accountability. So far, only 8 countries have implemented or are implementing EITI, although 14 more have endorsed it. Other participants include international financial institutions (such as the World Bank), bilateral donors, mining and oil companies, and nongovernmental organizations.

Global Witness is a nongovernmental investigative organization that aims to break the link between the exploitation of natural resources and the funding of conflict and corruption. It does this by gathering firsthand information and documenting evidence to feed an intensive campaign for reform. One of the organization's breakthrough successes was the eventual demise of the Khmer Rouge after undercover investigations unearthed an illegal multimillion-dollar log trade between the Cambodian communist group and Thai logging companies. The evidence presented by Global Witness, along with international pressure, forced the Thai government to close the border, thus starving the Khmer Rouge of funds. Global Witness is using the experience from this case to launch similar campaigns in conflict and natural resource–rich areas of Asia and Africa.

The Global Organisation of Parliamentarians Against Corruption (GOPAC) is a network of over 400 parliamentarians from 70 countries committed to fighting corruption. GOPAC enlists anticorruption experts to help members develop tools and initiatives to combat corruption and strengthen parliamentary oversight capabilities through knowledge sharing, training, and mutual support. The goals are to help parliamentarians improve and better implement international and national accountability and transparency standards and to fulfill their oversight role.

In the past decade, in tandem with the proliferation of national disclosure laws, international organizations and government financial institutions have also been working to improve international disclosure standards in the corporate sector:

- The first version of the International Accounting Standards was developed by 10 countries in 1974. To date, over 70 countries have adopted the standards or use them as national standards.
- The International Chamber of Commerce first published its Rules of Conduct to Combat Extortion and Bribery in 1977. Last revised in 1999, the rules include disclosure procedures as national preventive measures against extortion and bribery.
- In 1998, the International Organization of Securities Commissions (IOSCO) adopted a comprehensive set of Objectives and Principles of Securities Regulation that sets international benchmarks (including

benchmarks for transparency) for all securities markets. IOSCO members regulate more than 90 percent of the world's securities markets.

- In June 2000, the Global Reporting Initiative (GRI) released the first set of GRI Sustainability Reporting Guidelines for public disclosure of corporate financial, environmental, and social performance. As of March 2006, over 800 corporations from 80 countries had filed reports under these guidelines.
- In June 2002, George Soros, chairman of the Open Society Institute, launched the Publish What You Pay campaign. As of 2006, the campaign had grown into a coalition of over 280 nongovernmental organizations worldwide calling for the mandatory disclosure of payments made by companies in the extractive industry to all governments.
- Eleven major international banks were brought together by Transparency International in 2000 to form the Wolfsberg Group. In October of that year, the group published the Wolfsberg Anti–Money Laundering Principles of Private Banking (revised in May 2002), followed by guidelines for correspondent banking in November 2002. These and other documents set global standards for banks in terms of knowing their clients and ensuring that clients' funds are from legitimate sources.
- In 2004, member companies of the World Economic Forum and Transparency International launched the Partnership Against Corruption Initiative (PACI), designed to help consolidate efforts to fight corruption in the private sector. The PACI Principles call for a commitment to improving business standards of transparency in private sector operations, among other anticorruption strategies.
- In 2004, a 10th principle against corruption was added to the UN Global Compact, an initiative of UN Secretary General Kofi Annan. Hundreds of companies have since committed to the compact, which urges them to lobby for the ratification and implementation of UNCAC and to use anticorruption tools and collaborate in international anticorruption efforts such as those of Transparency International, the International Chamber of Commerce, EITI, and Publish What You Pay.

Much More Can Be Done

The Oil-for-Food Programme, described above, became notorious as an example of corruption on a global scale. The corruption was so extensive and involved so many international institutions, companies, and high-level officials of various countries that it made clear that the international safeguards and agreements against corruption in place at the time were inadequate to the task. Changes in the international financial system, antibribery agreements, and mechanisms for the settlement of disputes between multilateral investors and states are therefore needed to counteract the increasing sophistication and the persistence of corruption. Several researchers have proposed ideas for such changes:

- Theodore Moran of Georgetown University suggests that the OECD Convention Against Bribery could change its definition of bribery from the present one, which simply criminalizes certain payments to public officials by an international company, to the broader definition in the OECD Guidelines for Multinational Enterprises.[7] Those guidelines state that "Enterprises should not, directly or indirectly, offer, promise, give, or demand a bribe or other undue advantage to obtain or retain business or other improper advantage. . . . In particular, enterprises. . . should not use sub-contracts, purchase orders or consulting agreements as means of channeling payments to public officials, to employees of business partners, or to their relatives or business associates." This, Moran feels, would close a major loophole.
- Kathryn Nickerson of the U.S. Department of Commerce has reported a number of concerns that have emerged from reviews of the implementation of the OECD Antibribery Convention, including lack of awareness by government officials (including prosecutors, police, and officials stationed abroad), and relevant government agencies, of the pertinent laws; insufficient training and resources to enforce the laws; lack of public awareness, especially on the part of small and medium-size enterprises; poor enforcement of accounting rules; short statutes of limitation; weak sanctions; and narrow jurisdictions.[8]
- Moran has also suggested that, in the area of multilateral investor-state dispute settlement mechanisms, host states must be protected against misbehavior by international investors. Any international investor proven to have engaged in a corrupt act, such as paying a bribe, should lose the right to be compensated through international arbitration for actions a host state may have taken against it, such as confiscating assets or cancelling payments.
- In addition, Moran feels that the push for full transparency in international transactions must be expanded geographically and cover more sectors. Countries must require both state-owned and private companies to make records of all payments available to the public, and host governments must in turn be transparent regarding expenditure. These

records can then be audited and monitored by independent bodies, through initiatives such as EITI, which can be expanded to cover other sectors, including infrastructure.

- Glenn Ware and Gregory Noone have suggested that multilateral development banks could also more aggressively investigate cases of corruption affecting their resources and programs and be bolder in publicizing all findings of impropriety or illegality.[9] They noted that organizations could share information with each other and maintain a common database of corruption intelligence that would aid each other's investigations. Ware and Noone also maintained that collective sanctions against offenders—whether companies or governments—could evolve into an effective deterrence system and would greatly increase the risk of detection and levels of punishment. In February 2006, the multilateral development banks took initial steps in this direction when they agreed to strengthen information sharing and to support each other's compliance and enforcement actions. A task force was formed to develop a uniform Framework for Preventing and Combating Fraud and Corruption by September 2006.

- Ware and Noone also proposed that voluntary disclosure programs, such as the one used by the World Bank, could be adopted by the other multilateral development banks. Under such programs, contractors would voluntarily disclose information on corruption and fraud in programs funded by the bank, including (and indeed especially) in the contractor's own operations. In exchange for this voluntary disclosure, the bank would agree not to debar the contractor from future contracts. However, the contractor would have to make restitution of any damages to the bank, allow itself to be audited, and agree to improve its compliance programs. This would shift the responsibility of disclosure to the contractors and result in savings for the bank, not just in its programs but also from decreased investigative requirements.

- Vinay Bhargava and Emil Bolongaita reported on public hearings of the U.S. Senate Foreign Relations Committee from May 2004 to April 2005 on combating corruption in the multilateral development banks.[10] Among the key recommendations for bank action that emerged from these hearings were the following: write off "criminal debt"; change corporate cultures and staff incentives so as to achieve greater anti-corruption accountability; improve the auditing and supervision of loans and projects by, among other things, adopting stricter governance criteria, promoting civil society and media participation in operations, and harmonizing anticorruption policies, including debarment of firms; strengthen internal and external anticorruption capabilities, including in investigation and prosecution; and prioritize corruption risks in policy-based or programmatic lending, condition financial support on transparency reforms, and support governments in meeting transparency and accountability goals.

The Role of the World Bank in Combating Corruption

The World Bank confronts corruption globally by helping countries combat corruption more effectively, by making a country's anticorruption efforts a significant factor in lending decisions regarding that country, by working to prevent corruption from infecting Bank-financed projects, and by actively participating and often leading international efforts to fight corruption.

The World Bank undertakes extensive analytical and operational work on corruption through its regional operations and through its Poverty Reduction and Economic Management department, the World Bank Institute, and the Legal Department. It uses this knowledge and expertise to help countries improve public service transparency and accountability.

The World Bank requires that all Country Assistance Strategies, which are the basis for the Bank's lending decisions, address governance issues. In countries where corruption is widespread, governance issues often dominate the Country Assistance Strategy. In 2005, almost half of all new Bank projects addressed governance issues. The Bank also refuses to grant loans or suspends the disbursement of loans and debt forgiveness in cases where the government or the funded projects are plagued with corruption.

The World Bank's Department of Institutional Integrity participates in fiduciary reviews of Bank-funded projects that are perceived as vulnerable to corruption and fraud. As a result of the department's investigations, over 330 companies and individuals had been sanctioned as of June 2005.

Among the multilateral development banks and other international financial institutions, the World Bank has led the way in the breadth and depth of its anticorruption and governance strategy and approach. In addition to mainstreaming corruption and governance issues into all facets of its operations, the Bank aims to set high standards by which it hopes governments and other international financial and development institutions will measure their own efforts and strive to attain or even exceed them.

In February 2005, the World Bank released its first annual report on corruption and fraud investigations involving Bank-financed projects as well as cases internal to the Bank.[11] The report's publication, together with other research and information produced by the Bank, provided an overview of its anticorruption efforts from 1999 onward with other agencies and groups. The report showed that the Bank spends $10 million annually, more than all the other multilateral development banks combined, on investigations and sanctions. Its investigative department has over 50 staff members, more than that of any similar organization. The Bank is also pioneering the use of such techniques as voluntary disclosure, by reducing sanctions and giving assurances of confidentiality for firms that provide information on their involvement in corrupt or fraudulent acts on Bank-financed projects.

The World Bank recognizes that a concerted effort is needed to win more battles against corruption, and it actively supports international and interagency programs that aim to do so. The Bank has joined the International Monetary Fund and the regional development banks in reaching a consensus agreement on the broad policies and practices needed to address corruption within the organizations as well as in member countries.

This progress on improving coordination among the development institutions builds on ongoing and expanding programs in research, reform, enforcement, and other governance and corruption-related issues, through different partnership configurations. The World Bank, for example, has partnered with other institutions to undertake research, such as its work with the European Bank for Reconstruction and Development to develop the Business Environment and Enterprise Performance Survey.

The work of the World Bank Institute on governance and anticorruption focuses on improving countries' governance capacity and is based on pioneering research gathered in a highly participative manner. The Institute has partnership agreements with nearly 200 organizations, and more than half of its activities are developed with partners in client countries. These partners include government ministries, nongovernmental organizations, professional organizations, interagency groups, bilateral aid agencies, media groups, think tanks, parliamentary associations, and research organizations, among others.

Notes

1. Wolfensohn (1996, p. 50).
2. The text of the Millennium Development Goals may be found in chapter 21 of this volume.
3. European Parliament, Council of Europe, and European Commission (2006).
4. Pope (2000).
5. See article 31 of the convention. The text of the convention is available at http://www.unodc.org/ pdf/crime/convention_corruption/signing/Convention-e.pdf.
6. The text of the convention is available at http://www.olis.oecd.org/olis/1997doc.nsf/LinkTo/ daffe-ime-br(97)20.
7. Moran (2006). The text of the OECD guidelines is available at http://www.oecd.org/dataoecd/ 56/36/1922428.pdf.

8. Nickerson (2005).
9. Ware and Noone (2005).
10. Bhargava and Bolongaita (2005).
11. World Bank (2005).

Selected Readings and Cited References

Banisar, David. 2004. "The Freedominfo.org Global Survey: Freedom of Information and Access to Government Record Laws Around the World." Washington, DC: Freedominfo.org.

Bhargava, Vinay, and Emil Bolongaita. 2004. *Challenging Corruption in Asia: Case Studies and a Framework for Action.* Washington, DC: World Bank.

————. 2005. "Combating Corruption in Multilateral Development Banks." Washington, DC: World Bank.

European Parliament, Council of Europe, and European Commission. 2006. "The European Consensus on Development." *Official Journal of the European Union,* February 24. http://ec.europa.eu/comm/development/body/development_policy_statement/docs/edp_statement_oj_24_02_2006_en.pdf.

Group of Eight. 2003. "Fighting Corruption and Improving Transparency: A G8 Declaration." June 1–3.

Independent Inquiry Committee into the United Nations Oil-for-Food Programme. 2005. *Report on Programme Manipulation.* October 27.

Kaufmann, Daniel. 2006. "Myths and Realities of Governance and Corruption." In *Global Competitiveness Report 2005–2006.* Geneva: World Economic Forum.

Moran, Theodore H. 2006. "How Multinational Investors Evade Developed Country Laws." Working Paper 79, Center for Global Development, Washington, DC.

Nickerson, Kathryn. 2005. "International Enforcement of the OECD Antibribery Convention." *Federal Ethics Report* 12(3).

Pope, Jeremy. 2000. *Confronting Corruption: The Elements of a National Integrity System (TI Source Book 2000).* London: Transparency International.

Transparency International. 2004. *Global Corruption Report 2004.* London: Pluto Press.

————. 2005. *Report on the Transparency International Global Corruption Barometer.* Berlin: Transparency International.

Ware, Glenn T., and Gregory P. Noone. 2005. "The Anatomy of Transnational Corruption." *International Affairs Review* 14(2).

Wolfensohn, James D. 1996. "People and Development." Address to the Board of Governors at the Annual Meetings of the World Bank and the International Monetary Fund. Reprinted in *Voice for the World's Poor: Selected Speeches and Writings of World Bank President James D. Wolfensohn, 1995–2005.* Washington, DC: World Bank.

Wolfowitz, Paul. 2005. "Charting a Way Ahead: The Results Agenda." Address to the Board of Governors at the Annual Meetings of the World Bank and the International Monetary Fund, Washington, DC, September 24.

Wolfsberg Group. "Global Banks: Global Standards." http://www.wolfsberg-principles.com.

World Bank. 2005. *Annual Report on Investigations and Sanctions of Staff Misconduct and Fraud and Corruption in Bank-Financed Projects.* Washington, DC.

World Economic Forum. 2005. *Global Competitiveness Report 2005–2006.* Geneva.

Selected Web Links on Governance and Corruption

ADB/OECD Anti-Corruption Initiative for Asia-Pacific	http://www1.oecd.org/daf/asiacom
BEEPS (Business Environment and Enterprise Performance Survey) Interactive Data Set	http://info.worldbank.org/governance/beeps/
Doing Business database	http://www.doingbusiness.org
Extractive Industries Transparency Initiative	http://www.eitransparency.org
Financial Action Task Force	http://www.fatf-gafi.org
Global Organisation of Parliamentarians Against Corruption	http://www.gopac.org
Global Reporting Initiative	http://www.globalreporting.org
Global Witness	http://www.globalwitness.org
International Chamber of Commerce	http://www.iccwbo.org
International Organization of Securities Commissions	http://www.iosco.org
Publish What You Pay	http://www.publishwhatyoupay.org
Transparency International	http://www1.transparency.org/index.html
UN Convention Against Corruption	http://www.unodc.org/unodc/crime_convention_corruption.html
World Economic Forum	http://www.weforum.org

ANNEX 18.1: Recommended Measures in the ADB/OECD Anticorruption Action Plan for Asia and the Pacific

Pillar 1: Developing effective and transparent systems for public service	Pillar 2: Strengthening antibribery actions and promoting integrity in business operations	Pillar 3: Supporting active public involvement
Establish systems of government hiring of public officials that ensure openness, equity, and efficiency, and promote the hiring of people with the highest levels of competence and integrity through the following:	Take effective measures to actively combat bribery as follows:	Take effective measures to encourage public discussion of the issue of corruption through the following:
■ Development of systems for compensation adequate to sustain appropriate livelihood and according to the level of the economy of the country in question ■ Development of systems for transparent hiring and promotion to help avoid abuses of patronage, nepotism, and favoritism; help foster the creation of an independent civil service; and help promote a proper balance between political and career appointments ■ Development of systems to provide appropriate oversight of discretionary decisions and of personnel with authority to make discretionary decisions	■ Ensuring the existence of legislation with dissuasive sanctions that effectively and actively combat the bribery of public officials ■ Ensuring the existence and effective enforcement of anti-money laundering legislation that provides for substantial criminal penalties for laundering the proceeds of corruption and crime consistent with the law of each country ■ Ensuring the existence and enforcement of rules to ensure that bribery offenses are thoroughly investigated and prosecuted by competent authorities; these authorities should be empowered to order that bank, financial, or commercial records be made available or be seized and that bank secrecy be lifted ■ Strengthening investigative and prosecutorial capacities by fostering interagency cooperation, by ensuring that investigation	■ Initiation of public awareness campaigns at different levels ■ Support of NGOs that promote integrity and combat corruption by, for example, raising awareness of corruption and its costs, mobilizing citizen support for clean government, and documenting and reporting cases of corruption ■ Preparation and implementation of education programs aimed at creating an anti-corruption culture.

(Continues on the following page)

ANNEX 18.1: Recommended Measures in the ADB/OECD Anticorruption Action Plan for Asia and the Pacific (Continued)

Pillar 1: Developing effective and transparent systems for public service	Pillar 2: Strengthening antibribery actions and promoting integrity in business operations	Pillar 3: Supporting active public involvement
■ Development of personnel systems that include regular and timely rotation of assignments to reduce insularity that would foster corruption.	and prosecution are free from improper influence and have effective means for gathering evidence, by protecting those people helping the authorities in combating corruption, and by providing appropriate training and financial resources ■ Strengthening bilateral and multilateral cooperation in investigations and other legal proceedings by developing systems that, in accordance with domestic legislation, enhance (a) effective exchange of information and evidence, (b) extradition where expedient, and (c) cooperation in searching for and discovering forfeitable assets as well as prompt international seizures and repatriation of those forfeitable assets	Ensure that the general public and the media have freedom to receive and impart public information (particularly information on corruption matters) in accordance with domestic laws and in a manner that would not compromise the operational effectiveness of the administration or in any other way be
Establish ethical and administrative codes of conduct that proscribe conflicts of interest, ensure proper use of public resources, and promote the highest levels of professionalism and integrity through the following:	Take effective measures to promote corporate responsibility and accountability on the basis of existing relevant international standards through: ■ Promotion of good corporate governance that provides for adequate internal company controls such as codes of conduct, the	

- Prohibitions or restrictions governing conflicts of interest
- Systems to promote transparency through disclosure and monitoring of, for example, personal assets and liabilities
- Sound administration systems to ensure that contacts between government officials and business services users, notably in the areas of taxation, customs, and other corruption-prone matters, are free from undue and improper influence
- Promotion of codes of conduct that take due account of the existing relevant international standards as well as each country's traditional cultural standards, and regular education, training, and supervision of officials to ensure proper understanding of their responsibilities
- Measures to ensure that officials report acts of corruption and measures that protect the safety and professional status of those who do

Safeguard accountability of public service via effective legal frameworks, management practices, and auditing procedures through the following:

- Institution of measures and systems to promote fiscal transparency

establishment of channels for communication, the protection of employees reporting corruption, and staff training
- The existence and the effective enforcement of legislation to eliminate any indirect support of bribery, such as tax deductibility of bribes
- The existence and thorough implementation of legislation requiring transparent company accounts and providing for effective, proportionate, and dissuasive penalties for omissions and falsifications for the purpose of bribing a public official, or hiding such bribery, in respect of the books, records, accounts, and financial statements of companies
- Review of laws and regulations governing public licenses, government procurement contracts, or other public undertakings, so that access to public sector contracts can be denied as a sanction for bribery of public officials

detrimental to the interest of governmental agencies and individuals, through the following:

- Establishment of public reporting requirements of justice and other governmental agencies that include disclosure about efforts to promote integrity and accountability and to combat corruption
- Implementation of measures providing for a meaningful public right of access to appropriate information

Encourage public participation in anticorruption activities, in particular through the following:

- Cooperative relationships with civil society groups, such as chambers of commerce,

(Continues on the following page)

ANNEX 18.1: Recommended Measures in the ADB/OECD Anticorruption Action Plan for Asia and the Pacific (Continued)

Pillar 1: Developing effective and transparent systems for public service	Pillar 2: Strengthening antibribery actions and promoting integrity in business operations	Pillar 3: Supporting active public involvement
▪ Adoption of existing relevant international standards and practices for regulation and supervision of financial institutions ▪ Adoption of appropriate auditing procedures applicable to public administration and the public sector and of measures and systems to provide timely public reporting on performance and decision making ▪ Adoption of appropriate, transparent procedures for public procurement that promote fair competition and deter corrupt activity and establishment of adequate simplified administration procedures ▪ Enhancement of institutions for public scrutiny and oversight ▪ Adoption of systems for information availability, including information on issues such as application processing procedures, funding of political parties, and electoral campaigns and expenditures ▪ Simplification of the regulatory environment by abolishing overlapping, ambiguous, or excessive regulations that burden business		professional associations, NGOs, labor unions, housing associations, the media, and other organizations ▪ Protection of whistleblowers ▪ Involvement of NGOs in monitoring of public sector programs and activities

Source: Bhargava and Bolongaita 2004. Adapted from the ADB/OECD Anticorruption Action Plan for Asia and the Pacific, November 30, 2001.

NGOs = nongovernmental organizations

19

The United Nations Economic and Social System: An Organization in the Midst of Change

OSCAR AVALLE AND GASPARD CURIONI

Management of global issues requires effective international cooperation, and the United Nations (UN) is the primary body created for achieving such cooperation. This chapter provides an overview of the UN, its mandates, and its finances. It looks at the role that the UN plays in global issues management and the constraints the UN faces in this role. The chapter ends by discussing some key reforms that will help the UN be more effective in managing global issues.

An Overview of the United Nations System

On a single day, April 28, 2006, the UN's World Food Programme cut food aid to the war-torn Darfur region in Sudan, Iran curtailed its cooperation with UN nuclear inspectors, and a vote sponsored by a large group of developing countries (the Group of 77) in the UN's Budget Committee blocked a major management reform proposal offered by the secretary-general.[1] By the end of that fateful day in April, calls for change were once again resonating across the UN and beyond. Media commentators and leaders of civil society

We would like to thank Joanne Dickow and Audrey Liounis for their advice, cooperation, and assistance in putting this chapter together.

organizations demanded that the organization reform itself to respond to an increasingly complex and difficult world but at the same time questioned its capacity to do so. The stalemate also marked a clear division between developed and developing countries, one that would make future movement on reform extremely difficult. As delegates and observers left UN headquarters late that Friday night, it was clear that the organization was facing one of the most serious crises in its 60 years of existence. Asked if they saw a way out, veteran UN delegates just shook their heads.

The UN came into existence at the end of World War II, in 1945, when representatives of 51 nations met in San Francisco to draw up the charter of a new organization. After a short but intense deliberation, the UN Charter came into force in October 1945 after being ratified by the countries that would become the five permanent members of the UN Security Council (China, France, the Soviet Union, the United Kingdom, and the United States) and the majority of signatory nations. In contrast to its predecessor, the League of Nations, the new organization enjoyed the support of all the great powers of the world, and despite the onset of the Cold War, the UN would become an important and effective forum for managing global issues.

The Charter of the UN sets out the basic principles of international relations and entails obligations that all member states agree to accept. According to the Charter, the UN has four purposes:

- To maintain international peace and security
- To develop friendly relations among nations
- To cooperate in solving international problems and in promoting respect for human rights
- To be a center for harmonizing the actions of nations.

To put these principles into practice, the UN Charter establishes five main bodies: the Security Council, the General Assembly, the Economic and Social Council, the Trusteeship Council, and the International Court of Justice. This chapter will focus on the first three. In addition to these, the UN Secretariat administers the policies and programs of these main bodies and carries out the day-to-day work of the organization.

The Security Council is made up of 15 member nations: the 5 permanent members listed above and 10 members elected by the General Assembly for 2-year terms. Each council member has one vote. However, each of the permanent members has the right to veto decisions passed by the council. Through this veto mechanism, the victorious powers in World War II effectively were granted an instrument by which to control intergovernmental relations in the area of peace and security.

Within the new organization, the Security Council was balanced by the inclusive and open General Assembly, a forum where all nations have an equal vote. Today, 191 countries—nearly all the countries of the world—are members of the UN and have seats in the General Assembly.

The Economic and Social Council (ECOSOC) is the central forum for discussing and managing global issues outside the security domain, such as higher standards of living, full employment, and economic and social progress around the world; for identifying solutions to international economic, social, and health problems; for facilitating international cultural and educational cooperation; and for encouraging universal respect for human rights and fundamental freedoms. With 54 voting member states (none holding veto power) elected by the General Assembly for overlapping three-year terms, ECOSOC meets annually for a four-week substantive session each July, alternating between New York and Geneva.

In addition to the principal organs established by the Charter, the UN now includes a network of international organizations, subsidiary bodies, agencies, funds, and programs, which together are known as the UN system. Among them are the Office of the UN High Commissioner for Refugees, the UN Development Programme (UNDP), and the UN Children's Fund (UNICEF). These bodies are closely linked to the central organization and report to the General Assembly or to ECOSOC.

Specialized agencies, by contrast, are independent organizations created by intergovernmental agreements and treaties. The International Monetary Fund (IMF) and the World Bank—called the Bretton Woods institutions after the location of their founding in 1944—and 12 other independent organizations, such as the World Health Organization and the International Civil Aviation Organization, cooperate with other entities in the UN system on a wide range of global issues in the economic, social, cultural, humanitarian, environmental, and related fields. Table 19.1 lists the programs, funds, and other organs of the UN system and the specialized agencies. Figure 19.1 is an organizational chart of the system.

All of the specialized agencies have their own governing bodies, budgets, and secretariats. At the intergovernmental level, they interact through the coordinating function of ECOSOC. However, under the provisions included in the legal agreements that rule the relationship between the specialized agencies and the UN, many of the organizations within the system behave as independently of the UN as if they were not part of the system at all. Within ECOSOC, countries' diplomatic representatives are supposed to decide on technical issues and agendas on the basis of reports prepared by the secretariats of the specialized agencies. These reports are often long and technical,

TABLE 19.1   Programs, Funds, and Other Organs of the United Nations System and Specialized Agencies, Selected Programs

Entity and standard abbreviation	Year created	Headquarters	Web site
Programs, funds, and other organs			
United Nations Capital Development Fund (UNCDF)	1966	New York	http://www.uncdf.org
United Nations Conference on Trade and Development (UNCTAD)	1964	Geneva	http://www.unctad.org
United Nations Development Programme (UNDP)	1965	New York	http://www.undp.org
United Nations Environment Programme (UNEP)	1972	Nairobi	http://www.unep.org
United Nations Population Fund (UNFPA)	1969[a]	New York	http://www.unfpa.org
Office of the United Nations High Commissioner for Refugees (UNHCR)	1950	Geneva	http://www.unhcr.org
United Nations Human Settlements Programme (UN-HABITAT, UNHSP)	1978	Nairobi	http://www.unhsp.org
United Nations Children's Fund (UNICEF)	1946	New York	http://www.unicef.org
United Nations Institute for Training and Research (UNITAR)	1965	Geneva	http://www.unitar.org
United Nations Relief and Works Agency for Palestine Refugees in the Near East (UNRWA)	1949	Gaza City and Amman	http://www.unrwa.org
United Nations University (UNU)	1969	Tokyo	http://www.unu.edu
World Food Programme (WFP)	1962	Rome	http://www.wfp.org
Specialized agencies			
Food and Agriculture Organization (FAO)	1945	Rome	http://www.fao.org
International Atomic Energy Agency (IAEA)	1957[b]	Vienna	http://www.iaea.org
International Civil Aviation Organization (ICAO)	1944	Montreal	http://www.icao.org
International Labour Organization (ILO)	1919[c]	Geneva	http://www.ilo.org
International Maritime Organization (IMO)	1948	London	http://www.imo.org
International Telecommunication Union (ITU)	1865[d]	Geneva	http://www.itu.org
United Nations Educational, Scientific and Cultural Organization (UNESCO)	1945	Paris	http://www.unesco.org
United Nations Industrial Development Organization (UNIDO)	1966[e]	Vienna	http://www.unido.org
Universal Postal Union (UPU)	1874[f]	Bern	http://www.upu.org

(*Continues on next page.*)

TABLE 19.1 *(Continued)*

Entity and standard abbreviation	Year created	Headquarters	Web site
World Health Organization (WHO)	1948	Geneva	http://www.who.int
World Intellectual Property Organization (WIPO)	1893[g]	Geneva	http://www.wipo.org
World Meteorological Organization (WMO)	1873[h]	Geneva	http://www.wmo.ch
Specialized agencies with independent governance			
International Monetary Fund (IMF)	1944	Washington, DC	http://www.imf.org
World Bank[i]	1944	Washington, DC	http://www.worldbank.org

Sources: Agency Web sites.
a. Originally the UN Fund for Population Activities, UNFPA took its present name in 1987.
b. IAEA was originally called Atoms for Peace.
c. ILO became a specialized agency of the UN in 1946.
d. Originally the International Telegraph Union, ITU took its present name in 1934 and became a specialized UN agency in 1947.
e. Originally an integrated organ of the UN, UNIDO became a specialized UN agency in 1985.
f. UPU became a specialized UN agency in 1948.
g. Originally formed from separate organizations (for patents and trademarks and for copyright) as the United International Bureaux for the Protection of Intellectual Property, WIPO took its present name in 1970 and became a specialized UN agency in 1974.
h. Originally the International Meteorological Organization, WMO took its present name in 1950 and became a specialized UN agency in 1951.
i. The World Bank comprises the International Bank for Reconstruction and Development and the International Development Association; the World Bank Group comprises these two organizations and the International Finance Corporation, the Multilateral Investment Guarantee Agency, and the International Centre for Settlement of Investment Disputes.

and in many cases, ECOSOC does not spend enough time and attention discussing them.

Originally, ECOSOC was intended to perform quite a different role. The San Francisco conference in 1945 adopted an understanding that the word *economic* in the UN Charter would cover international trade, finance, communications, transport, economic reconstruction, and, where economic problems emerge, access to raw materials and capital flows. From the work of the Preparatory Commission, it is clear that the governments whose representatives met in San Francisco intended the UN and ECOSOC to be the world's central body for the formulation of global macroeconomic policy. The subsequent record shows an important failure by those same governments and by the international community to fulfill their commitments in this regard. Political will, or lack thereof, is the critical factor in international affairs, and the UN, at its best, can only contribute to catalyzing the will of governments.

FIGURE 19.1 The United Nations System

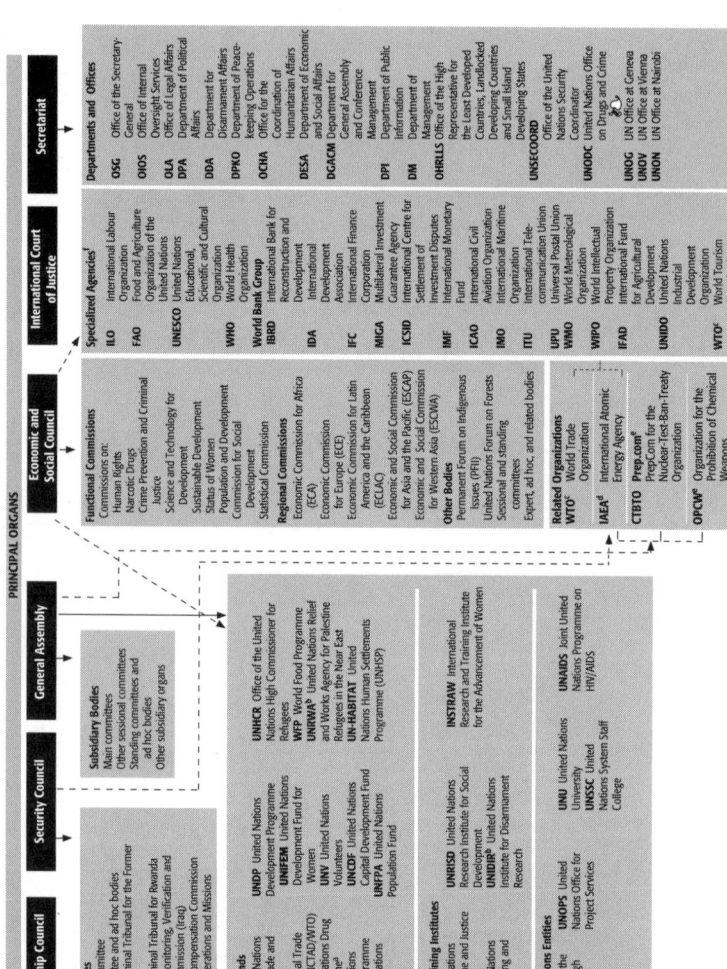

PRINCIPAL ORGANS

| Trusteeship Council | Security Council | General Assembly | Economic and Social Council | International Court of Justice | Secretariat |

Trusteeship Council

Subsidiary Bodies
Military Staff Committee
Standing Committee and ad hoc bodies
International Criminal Tribunal for Rwanda
International Criminal Tribunal for the Former Yugoslavia
United Nations Monitoring, Verification and Inspection Commission (Iraq)
United Nations Compensation Commission
Peacekeeping Operations and Missions

Programs and Funds
UNCTAD United Nations Conference on Trade and Development
  ITC International Trade Centre (UNCTAD/WTO)
UNDCP United Nations Drug Control Programme[a]
UNEP United Nations Environment Programme
UNICEF United Nations Children's Fund

Research and Training Institutes
UNICRI United Nations Interregional Crime and Justice Research Institute
UNITAR United Nations Institute for Training and Research

Other United Nations Entities
OHCHR Office of the United Nations High Commissioner for Human Rights

Security Council

UNDP United Nations Development Programme
UNIFEM United Nations Development Fund for Women
UNV United Nations Volunteers
UNCDF United Nations Capital Development Fund
UNFPA United Nations Population Fund

UNRISD United Nations Research Institute for Social Development
UNIDIR[b] United Nations Institute for Disarmament Research

UNOPS United Nations Office for Project Services

General Assembly

Subsidiary Bodies
Main committees
Other sessional committees
Standing committees and ad hoc bodies
Other subsidiary organs

UNHCR Office of the United Nations High Commissioner for Refugees
WFP World Food Programme
UNRWA[b] United Nations Relief and Works Agency for Palestine Refugees in the Near East
UN-HABITAT United Nations Human Settlements Programme (UNHSP)

INSTRAW International Research and Training Institute for the Advancement of Women

UNU United Nations University
UNSSC United Nations System Staff College

UNAIDS Joint United Nations Programme on HIV/AIDS

Economic and Social Council

Functional Commissions
Commissions on:
Human Rights
Narcotic Drugs
Crime Prevention and Criminal Justice
Science and Technology for Development
Sustainable Development
Status of Women
Population and Development
Commission for Social Development
Statistical Commission

Regional Commissions
Economic Commission for Africa (ECA)
Economic Commission for Europe (ECE)
Economic Commission for Latin America and the Caribbean (ECLAC)
Economic and Social Commission for Asia and the Pacific (ESCAP)
Economic and Social Commission for Western Asia (ESCWA)

Other Bodies
Permanent Forum on Indigenous Issues (PFII)
United Nations Forum on Forests
Sessional and standing committees
Expert, ad hoc, and related bodies

Related Organizations
WTO[c] World Trade Organization
IAEA[d] International Atomic Energy Agency
CTBTO Prep.Com[e] PrepCom for the Nuclear-Test-Ban-Treaty Organization
OPCW[e] Organization for the Prohibition of Chemical Weapons

International Court of Justice

Specialized Agencies[f]
ILO International Labour Organization
FAO Food and Agriculture Organization of the United Nations
UNESCO United Nations Educational, Scientific and Cultural Organization
WHO World Health Organization
World Bank Group
IBRD International Bank for Reconstruction and Development
IDA International Development Association
IFC International Finance Corporation
MIGA Multilateral Investment Guarantee Agency
ICSID International Centre for Settlement of Investment Disputes
IMF International Monetary Fund
ICAO International Civil Aviation Organization
IMO International Maritime Organization
ITU International Telecommunication Union
UPU Universal Postal Union
WMO World Meteorological Organization
WIPO World Intellectual Property Organization
IFAD International Fund for Agricultural Development
UNIDO United Nations Industrial Development Organization
WTO[c] World Tourism Organization

Secretariat

Departments and Offices
OSG Office of the Secretary-General
OIOS Office of Internal Oversight Services
OLA Office of Legal Affairs
DPA Department of Political Affairs
DDA Department for Disarmament Affairs
DPKO Department of Peacekeeping Operations
OCHA Office for the Coordination of Humanitarian Affairs
DESA Department of Economic and Social Affairs
DGACM Department for General Assembly and Conference Management
DPI Department of Public Information
DM Department of Management
OHRLLS Office of the High Representative for the Least Developed Countries, Landlocked Developing Countries and Small Island Developing States
UNSECOORD Office of the United Nations Security Coordinator
UNODC United Nations Office on Drugs and Crime
UNOG UN Office at Geneva
UNOV UN Office at Vienna
UNON UN Office at Nairobi

Source: United Nations Department of Public Information 2004.
Note: Solid lines from a Principal Organ indicate a direct reporting relationship; dashes indicate a nonsubsidiary relationship.
a. The UN Drug Control Programme is part of the UN Office on Drugs and Crime.
b. UNRWA and UNIDIR report only to the General Assembly.
c. The World Trade Organization and World Tourism Organization use the same acronym.
d. IAEA reports to the Security Council and the General Assembly.
e. The CTBTO Prep.Com and OPCW report to the General Assembly.
f. Specialized agencies are autonomous organizations working with the UN and each other through the coordinating machinery of ECOSOC at the intergovernmental level, and through the Chief Executives Board for coordination at the inter-secretariat level.

The challenges faced by the system in achieving effective cooperation on global issues are compounded by the decision of many governments to send officials of their foreign ministries to the General Assembly and ECOSOC, while sending officials from other sector ministries, such as finance, health, or international development, to the governing bodies of the specialized agencies. Given that coordination at the national level between ministries is not always fluid, it is easy to imagine how disconnected representatives of different ministries in the various specialized agencies, working in different cities and guided by their own agendas and cultures, might become.

This difficulty did not go unnoticed. The UN, and in particular ECOSOC, were not in a position to provide the systemwide coherence needed. Duplication and fragmentation became a common feature, leading to inefficient use of resources and ultimately a clear lack of results. It is therefore not surprising that calls for reform increased significantly over time.

How the United Nations System Is Funded

If the institutional design of the UN seems complex, the funding modalities established to provide the resources it needs are at least as cumbersome and complicated. The UN system is financed primarily through assessed and voluntary contributions from the member states. The Regular Budget, the Peacekeeping Budget, and the international tribunals' budget are funded through assessments on the member countries. The various UN programs and funds are financed through voluntary contributions from members. The specialized agencies are funded partly through assessments and partly through voluntary contributions, except for IMF and the World Bank, which are mostly self-funding. The expenditures of the UN system amounted to approximately $45 billion for the biennium 2004–05. This includes the Regular Budget, the Peacekeeping Budget, and the budgets of the specialized agencies (assessed and voluntary). It also includes voluntary contributions to cover the operational expenditures of the funds, programs, and specialized agencies (other than IMF and the World Bank). Figure 19.2 shows how UN system expenditures were distributed among the Regular Budget, the Peacekeeping Budget, the programs and funds, and the specialized agencies in a recent year.

The General Assembly sets the Regular Budget every two calendar years. This budget funds the UN's core activities, including staffing costs, in the system's eight headquarters locations in the United States, Europe, Asia, Africa, and Latin America. It also covers international conferences, dissemination of public information, human rights promotion, and special UN missions to conflict areas. The Regular Budget is financed through

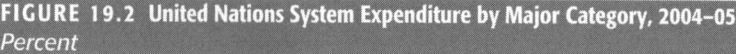

FIGURE 19.2 United Nations System Expenditure by Major Category, 2004–05
Percent

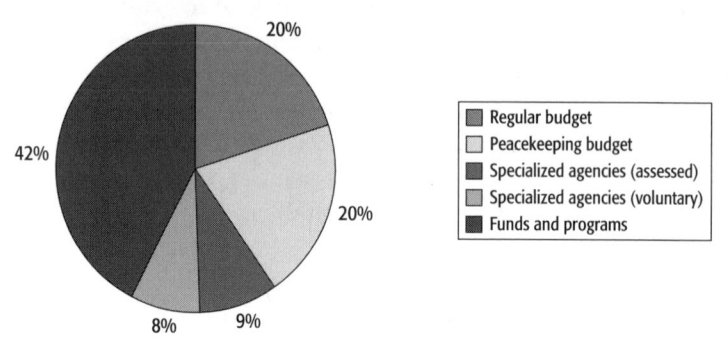

Source: United Nations data.
Note: Percentages do not sum to 100 because of rounding.

assessments on all UN member states. Countries pay according to their economic capacity, except that no country may pay more than 22 percent of the total; this ceiling rate is intended to prevent the UN from becoming overly dependent on any one member state. The United States is the only country that would exceed this ceiling based on economic capacity; consequently, it pays much less than its share of the global economy would indicate. However, over 80 percent of all member states fail to pay their dues to the UN in full and on time. Many countries, including some of the largest contributors, transfer just about enough to maintain their vote in the General Assembly.

The Peacekeeping Budget pays for UN peacekeeping operations all over the world. This budget is financed through assessments on all the member states, based on the scale of assessments for the regular budget. The five permanent members of the Security Council, which approve all peacekeeping operations, pay a surcharge on top of their regular assessments. Poor countries get a discount on their rates. In the 1990s, as the Security Council launched an unprecedented number of peacekeeping operations, the Peacekeeping Budget and total debt to the budget rose quickly. The General Assembly also sets a fiscal-year Peacekeeping Budget. However, the committee reviews and adjusts the budget throughout the year. Since peacekeeping missions vary in number, size, and duration, contributions to the Peacekeeping Budget are extremely volatile.

Some of the specialized agencies, funds, and programs are financed through voluntary contributions from member countries, and in some cases also from private sector and nongovernmental organizations (NGOs). UNICEF has developed this modality extremely well, through the establishment of its national committees. However, the Food and Agriculture Organization, the International Labour Organization, the United Nations Educational, Scientific and Cultural Organization, and the World Health Organization are funded through assessments and voluntary contributions. IMF and the World Bank are funded and governed outside of the UN system. UN programs and funds remain particularly vulnerable, as they rely entirely on voluntary contributions from a handful of donor countries. Thus the capacity of these agencies and funds to develop longer-term programs is extremely limited. Improving the predictability of funding has therefore become one of the key objectives of the reform process. Some NGOs argue that these organizations should be funded at least partly through assessments. Additional funds could be raised through alternative sources such as global taxes. Since the Millennium Summit in 2000 agreed on the principles that would become the Millennium Development Goals (MDGs), these proposals have lately regained momentum and are being discussed in several forums.

The United Nations' Role in Global Issues Management: Actions and Limitations

The UN, as a universal meeting place and forum, has been entrusted since its creation with promoting stability and good relations between states. The UN has evolved over the years to fulfill this mandate and to perform its critical role in global issues management. Adaptation to new geopolitical contexts and circumstances has not always been easy, but the UN system has made commendable attempts, notably during the major international conferences of the 1990s, to forge international cooperation to address global challenges in areas such as the environment, human development, and peace and security.

The 1960s and 1970s: Putting Together a System to Manage Global Issues

From time to time, the UN has had to catch up with political, social, and economic change around the world. In the 1960s, UN reform was driven by the decolonization process and the need to provide greater assistance to newly independent countries and developing countries. From a global issues perspective, the main focus was on how the system could support the efforts of these countries to accelerate their economic growth and development.

In 1969, two reports examined the capacity of the UN system to respond to the development challenges of that time. *Partners in Development,* better known as the Pearson Report,[2] was prepared by the Commission on International Development at the request of then–World Bank President Robert McNamara and under the leadership of Lester B. Pearson, former prime minister of Canada. The so-called Jackson Report was commissioned by the UNDP's Governing Council to study the capacity of the UN development system.[3]

The final Pearson Report stated that the UN system was suffering from a proliferation of agencies, which resulted in dispersed and unrelated efforts at the country level. The report also stressed the urgent need for improved coordination and proposed that donor countries' total aid should amount to at least 1 percent of their gross national product (GNP) by 1975, and that official aid should reach 0.7 percent of GNP. The Jackson Report concluded that "the UN development machine had evolved into probably the most complex organization in the world . . . [with] no real central coordinating organization, which could exercise effective control at headquarters and with *administrative tentacles* that ran down to a vast complex of regional, sub-regional, and field offices" [emphasis in the original]. Among the report's recommendations was that UNDP be anchored firmly as the central financing mechanism for technical cooperation and pre-investment for the whole UN system. The report pleaded in favor of "country ownership," argued against "one size fits all templates and blueprints" for development, and indicated an early interest in management for results. Both reports addressed the issue of systemwide coordination of the aid machinery, including the Bretton Woods institutions.

The Jackson Report enjoyed greater support than the Pearson Report, most likely because it focused more on the UN system and incorporated concrete reform proposals for the UN development framework. Some of the Jackson Report's main recommendations were phased in, such as a new system of country programming based on indicative planning figures and the creation of UNDP resident representatives (later called resident coordinators).

It was several years before the topic was taken up again, this time in the 1975 Gardner Report,[4] which again looked at the need for greater coherence in the planning, programming, and budgetary processes of the UN system. The report also recommended the establishment of a UN Development Authority, which would consolidate funds for technical cooperation and the pre-investment activities of agencies throughout the system with the exception of UNICEF.

Some of the Gardner Report's reform proposals, in a much-weakened form, were taken up in 1975–77 by the Ad Hoc Intergovernmental

Committee on the Restructuring of the Economic and Social Sectors. The committee endorsed a single annual pledging conference for all UN operational activities for development. It called for measures to achieve maximum uniformity of administrative, financial, budgetary, personnel, and planning procedures and for improved coherence of action and effective integration at the country level. The committee decided that the UNDP country programming process would become the framework for systemwide operational management of global issues.

The 1980s and 1990s: Building a Common Future

A new reform process began in 1987 and gathered momentum with the optimism that emerged with the end of the Cold War. It was widely believed that the world was facing a unique opportunity to construct a better world for current and future generations, if it could address effectively the management of common global issues such as environmental protection, population growth, and human rights at the global level. In light of this opportunity, the international community launched a series of global summits to discuss these issues. One such summit was the UN Conference on Environment and Development in 1992 (also known as the Rio Earth Summit), followed by the Cairo Conference on Population and Development in 1994 and the Copenhagen Social Summit in 1995.

The impetus for these conferences came from outside expert reports. One key document, the Brundtland Report, was produced by the World Commission on Environment and Development in 1987.[5] This pivotal report resulted in the landmark Rio Earth Summit in Rio de Janeiro in 1992. In terms of UN system dynamics, the Rio summit and the "Agenda 21" that it produced marked a turning point in the relationship between the UN and nonstate actors. Until then, diplomacy had been considered a privileged affair in which secrecy and backroom deals were not only expected but viewed as legitimate. In this instance, intense pressure from civil society and NGOs resulted in a change in the usual course of events—this time, civil society drove the agenda for the summit.

All these reports and conferences seemed to mark a new awakening—a renaissance of trust in the capacity of the international system to manage global issues effectively. However, the new dynamic of the intergovernmental normative process was not accompanied by parallel processes for the provision of resources to pay for the conferences' ambitious plans. Although it had been agreed, in Agenda 21, that new and additional financial resources would be used to fund sustainable development, the result was that official development assistance, core contributions, and noncore UN contributions remained roughly the same. Heads of state gathered to discuss ways to improve the system, but the ideas they generated were not transformed into reality on the ground.

It is not surprising, then, that shortly after the conclusion of the Rio and Cairo conferences, a new set of studies were conducted dealing with financing options. Given the new tasks that had been taken on, the international community and the UN in particular needed to find appropriate means of financing these new tasks. In 1993, the Ford Foundation supported an effort to review UN financing. The report of the Independent Advisory Group on UN Financing (also known as the Ogata-Volcker Group after its chairs Sadako Ogata and Paul Volcker), *Financing an Effective United Nations*,[6] concluded that, as confidence in the effectiveness and efficiency of the UN grew, governments might start to look more favorably at alternative financing mechanisms, such as that of the World Intellectual Property Organization, which is authorized to collect payment for services rendered with respect to intellectual property rights. Although the report was generally well received, few of its recommendations were ever implemented.

All of these efforts and the human development commitments that had been made in New York, Rio, and Cairo were synthesized in a 1994 report of the then–Secretary-General Boutros Boutros-Ghali.[7] Titled "An Agenda for Development" and intended as an accompaniment to the 1992 report "An Agenda for Peace,"[8] the report sought to "revitalize a vision of development and to stimulate intensified discussion of all its aspects." The report addressed concerns that the UN was placing greater emphasis on peacekeeping than on development issues, and it established a clear link between peace and development. It also emphasized that coordination of activities and assistance was essential for development resources to achieve their maximum impact, and it presented once again the concept of a global tax as a potential development funding source.

There was a clear desire to make the system work. The follow-up to these reports was undertaken by five thematic intergovernmental high-level working groups on UN reform within the General Assembly. The working groups looked specifically at finance, Security Council reform, peace and security issues, and development, as well as the overall strengthening of the UN system. Unfortunately, member states could not agree on a specific reform proposal, in part because of lack of political will and of new ideas that could be implemented without a commitment to new and additional resources, and in part, near the end of the process, because of dwindling interest and growing frustration in national capitals and among UN delegations. Four out of the five groups closed their deliberations in 1996, just as the UN was marking its 50th anniversary, without showing concrete results; only the working group on Security Council reform continued to function.

From that point onward until the end of the millennium, numerous additional reports researched and discussed structural reform of the UN, but with little practical impact. Some of these reports included the following:

- The secretary-general's 1994 report, "Funding Operational Activities for Development Within the UN System,"[9] reviewed the funding of UN development operations and examined the funding mechanisms used by other multilateral organizations, including replenishment systems and negotiated pledges.
- *Our Global Neighbourhood,*[10] the 1995 report of the Commission on Global Governance, made numerous specific proposals such as a global tax, a standing U.N. army, an Economic Security Council, UN authority over the global commons, an end to the veto power of the permanent members of the Security Council, a new parliamentary body of representatives of civil society, a new Petitions Council, a new Court of Criminal Justice, binding verdicts of the International Court of Justice, and expanded authority for the secretary-general.
- More influential in the reform debate was a review of the UN system undertaken by Sir Brian Urquhart and Erskine Childers in 1994–96 under the auspices of the Dag Hammarskjold Foundation. In their report, titled "Renewing the UN System,"[11] the authors advanced innovative reform proposals to "gradually transform [the UN] into the effective mechanism of a future world community." They recommended reempowering the UN to formulate global macroeconomic policies and to consolidate the authority of the United Nations at the global and field level around a single UN development authority.
- From 1991 to 1997, a Nordic UN Project was undertaken. The project's report described in detail the urgent need for UN reform in general and of its development system in particular.[12] Recommendations for operations at the country level included support for integrated development and local ownership. At the headquarters level, the project recommended integrated support of country-level operations. In terms of governance by the member states, it called for further integration of intergovernmental mechanisms and a better division of labor among governing bodies, as well as for financial reform and predictable funding—a combination of voluntary contributions, pledges and assessed contributions, and innovations in funding.

Shortly after his appointment as secretary-general, Kofi Annan presented his 1997 report, "Renewing the United Nations: A Programme for Reform,"[13] to the 51st session of the General Assembly. This early reform appraisal focused on renewal and revitalization of the institution, with recommendations that would establish a new leadership and management structure and, through it, a new culture intended to lead to greater unity of purpose, coherence of effort, and agility to respond to the goals expressed in major international conferences. The report called for a strengthening of UN operations at the country level, with a view to improving policy and program coherence. The establishment of the UN Development Assistance Framework, the Common Country Assessment, and the UN Development Group were among the key outcomes of these 1997 reforms. Executive committees were created to address global issues in the areas of peace and security, economic and social affairs, development cooperation, and human affairs, among others.

The New Millennium: The Awakening

As the new millennium began, hopes for a world at peace had not materialized. Neither had the much-expected peace dividend—resources no longer needed to finance the Cold War that could have been channeled to development assistance. Despite the expected benefits of globalization, the implementation of the commitments agreed upon in the global conferences remained far from becoming a reality. In this context of increasing demands on an already overextended system, the UN agreed in 2001 on the MDGs, which, for the first time, established comprehensive and clearly defined goals and targets for development and poverty relief, reflecting the multidimensional nature of development, while linking its income and nonincome dimensions. As the 2004 *Global Monitoring Report* stated, "Higher incomes and less poverty mean better human development outcomes. Better health and education contribute to higher productivity and higher incomes."[14]

There was a consensus among the member states that, in order to manage global issues, a more coherent global development approach was needed—the question was not only one of resources but also one of coordination, country ownership of reform, and quality of assistance. Starting from these principles, the UN undertook a new reform process, which continues today.

In 2003, at the 57th session of the General Assembly, Secretary-General Annan presented a new set of proposals in a new report, "Strengthening of the United Nations: An Agenda for Further Change."[15] This report called for a thorough review of the organization's work, to "make sure we are concentrating our efforts on what matters to . . . the peoples of the world." The secretary-general noted the need to clarify the roles and responsibilities of UN entities, to make coordination more effective and better serve member states, and he presented a number of proposals for improving performance in the areas of human rights and public information. The report also established a "panel of eminent persons" to review the relationship between the UN and civil society.

Secretary-General Annan's 2005 report to the 59th Session of the General Assembly—prepared in the context of the "Year of Development" that marked the five-year point since the adoption of the MDGs—went a step further. Titled "In Larger Freedom: Towards Development, Security and Human Rights for All,"[16] the report addressed a wide range of critical issues, including the threat of terrorism, the means to finance development, enlargement of the Security Council, and the replacement of the Human Rights Commission. On the issue of improving systemwide coherence to manage global issues, the report emphasized the secretary-general's commitment to the UNDP and a further strengthening of the role of the resident coordinators, giving them more authority. Annan called on member states to improve coordination among their representatives on the various governing boards, to ensure coherent policy in assigning mandates and allocating resources throughout the system. He also requested that member states consider a more integrated structure for the management of global issues in the areas of environmental standards setting, scientific discussion, and monitoring of treaty compliance.

The 2005 World Summit took up the question of UN reform and the status of progress in reducing poverty and improving livelihoods since the 2000 Millennium Declaration. The summit's outcome document supported systemwide coherence and noted that it would require policy measures to create stronger linkages between the organization's normative and operational work, as well as coordination of representation on the governing boards of the various development and humanitarian agencies. On the operations side, the document called for implementation of reforms aimed at a more effective, efficient, coherent, coordinated, and better-performing UN country presence, and it asked the secretary-general to launch an effort to further strengthen management and coordination of UN operational activities, including proposals for tighter management of entities in the fields of development, humanitarian assistance, and the environment.

Among the proposals of "In Larger Freedom" lay the genesis of two significant changes made to the UN system structure following the 2005 summit:

- The new Peacebuilding Commission, which started its deliberations in June 2006, is designed to coordinate efforts in postconflict situations across the UN system. It will propose integrated strategies for post-conflict recovery, focusing attention on reconstruction, institution building, and sustainable development. It will coordinate systemwide efforts in conflict prevention, mediation, peacekeeping, respect for human rights, the rule of law, humanitarian assistance, reconstruction, and long-term development, and it will help ensure predictable financing for early recovery and sustained reconstruction following the cessation of conflict.
- In March 2006, the General Assembly adopted a resolution replacing the highly politicized Geneva-based Commission on Human Rights with a 47-member Human Rights Council. The new council will address violations of human rights, including gross and systematic violations, and promote effective coordination and the mainstreaming of human rights within the UN system. The council began its work on June 19, 2006.

The United Nations at a Crossroads

The adoption of the MDGs at the beginning of the century marked a turning point for the role of the UN in the management of global issues. For the first time, the international community, acting with remarkable unity to face the new challenges of globalization, agreed on a comprehensive plan for a world free of poverty. By setting clear and monitorable goals, the UN was leading the way toward a new and enhanced partnership for development cooperation. But as the 2005 World Summit's five-year assessment showed, the world is currently not on track to meet the MDGs by 2015.[17] The UN has a crucial role to play to move the agenda forward and build the required momentum for significant results on the ground. But urgent reforms are needed for the UN to play a more effective role.

It is clear that enormous effort has gone into scrutinizing the structure of the UN and identifying reforms that would enable it to respond to the needs of a changing world and the development challenges it faces. However, it is also clear that the longer the implementation of much-needed reforms are delayed, the more difficult it will be for the organization to tackle the global issues of our time, from pandemics to climate change and humanitarian crises. Inaction not only would be detrimental to the organization's future but would also signify a collective failure to move the world closer to peace and prosperity for all.

At the intergovernmental level, the main issue on the minds of the negotiators has been the need to coordinate the activities, agencies, and programs of the UN system in the economic and social arena. Analysis of the work to date indicates no lack of ideas but, rather, a lack of political will to make the system work. It is seldom possible to use the word *new* about proposals for reorganization or better coordination in the UN system. Rather, the latest proposals are almost always carried over from a previous round. Poor institutional memory at the UN sometimes accounts for this and often gives UN veterans and current staff members a depressing sense of déjà vu. For example, the recent debates on development cooperation and the terms of reference of recent ECOSOC reform efforts echo the criticism leveled in 1966—and some of the remedies being proposed now were actually adopted by the General Assembly in that year. For example, in 1966, the General Assembly called for sharply reducing the burden of reporting and program request procedures on developing countries, yet in 1990, the General Assembly requested a new study to assess the burden of existing procedures on developing countries. In the late 1950s, then–Secretary-General Dag Hammarksjöld urged the creation of a High Level Segment of ECOSOC and a streamlining of its agenda. In 1991, the same request was repeated and decided on all over again.

At the interagency level, the discussion has focused mainly on two issues: the programmatic relationship between funds and programs and the relationship between funds and agencies at the field level. To these a third has to be added, to deal with the UN Secretariat.

The Programmatic Relationship Between Funds and Programs

The capacity to establish a clear programmatic relationship between funds and programs is directly linked to the ability of the intergovernmental machinery to improve interagency coordination. Currently, three models are being discussed in response to the secretary-general's recommendation in his 2006 report,[18] proposing the grouping of UN operational activities around three pillars: development, humanitarian affairs, and the environment:

- Under the *fundamental restructuring approach,* the policy and program activities of the existing funds and programs would be consolidated into three self-contained agencies, each with a much broader mandate: one for development, one for humanitarian affairs, and one for the environment.
- The *grouping approach* is based on development of a common governance and policy direction for organizations acting in the three pillar areas, as well as a more integrated management. The existing

institutions would be largely left intact but made subject to some form of governance or management by a higher entity.

- Under a *business-as-usual approach,* the basic structure of the UN operational system would not change, but management and operational reforms would be introduced to make the system more efficient and effective.

Whatever the solution, the critical element for success is the capacity to create an effective coordination mechanism capable of identifying and deciding on program priorities.

The Relationship Between Funds and Agencies at the Field Level

Who should be in charge of UN operational programs at the field level? Currently, most agencies with a field presence have their own representative in the field to interact with the host government. The UN resident coordinator in each country tries to introduce a certain level of interagency coordination through the UN country team and the UN Development Assistance Framework. The resident coordinator, however, has no authority to manage the overall UN program at the field level.

The models currently being discussed focus on the role of the resident coordinator and how much power he or she could or should have over management of the country program. Here, again, the main question is how much coordination power should the position of resident coordinator have? As long as this question remains unresolved, the Gordian knot will not be untied.

Reform of the United Nations Secretariat

Currently, the secretary-general has limited capacity to reform the structure of the administrative system that he or she is in charge of—the UN Secretariat. The Budget Committee, not the secretary-general, authorizes the use of funds for each and every program; the secretary-general cannot move resources from one program to another, as any serious reform would require, without the committee's approval. Recently, the Budget Committee turned down a proposal to give the secretary-general more budget authority and to let the secretary-general manage the organization, including personnel appointments, without major interference.

Conclusions

Few UN reforms in the past have been given enough time for implementation: new calls for reform often come along before the previous reform has had a chance to show results. Moreover, those reforms that have been adopted are typically watered down, during an often-lengthy negotiating process, from what was originally proposed. Reform resolutions produced or endorsed by high-level representatives are often extremely detailed and sophisticated, with resounding rhetoric and idealism in abundance, but in reality they usually call for changes that would be difficult to implement, or for new organizational units that, if created at all, may prove unable to show adequate results because the original supporting structure could not be agreed upon or financed. A compromise reform may fail to remedy the real weaknesses, and it virtually guarantees that sooner or later the reform process will start again, under even more difficult conditions.

The above problems notwithstanding, the response to the question posed to the delegates leaving the UN on April 28, 2006, is yes. There is a way out of the UN's dilemma. The UN has a future as long as the member states and the organization itself have the political commitment to make the system work.

At the intergovernmental level, ECOSOC, or a new institution such as an Economic Security Council, has to be given real authority to coordinate the system and to manage global issues. Real authority means high-level and relevant representation in the institution, as well as at meetings, and a commitment to decide on priorities that the governing bodies of each fund and program can then translate into operational guidelines. Regardless of the model adopted—whether it be the fundamental approach, the grouped approach, or business as usual—at the interagency level, the funds and programs will be able to implement the reform decisions only if enough political will exists to allow for effective coordination and priority setting across agencies. At the country level, the key is to give enough authority to the resident coordinator while ensuring that the other players—agencies, funds, governments, donors, and others—recognize the resident coordinator as the principal UN authority in the field. At the same time, the UN and its funds and programs have to be given predictable funding scenarios that allow them, their government counterparts, and other partners such as the World Bank to develop meaningful development plans that have results in the real world.

With respect to reform of the UN Secretariat, the legitimacy and leadership of the position of the secretary-general are critical for the success of the entire organization. If the secretary-general lacks the recognition and support of all member states; any reforms that he or she may propose will not be implemented.

When asked about democracy, Winston Churchill once said that many forms of government have been tried and will be tried in this world of sin and woe. No one pretends that democracy is perfect or all-wise. Indeed, it has been said that democracy is the worst form of government except for all the others that have been tried. The same applies to the UN.

Notes

1. United Nations (2006). The Group of 77 is the largest coalition of developing countries at the United Nations.
2. Commission on International Development (1969).
3. United Nations Development Programme (1969).
4. United Nations Group of Experts on the Structure of the United Nations System (1975).
5. World Commission on Environment and Development (1987).
6. Independent Advisory Group on United Nations Financing (1993).
7. United Nations (1995a).
8. United Nations (1992).
9. United Nations (1997a).
10. Commission on Global Governance (1995).
11. Childers and Urquhart (1994).
12. Nordic Council (1991).
13. United Nations (1997b).
14. World Bank (2004, p. 23).
15. United Nations (2003).
16. United Nations (2005).
17. World Bank (2005).
18. United Nations (2006).

Selected Readings and Cited References

Childers, Erskine, and Sir Brian Urquhart. 1994. "Renewing the UN System." Uppsala, Sweden: Dag Hammarskjold Foundation.

Commission on Global Governance. 1995. *Our Global Neighbourhood: The Report of the Commission on Global Governance.* Oxford and New York: Oxford University Press.

Commission on International Development. 1969. *Partners in Development.* New York: Henry Holt.

Independent Advisory Group on United Nations Financing. 1993. *Financing an Effective United Nations. Report of the Independent Advisory Group on UN Financing.* New York: Ford Foundation.

Independent Working Group on the Future of the United Nations. 1995. *The United Nations in Its Second Half-Century.* New York: Ford Foundation.

New Zealand. Ministry of Foreign Affairs and Trade. 2005. *United Nations Handbook,* 43rd ed. Wellington.

Nordic Council. 1991. *The United Nations: Issues and Options: Five Studies on the Role of the UN in the Economic and Social Fields.* Stockholm: Nordic UN Project.

United Nations. 1992. "An Agenda for Peace: Preventive Diplomacy, Peacemaking and Peace-keeping." Report of the Secretary-General. Document DPI/1247. New York.

_____. 1995a. "An Agenda for Development, 1995, with Related UN Documents." Document DPI/1622/DEV. New York.

_____. 1995b. "Strengthening of the United Nations System." Document A/RES/49/252. New York.

_____. 1997a. "Funding Operational Activities for Development Within the UN System." Document A/48/940. New York.

_____. 1997b. "Renewing the United Nations: A Programme for Reform." Report of the Secretary-General. Document A/51/950. New York.

_____. 2003. "Strengthening of the United Nations: An Agenda for Further Change." Report of the Secretary-General. Document A/57/387. New York.

_____. 2005. "In Larger Freedom: Towards Development, Security and Human Rights for All." Report of the Secretary-General. Document A/59/2005. New York.

_____. 2006. "Investing in the UN: For a Stronger Organization Worldwide." Report of the Secretary-General. Document A/60/692. New York.

United Nations. Group of Experts on the Structure of the United Nations System. 1975. "A New United Nations Structure for Global Economic Co-operation." Document E/AC.62/9. New York.

United Nations Department of Public Information. 2004. New York.

United Nations Development Programme. 1969. *A Study of the Capacity of the United Nations Development System.* 2 vols. Geneva: United Nations.

World Bank and the International Monetary Fund. 2004. *Global Monitoring Report 2004.* Washington, DC.

_____. 2005. *Global Monitoring Report 2005.* Washington, DC.

World Commission on Environment and Development. 1987. *Our Common Future.* New York: Oxford University Press.

_____. 1987.

20

The Role of the International Financial Institutions in Addressing Global Issues

VINAY BHARGAVA

ddressing the many global issues discussed in this volume will require international cooperation in the economic as well as the political sphere. The key global institution mobilizing political cooperation among nations on these issues is the United Nations (UN) system, discussed in chapter 19. Mobilization of economic and financial cooperation, including issues related to the transfer of resources, is one of the key responsibilities of the international financial institutions (IFIs). Together, the UN and IFIs make up the bulk of the global governance system in place today. This chapter provides an overview of IFIs, the role they play in addressing global issues, and the main current proposals to improve their effectiveness.

International Financial Institutions: An Overview

IFIs are institutions that provide financial support and professional advice for economic and social development activities in developing countries and promote international economic cooperation and stability. The term

The information for this chapter is based mostly on publicly available materials on the Web sites of the International Monetary Fund, the World Bank, and the regional development banks. Information about the global programs is based on the Annual Global Monitoring Reports. These contributions are gratefully acknowledged.

international financial institution typically refers to the International Monetary Fund (IMF) and the five multilateral development banks (MDBs): the World Bank Group, the African Development Bank, the Asian Development Bank, the Inter-American Development Bank, and the European Bank for Reconstruction and Development. The last four of these each focus on a single world region and hence are often called regional development banks. IMF and the World Bank, in contrast, are global in their scope; they are also specialized agencies in the UN system but are governed independently of it.

All IFIs admit only sovereign countries as owner-members, but all are characterized by a broad country membership, including both borrowing developing countries and developed donor countries; membership in the regional development banks is not limited to countries from the region but includes countries from around the world. Each IFI has its own independent legal and operational status, but because a considerable number of countries have membership in several IFIs, a high level of cooperation is maintained among them.

Broadly speaking, IMF provides temporary financial assistance to member countries to help ease balance of payments adjustment. MDBs provide financing for development to developing countries through the following:

- Long-term loans (with maturities of up to 20 years) based on market interest rates. To obtain the financial resources for these loans, MDBs borrow on the international capital markets and re-lend to borrowing governments in developing countries.
- Very-long-term loans (often termed credits, with maturities of 30 to 40 years) at interest rates well below market rates. These are funded through direct contributions by governments in the donor countries.
- Grant financing is also offered by some MDBs, mostly for technical assistance, advisory services, or project preparation.

All IFIs are active in supporting programs that are global in scope, in addition to their primary role of financing and providing technical assistance to programs at the country level. Their global activities are discussed later in the chapter.

Several other publicly owned international banks and funds also lend to developing countries, and these are often grouped together as other multilateral financial institutions rather than as IFIs. They usually have a relatively narrow ownership or membership structure or focus on particular sectors or activities. Among these are the European Investment Bank, the International Fund for Agricultural Development, the Islamic Development Bank, the Nordic Development Fund and the Nordic Investment Bank, and the Organization of the Petroleum Exporting Countries Fund for International Development.

A number of subregional banks established for development purposes are also classified as multilateral banks rather than as IFIs, as they are owned by a group of countries (typically borrowers and not donors). Among these are the Corporación Andina de Fomento (Andean Development Corporation), the Caribbean Development Bank, the Central American Bank for Economic Integration, the East African Development Bank, and the West African Development Bank.

Some other international institutions, such as the Bank for International Settlements, the Financial Stability Forum, and the Basel Committee, also perform important roles in the international financial system but are not involved in lending. These, too, are not counted among IFIs and are not discussed in this chapter, which discusses IMF and MDBs only.[1]

The International Monetary Fund

IMF was established by international treaty in 1945 as the central institution of the international monetary system—the system of currency trading and exchange rates that enables business to take place between countries with different currencies. IMF aims to prevent crises in the system by encouraging countries to adopt sound economic policies and monitoring their adherence to such policies; it is also—as its name suggests—a fund that can be tapped by members needing temporary financing to address balance of payments problems.

More specifically, IMF's statutory purposes include promoting the balanced expansion of world trade, the stability of exchange rates, the avoidance of competitive currency devaluations, and the orderly correction of balance of payments problems. To serve these purposes, IMF engages in three types of activities: (a) it monitors economic and financial developments and policies, both in its member countries and at the global level, and offers policy advice to its members based on its more than 50 years of experience; (b) it lends to member countries experiencing balance of payments problems, not just to provide temporary financing but also to support economic adjustment and reforms aimed at correcting the underlying problems; and (c) it provides the governments and central banks of its member countries with technical assistance and training in its areas of expertise.

Headquartered in Washington, D.C., IMF is governed by its almost-global membership of 184 countries. IMF is also the principal forum for discussing

not only national economic policies in a global context but also issues important to the stability of the international monetary and financial system. These
include countries' choice of exchange rate arrangements, the risks of destabi-
lizing international capital flows, and the design of internationally recognized
standards and codes for policies and institutions.

The World Bank Group

Founded in 1945 at the same international conference as IMF, the World
Bank at first was involved mainly in the reconstruction of countries devas-
tated by World War II. As those countries recovered, the Bank turned its
primary focus to the second task envisioned for it, namely, the economic
development of the world's nonindustrialized countries, with the goal of
lifting the world out of poverty.

The World Bank is organized much like a cooperative, whose shareholders are the same 184 countries that make up IMF's membership. The share-
holding countries are represented by a Board of Governors, which is the
Bank's ultimate policy making body. As a rule, the governors are member
countries' ministers of finance or of development. Because they meet only
annually, the governors delegate much of the Bank's decision making to 24
executive directors, who work on site at the Bank. The governors have also
established a Development Committee at the ministerial level. The committee's task is to facilitate intergovernmental consensus building on development issues, as well as to advise the boards of governors of both the Bank and
the IMF on critical development issues and on the financial resources
required to promote development.

The World Bank Group, which is headquartered in Washington, D.C., is
made up of five institutions: the International Bank for Reconstruction and
Development (IBRD), the International Development Association (IDA), the
International Finance Corporation (IFC), the Multilateral Investment Guarantee Agency (MIGA), and the International Centre for Settlement of Investment Disputes (ICSID). Each institution plays a different but important role
in the group's corporate mission of reducing global poverty and improving
living standards in the developing world. Together, they provide low-interest
loans, interest-free credits, and grants to governments and the private sector
in developing countries for investments in education, health, infrastructure,
communications, and many other purposes, as well as services in support of
those investments.

IBRD focuses on middle-income countries and creditworthy low-income
countries, whereas IDA focuses on the poorest countries in the world. IBRD

lends only to governments, financing these loans primarily by selling triple-A-rated bonds in the world's financial markets. Although IBRD earns a small margin on this lending, the greater proportion of its income comes from lending out its own capital. This capital consists of reserves built up over the years and money paid in from the World Bank's shareholders. This income also pays the World Bank's operating expenses, and part of it has been contributed to IDA and debt relief.

IDA is the world's largest source of interest-free loans and grant assistance to the governments of the poorest countries. Its funds are replenished every 3 years by its 40 donor country members. Additional funds are generated through repayments of principal on its 35- to 40-year no-interest loans; these funds are then available for re-lending. IDA lending amounts vary from year to year but generally account for about 40 percent of total World Bank Group lending.

IFC focuses on financing private sector projects, in which it may take an equity stake in addition to lending. MIGA promotes foreign direct investment in developing countries by insuring investors against political or noncommercial risks in those countries. ICSID provides a forum for mediating disputes between investors and governments and advises governments in their efforts to attract investment.

The Inter-American Development Bank

The Inter-American Development Bank (IDB) was established as a development institution in 1959, which makes it the oldest of the regional development banks. It is owned by its 47 member countries, which include 26 Latin American and Caribbean states, the United States, Canada, 16 European countries, Israel, the Republic of Korea, and Japan. It is headquartered in Washington, D.C. Within its region, IDB is the main source of multilateral financing for economic, social, and institutional development projects in both the public and the private sectors, as well as for trade and regional integration programs.

IDB's main goals are to promote poverty reduction and social equity, as well as environmentally sustainable economic growth. To attain these goals, IDB focuses its work on four priority areas:

- Fostering competitiveness through support for policies and programs that increase a country's potential for development in an open global economy
- Modernizing the state by strengthening the efficiency and transparency of public institutions

- Investing in social programs that expand opportunities for the poor
- Promoting regional economic integration by forging links among countries to develop larger markets for their goods and services.

IDB supports regional initiatives by producing information and knowledge for policy discussion and funding technical cooperation to strengthen regional integration. It provides technical support to governments on trade and integration issues and conducts public outreach activities to promote such integration.

The Asian Development Bank

The Asian Development Bank (ADB) is owned by its 65 members, 47 from the region and 18 from other parts of the globe. Its highest policy making body is its Board of Governors, which meets annually and consists of one representative from each member. The governors elect the 12 members of the Board of Directors. ADB was founded in 1966 and is headquartered in Manila.

ADB's vision is a region free of poverty. Its mission is to help its developing member countries reduce poverty and improve the quality of life of their citizens through policy dialogue, loans, technical assistance, grants, guarantees, and equity investments. ADB's operations are financed by bonds, recycled repayments on its loans, and contributions from members. About 70 percent of its cumulative lending comes from its ordinary capital resources, but ADB also provides loans from several special funds. Among these is the Asian Development Fund, which provides concessional loans to the least-developed member countries. ADB also manages several trust funds and channels grants provided by bilateral donors to their ultimate recipients.

The African Development Bank

The African Development Bank (AfDB) is engaged in promoting the economic development and social progress of its shareholder countries in Africa. Established in 1964, with headquarters in Abidjan, Cote d'Ivoire (but temporarily located in Tunis), AfDB is owned by 53 African countries and by 24 countries in the Americas, Europe, and Asia. AfDB's principal functions include the following:

- Making loans and equity investments for the economic and social advancement of the regional member countries
- Providing technical assistance for the preparation and execution of development projects and programs
- Promoting the investment of public and private capital for development purposes

- Responding to requests for assistance in coordinating the development policies and plans of the regional member countries.

In its operations, AfDB is also required to give special attention to national and multinational projects and programs that promote regional integration.

AfDB gets its financial resources from subscribed capital, reserves, funds raised through borrowings, and accumulated net income. Its capital is subscribed such that the regional member countries hold two-thirds of the total and the nonregional members one-third. AfDB's highest policy making body is its Board of Governors, which consists of one governor for each member country. The Board of Governors delegates many of its powers to the Board of Directors, which is composed of 18 executive directors: 12 representing the regional members and 6 representing the nonregional members. Under AfDB's founding agreement, its president must be a national of one of the regional members.

AfDB lends on a nonconcessional basis at a variable lending rate calculated on the basis of the cost of its borrowing. The other terms include a commitment charge of 1 percent and maturities of up to 20 years, including a 5-year grace period. AfDB also provides development finance on concessional terms to its low-income member countries that are unable to borrow on the above nonconcessional terms. Money for such loans comes from the 24 nonregional shareholders in the form of grant contributions.

The European Bank for Reconstruction and Development

The European Bank for Reconstruction and Development (EBRD) was established in 1991, when communism was crumbling in central and eastern Europe and these countries needed support to nurture a new private sector in a democratic environment. EBRD's charter is unique among MDBs in that it stipulates that EBRD may work only in countries that are committed to democratic principles.

EBRD, which is headquartered in London, is owned by 60 countries and 2 intergovernmental institutions, the European Union and the European Investment Bank. EBRD's share capital is provided by its members. EBRD does not directly use shareholders' capital to finance its loans. Instead, its triple-A creditworthiness rating enables it to borrow funds in the international capital markets by issuing bonds and other debt instruments at highly favorable market rates. Although its shareholders are in the public sector, EBRD invests mainly in private enterprises, usually together with commercial partners.

Today, EBRD uses its investment tools to help build market economies and democracies in 27 countries from central Europe to central Asia. It provides project financing for banks, industries, and individual businesses, in the form of both new ventures and investments in existing companies. It also works with publicly owned companies to support privatization, restructuring of state-owned firms, and improvements in municipal services. EBRD uses its close relationship with governments in the region to promote policies that will bolster the business environment.

International Financial Institutions and Global and Regional Issues

All IFIs have two major product lines that help address global and regional issues: their country programs and their global and regional programs.[2] By definition, the country programs support the development strategies and investment projects of individual countries, but taken together, these programs contribute to advancing the well-being of the country's region and of the world as a whole. The global and regional programs provide financial resources that address global and regional issues directly and increase the supply of global public goods. They also promote international cooperation. A good overview of the activities of IFIs at the country, regional, and global levels can be found in the annual *Global Monitoring Report* series jointly produced since 2004 by the staff members of the World Bank and IMF. Although the primary purpose of these reports is to assess the implementation of policies and actions aimed at achieving the Millennium Development Goals, each report also contains a chapter on IFIs, which summarizes their contributions on global issues through their global and regional programs. The rest of this section draws heavily on the 2004 and 2005 reports.

The International Monetary Fund

IMF plays a central role in addressing those global issues related to promoting a stable and open global economic and financial environment (see chapter 3 of this volume). First, it does so through its surveillance of the economic policies of those countries that, because of their size or their critical role in international trade or finance, are important to the health of the global economic system. The consultations with industrial countries that IMF conducts under Article IV of its Articles of Agreement are a vehicle for promoting appropriate policies, such as curbing domestic imbalances that may pose risks for the global economy. IMF is also becoming increasingly active in multilateral surveillance, highlighting both macroeconomic and financial risks as they emerge at the global level. IMF is planning to make its surveillance more effective through more-incisive analysis of specific weaknesses and distortions in the global financial system that raise the risk of crisis or contagion or hinder adjustment to globalization. It will also promote international dialogue within the international community on multilateral actions necessary to ensure global financial stability.

Second, IMF provides financial support to member countries experiencing protracted balance of payments difficulties. Such lending helps stabilize the affected economy while also safeguarding global financial stability. Stabilization loans are extended at market interest rates for high- and middle-income countries and on concessional terms for low-income countries.

The World Bank

A critical part of the World Bank's work is devoted to analysis and advocacy in the global arena, especially with respect to the policies and actions of developed countries on trade, aid, and debt relief, given their importance in addressing these global issues and reducing poverty. The Bank's support for global programs began three decades ago, with the establishment of the Consultative Group on International Agricultural Research (CGIAR), for which the Bank serves as both convener and donor, as well as a lender to developing countries for complementary activities. CGIAR, which brings together leading agricultural research institutes from around the world, has had some notable successes in creating global public goods such as the high-yielding varieties of crops that are the backbone of the Green Revolution.

As the only global institution among MDBs, the World Bank has increased its support for global programs rapidly in recent years; 70 different programs involving many of the global issues covered in this book are now under way. A major expansion of the Bank's work on global issues began in the late 1990s, when the Bank increased its orientation toward global partnerships and associated program support activities. This change in policy reflected the Bank's recognition of the rapid pace of globalization and the sharply increased attention to global policy issues within the development community. Many of these programs feature partnerships focused on the delivery of global and regional public goods, including the provision of seed money. In September 2000, the Development Committee endorsed the Bank's priorities in supporting global public goods; those priorities focus on five areas: public health, protection of the global commons, financial stability, trade, and knowledge.

The Regional Development Banks

The regional development banks are also actively involved in global and regional programs covering financial stability, trade, the environment, post-conflict assistance, and knowledge; all but EBRD are also involved in the control of infectious diseases. In many cases, the regional banks' focus is on provision of regional public goods (RPGs) or on regional aspects of global public goods; in this regard, they complement the World Bank's global and regional efforts. The regional banks are also involved in helping their regional members build capacity to meet members' obligations under recent global agreements.

IDB has five priority areas in the provision of regional and global public goods: financial sector assessments, regional integration, curbing of infectious diseases, promotion of environmental services, and support for research in agriculture and regional policy dialogue. IDB has prepared a new policy framework for its support for RPGs, including a financing facility geared to providing grant financing for what it calls *early-stage RPGs*, where the greatest need is for dialogue among countries; *later-stage RPGS*, where more institutional resources to manage the emerging program are needed; and the initial stages of *club RPGs*, which will likely be financially self-sustaining once they are up and running.

For AfDB, critical regional issues include postconflict assistance and public health measures, especially in the face of the HIV/AIDS epidemic. For ADB, key issues are the environment, health, and knowledge, with a particular focus on those issues where spillover effects exist within the region or its subregions.

Finally, for EBRD, nuclear safety is an area of special focus. It has taken the lead internationally in supporting countries in transition from socialism in the decommissioning of nuclear capacity, along with the resolution of other environmental liabilities from the socialist era. Another area of focus is financial stability, especially the adoption by EBRD's regional members of the financial standards and codes underpinning market economies.

Taken together, MDBs support a number of regional and subregional programs and initiatives in collaboration with other partners. These regional programs include a mix of RPG programs, including regional infrastructure projects, and multicountry programs. Examples include the following:

- AfDB is supporting the New Partnership for Africa's Development, the African Union, the Global Environment Facility (especially on the development of an Environmental Action Plan for Africa), and the Africa Regional Coordination Unit for the UN Convention to Combat Desertification.

- ADB is supporting the Greater Mekong Subregion Program, which promotes cross-country cooperation in a number of sectors through investments in infrastructure, policy initiatives, and institutional mechanisms. ADB is also supporting regional programs for the Pacific Islands; subregional economic cooperation in Central Asia and South Asia; and cooperation in the Indonesia-Malaysia-Thailand growth triangle and among the countries of Brunei, Indonesia, Malaysia, and the Philippines. Particularly noteworthy is ADB's leadership on tsunami-related work, including its organization of a recent high-level conference and the support it has pledged for an interim tsunami warning system.
- IDB's approach to regional issues has focused on facilitating cross-fertilization of ideas on policy issues. Its Regional Policy Dialogue provides a forum for policy makers to discuss issues of common concern in its seven network areas: education, natural disasters, environment, central banks and finance ministries, poverty and social protection, public policy management, and transparency.
- An example of collaboration between regional development banks on RPGs is the joint sponsorship by ADB and IDB of the recent Tokyo Forum on the Operational Dimensions of Supplying Regional Public Goods through Regional Development Assistance.
- EBRD supports a number of regional programs for private sector development, including for trade facilitation and small and medium-size enterprise development. In addition, a growing number of EBRD projects cover more than one country: examples include regional equity funds, energy trade, and projects in which sponsors from one country invest in another.
- The World Bank supports a large number of regional programs and initiatives in cooperation with other MDBs and other relevant partners. Examples include the Trade and Transport Facilitation in Southeast Europe Program, which promotes more efficient and less costly trade flows and provides customs standards compatible with the European Union; the Latin American regional initiative on infrastructure, in cooperation with IDB; and the strategic framework for IDA assistance to Africa, in cooperation with AfDB and other partners.

Reform of the International Financial Institutions

IFIs' unique comparative advantage and the contributions they have made toward addressing global issues are well recognized. Yet there is a rising expectation on the part of almost all stakeholders—developed and developing country shareholders, academics and think tanks, civil society organizations, and business leaders—that IFIs need to do still more in this domain. However, a number of concerns about IFIs raise questions about the role they can play in global issues management.[3] Many suggestions have been put forward for reform of IFIs. IFIs themselves agree that reform is needed if their shareholders expect them to play an increasing role in regional and global development issues. The suggested reforms can be categorized under the headings of legitimacy, effectiveness, conditionality, and financial capacity and sustainability.

Legitimacy

Legitimacy concerns relate to the extent to which IFIs are perceived as impartial advisers, given that their ownership structure and their policy making powers are skewed in favor of the rich nations. Many in developing countries—officials and citizens alike—as well as international nongovernmental organizations (NGOs) and researchers believe that the developed countries, particularly the United States and the European countries, have an undue influence on IFIs' policies, policy advice, and allocation of funds. Their influence is so great, in this view, that IFIs' advice cannot be trusted to be impartial but, rather, is infected by political and ideological bias. Those who hold this view also criticize the way the heads of IFIs are chosen: by convention, the head of IMF has always been a European, the head of the World Bank an American, the head of the EBRD a European, and the head of ADB a Japanese. (However, the head of AfDB is always an African, and the head of IDB a Latin American.) The critics argue that leadership selections should be made on the basis of merit and in public hearings, not on the basis of national origin.

Given their global nature and influence, concerns over legitimacy are most acute in the case of IMF and the World Bank, and, in response, proposals for reform of these institutions have been tabled for consideration by their shareholders. IMF's medium-term strategy paper proposes the reallocation of existing shareholdings (called quotas) so as to improve the share of developing countries. Other proposals would give more votes to developing countries with large and growing shares of the global economy (such as Brazil, China, India, and South Africa) and to smaller nations (particularly in Africa) that represent a significant share of the work of the two institutions.[4] At the Spring 2006 meetings of IMF and the World Bank, some promising breakthroughs were made when the International Monetary and Financial Committee of the Board of Governors of IMF agreed on the need for fundamental reform and called on IMF's managing director to present concrete proposals for agreement at the annual meetings in September 2006.

Effectiveness

Concerns about effectiveness relate to the adequacy of the results produced by IFIs' development assistance programs, the soundness of their policy advice (for example, on privatization and the liberalization of financial markets), the relevance of such advice for countries' realities, and the need for safeguards both to prevent the loss of development assistance to fraud and corruption and to protect the environment and the rights of people who may be adversely affected by development projects.

IFIs are heeding the call for greater effectiveness in all these areas of concern. In 2002, they launched a Managing for Development Results Initiative, which led to the adoption of the Paris Declaration on Aid Effectiveness. The Paris Declaration, endorsed on March 2, 2005, is an international agreement by nearly 100 ministers, heads of agencies, and other senior officials to continue and increase efforts toward harmonization, alignment, and managing aid for results with a set of monitorable actions and indicators.

In April 2006, MDBs agreed on a Common Performance Assessment System to provide a consolidated source of data on how MDBs are contributing to positive development results. Data will be provided in seven categories: country-level capacity development, performance-based concessional financing, results-based country strategies, projects and programs, monitoring and evaluation, learning and incentives, and interagency harmonization. MDBs hope that this system will improve accountability.

In the area of safeguards on the proper use of funds, all MDBs have policies and procedures in place to prevent fraud and corruption and to protect people and environmental resources that the projects they finance might endanger. However, MDBs have acknowledged that there is room to do more and to do better in this domain, and they have launched efforts to improve and harmonize their policies so as to improve the policies' effectiveness.

IMF's medium-term strategy also lays out several proposals to improve the organization's effectiveness in several areas: country and global surveillance to promote global financial stability; prevention and resolution of crises in emerging markets; and IMF's role in low-income countries to promote a stable macroeconomic environment that promotes growth and poverty reduction.

Conditionality

Conditionality is a standard feature of the loans provided IFIs. It typically refers to the actions that a borrower must take in order to obtain the loan; failure to comply with these conditions may result in suspension, cancellation, or recall of the loan. The purpose of conditionality is to ensure that borrowers take the necessary actions—in terms of policies, provision of technical inputs, implementation, and safeguard measures—to produce the intended development results.

Most observers agree that conditionality related to procurement, financial bookkeeping, auditing, environmental issues, resettlement, and organizational change is needed if development projects are to be implemented effectively. In fact, such conditionality has always been a part of development assistance, and some conditionality is in response to advocacy by NGOs with respect to environmental issues and indigenous peoples' rights. What is controversial about conditionality relates mostly to policy and institutional reforms such as privatization, trade and capital account liberalization, elimination of subsidies, and limits on public expenditure. All of these often feature prominently in adjustment lending (more recently called *development policy lending* or *budget support lending*) by MDBs and IMF. Critics argue, sometimes on the basis of credible evidence, that this type of conditionality has not worked and sometimes has done more harm than good. They also argue that some conditions are merely an attempt to impose Western free-market policies on developing countries where they are neither appropriate nor desired.

IFIs generally agree that policy and institutional conditionality is most effective when it supports reforms on which the country is already taking the lead and that it is ineffective when there is little or no political will to undertake the reforms. At the same time, IFIs face the challenge of assessing whether a country's proposed reforms really address the key policy distortions hampering equitable (pro-poor) growth and whether the borrower is genuinely committed to reform. Without such reform the development objectives supported by the lending cannot be achieved—hence the conditionality.

IFIs are beginning to take a more flexible approach to conditionality. They are looking for more evidence of borrowers' commitment to reforms and are rewarding reforms already undertaken; they are reducing the average number of conditions per lending operation; they are focusing more on long-term institutional issues and on the actions that are most critical for achieving results; and they are increasing transparency and encouraging public debate on the need for reform.

Financial Capacity and Sustainability

Concerns about the financial capacity of IFIs grounded in the fact that the resources needed for the enormous challenges they face—achieving MDGs, avoiding unbalanced growth of the world economy, and providing emergency financing should another global financial crisis occur—far exceed what

IFIs can mobilize today. This capacity shortfall is particularly acute for the concessional financing needed to help the poorest countries and to bridge the huge gap in the supply of global public goods. The undersupply of concessional financing is compounded by recent moves to make more of it available as grants, which, unlike loans, do not generate flows of funds back to the lending institutions for recycling.

These issues of financial viability and sustainability arise from the fact that IFIs' income base is narrow and diminishing, even as the range of services demanded of them is growing. One reason why IFIs' incomes are declining is reduced demand for loans on the part of the middle-income countries, which in turn may be due to the relatively high cost of doing business with IFIs, the conditionality attached to IFI loans, and, in some cases, countries' ability to borrow from private markets at interest rates competitive with those charged by IFIs. The resulting constraints on the incomes of IFIs undermine their ability to devote more resources to global and regional issues.

Awareness of these concerns led developed countries to make new pledges of financial support at the Monterrey Conference on Financing for Development in 2002. As a result, the decline in development assistance has been reversed and aid flows have increased, although not by the full amounts pledged (see chapter 4). Some of the increased funding is being earmarked for global public goods such as prevention and treatment of communicable diseases. Concerns about financial sustainability are also receiving attention, and all IFIs are looking into the causes and possible remedies. All of them are seeking to make their services more attractive by reducing the cost of doing business with them, widening the range of financial products and services they offer, and better leveraging their financial strength so as to boost their own market borrowings. They are also supporting innovative financing mechanisms that can attract private sector funding on concessional as well as on market terms.

Conclusions

IFIs, and particularly IMF and the World Bank, have a mandate from their shareholders to provide both sophisticated analysis and effective financing to address global issues such as those discussed in this volume. IFIs undoubtedly have comparative advantage in mobilizing resources and channeling them into projects that can effectively address these issues. Indeed, IFIs have been playing this role for many years but never on a scale commensurate with the problems. Their efforts are hampered by concerns relating to their legitimacy, their effectiveness, their use of conditionality, and their financial capacity.

Many proposals for reforming IFIs have been put forward, and some of these are being implemented. Successful reform of IFIs will go a long way toward improving their capacity to address the global issues identified in this book.

Notes

1. The information in this section relating to each IFI draws heavily on the publicly available pages of their Web sites. See the list of Web links at the end of the chapter. For information on some of the other institutions mentioned here, see chapter 3 of this volume.
2. This section draws extensively on the *Global Monitoring Report* for 2004 and 2005.
3. A number of books have been written on how to improve the effectiveness of IFIs; some of the most frequently mentioned are those by Buira (2003, 2005), Easterly (2001), Koeberle and others (2005), Mallaby (2004), and Woods (2006).
4. For details of these proposals, see the paper on the Development Committee Web site, http://web.worldbank.org/WBSITE/EXTERNAL/DEVCOMMEXT/0,menuPK:60001663~pagePK:64001141~piPK:64034162~theSitePK:277473,00.html papers.

Selected Readings and Cited References

Blustein, Paul. 2001. *The Chastening: Inside the Crisis that Rocked the International Financial System and Humbled the IMF.* New York: Public Affairs Press.

Buira, Ariel, ed. 2003. *Challenges to the World Bank and IMF: Developing Country Perspectives.* London: Anthem Press.

————. 2005. *The IMF and the World Bank at Sixty.* London: Anthem Press.

Clark, Dana, Jonathan Fox, and Kay Treakle, eds. 2003. *Demanding Accountability: Civil Society Claims and the World Bank Inspection Panel.* Lanham, MD: Rowman and Littlefield.

De Soto, Hernando. 2000. *The Mystery of Capital: Why Capitalism Triumphs in the West and Fails Everywhere Else.* New York: Basic Books.

Easterly, William. 2001. *The Elusive Quest for Growth.* Cambridge, MA: MIT Press.

Koeberle, Stephan, Harold Bedoya, Peter Silarszky, and Gero Verheyen, eds. 2005. *Conditionality Revisited: Concepts, Lessons and Experiences.* Washington, DC: World Bank.

Mallaby, Sebastian. 2004. *The World's Banker: A Story of Failed States, Financial Crises, and the Wealth and Poverty of Nations.* New York: Penguin Press.

Roubini, Nouriel, and Brad Setser. 2004. *Bail Outs or Bail Ins? Responding to Financial Crises in Emerging Economies.* Washington, DC: Institute for International Economics.

Sachs, Jeffrey D. 2005. *The End of Poverty: Economic Possibilities for Our Time.* New York: Penguin Press.

Stiglitz, Joseph E. 2002. *Globalization and Its Discontents.* New York: Norton.

World Bank. 2003. *A Guide to the World Bank.* Washington, DC.

World Bank and the International Monetary Fund. 2004. *Global Monitoring Report 2004.* Washington, DC.

————. 2005. *Global Monitoring Report 2005.* Washington, DC.

Woods, Ngaire. 2006. *The Globalizers: The IMF, the World Bank and Their Borrowers.* Cornell University Press.

Selected Web Links on International Financial Institutions

African Development Bank	http://www.afdb.org
Asian Development Bank	http://www.adb.org
European Bank for Reconstruction and Development	http://www.ebrd.org
Global Monitoring Report	http://www.worldbank.org/globalmonitoring
Inter-American Development Bank	http://www.iadb.org
International Monetary Fund	http://www.imf.org
Managing for Development Results	http://www.mfdr.org
World Bank	http://www.worldbank.org

Global Compacts: Building a Better World for All

VINAY BHARGAVA AND ASLI GURKAN

The list of global issues discussed in this book is long, and the list will surely grow as the world becomes ever more connected—by trade, by finance, by concern for the environment and the natural resources that we all share, by people migrating across borders in ever larger numbers, by the spread of diseases old and new, by education that awakens us to how people live elsewhere, by inequities in incomes and opportunities both within and across countries, by crime, and by terror. The challenge we face in the 21st century is how to address these global issues that affect us all.

The solutions to many of these problems remain largely unknown. One thing that is certain, however, is that none of them will be resolved satisfactorily unless people in all countries come together to share their views and, ultimately, agree on how to act in concert. Several such global meetings of world leaders and of minds have already begun to make a difference. This chapter reviews the key international agreements—*global compacts*—that have already been concluded, discusses the progress made so far toward their implementation, and considers what more needs to be done.

These global compacts build on a number of notable successes in international development over the past 50 years. Among those commonly agreed upon are the following:

- Greater agricultural productivity has increased world food production to match a growing world population. From 1980 to 1996, the value of food production worldwide increased by 57 percent, while population grew by a much smaller 31 percent.
- Science and technological progress have brought prosperity and good health to many. The share of the population in poverty in developing countries has fallen from 40 percent to 21 percent. Average life expectancy worldwide has increased from 44 years to 64 years.

- Diseases such as smallpox and river blindness that formerly afflicted millions of people a year have been virtually eradicated.
- Overall literacy rates in developing countries have increased from 70 percent to 76 percent over the past decade.
- Thirty million fewer primary school–age children are out of school than in 1990, and the average number of years in school has climbed by half a year.
- The share of adults worldwide who are illiterate has been cut by half, to 22 percent.
- Incomes per capita have risen in most countries of the world. China, Hungary, India, Ireland, the Republic of Korea, Singapore, and Thailand are all among the economic success stories of the past 20 years.
- International trade has boomed.
- Colonialism has ended.
- More countries have free and independent media.
- Democracy has spread to many more countries, and more people around the world enjoy secure and meaningful civil liberties.

It is in large measure the optimism that grows out of these major successes already achieved that gives an impetus to further cooperation.

Today's global compacts build upon a growing global convergence on the belief that collective world action is needed to make a better world for all. This convergence has its roots in several major international conferences of the 1990s, which set common global goals and decided on actions to achieve them. These conferences sought to mobilize governments and non-governmental organizations (NGOs) to take action on major global challenges, to establish international standards and guidelines, to serve as a platform for reaching consensus and discussing new ideas and proposals, and to reinforce a process whereby governments' commitment will be clearly heard and governments will be responsible to report back to the United Nations on actions undertaken. The most notable global conferences of the 1990s include the following:

- The World Summit for Children, New York, September 1990
- The United Nations Conference on Environment and Development (the Rio Earth Summit), Rio de Janeiro, June 1992
- The World Conference on Human Rights, Vienna, June 1993
- The World Summit for Social Development, Copenhagen, March 1995
- The Fourth World Conference on Women, Beijing, September 1995
- The Second United Nations Conference on Human Settlements (Habitat II), Istanbul, June 1996.

As they confront the challenges ahead, the members of the international community are also taking note of lessons learned from international development efforts over the past few decades:

- *Globalization and inequality:* World leaders have increasingly realized that globalization does not take place in a just and equitable manner unless it is well managed and governed. Although greater economic and technological interconnectedness has contributed to remarkable achievements in economic growth and poverty reduction, globalization has also widened the income gap between rich and poor, ignited conflicts in poorer regions, and led to rapid degradation of the environment in some parts of the world. These mounting challenges have led many leaders to call for corrective measures to expand the benefits of globalization to those currently disadvantaged.
- *The need for partnership between developed and developing countries.* World leaders have also acknowledged that developing countries cannot address their challenges alone; they need the cooperation of developed countries, especially on trade, aid, and debt relief. As Jeffrey Sachs, director of the Earth Institute at Columbia University, explains, "Ending global poverty . . . will require concerted actions by the rich countries as well as the poor, beginning with a 'global compact' between the rich and poor countries."[1] In this line of thinking, the poor countries need to devote more national attention and resources to reduce poverty, rather than to war and corruption, whereas the rich nations need to deliver on their promises of resources and technical assistance. Furthermore, the global spread of conflict, terrorism, and HIV/AIDS has shown that global cooperation is not only an ethical responsibility but indeed a necessity. These challenges threaten rich and poor nations alike and will not be met unless measures are taken on a global scale.
- *The need for clear benchmarks.* The major conferences of the 1990s—and in particular the Millennium Summit and the Doha, Johannesburg, and Monterrey gatherings that followed in this decade—highlighted the importance of setting clear goals and benchmarks on the path toward development. Without them, it is very difficult to evaluate progress and to push the implementation process forward when shortcomings emerge.
- *The inexorable interlinking of many global challenges.* The international community now recognizes the difficulty of tackling any single development challenge apart from others. For example, the conflict-prone countries in Africa have not been able to preserve the peace without

addressing the factors that create the conditions for conflict, such as poverty, unemployed youth, the weapons trade, and lack of educational opportunities. Likewise, it is hard to address the issue of universal primary education without also promoting gender equality, reducing poverty, and ensuring that children are well nourished and protected from disease.

Four Global Compacts for the 21st Century

As the 21st century began, the heads of more than 190 countries, acting with remarkable unity, agreed on a series of global compacts for a more prosperous and sustainable world for all. These compacts had several distinguishing features: they set clear and monitorable goals; they were concluded under the auspices of the United Nations (UN) (although they are not legally binding); they describe the mutual roles and responsibilities of developing as well as developed countries; and they call for a new partnership among governments, civil society organizations, and the private business sector to work together to achieve the agreed goals. The four global compacts are the following:

- The Millennium Declaration, adopted at the UN Millennium Summit, New York, September 6–8, 2000
- The Doha Declaration on Trade, adopted at the Fourth Ministerial Conference of the World Trade Organization, Doha, Qatar, November 9–14, 2001
- The Monterrey Declaration on Financing for Development, adopted at the International Conference on Financing for Development, Monterrey, Mexico, March 18–22, 2002
- The Johannesburg Declaration on Sustainable Development, adopted at the World Summit on Sustainable Development, Johannesburg, August 26–September 4, 2002.

Of these four, the best-known and most closely monitored is the Millennium Declaration, which set forth the eight Millennium Development Goals (MDGs) listed in box 21.1. Two of the MDGs include targets for an improved trading environment for developing countries, for expanded official development assistance and debt relief, and for progress toward environmental sustainability. These, in turn, were elaborated further under the Doha, Monterrey, and Johannesburg declarations, respectively.

The Millennium Declaration

The world leaders of 189 countries adopted the Millennium Declaration during the September 2000 Millennium Summit at UN headquarters in

BOX 21.1 The Millennium Development Goals

Goal One: Eradicate Extreme Poverty and Hunger
- Reduce by half the proportion of people living on less than a dollar a day
- Reduce by half the proportion of people who suffer from hunger.

Goal Two: Achieve Universal Primary Education
- Ensure that all boys and girls complete a full course of primary schooling.

Goal Three: Promote Gender Equality and Empower Women
- Eliminate gender disparity in primary and secondary education, preferably by 2005, and at all levels by 2015.

Goal Four: Reduce Child Mortality
- Reduce by two-thirds the mortality rate among children under 5.

Goal Five: Improve Maternal Health
- Reduce by three-quarters the maternal mortality ratio.

Goal Six: Combat HIV/AIDS, Malaria, and Other Diseases
- Halt and begin to reverse the spread of HIV/AIDS.
- Halt and begin to reverse the incidence of malaria and other major diseases.

Goal Seven: Ensure Environmental Sustainability
- Integrate the principles of sustainable development into country policies and programs; reverse loss of environmental resources.
- Reduce by half the proportion of people without sustainable access to safe drinking water.
- Achieve significant improvement in the lives of at least 100 million slum dwellers by 2020.

Goal Eight: Develop a Global Partnership for Development
- Develop further an open trading and financial system that is rule-based, predictable, and nondiscriminatory and includes a commitment to good governance, development, and poverty reduction—nationally and internationally
- Address the least developed countries' special needs, including tariff- and quota-free access for their exports; enhanced debt relief for heavily indebted poor countries; cancellation of official bilateral debt; and more generous official development assistance for countries committed to poverty reduction.
- Address the special needs of landlocked and small island developing States.
- Deal comprehensively with developing countries' debt problems through national and international measures to make debt sustainable in the long term.
- In cooperation with the developing countries, develop decent and productive work for youth.
- In cooperation with pharmaceutical companies, provide access to affordable essential drugs in developing countries.
- In cooperation with the private sector, make available the benefits of new technologies—especially information and communications technologies.

Source: United Nations Web site, http://www.un.org/millenniumgoals.

New York. The central mission of the declaration was to make globalization a positive force for all people. The declaration states that this mission can only be fulfilled though consistent efforts to create a shared future for all of humanity. It calls, among other things, for halving the share of people in poverty worldwide; for reducing infant mortality by two-thirds and maternal mortality by three-quarters; for getting all children into school; and for ensuring environmental sustainability. To achieve these goals, it calls on the world's rich countries to mobilize resources to finance initiatives that will benefit the developing countries. The document also urges measures to ensure duty-free and quota-free access for essentially all exports from the least developed countries and to enhance plans to provide debt relief to heavily indebted poor countries.

The declaration also calls for supporting local initiatives through necessary policies and measures at the global level. It underlines the essential fundamental values that support global cooperation, namely, freedom, equality, solidarity, tolerance, respect for nature, and shared responsibility. In adopting the declaration, world leaders pledged to curb the adverse effects of economic sanctions on innocent publics, and they called for strengthening the rule of law and supporting the decisions of the International Court of Justice. The leaders also made a commitment to accelerate disarmament efforts through cooperation among regional and international organizations such as the UN. The leaders further agreed to provide the UN with the resources it needs for conflict prevention and peaceful resolution of disputes and to take action against the global drug trade, weapons of mass destruction, and terrorism.

The MDGs are significant in several respects:

- They are owned by all member states of the UN system as well as all of the shareholders and management of the International Monetary Fund, the World Bank, and the other multilateral development banks. In that sense, they strive to create a common ground and help narrow the ideological differences among these institutions.
- They establish a consensus that poverty is the biggest challenge facing humanity. World leaders made commitments to halve, by 2015, the share of people worldwide with incomes of less than a dollar a day and the share of people suffering from hunger. They also pledged to significantly improve the lives of at least 100 million slum dwellers by 2020.
- They contributed to the convergence of the global agendas of developed and developing countries and strengthened the prospects for an increase in official development assistance.

- The fact that these important global development issues were addressed through a UN conference fosters a renewed belief in multilateralism and the relevance of the UN system.
- They have helped make international decision-making processes more inclusive, with increased participation of NGOs in the preparatory work.

The Doha Declaration on Trade

The Fourth Ministerial Conference of members of the World Trade Organization (WTO) was held in Doha, Qatar, in 2001. There, the ministers agreed to take measures to improve the global trading system in ways that would benefit the world's least-developed countries. Specifically, the declaration adopted at Doha calls on developed countries to provide greater access to their markets to products from least-developed countries. It proposes a special mechanism for achieving the objective of greater access. It pledges a comprehensive examination of activities to provide technical cooperation and build negotiating capacity in least-developed countries. And it establishes procedures to ensure more active and effective participation of all member governments in the WTO itself. The declaration adopted at Doha also calls for fundamental reform in agriculture, with a view to reducing or phasing out export subsidies and trade-distorting domestic support. In all, the participating ministers agreed to adopt some 50 decisions clarifying the obligations of developed country member governments on topics such as agriculture, subsidies, textiles and clothing, technical barriers to trade, trade-related investment measures, and rules of origin.

To address these challenges, donor countries were urged to contribute to the WTO trust fund for training developing country officials in WTO rules. The inadequate implementation by developing countries of their commitments under the previous round of trade negotiations, the Uruguay Round, was explicitly addressed by granting countries longer grace periods for meeting those commitments. However, the declaration does stop short of tangible commitments in this regard.

The significance of the Doha Declaration and of the Doha Development Round of trade talks that it launched was that, for the first time, it placed developing country interests were placed at the center of a multilateral round of trade negotiations. Recognizing that any progress within the new round would depend on ensuring more-equitable outcomes for developing countries, members pledged to expand market access to developing countries, adopt more balanced rules, and strengthen the provisions of the trading system that grant differential treatment to developing country goods. The Doha meeting thus signaled a turnaround after the disappointing experience at the Seattle ministerial in 1999, where ministers were unable to agree on the launch of a new round of trade talks. By promising to help build the currently weak capacity of many developing countries to hold their own in the multilateral trade negotiations, the declaration also acknowledged an increasing effort on the part of the developing world to make its voice heard in the global trade arena.

The Monterrey Consensus

The International Conference on Financing for Development, held in Monterrey, Mexico, in 2002, discussed opportunities to expand the amount of all types of financial resources made available to developing countries. It signaled a reversal in what had been a declining trend of official development assistance flows. Within the conference declaration, pledges by the developed countries to increase their official assistance and make it more effective were complemented by promises by the developing countries to improve their *enabling domestic environment* by strengthening good governance, promoting private sector development, improving the investment climate, building democratic institutions, and investing in basic economic and social infrastructure. The conference also stressed that trade and foreign direct investment are additional crucial avenues for providing financing for development.

The Monterrey declaration explicitly supports the harmonization of the policies and procedures of international institutions. It also reiterates the need for developed countries to cease the practice of tying their foreign aid to purchases of certain goods and services from the donor countries. The declaration calls for focusing all development activities more closely on poverty reduction, and it stresses the need for new development frameworks that are nationally owned and driven by the developing countries themselves.

The Johannesburg Action Plan for Sustainable Development

The World Summit on Sustainable Development, held in Johannesburg in 2002, was also known as Rio +10 because it took place 10 years after the UN Conference on Environment and Development was held in Rio de Janeiro. Participants at the summit pledged to improve the effectiveness of development initiatives through a greater focus on issues relating to water, energy, health, agriculture, and biodiversity—the WEHAB priority areas.

The Action Plan includes about 280 partnerships among government, NGOs, and business and international financial institutions for promoting sustainable development in water, energy, health, agriculture, and biodiversity. Africa was singled out for increased attention at the conference because of the region's dire needs on many fronts. From the development community's perspective, two other outcomes—a call for sustainable production and consumption patterns and strengthened corporate social responsibility—were noteworthy because of their crucial importance for sustainable development. The all-inclusive nature of *sustainable development,* combined with the summit's closeness in time to the Monterrey conference, made it difficult to reach agreement on a common agenda. The key outstanding environment issue, climate change, was left off the negotiating table because of U.S. resistance to continuing the Kyoto Protocol track.

Controversy and Alternative Views on the Usefulness of Global Compacts

Not everybody agrees that setting ambitious development goals is a useful approach. Some argue that global compacts embody utopian dreams, rather than practical operational targets. One of the most outspoken critics has been New York University professor and former World Bank economist William Easterly. In an article in *Foreign Policy* titled "The Utopian Nightmare," Easterly (2005) argues that although the MDGs are well intentioned, they promise the world's poor more than the international community can deliver. In his view, "[The MDG approach] places too much faith in altruistic cooperation and underestimates self-seeking behavior. It is expecting great things from schemes designed at the top, but doing nothing to solve the bigger problems at the bottom."[2] If the MDGs are not met, as is likely, Easterly argues, it will create deep disappointment and discourage societies from continuing to implement development projects.

Easterly proposes that, instead of setting multiple and overambitious goals to be fulfilled simultaneously, the world community should focus on smaller tasks, such as providing enough vaccines to reduce malaria in Africa. He also contends that the development agenda needs an accountability mechanism that reviews not only the performances of individual governments but also those of development agencies—both multilateral agencies such as the World Bank and the development agencies of individual developed countries. In his most recent book, *The White Man's Burden,*[3] Easterly reiterates that "development planners" should not construct broad agendas.

Easterly's critique particularly targets the views expressed in Jeffrey Sachs' 2005 book *The End of Poverty,*[4] which lays out an MDG-based poverty reduction strategy with five main parts:

- A differential diagnosis aimed at identifying policies to fulfill the MDGs
- An investment plan to lay out the costs and timing of necessary investments
- A financial plan that includes a realistic assessment of the gap between resources needed and resources currently available
- A donor plan to solidify multiyear donor commitments for achieving the goals
- A public management plan outlining ways to ensure better governance at the local and the national level.

Sachs argues that ending poverty is much easier than it appears, if ideas and policies can be directed more practically toward promoting investments in specific areas such as roads, electricity, water, and disease control.

A third line of thinking, which lies in between those of Sachs and Easterly, is proposed in a recent book coauthored by Kemal Dervis, administrator of the UN Development Programme, titled *A Better Globalization*.[5] Dervis's focus is on redefining the global governance framework based on the new realities of the 21st century. He offers suggestions for reforming the governance structure of the UN so as to focus on long-term strategies to reduce poverty and global instability, rather than reacting to the immediate symptoms. Dervis also proposes that the international financial institutions—the International Monetary Fund (IMF), the World Bank, and the regional development banks—reformulate their policies in a way that gives them greater legitimacy among the people they seek to help.

Many other development players, including some NGOs and advocacy groups, hold the view that political will is not enough to solve development problems and that nation-states, despite the signing of global compacts, will continue to act according to their national interest rather than toward the global common good. In this view, most countries still consider global development a low priority, even trivial, compared with defense and security issues, which means that foreign aid will still be distributed according to the demands of security alliances (such as the United States' continuing aid to Israel and Egypt), rather than economic need.

Monitoring the Implementation of Global Compacts

All of the global compacts discussed above assign the task of regular monitoring and progress reporting to the Secretary-General of the UN. In addition, the shareholders of the World Bank and IMF have asked for an annual report on actions and policies necessary to achieve the MDGs, and a variety of civil society organizations are preparing their own regular interim assessments. Finally, individual countries prepare their own monitoring reports, which are supplemented by country scorecards issued by the UN Development Programme. Altogether, more attention was paid worldwide to global development targets in 2005 than in any year since the international community first identified the International Development Goals (the predecessors of the MDGs) in the mid-1990s. The rest of this section looks at the findings of these various assessments.

The 2005 United Nations World Summit

On September 15 and 16, 2005, a summit of the UN was dedicated to reviewing the progress made thus far in implementing the Millennium Declaration and the MDGs. The summit also provided an opportunity for leaders from 160 countries to announce their new action plans to ensure that the goals are met by 2015. A positive outcome of the summit was that all the UN member states made a concrete commitment to fulfill the MDGs and incorporate them into their domestic agendas. One of the summit's main messages was that achieving the MDGs cannot depend only on government officials or aid agencies. It will also require the active participation of the private sector, consumers, and civil society groups. The official summit declaration also made some other important announcements in the areas of peace, security, and global governance, which are summarized in box 21.2.

The following are some of the main points—and omissions—of the summit declaration:

- *Governance:* The declaration placed special emphasis on the commitment of both developing and developed countries to good governance, transparency, and accountability.
- *Aid:* The declaration noted that some progress had been made on the aid front. For the first time at a UN gathering, developed countries made a commitment to improve not only the quantity but also the quality of their foreign aid, although this commitment was not accompanied by concrete plans or targets. Although some developed countries committed to devote 0.7 percent of their gross domestic product to official development assistance by 2015, others expressed reservations and did not adopt the 0.7 percent target.
- *Debt relief:* The summit reemphasized the commitments made at the Group of Eight Summit in Gleneagles, Scotland, earlier that year (see below), but did not go beyond that commitment.

BOX 21.2   Key Provisions of the 2005 United Nations World Summit

*D*evelopment. Unambiguous commitment by all governments, in donor and developing nations alike, to achieve the MDGs by 2015; to honor pledges that would raise an additional $50 billion a year by 2010 for fighting poverty; and to agree to consider additional measures to ensure long-term debt sustainability through increased grant-based financing, cancellation of 100 percent of the official multilateral and bilateral debt of heavily indebted poor countries.

Terrorism. Unqualified condemnation by all governments of terrorism "in all its forms and manifestations, committed by whomever, wherever and for whatever purposes"; strong political push for a comprehensive convention against terrorism within a year; support for early entry into force of the Nuclear Terrorism Convention; and agreement to fashion a strategy to fight terrorism in a way that makes the international community stronger and terrorists weaker.

Peacebuilding, Peacekeeping, and Peacemaking. Creation of a Peacebuilding Commission to help countries transition from war to peace, backed by a support office and a standing fund; and new standing police capacity for UN peacekeeping operations.

Responsibility to Protect. Unambiguous acceptance by all governments of the collective international responsibility to protect populations from genocide, war crimes, ethnic cleansing, and crimes against humanity; and willingness to take timely and decisive collective action for this purpose, through the Security Council, when peaceful means prove inadequate and national authorities are manifestly failing to do it.

Human Rights, Democracy, and Rule of Law. Decisive steps to strengthen the UN human rights machinery and agreement to establish a UN Human Rights Council during the coming year; welcome for new Democracy Fund, which has already received pledges of $32 million from 13 countries; and commitment to eliminate pervasive gender discrimination, such as inequalities in education and ownership of property, and violence against women and girls, and to end impunity for such violence.

Management Reform. Broad strengthening of UN's oversight capacity, including the Office of Internal Oversight Services; expansion of oversight services to additional agencies; and call for independent oversight advisory committee and further developing of a new ethics office.

Environment. Recognition of the serious challenge posed by climate change and a commitment to take action through the UN Framework Convention on Climate Change; assistance to those most vulnerable, such as small island developing states; and agreement to create a worldwide early warning system for all natural hazards.

International Health. Scaling up responses to HIV/AIDS, tuberculosis, and malaria through prevention, care, treatment, and support, and the mobilization of additional resources from national, bilateral, multilateral, and private sources; and support for the Global Outbreak Alert and Response Network of the World Health Organization.

Humanitarian Assistance. Improved Central Emergency Revolving Fund to ensure that relief arrives reliably and immediately when disasters happen.

Updating of UN Charter. Decision to revise and update the Charter by winding up the Trusteeship Council, marking completion of UN's historic decolonization role, and deleting anachronistic references to "enemy States."

Source: *United Nations Daily News,* September 16, 2005, "UN World Summit Adopts Landmark Outcome Document on Raft of Crucial Issues." http://www.un.org/news/dh/pdf/english/2005/16092005.pdf.

- *Trade:* The declaration recognized trade as one of the centerpieces of the global development agenda. However, trade issues and the Doha development targets were not discussed in detail; in particular, no deadline was set for the elimination of developed country agricultural subsidies.

The 2005 United Nations Secretary-General's Report

Six months before the 2005 UN summit, UN Secretary-General Kofi Annan released his five-year progress report on progress toward the MDGs. Titled "In Larger Freedom,"[6] the report underlines that it is time for the world community to go beyond declarations and to take action to solve global development challenges in a pragmatic and systematic manner, in the name of peace, prosperity, and human rights. The report also emphasizes the need to strengthen the UN as an instrument to respond to these challenges. Although the report was promising in terms of its pragmatic messages, Annan refrained from elaborating on some of the items that he had mentioned in an earlier report, such as expanding the size of the UN Security Council, agreeing on a common definition of terrorism, and providing measures for preventive collective action.

The 2005 Group of Eight Summit at Gleneagles, Scotland

Despite disruption by terrorist bombings in London, the Group of Eight (G-8) summit held in Gleneagles, Scotland, on July 6–8, 2005, resulted in agreement on full support for implementing the commitments made under the global compacts. The leaders of the eight countries (Canada, France, Germany, Italy, Japan, Russia, the United Kingdom, and the United States) also agreed on special measures for development in Africa and on climate change, as well as on issues such as the Middle East peace process and the global fight against terrorism.

The G-8 leaders agreed to cancel the debt of 18 of the world's poorest countries and to double their aid by 2010. Debt relief promised under this agreement amounts to some $40 billion, and the deal on aid can be considered a turning point, in that it would bring an end to a decline in aid flows over the past two decades.

At Gleneagles, for the first time, the G-8 leaders signed a statement that underlined climate change as an important phenomenon that is caused by human activity. They also agreed to partner with the World Bank and other development banks to allocate more funds for clean technology in developing countries. Nevertheless, the summit failed to reach a consensus on setting emission targets.

Beyond the agreements reached, the Gleneagles Summit was also historic for its creation of a partnership between the G-8 countries and major NGOs and advocacy campaigns. The most noteworthy of these are the Make Poverty History campaign and the Live 8 concerts.

Global Monitoring Reports 2005 and 2006

The annual *Global Monitoring Report,* a joint publication of the World Bank and IMF, focuses on current progress in the implementation of the MDGs and provides a thorough review of policies and actions necessary to achieve them. The 2005 report, the second in the series, introduced a five-point agenda based on the Monterrey framework of mutual accountability:

- Anchor actions to achieve the MDGs in country-led development strategies
- Scale up human development services
- Improve the environment for stronger private sector–led economic growth
- Dismantle barriers to trade
- Substantially increase the level and effectiveness of foreign aid.

The report concluded that achievement of the MDGs will be at risk without additional efforts to accelerate progress, particularly in Sub-Saharan Africa, the region that is furthest from fulfilling the MDGs. Nevertheless, the report notes, Sub-Saharan Africa's growing capacity to improve its economic performance presents an important opportunity to push through domestic reforms and partnerships. For their part, the report stated, the developed countries need to keep their promises to lower trade barriers, increase the quantity and quality of foreign aid, finalize debt relief arrangements, and encourage pro-poor growth.

Global Monitoring Report 2006, which was released during the Spring 2006 meetings of IMF and the World Bank, continued the emphasis on the need to accelerate efforts toward achieving the MDGs. The report reiterates that although impressive economic growth has contributed to the reduction of poverty globally, performance across regions and individual countries remains uneven. The most discouraging news again comes from Sub-Saharan Africa, whose poverty rate is likely to remain at around 38 percent, far above the target of 22.3 percent.

The report also notes that progress in improving the business climate and access to infrastructure in developing countries has been too slow. Human development goals, such as those in health and education, are also off track, although there is evidence of progress in some regions. Success in this area will depend heavily on providing aid to cover recurrent costs (such as salaries of teachers and health workers), as well as better governance in delivering services to the poor. On trade, the report urges the acceleration of the multilateral trade negotiations. It also identifies several risks at the global level that might affect achievement of the MDGs, such as "abrupt adjustments in global external imbalances and sharp increases in interest rates, newer threats like an avian flu pandemic, and a risk of deeper pain from persistently high oil prices."[7] The report stresses that success in reducing poverty will depend on the domestic growth environment in developing countries themselves. In concluding, the report highlights the following key actions: strengthening of infrastructure and national investment climates; more flexible aid, with better coordination and improved governance on human development goals; better results on the ground; more vigilant monitoring of trade and debt relief issues; and greater accountability and greater insistence on further progress on governance, complemented by stronger global checks and balances.

The Cancún and Hong Kong World Trade Organization Ministerials

The annual WTO meetings in the aftermath of the Doha ministerial meeting have served as a stage for nations seeking to continue the multilateral trade negotiation process. Despite great hopes, the fifth WTO ministerial meeting, held at Cancún, Mexico, in 2003, collapsed over disagreements on agricultural issues, including cotton. The breakdown of the talks showed that moving forward with trade reforms remained a major challenge. Many analysts argued that WTO had set too ambitious an agenda, which prevented consensus from being reached.

WTO's sixth ministerial conference, held in Hong Kong in December 2005, focused on more realistic expectations in the hope of avoiding another collapse, and indeed it proved more successful than the Cancún meeting in narrowing the differences between developed and developing countries. The members reached an agreement to phase out agricultural export subsidies by 2013, to provide developing countries with extra flexibility to protect their small farmers, and to prevent the abuse of food aid as a disguised form of dumping. A new deadline for concluding the negotiations was set for the end of 2006, since the initial June 1, 2005, deadline had been missed.

Despite this progress, however, the Hong Kong ministerial left much to be done. According to a report by the British-based development NGO Oxfam, "The WTO Hong Kong ministerial meeting was once again a lost opportunity to make trade fairer for poor people around the world. Most of the difficult decisions were put off to a further meeting by the end of April 2006, but it is far from clear why rich countries that were unable to show the necessary leadership in Hong Kong will behave any differently in a few months' time."[8]

Views of Civil Society

Civil Society Organizations at the 2005 United Nations World Summit

Several representatives of civil society and business organizations were invited, along with the more than 150 heads of state, to present their views to the UN General Assembly during its September 2005 summit. Speaking on behalf of the private sector, the senior partner of the international management consulting group McKinsey & Company, Rajat Gupta, emphasized the crucial role of business and commerce in economic growth and poverty reduction and called on all development partners to "raise their game" to help achieve the MDGs. Professor Leonor Briones of the NGO Social Watch spoke on behalf of civil society. Briones criticized both developing and developed country governments for not doing enough on trade and aid to further achievement of the MDGs, and she called on them to fulfill all their promises, past and present. Another civil society representative, Virginia Vargas of Global Call for Action Against Poverty (GCAP), called for social and gender justice and the dismantling of neoliberalism, militarism, and fundamentalism of all kinds. Guy Rider, speaking on behalf of the International Confederation of Free Trade Unions and the World Confederation of Labour, called for an enabling global policy environment that would be supportive of the MDGs. The World Conservation Union's representative, Achim Steiner, expressed disappointment at the slow pace of progress in meeting the goals of the global compacts. He also stressed how much more needs to be done to achieve the MDG of environmental sustainability: 15 of the 24 essential services provided by ecosystems—from food production, to water quality and availability, to disease management, to climate regulation—are still being used unsustainably and persistently eroded. Together these statements made it clear that civil society considers the actions taken to date to be unsatisfactory and wants those efforts to be accelerated and expanded.

World Social Forum 2005

The fifth World Social Forum, held in January 2005 in Porto Alegre, Brazil, under the motto "Another World is Possible," was organized as a counterpoint to the annual World Economic Forum held simultaneously in Davos, Switzerland. The forum's organizers saw the Davos meeting as excluding the voice of civil society on global issues. Although the 2005 forum focused especially on debt relief, participants considered a broader range of issues—indeed broader than the MDGs themselves. They called for a different kind of globalization, one run not by big business or government leaders but by the people, and working toward "a fairer, healthier, cleaner version of global trade in which poorer countries have better opportunities to advance themselves." The forum set as its objective "to force world leaders to live up to their promises, and to make a breakthrough on poverty in 2005." The forum supported other campaigns such as the Global Week of Action on Trade—the group's "first major global mobilization of 2005"—and other advocacy campaigns led by NGOs such as Oxfam and Actionaid.

The Global Call for Action Against Poverty Network

GCAP is the largest global coalition of civil society and other individual and collective actors working toward an end to poverty. Its mission is to exert pressure on world leaders to fulfill their promises under the global compacts and implement their global development agendas. GCAP coordinates with other campaigns, such as the Millennium Campaign and the Make Poverty History Campaign, to bring attention to the global power inequalities that feed into the suffering of the world's poor, who are too often excluded from the opportunities brought about by a globalized world. Specific issues on which GCAP has focused are *missing MDGs,* human-centered security, the right to quality public services and resources, just democratic governance, debt cancellation, trade, justice, and a major increase in the quality and quantity of aid.

Live 8

On July 2, 2005, dozens of the world's biggest popular music stars gave simultaneous concerts in 10 cities around the world, including Berlin, Johannesburg, London, Moscow, Paris, Philadelphia, and Rome, to put pressure on political leaders to tackle poverty in Africa. Organized by Bob Geldof, with guest appearances by UN Secretary-General Kofi Annan, former South African president Nelson Mandela, and others, the concerts attracted hundreds of thousands of people and were seen on television by millions more.

The Clinton Global Initiative

The first meeting of former U.S. President Bill Clinton's Clinton Global Initiative took place on September 22–24, 2005. It was another recent example of celebrities and political figures using their public presence to bring global issues to the forefront of the international agenda. The inaugural meeting, which coincided with the World Summit of the UN General Assembly, included workshops on how to reduce poverty, use religion as a force for reconciliation and conflict resolution, implement new business strategies and technologies to combat climate change, and strengthen governance.

The 2005 World Economic Forum

The 2005 World Economic Forum, which took place on January 26–30, 2005, focused on planning immediate action by business, political, and social leaders on poverty, climate change, education, equitable globalization, and global governance. Participants called for a scaling up of long-term measures to reduce the emission of greenhouse gases, increase financial aid to the poorest nations, and remove barriers to trade. The forum's underlying message to its participants was, in the words of its executive chairman, Klaus Schwab, to exercise "self responsibility, global responsibility . . . and responsibility to the next generation."[9] One notable speech was that of China's Vice-Premier Huang Ju, who assured the world leaders that China's economic growth would not aggravate global economic and environmental concerns and that China would devote more resources to environmental sustainability, including smarter use of energy resources. On the economic front, economic and business leaders pledged to resolve international trade disputes and keep inflation under control in order to prevent global financial instability.

Consequences of Failure to Achieve the Goals of the Global Compacts

Meeting the MDGs and the other important objectives set forth in recent global compacts will no doubt come at a cost. Yet the cost of not meeting them, in terms of lives lost and opportunities forgone, would be far greater. According to *Global Monitoring Report 2005,*

> Without faster progress, the MDGs will be seriously jeopardized— especially in Sub-Saharan Africa, which is off track on all the goals. At stake are prospects not only for hundreds of millions of people to escape poverty, disease, and illiteracy, but also prospects for long- term global security and peace—objectives intimately linked to devel- opment. Behind cold statistics on the MDGs are real people, and lack of progress has immediate and tragic consequences.[10]

A brief look at just a few of the issues covered by the MDGs—poverty, communicable disease, and climate change—will demonstrate just how tragic the outcomes could be if the goals are not seriously addressed.

The fight against *poverty* is becoming an ever-greater challenge as the world's population grows from 6 billion today to an estimated 8 billion within the next five to ten years. Yet recent results on rural poverty indicate that, among the world's poorest countries, only in Ghana and Madagascar are poverty rates declining at a pace that, if sustained, will realize the MDG on poverty.[11] Failure to accelerate progress toward poverty reduction would mean neglecting a major issue that underlies the worsening of other global problems. Poverty and the distress it causes create a breeding ground for disease, environmental destruction, and violent conflict. Failure of poor countries to develop economically and socially would deal a severe blow to job and revenue creation and would raise the risk of instability in the international financial architecture and the global business and investment climate.

The continuing spread of *communicable diseases*, in particular HIV/AIDS, provides a striking example of the costs of inaction. Since the 1980s, 60 million people have been infected with HIV, and 25 million have died. The spread is accelerating in India, Russia, the Caribbean, and China. According to a 2006 report of the joint UN Programme on HIV/AIDS, an estimated 38.6 million people worldwide were infected with HIV in 2005.[12] The report also underscores that more than two-thirds of HIV/AIDS-infected adults are women, and more than two-thirds of newly infected teenagers are female. This finding is further corroborated by an Oxfam briefing paper, which noted that

> Women bear the heaviest burden of the under-financing of the MDGs, particularly where this impacts on public service provision. Women are the majority of the world's poor, often sacrificing their own health for the benefit of their families. A clear example of this is in Southern Africa, where the massive burden of care for HIV/AIDS victims is taken up primarily by women, in the face of woefully inadequate state resources.[13]

Life expectancy has already declined by more than 10 years in South Africa and Botswana, two countries among the hardest hit by AIDS. Failure to act now to stop AIDS and other major diseases would reverse decades of development and pose a serious threat to future generations.

Climate change is both an environmental and a development challenge, and failure to address it would threaten not only the well-being of natural ecosystems but also poverty alleviation, human health, and national and regional security. Climate change can also be considered an equity issue, as the debate continues over whether developed or developing countries will bear the primary burden of controlling greenhouse gas emissions. Failure to address climate change in an equitable way would put an unfair burden on developing countries and on the poor and the vulnerable people in those countries in particular.

In sum, the issues that make up the global development agenda affect all of humanity, and inaction on these issues would impose a burden not only on those living today but also on future generations. Guy Rider, speaking at the 2005 UN World Summit, summarized the consequences of inaction succinctly: it would mean a world no longer secure and no longer fit to pass on to our children.

How Is the World Bank Contributing to the Success of Global Compacts?

The World Bank is one of many institutions and players engaged in helping achieve the goals set out in the various global compacts described in this chapter. As the world's largest development financing agency, the Bank has important contributions to make, but what the Bank itself does will not be the determining factor in success. The Bank supports the MDGs through its financial and technical support for social services, such as education, health, and nutrition that complement the efforts of others toward meeting the MDGs. In doing so, the Bank emphasizes results at the country level, by promoting partnerships between development institutions to reconcile requirements with resources; by encouraging country ownership of their own poverty reduction strategies; and by helping build institutional capacity for monitoring and evaluation in developing countries.

The World Bank is active in virtually all of the issues covered in the global compacts. In the area of climate change, the Bank is currently facilitating the creation of a new management framework for trading in carbon emissions, as well as promoting clean energy in its financing of energy facilities. The Bank committed $378 million in grants and lending toward climate change–related efforts in fiscal 2005 alone. In the area of trade, the Bank advocates that the reform agenda should target agriculture, labor-intensive manufactures, services, aid for trade and trade facilitation, and special treatment for developing countries. In the area of education, the Bank is the world's largest provider of external funding and has transferred more than $35.6 billion in loans and credits since 1963. In the area of debt relief, the Bank has been a pioneer: through the Heavily Indebted Poor Countries initiative, it has provided debt relief to 28 low-income countries, most of them in Africa.

As part of its role in monitoring progress toward the MDGs, the Bank has started a new information system, called the Development Data Platform, whose purpose is to tackle a number of challenging data issues and improve accessibility to data around the globe. The Bank has also created multiple new Web sites as a part of its global monitoring project. The Bank's Development Economics Unit has played a key role in monitoring progress toward the MDGs through providing statistical data and analysis and technical recommendations.

In the near future, as described in *Global Monitoring Report 2006,* many of the actions of the World Bank will be aimed directly at helping achieve the MDGs. Key recommendations of the 2006 report for the Bank and other international financial institutions are the following:

> Their focus must shift from managing inputs to achieving real results on the ground. . . . Moving to a results management agenda will require a shift in institutional practices, such as developing a common performance measurement system (COMPAS) and integrating Management for Development results into multilateral development Banks. . . . Developing countries need to build statistical capacity to measure performance and put in place the elements of results management systems; IFIs and donors must scale up their support for these efforts.[14]

Conclusion

The global compacts adopted by the international community in recent years have created a historic common ground for setting clear and measurable international development goals. The world's leaders have come to an agreement that additional financing from donors will be needed to achieve these goals, reversing the decline in overseas development assistance in real terms witnessed over the past 20 years. The declarations of the various global conferences of the first part of this decade spell out the mutual obligations of developed and developing countries under the compacts. Civil society and other nonstate actors have also become more closely integrated into global decision making.

These global compacts have the potential to prevent the world from growing further out of balance. However, progress has been slow, and there are real concerns that little will be accomplished, at least within the time frame originally proposed. As World Bank President Paul Wolfowitz stated during his speech at the 2005 UN World Summit:

> Rapid progress has put many countries on track to meet the MDGs. But let us be honest. Many of the poorest countries, especially in Sub-Saharan Africa, will not meet the targets on time. We must develop realistic plans to get them on track.[15]

The reason for the lack of progress in some countries that President Wolfowitz identified is that the resources so far committed to meeting the MDGs have been inadequate to the need. As the developing countries see it, the proposals put forward by the rich nations have failed to correspond to the developing countries' central demands in agriculture, on which two-thirds of the world's poor depend for their livelihood. For their part, donors remain skeptical that the aid they provide will be used efficiently by national governments. As all the follow-up reports and conferences on the original global compacts have highlighted, generous words have so far not been translated into generous action. Now is the time for both developed and developing countries to demonstrate the political will to fulfill their promises, to make this world a better place to live for all its citizens.

Notes

1. Sachs (2005, p. 266).
2. Easterly (2005, p. 60).
3. Easterly (2006).
4. Sachs (2005).
5. Dervis (2005).
6. Annan (2005).
7. World Bank and IMF (2006, p. 21).
8. Oxfam (2005, p. 3).
9. World Economic Forum (2005).
10. World Bank and IMF (2005, p. 2).
11. Sahn and Stifel (2003).
12. Joint United Nations Programme on HIV/AIDS (2006).
13. Oxfam International (2003, p. 5).
14. World Bank and IMF (2006, p. xix).
15. Wolfowitz (2005).

Selected Readings and Cited References

Annan, Kofi. 2005. "In Larger Freedom: Towards Development, Security and Human Rights for All." New York: United Nations.

Dervis, Kemal. 2005. *A Better Globalization: Legitimacy, Governance, and Reform.* Washington, DC: Center for Global Development.

Easterly, William. 2005. "The Utopian Nightmare." *Foreign Policy* 150: 58–64.

————. 2006. *The White Man's Burden: Why the West's Efforts to Aid the Rest Have Done So Much Ill and So Little Good.* New York: Penguin Press.

Joint United Nations Programme on HIV/AIDS. 2006. *Report on the Global AIDS Epidemic.* Geneva.

Oxfam International. 2003. "The IMF and the Millennium Goals: Failing to Deliver for Low Income Countries." Briefing Paper 54, Oxfam, Oxford, United Kingdom.
————. 2005. "What Happened in Hong Kong?" Briefing Paper 85, Oxfam, Oxford, United Kingdom.
Sachs, Jeffrey D. 2005. *The End of Poverty: Economic Possibilities for Our Time.* New York: Penguin Press.
Sahn, David, and David Stifel. 2003. "Progress Toward the Millennium Development Goals in Africa." *World Development* 31(1): 23–52.
United Nations. 2000. "United Nations Millennium Declaration." http://www.un.org/millennium/index.html.
————. 2002a. "Monterey Consensus." http://www.un.org/esa/ffd/Monterrey-Consensus-excepts-aconf198_11.pdf.
————. 2002b. "Johannesburg Declaration on Sustainable Development." http://www.un.org/esa/sustdev/documents/WSSD_POI_PD/English/POI_PD.htm.
————. 2005. "U.N. World Summit 2005 Outcome Document." http://daccessdds.un.org/doc/UNDOC/GEN/N05/487/60/PDF/N0548760.pdf?OpenElement.
Wolfowitz, Paul. 2005. "Statement by World Bank President Paul Wolfowitz." http://www.un.org/webcast/summit2005/statements/wbank050914eng.pdf.
World Bank and International Monetary Fund. 2005. *Global Monitoring Report 2005: Millennium Development Goals: From Consensus to Momentum.* Washington, DC.
————. 2006. *Global Monitoring Report 2006: Strengthening Mutual Accountability—Aid, Trade, and Governance.* Washington, DC.
World Economic Forum. 2005. "Annual Meeting 2005: Taking Responsibility for Tough Choices." Geneva. http://www.weforum.org/site/homepublic.nsf/Content/Annual+Meeting+2006%5CAnnual+Meeting+2005#21.
World Trade Organization. 2001. "Doha WTO Ministerial 2001: Ministerial Declaration." Document WT/MIN(01)/DEC/1. Geneva. http://www.wto.org/English/thewto_e/minist_e/min01_e/mindecl_e.htm.

Selected Web Links on Global Compacts

Clinton Global Initiative	http://www.clintonglobalinitiative.org
Global Call for Action Against Poverty	http://www.whiteband.org
Group of Eight Gleneagles Summit	http://www.g8.gov.uk
International Conference on Financing for Development (Monterrey conference)	http://www.un.org/esa/ffd
Live 8	http://www.live8live.com/whathappened
UN Millennium Summit Web page	http://www.un.org/millennium/index.html
UN page on MDGs	http://www.un.org/millenniumgoals

UN World Summit 2005 — http://www.un.org/summit2005/index.html

World Bank page on global monitoring — http://www.worldbank.org/globalmonitoring

World Economic Forum — http://www.weforum.org

World Social Forum 2005 — http://www.forumsocialmundial.org.be/index.php?cd_language=2&id_menu

World Summit on Sustainable Development (Johannesburg conference) — http://www.johannesburgsummit.org

World Trade Organization page on ministerial conferences — http://www.wto.org/english/thewto_e/minist_e/minist_e.htm

Index